'This exciting edited collection documen[...] nificance in different but comparable cont[...] Moving beyond technological utopianis[...] nuanced analysis of the way in which social media both challenge and reproduce power relations.'

Dr Wendy Willems, Associate Professor, Department of Media and Communications, London School of Economics and Political Science

'This volume is a timely political biography of social media use in Africa. The book is guided by a desire to avoid the often decontextualized and totalizing narratives that routinely attend the study of social media in the continent. Its critical significance thus lies in its faithfulness to context and history. Bringing together contributors from a diverse range of disciplines, the volume is also methodologically innovative, rich in data and analytically profound. This is one of the most important studies of social media in Africa in recent times.'

George Ogola, Associate Professor of Journalism, University of Central Lancashire

'ICTs are changing our world in many different ways. In this volume we are confronted with interesting case studies from Africa about the ways ICTs, especially social media, change the political landscape. The detailed case studies highlight how political agency is moulded through these technologies and may indeed lead to revolutionary change. These are developments in the making and as such the book is an invitation to researchers to continue the work that the authors of this volume have started.'

Mirjam de Bruijn, Professor of Contemporary History and Anthropology of Africa, Leiden University

'What a brilliant, rich and much-needed collection! Maggie Dwyer and Thomas Molony have done a fantastic job of bringing social media to the core of the present, and future, of African politics. This edited volume sheds a fascinating light on the understudied use of social media across the continent. In doing so, it not only makes a powerful case for why Africanists should study social media, but also why social scientists interested in digital media and democracy ought to engage the diverse, complex, and enthralling landscape of African politics.'

Dr Toussaint Nothias, Post-doctoral Research Fellow, Stanford Center on Philanthropy and Civil Society

SOCIAL MEDIA AND POLITICS IN AFRICA

ABOUT THE EDITORS

Maggie Dwyer is a Lecturer in the Centre of African Studies at the University of Edinburgh. Her research focuses on politics, security, and international development, primarily in West Africa. She is author of the book *Soldiers in Revolt: Army Mutinies in Africa*.

Thomas Molony is Director of the Centre of African Studies at the University of Edinburgh. His geographic focus is mostly on East Africa, where he has written on history, information and communication technology, politics, elections and security.

SOCIAL MEDIA AND POLITICS IN AFRICA

DEMOCRACY, CENSORSHIP AND SECURITY

Edited by Maggie Dwyer and Thomas Molony

ZED

Social Media and Politics in Africa: Democracy, Censorship and Security, was first published in 2019 by Zed Books Ltd, The Foundry, 17 Oval Way, London SE11 5RR, UK.

www.zedbooks.net

Editorial Copyright © Maggie Dwyer and Thomas Molony 2019
Copyright in this Collection © Zed Books

The right of Maggie Dwyer and Thomas Molony to be identified as the editors of this work has been asserted by them in accordance with the Copyright, Designs and Patents Act, 1988

Typeset in Plantin and Kievit by Swales and Willis Ltd, Exeter, Devon
Index by Rohan Bolton
Cover design by Keith Dodds
Cover photo © Sven Torfinn/Panos Pictures

All rights reserved. No part of this publication may be reproduced, stored in a retrieval system or transmitted in any form or by any means, electronic, mechanical, photocopying or otherwise, without the prior permission of Zed Books Ltd.

A catalogue record for this book is available from the British Library

ISBN 978-1-78699-498-1 hb
ISBN 978-1-78699-497-4 pb
ISBN 978-1-78699-499-8 pdf
ISBN 978-1-78699-500-1 epub
ISBN 978-1-78699-501-8 mobi

CONTENTS

ILLUSTRATIONS

Figures

Tables

CONTRIBUTORS

Tanja Bosch is an Associate Professor of Media Studies and Production at University of Cape Town. Her research focuses on community radio, talk radio and citizenship, health communication, youth and mobile media and social networking.

Peter Chonka teaches in the Department of Digital Humanities at King's College London and is a post-doctoral research associate at Durham University's Global Security Institute. His research looks at relationships between media technologies, conflict, political identity and state (re)construction, with a regional focus on the Horn of Africa.

Charlotte Cross is a Lecturer in International Development at The Open University. Her research focuses on policing, politics and development in East Africa.

Stephanie Diepeveen is Deputy Director and Research Lead (Digital Media, Voice and Power) in the Centre of Governance and Human Rights, University of Cambridge. Her research interests lie in the ways that different forms of power are realised through communication technologies. With a focus on Kenya, she has examined this through the study of face-to-face political gatherings as well as mobile phones and social media.

Brian Ekdale is an Associate Professor in the School of Journalism & Mass Communication at the University of Iowa. He studies media work within global digital cultures. His work has appeared in a number of academic journals, including *Media, Culture & Society*; *African Journalism Studies*; and *Journalism Practice*.

Jean-Benoît Falisse is a Lecturer at the Centre of African Studies in the School of Social and Political Science, University of Edinburgh. His main research is on ordinary people's and community engagement with basic services (health care, education, justice) in contexts of 'fragility'. Recently, his mixed-methods research has focused on the African Great Lakes region, with a particular interest in the use and production of data at the community level.

Denis Galava is a PhD student at the University of Edinburgh. A career journalist, he served as a writer, columnist and managing editor of East Africa's largest newspapers, *The Daily Nation* and *The Standard*.

Jamie Hitchen is a research analyst and evaluation expert who has almost a decade of experience working across Africa on projects related to elections, corruption, politics and urbanisation. He has particular expertise on the issues in Sierra Leone, Ghana, Nigeria and Uganda. Jamie is a regular commentator for *World Politics Review* and his analysis has also been published in *The Mail & Guardian* and *Washington Post*. He was part of a research team awarded a grant by WhatsApp to look into the use of the platform during Nigeria's 2019 election.

George Hamandishe Karekwaivanane is a Lecturer in African Studies at the University of Edinburgh and his research focuses on two main areas. The first is the shifting relationship between law and politics in Zimbabwean history, and the second is the social, political and economic impacts of digital media in Zimbabwe.

Admire Mare is a Senior Research Associate at the Department of Journalism, Film and Television, University of Johannesburg. His research focuses on the intersection between technology and society. He has done work focusing on the relationship between digital media and journalism, politics, digital campaigns in hybrid electoral systems, communications surveillance, digital literacy and internet freedom.

Bruce Mutsvairo is an Associate Professor in Journalism Innovation at the University of Technology Sydney, Australia. His research interests span the interplay of social media, citizen journalism and democratisation in Africa.

Hugues Nkengurutse is an independent journalist based in Burundi. He teaches communication studies and political science at the Université du Lac Tanganyika in Bujumbura. Hugues' recent research work has focused on governance and the media in the African Great Lakes region.

Nkwachukwu Orji is a Senior Research Fellow at the Institute for Development Studies, University of Nigeria. His research interest focuses on elections, democratisation, conflict and peace-building. He is actively involved in several learned associations including the International Political Science Association (IPSA), International Society for Third-Sector Research (ISTR) and Council for the Development of Social Science Research in Africa (CODESRIA).

Alisha Patel was a research associate at the University of Oxford and political risk analyst at AKE International at the time of writing. Her research has focused on the role of the media in conflict and democratisation processes, corruption, political risk, and political economy of state-owned enterprises in sub-Saharan Africa. She currently works at the UK Department for International Development as a Governance Adviser.

Emily Riley is the Assistant Director of the Kansas African Studies Center at the University of Kansas, with a PhD in cultural anthropology from Michigan State University. She has conducted research in Wolof and French in Senegal for more than ten years. Her research includes the ethnography of power and cultural production of women in politics and the engagement of social media activists in debates about democracy across Africa.

Kate Wright is a Chancellor's Fellow in the Cultural and Creative Industries at the University of Edinburgh's Centre for African Studies. Dr Wright has published extensively on the media representation of Africa, international news and mediated advocacy. This includes research into media production in Chad, the Democratic Republic of Congo, Kenya, Mali and South Sudan.

ACKNOWLEDGEMENTS

Many of the contributions to this volume were part of a workshop held in Edinburgh in April 2017, titled 'Social Media in Africa: Beyond the Hashtag'. The event was possible through generous funding from an ESRC/DFID grant (ES/M008983/1) for a project titled 'Social Media and Security in Africa' (SMS:Africa). We are grateful to Louise McKenzie and Brooks Marmon for all their hard work in coordinating the workshop. Many thanks also go to Abu Brima and Sallieu Kamara from the Network Movement for Justice and Development (NMJD) in Sierra Leone, Alexander Makulilo from the Department of Political Science and Public Administration at the University of Dar es Salaam in Tanzania, and Mutuma Ruteere from the Centre for Human Rights and Policy Studies (CHRIPS) in Kenya, all of whom have been central to the SMS:Africa project since its inception. We are also very appreciative of the assistance from Robert Macdonald in helping to compile the volume.

1 | MAPPING THE STUDY OF POLITICS AND SOCIAL MEDIA USE IN AFRICA

Maggie Dwyer and Thomas Molony

In Africa, like in most parts of the world, it is hard to imagine contemporary politics devoid of engagement on social media. Voters across the continent subscribe to politicians' and parties' feeds in order to be up to date; during elections it is commonplace to see people bent over smartphones, keeping abreast of the latest developments. More traditional forms of campaigning such as rallies and posters are still in place, but the messages are now amplified by supporters' photos and videos that circulate on social media. Social media is also used to share first-hand recordings of crime and security incidents that have subsequently led to criticism of state security forces. Civil society organisations frequently try to gain support nationally and internationally by creating attention-grabbing hashtags for their campaigns. Radio and television call-in shows in Africa debate the latest trending topics, while journalists on the continent now regularly source many of their leads from social media.

The term 'social media' is understood in a variety of ways. Approached narrowly, it can describe person-to-person relations on social networking services such as Facebook and Twitter. Others consider Web 2.0 internet-based applications more broadly, and include photos, videos and other user-generated content (Hunsinger & Senft 2014: 1). The definition that most succinctly encapsulates the understandings of social media as discussed by the authors of this volume follows Jan Kietzmann et al. (2011: 241), who describe social media as 'interactive platforms via which individuals and communities share, co-create, discuss, and modify user-generated content'.

This book deals with a variety of social media platforms that are used in sub-Saharan Africa. These include those with the highest number of users, as well as other platforms such as Twitter with a smaller but growing subscriber base. Figures published in 2018 show WhatsApp to be in clear first place in terms of the most active platforms in sub-Saharan Africa, followed by Facebook, and then any of YouTube, Instagram or Facebook Messenger in either third, fourth or fifth place (We Are Social 2018a; 2018b; 2018d). While most countries in sub-Saharan Africa have these platforms in the top five of most popular social media, there are a small number of anomalies for the highest ranking, including Telegram in Ethiopia (We Are Social 2018a: slide 12).

Social media in Africa: disparities in use

Social media uptake rates are likely to rise significantly as new users come online for the first time. The number of internet users in Africa is up by more than 20 percent year on year, with reported users in Benin, Sierra Leone, Niger, and Mozambique more than doubling between January 2017 and January 2018, and those in Mali increasing by almost six times over the same period (Kemp 2018b). The country-level data for the year-on-year increase in the total amount of people using social media between 2017 and 2018 adds to the narrative of growth, with a number of African countries placed well above the worldwide growth average of 13 percent. Data on social media use (Kemp 2018a: 56) points to large increases in Ghana and South Africa – 22 and 20 percent respectively – but a closer look at other African countries reveals even higher growth rates from the likes of Somalia (33 percent) and Sierra Leone (32 percent) (We Are Social 2018a: 138; 2018c: 131). Both the latter two countries start from more modest baselines of active social media users as a percentage of the population. Tanzania (at 8 percent penetration) and Burundi (3 percent) are particularly interesting in that they record a *decrease* in active social media users as a percentage of the population. These countries are covered here in chapters by Jean-Benoît Falisse and Hugues Nkengurutse (Burundi) and Charlotte Cross (Tanzania), whose focus on the actions of the state provide contextual explanations as to how the political environment may shape social media use and provide an explanatory factor for these figures.

The growth of social media use across much of Africa should not disguise disparities concerning access. Each of sub-Saharan Africa's regions is below the global average (42 percent) for social media penetration, with the highest level of users in southern Africa (31 percent), the next closest western Africa (11 percent), followed by eastern and central Africa (7 and 6 percent respectively).[1] Of the ten countries with the lowest social media penetration in the world, eight are African (Kemp 2018a: 55).

Some of the factors that have been selling points for the advantages of social media in Western democracies – such as its general widespread accessibility and affordability – have not translated to many parts of Africa. Those wanting to access the internet in some countries on the continent will pay among the highest rates in the world. Countries with no navigable route to the sea are especially vulnerable to high internet prices, with users in some paying on average double per month for broadband internet than users in coastal African countries (World Bank 2016: 212). The price of mobile data follows less of a pattern, with data charges fluctuating widely across the continent. The countries with the highest cost of mobile data include Angola, Chad, Guinea Bissau, South Sudan, Swaziland and Zimbabwe. In the case of Zimbabwe, mobile-data users pay on average nearly four times the amount per 1GB than the average paid by users in neighbouring countries (Research ICT Africa 2017b). Still, even for countries with lower mobile-data rates, low and inconsistent wages across much of the continent means mobile data, and the devices needed to get online, remain unaffordable to many.

Disparities in access to social media often overlap with broader issues of socio-economic gender inequalities. Many African countries perform poorly in terms of women's access to social media (Bailur et al. 2018; Wyche & Olson 2018). The latest available data from Facebook shows a particularly strong male skew in South Sudan and some central and western African countries such as Chad, Niger and Mali (Kemp 2018a: 66). Informal sector, household and individual surveys covering close to 10,000 respondents in seven African countries – Ghana, Kenya, Mozambique, Nigeria, Rwanda, South Africa and Tanzania – suggest a similar trend, with women recorded as being in a disadvantaged position vis-à-vis men on all counts in relation to mobile phone penetration, smartphone penetration, years of internet use, and social media use (Research ICT Africa 2017a: 12–17). This gendered gap in access to social media has the potential to further 'entrench or exacerbate unequal gendered or classed power relations' (Wasserman 2011: 149).

Urban/rural disparities provide another aspect of the unequal access seen within and between African countries. Social media use is greater in urban settlements (Research ICT Africa: 18–22) and often especially prominent in capital cities. The chapters in this book reflect the current urban-centric nature of social media. However, the expansion of mobile phone networks into more rural areas suggests the potential for a narrowing of this gap and the need for more research into ways social media may affect dynamics and relations in rural communities (Porter 2016).

While African countries have some of the highest social media growth rates in the world, Nyabola (2018: 101) warns against assuming that social media users are the norm. Rather the people who are active online are 'a subset of a subset of another subset – those who have access to electricity, those who have access to the internet and finally those who have accounts on social media'. Studies from Africa are now emerging that make visible the sizeable non-user population that has largely been rendered analytically invisible in earlier social media studies (for example, Wyche & Baumer 2017). Still, one should be wary of a clear-cut user/non-user dichotomy. As explained above, data costs in Africa can be very high, especially in the context of low and inconsistent wages. As a result, even those who use social media may do so irregularly, only buying small amounts of data when they have available funds, or intentionally restricting their use to sites or downloads that are not data heavy. Additionally, as the chapter on Sierra Leone by Maggie Dwyer, Jamie Hitchen and Thomas Molony demonstrates, information that originates on social media is often spread by word of mouth to those not using smartphones or the internet. This raises the importance of the role of 'information brokers' who spread (selective) information among their local interpersonal networks.

Researching social media in Africa

Social media handbooks, readers and primers tend to focus on the Global North. At times the approach is location-blind, but the implicit context is usually Europe or North America, with frequent reference to politics and popular culture in the United Kingdom or, more often, the United States (for example, Mandiberg 2012). Where introductory or general texts on social media do make reference to the Global South, it is often through the potent example of the 'democratising' role of Facebook, Twitter and other platforms in the 'Arab Spring' political unrest that swept North Africa and the Middle East from late 2010 (for example, Howard & Hussain 2013; Rane & Salem 2012; Wilson & Dunn 2011).

While earlier studies of social media often side-lined sub-Saharan Africa in its entirety, volumes dedicated to Africa (for example, Mutsvairo 2016; 2018) and in-depth country specific studies (for example, Gyampo 2017; Masilo & Seabo 2015; Nyabola 2018) are emerging. In many ways these works build on and provide continuity to debates from a decade earlier about the mobile phone 'revolution' in Africa (for example, Ekine 2010; Etzo & Collender 2010; Molony 2008), and discussion of 'digital divides' (for example, Armenta et al. 2012; Buys et al. 2008; Fuchs & Horak 2008; Norris 2001; *The Economist* 2005; Thompson 2004; Warschauer 2003). While acknowledging these earlier conversations, current social media scholarship on Africa shows much promise with the recent call to rejuvenate (de-Westernise) how we think about publics in our profoundly digital age (Srinivasan et al. 2019).

The networks enabled by social media, and the wide range of topics discussed, have drawn a strong and growing interest from scholars across disciplines. The interdisciplinary nature of research on social media is also represented in this volume, with the inclusion of chapters by authors from fields such as African studies, anthropology, communication studies, development studies, history, journalism studies and political science. The wide variety of academic research backgrounds brings to the study of social media a diverse range of theories and perspectives.

At the same time research on social media is helping guide the trajectory of many disciplines, especially through the adaptation of methodologies to explore the digital realm. This volume reflects the diversity of research techniques used to investigate the uses and effects of social media. Some authors have looked for qualitative trends using datasets collected from social media platforms. For example, in her study of public discussion about 'Operation Usalama Watch' in Somali neighbourhoods of Nairobi, Alisha Patel uses quantitative and qualitative analysis to explore whether alternative and subversive narratives of the crackdown were advanced on social media compared to print media, and to identify voices that were able to gain prominence. Similarly, Jean-Benoît Falisse and Hugues Nkengurutse combine quantitative and qualitative methods to show how, in a context marked by suspicion and limited political rights, differences in the nature of three social media platforms affect citizens' use of social media during and after a failed coup in Burundi. Others have adapted long-standing methodological approaches, such as ethnography, to the digital realm. Emily Riley, for example, uses ethnographic techniques to capture the virtual worlds of social media and its intersections with physical reality, revealing the creative ways that Senegalese activists use social media to 'talk back' to its institutions as a way of participating in democratic processes during the country's 2017 parliamentary elections. Many authors in this book use interviews to provide greater contextual depth that goes beyond text posted online. Their informants include a range of stakeholders, from political and government leaders at various levels, civil servants and security personnel, to journalists, activists, students and other ordinary citizens. Content analysis is a method that is used in a number of chapters. Visual analysis is especially important given the popularity in many social media posts of photographs (for example Peter Chonka), video (Brian Ekdale), memes (George Karekwaivanane and Admire Mare) and cartoons (Alisha Patel). As can be seen in the following chapters, most authors found the need to draw on more than one approach to capture the complex dynamics that are often under the surface of social media messages and interactions.

Democracy and social media

The rise in social media use in Africa coincides with a sense of ambivalence about the state of democracy in Africa. The 'third-wave of democracy' of the 1990s followed decades of authoritarian leadership across much of the African continent. This brought high expectations for increases in adherence to democratic principles and advances in civil liberties and human rights. Most countries did move to multi-partyism, but in many cases the path to democratisation quickly stalled (Cheeseman 2015: 94). While progress was made on many fronts, even by the late 1990s concern began to grow about democratic backsliding and a rise in new forms of authoritarianism across the continent (Diamond 1996; Joseph 1999; Mustapha & Whitfield 2009). In countries where democracy has struggled to take hold, social media has been viewed by some as a potential 'liberation technology' (Diamond 2010), which could help counter repressive leaders through new avenues of mobilisation. Likewise, even in countries with more entrenched political freedoms, the technology has been seen to provide the opportunity for citizens to become more informed (Abbott 2012; Abbott et al. 2013; Boulianne 2015). Yet, the hopeful tone of techno-determinists was not matched by some academics who quickly began to draw attention to the more troubling and divisive aspects of social media. These have included the issue of political polarisation and the extent to which it can be exacerbated by online bubbles (Lee et al. 2014; Sunstein 2017) and ways that patterns of offline discrimination, including threats, can be replicated and magnified online (Nyabola 2018: 146–147). In line with developments in the Global North, concerns about paid manipulation and bots in digital spaces are also emerging in the African context (Nyabola 2018: 90–92; Ogola & Owuor 2016: 240).

In practice, the ways in which social media is shaping democracy across the African continent do not fit one pattern. The contributions to this volume are united in demonstrating that the effects of social media on the political landscape cannot be viewed in binaries of positive or negative. They show that the distinction between online and offline political actions is often muddled, and that social media platforms are used in diverse ways that are entangled in complex historical and political contexts.

This volume explores the practice of politics through many facets including elections, activism and protest movements. The contributions demonstrate the wide range of political activity taking place in digital spaces as well as the breadth of actors involved. Many of the chapters, including those by Bosch, Dwyer et al., Karekwaivanane and Mare, and Riley, question if and how social media can be used to build new spaces for democratic engagement. The intersection of local and global is a key notion and goal for many of these spaces. The international reach of social media allows localised campaigns to swiftly reach international audiences, and creates opportunities for the development of transnational networks. Emily Riley provides evidence of this in her chapter on 'Africtivistes', a small yet active group of journalists and civil society activists from a variety of African countries who use social media in their attempts to change the political landscape in West Africa. From southern Africa, George Karekwaivanane and Admire Mare's chapter shows how social media platforms provided alternative spaces of participation within which Zimbabweans both in the country's urban locations and also among its considerable diaspora gathered around the #ThisFlag campaign to criticise Robert Mugabe's ZANU-PF government that actively sought to exclude dissenting voices from the public sphere.

Related to questions of new digital spaces for democratic engagement, chapters by Chonka, Diepeveen, Dwyer et al. and Patel have explored how politicians are using social media to engage with the electorate. For example, Dwyer, Hitchen and Molony demonstrate variations in social media engagement across candidates from three political parties in the 2018 Sierra Leone elections and explain the differences in the digital sphere based on the history of the parties and their leadership. The studies of online messages from political figures in this volume build on existing studies which have shown the limits of social media engagement by politicians in Africa. Both Tanja Bosch's (2018) study of South Africa and Teke Ngomba's (2016) study of Cameroon describe a situation in which politicians' social media accounts are mostly used to broadcast their messages rather than to engage voters in dialogue. Ngomba (2016: 448) observes that these accounts often go dormant between elections.

Another focus that spans several chapters, including those by Chonka, Falisse and Nkengurutse, and Orji, is social media's role as a platform for alternative information. As Herman Wasserman (2011: 151) notes, while 'mainstream media channels are often captured by elites or the state', social media has proven a valuable source of news stories that would not otherwise have been covered. Although social media may expose people to a wider range of opinions and information to make informed choices, it also allows for the spread of rumours and misinformation. Dwyer, Hitchen and Molony explore how new informal norms were created in Sierra Leone by citizens attempting to verify election-related news spread on social media. This verification process often relied on traditional forms of documentation applied to the digital realm. Nkwachukwu Orji also considers some of the questions that have emerged about the reliability of the information collected and shared through social media during the 2011 and 2015 election campaigns in Nigeria, and suggests that 'reliability may improve if independent verification checks are built into the system; for example, if a random sample of reports are vetted by a trusted and independent agency'. The inability to decipher accurate information from 'fake news' is a worldwide concern, while the spreading online of hate speech has been a more particular concern for some African countries. Finding ways to reduce online hate speech, for example, has been both a local and international focus during the last few election cycles in Kenya (Mutahi & Kimari 2017).

The unequal distribution of power and influence on social media platforms is an observation that spans many of the chapters, including those by Diepeveen, Falisse and Nkengututse, and Patel. Their work demonstrates that social media, like other technologies, 'are not socially neutral tools' (Wasserman 2011: 149) and can increase rather than bridge inequalities and hierarchies. Jean-Benoît Falisse and Hugues Nkengurutse reveal how in Burundi some social media platforms are monopolised by a few key individuals who act as brokers or 'notaries of citizenship'. These actors have disproportionate influence, construct opinions and decide whose voices will be heard. Likewise, both Alisha Patel and Stephanie Diepeveen show how in Kenya social media often reinforces attention on established, elite voices and familiar tropes. Patel's analysis of the interaction between traditional print media and Twitter during Operation Usalama Watch suggests that many of the power structures prevalent in the Kenyan political landscape are replicated in the online space. Focusing on a similar time period of insecurity in Mombasa, Diepeveen's examination of public information on Facebook reveals that while the platform is diversifying who informs public information flows, it is also reinforcing attention on dominant personalities and well-known narratives. Emerging research, again from Kenya, that compares traditional media and social media as sources of data to support emergency and crisis response during times of tension (such as elections) also recognises the biases in both 'new' and 'old' media, and so points to the continuing importance of diversifying sources of information (Dowd et al. 2018).

The diverse effects of social media also reflect the wide range of political systems in Africa. The authors explore how social media use is shaped by the political context of the countries they cover. For example, Charlotte Cross discusses the risks to those using social media in President Magufuli's Tanzania, a country that *The Economist* has described as undergoing 'a sickening lurch to despotism' (*The Economist* 2018), and where a recent poll shows that while 80 percent of respondents say citizens should be allowed to criticise the President, only 36 percent feel free to do so in practice (Twaweza East Africa 2018: 7–8). Drawing on interviews with police officers and local government officials in Dar es Salaam and Mwanza, Cross discusses how in Tanzania interpretations of what constitutes 'cyber-crime' have been influenced by political calculations. Understanding the impact of increased social media use on politics across the continent, she argues, requires consideration of the ways in which policing and politics are connected.

Security, surveillance and social media

While the potential and possible pitfalls of social media in relation to democratic participation have been the subject of debate globally over the last decade, the technology's salience to discussion of security is a newer phenomenon, particularly in Africa. In many parts of the continent political leadership frames social media as a threat to national and community security. This narrative has often been used to curtail advancements in civil liberties, human rights, and democratic freedoms to which many optimists had hoped social media could contribute. One of the most extreme – although increasingly familiar – measures taken by African states has been complete shutdowns of mobile networks and internet services or targeted blocking of social media sites (for example, BBC 18 January 2019; Chibita 2016: 87; Dahir 22 January 2019), at such a rate that countries on the continent now hold the ignominious accolade of disrupting internet connectivity more than anywhere else (Dahir 19 November 2018). During 2016 and 2017, Africa endured 43 social media blackouts and 237 days of delayed internet, and no fewer than 119 total internet shutdowns (Dendere 30 January 2019). These shutdowns are typically undertaken with little notice or explanation, and tend to occur around elections (e.g., Democratic Republic of the Congo: Dahir 2 January 2019) and/or growing anti-government protests (e.g., Sudan: Dahir 28 December 2018) – suggesting the action is used to disrupt conversations, information sharing and the organisation of events that could be deemed a threat to incumbents.

While social media is frequently touted as a safe place to openly share opinions, in many African countries activism – or simply having 'unpatriotic' conversations online – can be risky. Lately, many countries have proposed and/or passed legislation which criminalises aspects of social media use. In Nigeria, for example, the 'Act to prohibit frivolous petitions; and other matters connected therewith', as it was officially named, was widely seen as a means to restrict freedom of expression and, specifically, to gag Nigerians on social media. The Bill was withdrawn after the Senate refused to pass it (Kazeem 17 May 2016), but the National Council on Information has since recommended the establishment of a Council to regulate the use of social media in Nigeria (Agency Report 24 July 2017). Another notable example is Tanzania, where the Cybercrimes Act (2015) contains provisions addressing significant challenges such as child pornography, cyber bullying and computer fraud, but, as Charlotte Cross outlines, it has widely been used to delegitimise political dissent aimed at President Magufuli and to suppress information that challenges the government's official narrative about Tanzania's development. The Cybercrimes Act has since been supplemented by the Electronic and

Postal Communications (Online Content) Regulations (2018), and together they form a catalogue of – at times confusing and ambiguous (Taylor 12 April 2018) – legislation for online content that threatens citizens' constitutionally guaranteed rights to privacy and freedom of expression (Kalemera 12 April 2018). These laws have often been framed as a security measure, but in practice for social media users they have created a high level of insecurity and uncertainty.

Elsewhere other laws, that at times were created decades before the advent of social media, have been used to crack down on online 'dissent'. Only in April 2017, for example, did Kenya's High Court rule as unconstitutional Section 132 of the penal code, enacted in 1948, that had penalised 'undermining the authority of public officers' – though not before several bloggers and social media users were arrested for criticising government officials online (Bloggers Association of Kenya 2015: 7; Freedom House 2017). As Denis Galava discusses in his chapter on surveillance and social media in East Africa, a new Computer Misuse and Cybercrimes law has since been passed in Kenya. As in Tanzania, President Kenyatta justified this decision by raising concerns about pornography and fraud. However, activists are also concerned that under this new law the threat of prosecution for spreading 'false information' will further muzzle freedom of speech (Olewe 16 May 2018). Not to be outdone by their East African neighbours, Uganda's parliament has now passed a law to impose a controversial tax on people using social media platforms, to help the country 'cope with consequences of *olugambo* [gossiping]', as President Museveni explained in a letter to his Finance Minister (Byaruhanga 31 May 2018). Despite growing government scrutiny of political discussions using internet-enabled technologies, activists and whistleblowers in other sub-Saharan African countries have not been deterred from taking their cause online. The chapters by Tanja Bosch, which covers the #ZumaMustFall movement's attempts to remove Jacob Zuma from the presidency of South Africa, and by George Karekwaivanane and Admire Mare on the #ThisFlag campaign's efforts to remove Robert Mugabe from power in Zimbabwe, detail the role that social media played in toppling both political leaders.

While some of the framing of social media as a security threat clearly has political undertones and motivations, the platforms have led to a number of practical complications for state security forces. State authorities often have a monopoly on security-related information, particularly in countries where the state controls the media, but this has rapidly changed in recent years with the large increase in smartphone ownership. Platforms such as Ushahidi and other similar crowd-sourced applications have created independent avenues to organise and map data connected to incidents of violence that is often then shared on social media. Yet much of the information related to violence is exchanged via social media in a more diffuse and difficult-to-verify manner. Analysis of social media use during Al Shabaab's September 2013 assault on Nairobi's Westgate shopping mall where 67 civilians were killed, for example, identifies a lack of coordination over what could be made public, how and when, and reveals that security breaches within emergency organisations led to the relay of sensitive information on Twitter that benefitted the attackers (Mair 2017; Simon et al. 2014). The Somalia-based Al Shabaab have shown how social media remains an instrument with great potential for Africa-based non-state armed actors to shape public opinion during an on-going incident, as well as for propaganda, fundraising and recruitment (Anzalone 2016: 13–20; Joosse et al. 2015: 818–820; Meleagrou-Hitchens et al. 2012: 29–39). Boko Haram, a violent Islamist movement with expanding operations across West Africa, is using internet and social media platforms with increasing sophistication (Abubakar 2016: 206–207; Meehan & Speier 2011: 20–23), and in March 2015 used its newly opened Twitter account to pledge allegiance to ISIS (Comolli 2017: 164).

The wider framing of social media as a potential security threat – which has been both politicised, as well as a response to recognised armed groups that undoubtedly pose a threat to stability – has created an incentive for government agencies to attempt to monitor social media platforms. As the chapters on Burundi, Tanzania and Zimbabwe detail, while monitoring of social media content can be a resource-intensive undertaking, 'online patrols' can be assisted by informants who provide state security personnel with information discussed in, for example, WhatsApp groups. Other states are more open in their interventions, as Brian Ekdale shows in his discussion of a Kenyan government official's treatment of a local art collective's remix of a music video uploaded to YouTube. The posting led to much discussion on social media about 'appropriate' African online content, moral values and threats to national security.

Scrutiny of information attached to and posted on social media extends beyond governments to the private sector. For example, in the fintech sector – where technology is used to support or enable banking and financial services – 'alternative credit scoring' in Kenya includes the use of social media data sources to make judgements about credit applicants (Privacy International 2017). This raises questions of consent and privacy, if not the surveillance that Galava argues is an attempt to control public thought and secure political centres. However, as is so often the case with social media use, citizens usually find their own ways around those who seek to control their online actions, only for new measures to then be put in place in response (Duncan 2018), in a constant game of online cat and mouse over freedoms and monitoring.

The ordering of chapters of this volume loosely follows the book's subtitle. Social media as a tool for political expression is considered by all contributors, with the earlier chapters primarily engaged with the topic of democratic participation and the later chapters focused more on issues of security. The contributions in this book are immersed in context, provided by country specialists who are familiar with the languages and understand the local circumstances where these very global social media platforms are being used. In his analysis of Somali-language discussions on social media about a series of controversies under the two most recent Federal Government of Somalia administrations, for example, Peter Chonka shows that an understanding of the country's specific political circumstances, and its media/political-cultural history, is essential in appreciating the ways in which the 'double-edged sword' of social media plays out in a political centre such as Mogadishu. Similarly, Jean-Benoît Falisse and Hugues Nkengurutse's chapter on the transition in Burundi from FM radios to social media shows that an understanding of the linguistic nuances of Kirundi (as well as French, Kinyarwanda and English) is crucial when capturing debates that seek to engage with or avoid particular communities. The chapters by Nkwachukwu Orji and Tanja Bosch both demonstrate the importance of offering a wider, long-term perspective in situating what are sometimes assumed to be novel, contemporary topics of contestation because of the new medium – often prefixed with a hashtag – on which they are being discussed. The contextual richness the authors bring to the chapters here are evidence that Kandy Woodfield's 'capability challenge' of social media research (Woodfield 17 May 2014) – 'How many of us are really au fait with the worlds we are researching on social media platforms?' – can be met. As this volume shows, rising to the challenge often involves investigating *beyond* social media platforms, to engage with the real-world context and the people – not just the technologies – that inhabit it.

Note

1 In this context 'social media penetration' is defined as active social media users as a percentage of the population. Note, the survey considers Mozambique and Zimbabwe to be in Eastern Africa (South), not Southern Africa, and for Angola to be in 'Middle Africa' – here described as Central Africa (We Are Social. 2018b, slide 9).

References

Abbott, J. (2012) 'Democracy@internet. org revisited: analysing the socio-political impact of the internet and new social media in East Asia'. *Third World Quarterly*, 33(2): 333–357.

Abbott, J. et al. (2013) 'New social media and (electronic) democratization in East and Southeast Asia Malaysia and China compared'. *Taiwan Journal of Democracy*, 9(2): 105–137.

Abubakar, A.T. (2016) 'Communicating violence: the media strategies of Boko Haram'. In M. Bunce et al. (eds.), *Africa's Media Image in the 21st Century: from the 'Heart of Darkness' to 'Africa Rising'*. London: Routledge, pp. 200–210.

Agency Report (2017) 'Nigeria plans establishment of Council to regulate social media use in country'. 24 July. www.premiumtimesng.com/news/top-news/237933-nigeria-plans-establishment-council-regulate-social-media-use-country.html (accessed 11 May 2018).

Anzalone, C. (2016) 'The Resilience of al-Shabaab'. *CTC Sentinel*, 9(4): 13–20.

Armenta, A. et al. (2012) 'The new digital divide: the confluence of broadband penetration, sustainable development, technology adoption and community participation'. *Information Technology for Development*, 18(4): 345–353.

Bailur, S. et al. (2018) 'Gender, mobile, and development: the theory and practice of empowerment'. Introduction. *Information Technologies & International Development*, 14: 96–104.

BBC (2019) 'Zimbabwe blocks Facebook, WhatsApp and Twitter amid crackdown'. 18 January. www.bbc.co.uk/news/world-africa-46917259 (accessed 18 January 2019).

Bloggers Association of Kenya (2015) 'State of Blogging & Social Media in Kenya 2015 Report'. June. www.monitor.co.ke/wp-content/uploads/2015/06/The-State-of-Blogging-and-Social-Media-in-Kenya-2015-report.pdf (accessed 17 August 2016).

Bosch, T. (2018) 'Digital media and political citizenship: Facebook and politics in South Africa'. In B. Mutsvairo & B. Karam (eds.), *Perspectives on Political Communication in Africa*. London: Palgrave Macmillan, pp. 145–158.

Boulianne, S. (2015) 'Social media use and participation: a meta- analysis of current research'. *Information, Communication & Society*, 18(5): 524–538.

Buys, P. et al. (2008) 'Determinants of a digital divide in Sub-Saharan Africa: a spatial econometric analysis of cell phone coverage'. WPS4516, World Bank, Washington, DC.

Byaruhanga, C. (2018) 'Uganda imposes WhatsApp and Facebook tax "to stop gossip"'. 31 May. www.bbc.co.uk/news/world-africa-44315675 (accessed 1 June 2018).

Cheeseman, N. (2015) *Democracy in Africa: Successes, Failures, and the Struggle for Political Reform*. Cambridge: Cambridge University Press.

Chibita, M.B. (2016) 'Digital activism in Uganda'. In B. Mutsvairo (ed.), *Digital Activism in the Social Media Era*. London: Palgrave Macmillan, pp. 69–93.

Comolli, V. (2017) *Boko Haram: Nigeria's Islamist Insurgency*. London: Hurst.

Dahir, A.L. (2018) 'African countries disrupt internet connectivity more than anywhere else'. 19 November. https://qz.com/africa/1468491/ africa-internet-shutdowns-grow-longer-in-cameroon-chad-ethiopia/ (accessed 21 November 2018).

Dahir, A.L. (2018) 'Sudan has blocked Facebook, Twitter and Instagram to counter anti-govt protests'. 28 December. https://qz.com/africa/1510229/ sudan-shuts-down-facebook-twitter-instagram-amid-bread-protests/ (accessed 3 January 2019).

Dahir, A.L. (2019) 'An internet shutdown is the latest frustration hitting voters in DR Congo'. 2 January. https://qz.com/africa/1513023/ drc-shuts-down-internet-sms-ahead-of-election-results/ (accessed 3 January 2019).

Dahir, A.L. (2019) 'Chad Republic has kept social media shut for 300 days and counting'. 22 January. https://qz.com/africa/1530071/ chad-republic-blocks-social-media-for-300-days-sparking-campaign/ (accessed 25 January 2019).

Dendere, C. (2019) 'Why are so many African leaders shutting off the Internet in 2019?' 30 January. www.washingtonpost.com/news/ monkey-cage/wp/2019/01/30/ why-are-so-many-african-leaders-shutting-off-the-internet-in-2019/?noredirect=on&utm_term=. c71be7016af9 (accessed 2 February 2019).

Diamond, L. (1996) 'Is the Third Wave Over?' *Journal of Democracy*, 7(3): 20–37.

Diamond, L. (2010) 'Liberation technology'. *Journal of Democracy*, 21(3): 69–83.

Dowd, C. et al. (2018) 'Comparing "New" and "Old" Media for Violence Monitoring and Crisis Response in Kenya'. IDS Working Paper Report 520, Institute of Development Studies, Brighton.

Duncan, J. (2018) 'Taking the spy machine south: communications surveillance in sub-Saharan Africa'. In B. Mutsvairo (ed.), *The Palgrave Handbook of Media and Communication Research in Africa*. London: Palgrave Macmillan, pp. 153–176.

The Economist (2005) 'The real digital divide'. *The Economist*, 12–18 March, 374(8417): 9.

The Economist (2018) Tanzania's sickening lurch. *The Economist*, 17 March. www.economist.com/news/ leaders/21738885-start-containing-president-john-magufuli-how-save-tanzania (accessed 30 March 2018).

Ekine, S. (ed.) (2010) *SMS Uprising: Mobile Activism in Africa*. Oxford: Pambazuka Press.

Etzo, S. & Collender, G. (2010) 'The mobile phone "revolution" in Africa: rhetoric or reality?' *African Affairs*, 109(437): 659–668.

Freedom House (2017) 'Freedom on the Net 2017: Manipulating Social Media to Undermine Democracy – Kenya'. https://freedomhouse.org/sites/ default/files/FOTN%202017_Kenya. pdf (accessed 11 May 2018).

Fuchs, C. & Horak, E. (2008) 'Africa and the digital divide'. *Telematics and Informatics*, 25(2): 99–116.

Gyampo, R.E.V. (2017) 'Social media, traditional media and party politics in Ghana'. *Africa Review*, 9(2): 125–139.

Howard, P.N. & Hussain, M.M. (2013) *Democracy's Fourth Wave?: Digital Media and the Arab Spring*. Oxford: Oxford University Press.

Hunsinger, J. & Senft, T.M. (2014) 'Introduction'. In J. Hunsinger & T.M. Senft (eds.), *The Social Media Handbook*. New York: Routledge, pp. 1–4.

Joosse, P. et al. (2015) 'Narratives and counternarratives: Somali-Canadians on recruitment as foreign fighters to Al-Shabaab'. *British Journal of Criminology*, 55(5): 811–832.

Joseph, R. (ed.) (1999) *State, Conflict, and Democracy in Africa*. Boulder, CO: Lynne Rienner.

Kalemera, A. (2018) 'Tanzania Issues Regressive Online Content Regulations'. 12 April. https://cipesa.org/2018/04/tanzania-enacts-regressive-online-content-regulations/ (accessed 11 May 2018).

Kazeem, Y. (2016) 'Nigeria has finally killed its controversial anti-social media bill'. 17 May. https://qz.com/686237/nigeria-has-finally-killed-its-controversial-anti-social-media-bill/ (accessed 11 May 2018).

Kemp, S. (2018a) 'Digital in 2018: essential insights into internet, social media, mobile, and ecommerce use around the world'. New York: We Are Social and Hootsuite.

Kemp, S. (2018b) 'Digital in 2018: world's internet users pass the 4 billion mark'. https://wearesocial.com/blog/2018/01/global-digital-report-2018 (accessed 4 May 2018).

Kietzmann, J.H. et al. (2011) 'Social media? Get serious!'. *Business Horizons*, 54(3): 241–251.

Lee, J.K. et al. (2014) 'Social media, network heterogeneity, and opinion polarization'. *Journal of Communication*, 64(4): 702–722.

Mair, D. (2017) '#Westgate: a case study: how al-Shabaab used Twitter during an ongoing attack'. *Studies in Conflict & Terrorism*, 40(1): 24–43.

Mandiberg, M. (ed.) (2012) *The Social Media Reader*. New York: NYU Press.

Masilo, B. & Seabo, B. (2015) 'Facebook: revolutionising electoral campaign in Botswana?' *Journal of African Elections*, 14(2): 110–129.

Meehan, P. & Speier, J. (2011) 'Boko Haram: emerging threat to the U.S. Homeland'. U.S. House of Representatives Committee on Homeland Security, Subcommittee on Counterterrorism and Intelligence, Washington, D.C.

Meleagrou-Hitchens, A. et al. (2012) 'Lights, camera, jihad: Al-Shabaab's western media strategy'. International Centre for the Study of Radicalisation and Political Violence, London.

Molony, T.S.J. (2008) 'Running out of credit: the limitations of mobile telephony in a Tanzanian agricultural marketing system'. *Journal of Modern African Studies*, 46(4): 522–544.

Mustapha, A.R. & Whitfield, L. (eds.) (2009) *Turning Points in African Democracy*. Oxford: James Currey.

Mutahi, P. & Kimari, B. (2017) 'The Impact of social media and digital technology on electoral violence in Kenya'. IDS Working Paper 493, Institute of Development Studies, Brighton.

Mutsvairo, B. (ed.) (2016) *Digital Activism in the Social Media Era: Critical Reflections on Emerging Trends in Sub-Saharan Africa*. London: Palgrave Macmillan.

Mutsvairo, B. (ed.) (2018) *The Palgrave Handbook of Media and Communication Research in Africa*. London: Palgrave Macmillan.

Ngomba, T. (2016) 'Social media and election campaigns in Sub-Saharan

Africa: insights from Cameroon'. In A. Bruns et al. (eds.), *The Routledge Companion to Social Media and Politics*. New York and London: Routledge, pp. 447–459.

Norris, P. (2001) *Digital Divide: Civic Engagement, Information Poverty, and the Internet Worldwide*. New York: Cambridge University Press.

Nyabola, N. (2018) *Digital Democracy, Analogue Politics: How the Internet is Transforming Kenya*. London: Zed Books.

Ogola, G. & Owuor, M. (2016) 'Citizen journalism in Kenya as a contested "third space"'. In B. Mutsvairo (ed.), *Participatory Politics and Citizen Journalism in a Networked Africa: a Connected Continent*. London: Palgrave Macmillan, pp. 229–243.

Olewe, D. (2018) 'Kenya, Uganda and Tanzania in "anti-fake news campaign"'. 16 May. www.bbc.co.uk/news/world-africa-44137769 (accessed 17 May 2018).

Porter, G. (2016) 'Mobilities in rural Africa: new connections, new challenges'. *Annals of the American Association of Geographers*, 106(2): 434–441.

Privacy International (2017) 'Fintech: Privacy and Identity in the New Data-Intensive Financial Sector'. Privacy International, London.

Rane, H. & Salem, S. (2012) 'Social media, social movements and the diffusion of ideas in the Arab uprisings'. *Journal of International Communication*, 18(1): 97–111.

Research ICT Africa (2017a) 'Let the people speak: using evidence from the Global South to reshape our digital future'. Presented at 12th Internet Governance Forum, Geneva, 21 December 2017.

Research ICT Africa (2017b) RIA Africa Mobile Pricing (RAMP) Indices Portal. https://researchictafrica.net/ramp_indices_portal/ (accessed 7 May 2018).

Simon, T. et al. (2014) 'Twitter in the cross fire: the use of social media in the Westgate Mall terror attack in Kenya'. *PLoS ONE*, 9(8): 1–11.

Srinivasan, S. et al. (2019) 'Rethinking publics in Africa in a digital age'. *Journal of Eastern African Studies*, 13(1): 2–17.

Sunstein, C. (2017) *#Republic: Divided Democracy in the Age of Social Media*. Princeton: Princeton University Press.

Taylor, B. (2018) 'Fees, licences and lots of uncertainty: what's in Tanzania's new "online content" regulations?' 12 April. http://mtega.com/2018/04/fees-licences-and-lots-of-uncertainty-whats-in-tanzanias-new-online-content-regulations/#more-4793 (accessed 16 April 2018).

Thompson, M. (2004) 'Discourse, "development" and the "digital divide": ICT and the World Bank'. *Review of African Political Economy*, 31(99): 103–123.

Twaweza East Africa. (2018) 'Not to that extent? Tanzanians' views on information and public debate'. Sauti za Wananchi Report 46, March, Twaweza East Africa, Dar es Salaam.

Warschauer, M. (2003) *Technology and Social Inclusion: Rethinking the Digital Divide*. Cambridge, MA: MIT Press.

Wasserman, H. (2011) 'Mobile phones, popular media, and everyday African democracy: transmissions and transgressions'. *Popular Communication*, 9(2): 146–158.

We Are Social (2018a) Digital in 2018 in Eastern Africa Part 1 – North. www.slideshare.net/wearesocial/digital-in-2018-in-eastern-africa-part-1-north-86865720 (accessed 15 March 2018).

We Are Social (2018b) Digital in 2018 in Southern Africa. www.slideshare. net/wearesocial/digital-in-2018-in-southern-africa-86865907 (accessed 15 March 2018).

We Are Social (2018c) Digital in 2018 in Western Africa Part 1 – West. www.slideshare.net/wearesocial/digital-in-2018-in-western-africa-part-1-west-86865478 (accessed 15 March 2018).

We Are Social (2018d) Digital in 2018 in Western Africa Part 2 – East. www.slideshare.net/wearesocial/digital-in-2018-in-western-africa-part-2-east-86865566 (accessed 15 March 2018).

Wilson, C. & Dunn, A. (2011) 'Digital media in the Egyptian revolution: descriptive analysis from the Tahrir data sets'. *International Journal of Communication*, 5: 1248–1272.

Woodfield, K. (2014) 'Future challenges, take-down notices & social media research'. 17 May. http://nsmnss. blogspot.co.uk/2014/05/future-challenges-take-down-notices.html (accessed 6 March 2017).

World Bank (2016) 'World Development Report 2016: Digital Dividends'. Washington, D.C.: World Bank Group.

Wyche, S. & Baumer, E. (2017) 'Imagined Facebook: an exploratory study of non-users' perceptions of social media in rural Zambia'. *New Media & Society*, 19(7): 1092–1108.

Wyche, S. & Olson, J. (2018) 'Kenyan women's rural realities, mobile Internet access, and "Africa Rising"'. *Information Technologies & International Development*, 14: 33–47.

2 | '"*IGU SAWIR*" GONE TOO FAR?'

Social media and state reconstruction in Somalia

Peter Chonka

Introduction

In 2017, Somali rapper Ilkacase Qays released the music video for his track '*Igu sawir*' ('Take my picture') on YouTube. Clad in a turquoise-blue Somalia football team tracksuit, Ilkacase raps and sings in Somali over images of politicians taking pictures and 'selfies' with various citizens and symbols: "A disabled person? Yes – *Igu sawir*! A blind person? Yes – *Igu sawir*! The flag? Yes – *Igu sawir*!"[1] The catchy refrain encapsulated and intensified a social media-driven critique of Somali power holders' own use of social media in their attempts to connect with the public and legitimise the arduous process of state reconstruction that they are undertaking in a context of ongoing conflict, sporadic terrorist violence and perennial political instability. This online engagement highlighted the importance of social media platforms for state communications, as well as their role as arenas for debates around the re-establishment of government authority in Somalia after more than a quarter-century of effective statelessness.

Considering Somalia's unenviable international image as a location of chronic instability, terrorism and piracy, it is unsurprising that local efforts towards state reconstruction have frequently engaged with these mainstream narratives through the channels afforded by 'new' and 'social' media. This has been particularly true for the post-2012 period on which this chapter focuses. It was in the previous year that Harakaat Al Shabaab Al Mujahidiin (hereafter Al Shabaab) was expelled from Mogadishu by Western-backed forces. These military operations preceded the installation of Xasan Sheikh Maxamuud's Federal Government of Somalia (FGS), the first internationally recognised authority in Mogadishu since the collapse of Siyaad Barre's government in 1991. Military, security and political gains in this period (however modest) were frequently framed in local news and social media discourse in terms of a 'Somalia rising' narrative (Hammond 2013). Often such efforts were led by internationally connected and tech-savvy commentators in the city, many of whom were 'returnees' from the global Somali diaspora. Taking advantage of economic opportunities in the dynamic city, as well as earlier developments in the telecommunications industry, this transnational social media commentariat of entrepreneurs, civil society activists and government employees remains important, and has continued to challenge international stereotypes about the status and prospects of a modern Somalia in the midst of political and economic change. These interventions also take place within a broader transnational Somali-language public sphere of mediated political debate around state reconstruction and ongoing conflict.

This chapter first situates the Somali case study in relation to wider literature on social media and political contestation in zones of conflict or 'limited statehood'. It argues that the blurring of public/private boundaries inherent in the modern social media environment acutely affects the very basics of political communication for state actors in Somalia. This is related to the socio-political environment in which they operate: one that has been characterised by prolonged statelessness, and physical and discursive challenges to their legitimacy from an undefeated insurgency. It further argues that although social media can facilitate a groundswell of popular optimism around state reconstruction, it can be an equally potent force for the questioning of state legitimacy and the undermining of the communicative coherence of re-emerging structures of governance. Although this 'double-edged sword' argument is hardly novel, the analysis suggests that specific local political circumstances (and media/cultural history) are of great importance for understanding the ways in which this dialectic relationship plays out in a political centre such as Mogadishu – the city from which the federal reconstruction of the Somali state is being undertaken in collaboration with various external actors.

After outlining important features of the Somali conflict and developments in communications/media technologies, the chapter makes the above argument through analysis of a series of controversies that have played out through social media channels. These occurred between 2012 and 2017, during the two FGS administrations of Presidents Xasan Sheikh Maxamuud and Maxamed Cabdilaahi 'Farmaajo'. The chapter discusses the former administration in terms of the securitisation of media in relation to terrorism and counter-insurgency operations. It then explores incidents occurring under Farmaajo's subsequent administration that have highlighted the strategies and limitations of its communications through social media platforms (for example state actors engaging directly with constituents through Facebook) in relation to US military operations and Al Shabaab violence. Finally, the chapter examines tensions that relate to representations of political change for local and international audiences, and returns to the example of rapper Ilkacase Qays. Media texts relating to Ilkacase provide useful examples of the complex interplay between nationalist and Islamist discourses around Somali state reconstruction, which social media platforms and practices both reflect and facilitate. The analysis is informed by the author's experience of working for an international humanitarian organisation in Somalia (undertaking local-language media monitoring through the period analysed), and by fieldwork in Mogadishu and other cities on Somali-language media networks.

Social media scholarship and Somalia

The wider literature on social media's impact on politics in the Middle East and North/sub-Saharan Africa tends to focus on its potential for democratic mobilisation and challenges to consolidated authoritarian states (Banda, Mudhai & Tettey 2009; Lynch 2011; Tukefci and Wilson 2012; Bruns, Highfield & Burgess 2013; Wolfsfeld, Segev & Sheafer 2013). In the Somali case, despite their sporadic violence or attempted regulation of media, state structures remain nascent and contested, and do not constitute a coherent leviathan against which a 'civil society' mobilises. In Western contexts scholars have explored the opportunities and technical limitations of state structures' use of social media platforms to listen to and engage with citizens (Bertot, Jaeger & Grimes 2010; Kavanaugh et al. 2012). Literature on African states' utilisations of new media technology is emerging, but often highlights locations where state power is relatively 'hard' and can be exercised towards 'developmental state'-type transformative agendas (Gagliardone 2014).

Elsewhere, scholars have conceptualised ICTs (information and communications technology) as a potential means to achieve 'alternative governance modalities' in settings of 'limited statehood'. Livingston and Walter-Drop's (2014) volume addresses a diverse range of cases where empirical state capacity has historically been weak and where the popular use of new media technologies can allow for either collaborations between the state and civil society (for example crowd-sourcing of data that strengthens *government* monitoring capabilities) or the emergence of new practices of local *governance* that bypass the state or fill in gaps in its capabilities. A relatively small number of the contributions to that volume focus on state (as opposed to other actors') use of ICTs to govern, and these (Asmolov 2014; Singh 2014) explore locations such as Russia and India, countries where state institutions are big and highly visible, if 'limited' in terms of certain capacities. Clearly, such settings differ from Somalia where a nationally sovereign authority has been non-existent for over a quarter of a century, and where reconstruction involves the fundamental (re)articulation of the state's basic legitimacy. The Federal Government in Mogadishu cannot effectively project a monopoly of the legitimate means of violence beyond the city, and continues to compete with an armed organisation such as Al Shabaab that maintains parallel systems of governance (for example for taxation) not only in those hinterlands but also in the capital city itself.[2]

Given this distinctive context, the use of social media by state actors in Somalia raises a somewhat different set of questions. These concern the necessity or desirability (for the state) of communicating with populations through increasingly ubiquitous platforms, such as Facebook. Prior experiences of prolonged state collapse have often made distinctions between state and non-state authority highly fuzzy, and emerging Somali state-builders are constructing potentially new modalities of governance and communications through social media platforms that, by their very nature, further blur boundaries between public and private, or professional and personal realms (Lange 2007; Van Dijck 2013). The focus on social media here builds on other accounts of state–society media engagement in Somalia. For instance, Stremlau, Fantini and Gagliardone's (2015) discussion of radio call-in programmes, which argues persuasively that a sole focus on the media's supposed role as a tool for facilitating state accountability may overlook the ways in which various (state and non-state) power structures are reproduced in new forms. Eschewing, as they do, problematic normative assumptions about what media 'should' do or facilitate, this chapter examines what actually happens when the use of modern social media communications channels is almost unavoidable for state actors, but also affects the communicative coherence of embryonic institutions. This will be demonstrated below with reference to state actors using personal social media accounts to engage with publics around highly sensitive issues, and certain digitally mediated civil society initiatives that throw into question firm distinctions between 'state' and 'stakeholder' actions (Srinivasan 2014: 96).

Another emerging theme of contemporary media studies in the West highlights the impact of social media platforms on the nature of debate and the apparent ideological polarisations they encourage (Wodak, Mral & Khosravinik 2013; Gruzd and Roy 2014). Algorithmic curation of content is said to create the 'filter bubbles' in which media consumers are exposed only to the opinions that they are expected to respond to positively, while the physical detachment afforded by the cyber public sphere promotes increasingly intolerant language and the flouting of norms of debate that might otherwise characterise face-to-face interactions. Considering these important insights (very much the zeitgeist of an era of 'post-truth' politics, Brexit and Trump), it is necessary to problematise the influence of social media platforms as part of non-Western and non-English-language media ecologies. In Somali-language social media, it is difficult to ascertain the extent to which the tracking and algorithms that so characterise European-language social media are observable, operational and effective in influencing patterns of online interaction. This kind of technical analysis is beyond the scope of this chapter. Nonetheless it deserves future attention and will be influenced by the current capacity of online platforms to process and interpret Somali-language social media-generated content as a form of 'big data'.

This chapter instead provides a qualitative overview of types of debate that are playing out within the dynamic Somali media environment and between influential networks of media producers. Although debates may take on similarly vitriolic tones (unsurprising in a context of extreme political fragmentation where post-civil war national reconciliation has never taken place), binary ideological polarisations (for instance between 'militant Islamists' and FGS-supporting 'nationalists') are not always clearly visible, and may obscure the more nuanced and ambiguous contours of debate over the future of the Somali nation state. Examples of particular types of network and producer that cross between these discursive boundaries are provided in the subsequent analysis, demonstrating the potential impact of social media on complex 'assemblages' of ideological affiliation and transnational religious, political and socio-cultural orientation (Phillips 2006; Wise 2012; Hess 2015). Whilst the chapter demonstrates the novel features and affordances of social media platforms, it also highlights types of cultural production (for instance the political-responsive role of popular music) that should be understood with reference to historical trends in anti- and post-colonial oral literature

(Johnson 1974; Samatar 1982; Adam 2001; Kapteijns 2010). Poetry, theatre and popular music (along with 'old' mediating technologies of production and dissemination) played fundamental roles in historically defining the contested parameters of Somali ethno, cultural and religious nationalism, and themselves can be seen to feed into modern social media debates and practices.

Conflict and communications technology in Somalia

In the two decades following the collapse of dictator Siyaad Barre's military regime in 1991 – and the civil war which both preceded and followed on from this crucial juncture – Somalia remained without an internationally recognised or nationally sovereign state. The comparatively 'organic' emergence and consolidation of the Islamic Courts Union from the early 2000s (an initially decentralised network of Shariah courts funded by clan networks of business interests first in Mogadishu and then through wider swathes of south-central Somalia) was halted by the US-backed Ethiopian military intervention of 2006 (Barnes and Hassan 2007). This invasion and occupation paved the way for Al Shabaab to emerge as a 'radical' armed splinter of the former Courts movement. It claimed a certain degree of nationalist legitimacy in its campaign against Ethiopian forces, and moved to expand administrative systems of Islamist governance across the majority of the south-central regions (Hansen 2013). Broader historical dynamics of Islamist mobilisation, socio-religious change and growing Sunni-orthodoxy in the overwhelmingly Muslim Somali regions of the Horn helped create an environment where populations were at times willing to accept Al Shabaab's strict forms of governance, even if only as a trade-off for improved security conditions.

Al Shabaab was expelled from Mogadishu in 2011 through the military efforts of the strengthened multinational African Union Mission for Somalia (AMISOM) and local troops affiliated with the beleaguered Transitional Federal Government, the product of externally facilitated peace negotiations and international patronage. The year 2012 saw the installation of its successor, the FGS, under an administration led by President Xasan Sheikh Maxamuud. Maxamuud's bid for selection was heavily influenced by money from the Gulf, while his subsequent administration benefited from significant humanitarian, development and security largesse from increasingly important regional players such as Turkey. His government in Mogadishu was the first Somali government to gain diplomatic recognition from the United States since 1991.

Despite the FGS' dependence on international support, persistent political instability, the United Nations' bumpy orchestration of a national 'federalisation' process, and continued Al Shabaab violence, the post-2012 period witnessed a broadly optimistic shift in the popular discourse around the potential for Somalia to 'rise' from the ashes of past conflict. Taking advantage of perceived security gains, returnees and finance from the diaspora have contributed to economic change in Mogadishu. This is exemplified in symbolic locations such as the city's Makka Al Mukarama thoroughfare, re-paved by Turkish engineers and home to newly opened banks, hotels, restaurants and a vibrant retail sector. Other locations such as the city's Lido beach are similarly redolent with mediated imagery of Somalia's potential for 'rebirth' and serve as important sites where young locals and diaspora returnees relax and socialise.

A *dib-u-dhis* ('reconstruction') discourse has emerged in response to post-2012 political developments, and this period is broadly coterminous with an increased uptake of social media usage in Mogadishu and more broadly across (urban) Somalia. Modern internet penetration is closely related to the rapid expansions of the local telecommunications industry through earlier periods of statelessness (Feldman 2012). Mobile phone usage is nearly ubiquitous, as demonstrated by the extensive uptake of local innovations such as mobile money.[3] Such tools themselves emerged in response to local monetary and security conditions that contributed to the limited circulation of the Somali shilling, a reliance on US Dollars and fears around carrying large amounts of cash on one's person. Cheap (and not so cheap) smartphones have become significantly more prevalent and serve as important devices for communication and consumption of various forms of online and offline media – for instance in their common usage for listening to local private FM radio stations.

Comparative global statistics put internet penetration at only around 1–2% for the entire country (World Bank 2016). Nonetheless, such estimates may be hampered by a lack of more general census data and difficulties of gathering accurate quantitative data from multiple service providers across a highly fragmented business and political environment. As such, these figures should not obscure the wider importance of internet-based communications in urban centres such as Mogadishu. Furthermore, even fairly recent data may already be out of date, considering the rapid expansions of internet infrastructure brought with Somalia's connection to the East African network of undersea fibre-optic cables in 2013 (Reuters 2013). The author's observations of university students' media usage in different urban centres across Somalia since 2009 (including Mogadishu, which also has a booming private higher educational institution industry) highlight a prevalence of social use, primarily accessed through mobile devices. Similar to other African contexts (Parks & Mukherjee 2017), Facebook remains the platform accessed and engaged with in the Somali language by the broadest range of local users, whilst the Somali Twitter scene tends to be limited to a more 'elite' user base, with many discussions taking place in English.

The news media industry in Somalia is as fragmented and dynamic as the political space in which it operates. Protracted statelessness and ongoing division across the largely embryonic federal regions have created a media environment characterised by a proliferation of private online and radio news, often with particular regional focuses. In 2015, in Mogadishu alone there were over thirty private FM radio stations in operation and countless news websites cumulatively covering the entirety of the country. Such local networks of media entrepreneurs and young journalists coexist with (and overlap) what can be characterised as transnational Somali-language broadcasters. Based outside the country but reaching audiences across the region, this category encompasses the widely listened-to content of the British Broadcasting Corporation (BBC) and Voice of America (VOA) Somali Services, and diaspora-financed satellite television stations such as Universal TV. 'State' broadcasting exists but operates as merely a single (and not necessarily privileged) voice in a wider cacophony of Somali-language media production. In the capital, for instance, the FGS broadcasts through Radio Mogadishu and Somali National Television, but has a relatively limited capacity to control (particularly militant) opposition voices. This does not mean that journalism in Somalia is 'free'. Attacks against media workers are a common occurrence and have been perpetrated by state, armed opposition and private actors (NUSOJ 2014; Stremlau, Fantini & Osman 2015). Whilst Somalia is one of the most dangerous places in the world to be a journalist, the fragmented nature of the media ecology means that production is dynamic, and the social importance of news transmission ensures that markets exist for huge volumes of content to be broadcast.

As I have argued elsewhere, the ways in which all of the aforementioned types of broadcasters (and their audiences) engage with social media platforms helps create a transnational Somali-language 'digital public' that allows debates to take place across the multiple contested borders of the Somali Horn (Chonka 2019). Considering this, and given the recent history of fragmented media development in Somalia, it is unhelpful to draw firm distinctions between 'social media' on one hand and professional journalism or official state communication on the other. The parallel trajectories of reconfigured state power and digital, social media platform-linked journalism blur these boundaries, and weak institutionalisation of nascent political structures means that the state may communicate directly (and not always coherently) with citizens via social media. Furthermore, local and transnational networks of Somali-language news media interact and intersect through social media platforms, creating space for new types of network and producer.

The emergence of a group such as Dalsoor Media (primarily through social media platforms such as YouTube) is an instructive example of this process and also highlights some of the complex ideological fault lines that exist at the heart of the Somali state reconfiguration process. Dalsoor was founded by Jamaal Cusmaan, an internationally renowned British-Somali journalist who has produced content for UK media outlets such as Channel 4 News and the *Guardian*. Cusmaan's work has long been characteristically critical of foreign security-related intervention in Somalia, highlighting, for instance, the role of foreign intelligence agencies in the running of secret places of detention and interrogation in Mogadishu.[4] Apparently identifying a gap in the Somali-language news media market for critical nationalistic broadcasting of a high technical quality, Dalsoor Media emerged as a primarily online vehicle for Cusmaan and other journalists to bring such themes to local and diasporic Somali-speaking audiences. The majority of Dalsoor's output has constituted short polemic documentaries broadcast via their website and YouTube channel, often focusing on foreign interference and local corruption in Somali politics and society.

One of their most notable broadcasts was a filmed interview with Al Shabaab spokesman Sheekh Cali Maxamuud Raage 'Dheere'. The interview was conducted by another high-profile international journalist of Somali heritage (Al Jazeera English's Hamze Mohamed) on behalf of Dalsoor.[5] Cali Dheere is one of Al Shabaab's most visible representatives and is a high-value target for foreign (US) and FGS military capture/kill operations. Given the sensitivity of his location, the fact that Dalsoor and Mohamed were able to gain access to the interviewee demonstrates the efficacy of their network of contacts in the region. Whilst the journalist's questions were hardly uncritical, the very nature and facilitation of the interview was taken by some Somali commentators as evidence of Dalsoor's sympathy for a terrorist agenda and an undermining of the FGS. As such, the interviewer was subsequently detained by FGS authorities on his return to Mogadishu and interrogated by National Intelligence and Security Agency (NISA) operatives.

It is not the objective of this chapter to comment on the ethics of broadcasting the statements of militants, although this is a highly sensitive question in the Mogadishu context. Instead, observations of these types of network and the subsequent analyses of other social media controversies since 2012 demonstrate the affordances provided by social media platforms in settings of contentious politics to facilitate the diversification of elite and local journalistic production. Such processes both reflect and further condition the complexities of ideological and cultural expression which cannot simply be reduced to Global War on Terror binaries of militant-Islamist/liberal-secularist affiliations. The FGS is attempting to assert itself in a decentralised media ecology which it cannot dominate in any substantive fashion. Instead of studying the impact of social media from the perspective of a coherent authoritarian state (and attempts to manage or take advantage of new media technologies), the experiences of the FGS outlined below demonstrate the context-specific and coterminous emergence of new forms of state power alongside significant developments in popular media production, reception and utilisation.

The securitisation of media

As the first internationally recognised government to take power in Mogadishu since 1991, President Xasan Sheikh Maxamuud's administration (2012–2017) was frequently engaged in attempts to gain control of the media narrative around urban security, and discredit the displaced militants who retained the capacity to strike targets close to centres of state power. During this period Al Shabaab maintained a fairly consistent pace of targeted assassinations of MPs and other individuals broadly associated with the government, as well as complex suicide attacks on locations such as hotels, the fortified airport zone and government ministries.

Al Shabaab maintains a broad network of official and affiliated media organisations and employs a variety of platforms (including social media) to distribute multi-lingual propaganda of various themes, for instance 'documentaries' extolling the virtues of life under the 'Shade of Shariah' in various locations where the group has held administrative control (Chonka 2016). The dynamic nature of its communications can be seen through the networks involved in disseminating real-time information about ongoing 'operations' in Mogadishu (Chonka 2018) and in large-scale assaults on fixed AMISOM positions in the rural interior. There, embedded cameramen take battlefield footage which is incorporated in fast-produced communications about apparent victories. The technical quality of this often graphic footage contributes to its rapid spread across social media and the myriad Somali news websites.[6] Such sites may not be run by Al Shabaab supporters but they nonetheless use this material in order to document events that are deemed newsworthy to audiences. Considering the slim economic margins and reliance on advertising revenues for this vast and fragmented online news media ecology, the value of this content as potential 'clickbait' is an important consideration. Al Shabaab also occasionally communicates directly with foreign journalists and translates and deploys a range of external material (ranging from NGO reports to external policy briefings) to bolster its claims of continued vitality and the weakness or corruption of the FGS, who are portrayed as 'stooges' of Western imperialists.[7]

In response, the FGS has, at times, attempted to directly shape the media narrative through ambiguous directives on the use of the name 'Al Shabaab' (exhorting journalists to use the derogatory acronym 'UGUS' instead) and selectively prosecuting radio broadcasters ostensibly for their use of recorded militant statements.[8] Whilst news media cannot be described as 'free' in Somalia – given such moves and wider patterns of violence from state and non-state actors against journalists – the state has not been able to systematically block the rebroadcasting of Al Shabaab material through private news sites as it is unable to guarantee protection to such entities in the case of militant retaliation (UN 2016: 27).

Aside from this attempted regulation, the FGS developed its own media strategy designed to highlight security gains in the capital and the efforts of security forces such as NISA to investigate and thwart militant activity. An example of these efforts could be seen in the case of Xasan Xanafi, a journalist affiliated with an Al Shabaab's radio station who was extradited to Somalia from Kenya early in 2016 to face trial for his involvement in the killing of several other media professionals in the capital between 2007 and 2011. Before being sentenced to death by a military court, state-run Somali National Television (in collaboration with NISA) broadcast an extended interview (advertised and rebroadcast through social media platforms such as YouTube) with the accused in custody.[9] Xanafi was subsequently executed by firing squad in what was, essentially, a public execution: pictures in the Somali media appeared in Twitter and Facebook newsfeeds moments after it occurred.

Irrespective of judicial process, this incident highlighted both the capacity and challenges faced by the state in waging a public relations battle against Al Shabaab through interlinked 'state' and 'social' media. The broadcasting of Xanafi's apparent confession prompted the production of a counter-narrative by unidentified but presumably pro-Al Shabaab propagandists claiming to have obtained a voice recording of Xanafi in custody, distancing himself from what he alleged was a forced confession at the hands of local and Western intelligence operatives.[10] This YouTube 'documentary' ignored questions of Xanafi's alleged guilt and focused instead on the activities of foreign intelligence services. Characteristic of the militant media assemblages noted above, the bilingual (Somali–English) film featured material from the UK's *Channel Four News* (a piece by aforementioned British-Somali journalist Jamaal Cusmaan on foreign detention and interrogation in Mogadishu) and was produced by a self-styled human-rights advocacy group.[11] Such interaction demonstrates the range of formats employed by anti-state elements in their propaganda and the constant discursive interaction, via overlapping platforms of 'social' and 'official' media, between the FGS and Al Shabaab (and their supporters).

The nascent state's broadcasting of counter-terrorism or counter-insurgency efforts could also be seen to have had practical ramifications for how such operations are conducted. Prominent commentators, such as former head of the BBC Somali Service Yusuf Garaad, voiced concerns through Facebook, blog posts and private news websites that the FGS's broadcasting of images and interviews with Al Shabaab suspects was potentially detrimental to investigations and judicial processes.[12] Furthermore, the same high-profile figure (who was later appointed Foreign Minister under President Farmaajo) also criticised journalists' use of social media platforms in the midst of ongoing Al Shabaab attacks, suggesting that militants could follow the Twitter feeds of journalists to gain operational intelligence.[13] Garaad's use of Facebook is also illustrative here of the preferred platforms that prominent figures, public intellectuals and state officials use to communicate with various constituencies. The embryonic nature of state institutions in Mogadishu is accompanied by a high turnover of ministers, many of whom come from backgrounds outside of government. Habits of popular social media engagement by these individuals carry over into their state roles and this has implications for the maintenance of clear communications channels from government. This is a point returned to in the following section on more recent controversies.

The state, social media and 'Somalia rising' (again)

The sense of optimism that accompanied the parliamentary (s)election of President Maxamed Cabdilaahi 'Farmaajo' was reminiscent of the popular mood that greeted his predecessor in 2012. Then, Xasan Sheikh Maxamuud's background as a civil society activist (who had stayed in the country since the civil war) was viewed positively by many local and international commentators. Although the US–Somali dual citizen President Farmaajo could hardly be described as an outsider given his past stint as Prime Minister, this brief previous term in office had endeared him to a large segment of the population who saw him as a staunch (anti-Ethiopian) nationalist and a politician with the will and capacity to undertake technocratic reforms, particularly around payments for security forces. Although both Xasan Sheikh Maxamuud *and* Farmaajo were allegedly backed by Qatari money (Roble 2017), the latter's eventual selection by MPs was popularly perceived as being something of a surprise given the clout of former leaders who were standing against him, and significant amounts of foreign money bankrolling other 'campaigns' to ensure support amongst electors in the newly formed Parliament.

Although the selection process was live-streamed via Facebook, it can hardly be said that Farmaajo was brought to power by social media. Although commentators have pointed out that Farmaajo appeared to be the most popular candidate in online debates and Twitter 'polling' conducted by journalists (Mursal 2017), this was not a one-person-one-vote national election and the extent to which the involved MPs were influenced by candidates' respective social media strategies or standing is difficult to ascertain. Nonetheless, the narrative of his 'unexpected' victory was amplified by social media particularly on the streets of Mogadishu. '*Farmaajo ii geeya*' ('bring me to Farmaajo') was the chant of a young man leading an enthusiastic crowd celebrating in public that night, the video of which went 'viral' across social media, rapidly becoming an emblem for narrative and musical expressions of optimism around the political transition.

These popular discourses chimed with earlier articulations of the 'Somalia rising' narrative predating Farmaajo's elevation to the presidency. Increased numbers of diaspora returnees post-2012 brought with them (and contributed to) local social media practices designed to highlight an alternative perspective on Somalia's political and security situation. Many Somali social media users have been quick to highlight overly negative or sensationalist 'mainstream' and external media reporting on Somalia,[14] countering such narratives with trending visual material of Mogadishu's physical redevelopment, the beauty of its coastline or the quality of its culinary offerings.[15] The chapter will return to tensions that exist in this popular discursive environment between reporting of realities of violence and mediated 'solidarity' with Somalia below. However, it is first necessary to examine the ways in which state authorities themselves attempt to utilise these debates, and the potential blurring of communicative channels that occurs when government actors employ social media platforms themselves.

Like most other modern governments, the FGS is increasingly required to manage its social media profile, utilise different communicative platforms to engage with constituents and promote particular narratives of governance. Given the wave of popular sentiment that accompanied President Farmaajo's selection, the administration was quick to capitalise on this goodwill and intensify efforts to broadcast the new administration's activities and stance on various issues. These efforts often coalesced around a #*NabadIyoNolol* ('Peace and life') social media hashtag that denoted broad support for the new government. Farmaajo's widely broadcasted donning of military fatigues demonstrated an apparent commitment to intensified military engagements with Al Shabaab, while images of the President strolling on Lido beach in a 'team Somalia'-esque tracksuit was clearly intended to portray a 'man of the people' engaging at ease with ordinary folk at a location with high symbolic resonance for the 'Somalia rising' narrative.

This type of public relations strategy has become a topic of divisive popular debate, itself inevitably and recursively playing out through the same social media channels. Here a critique of the state's perceived immaterial self-promotion emerged around the *'Igu sawir'* debate, epitomised by Ilkacase Qays' pop song quoted at the beginning of the chapter. Both the governments of Xasan Sheikh Maxamuud and Maxamed Cabdullahi Farmaajo faced popular criticism for a lack of tangible support given to a female member of the armed forces who was injured in 2016.[16] The slogan (and music video) thus made reference to the eagerness of politicians to be photographed with such individuals or initiatives for (social) media purposes without demonstrating tangible improvements in governance capacity or the ability to actually get things done.

Whilst the levelling of such a criticism is hardly unique to Somalia, this trending topic and ensuing debate raised questions about government communication strategies in a context where social media platforms have become a primary vector for the dissemination of information from the state itself. Lacking a dominant or highly resourced state broadcaster, and competing in a highly fragmented digital media environment where private Somali-language commercial broadcasting overlaps almost seamlessly with social media, government figures have increasingly relied upon such platforms to communicate with various constituencies. Whilst this is the new media environment in which the nascent state finds itself, the proclivity of state officials to communicate via social media (such as President Farmaajo's 'tweeting' of his appointment of the Prime Minister before its announcement by state media[17]) presents new dilemmas for authorities in maintaining coherent lines of communication, particularly around contentious issues.

Few issues are more contentious than the presence and operations of foreign forces in Somali territory. US military involvement in operations against Al Shabaab has intensified since 2012 with an increase in drone strikes and Special Forces kill/capture raids being undertaken independently or alongside Somali troops. President Trump's March 2017 designation of the country as a 'zone of active hostilities' represented a continuation of this trend with increasing operational freedoms being devolved to commanders at lower levels of the military hierarchy. The coastal and agriculturally rich Lower Shabelle region south-west of Mogadishu is a primary theatre of such operations. Al Shabaab has maintained a significant presence in the region and its proximity to Mogadishu provides space for preparing attacks on the capital. On 25 August 2017, US Special Forces undertook a joint operation with Somali troops in the town of Bariire recently seized from Al Shabaab. In the course of the pre-dawn raid, ten civilians (reportedly including three children) were shot dead.

While pictures of the bodies were released and disseminated both by pro-Shabaab and unaffiliated local media, an initial statement from the Ministry of Information released both on the Minister's Facebook page and to the media suggested that no civilians had been killed in the operation.[18] In a separate post (in Somali) the Minister also stated that a full investigation would take place about the incident and that its findings would be released to the public.[19] Various other military, federal and local government officials then made contradictory statements through social and news media channels before it was established that ten civilians had, in fact, been killed in the raid (most of whom hailed from the politically influential and well-armed Habir Gedir subclan, whose elders would later negotiate sizeable compensation payments). The Minister's original Facebook post was subsequently removed and contradictory communications were explained as being the result of confusion about multiple military operations around Bariire that night.[20] Aside from igniting a popular social media debate between ordinary people and politicians (which the news media, as elsewhere, recursively reports as being news in and of itself[21]), the incident soon prompted the Office of the Prime Minister to issue a directive to all ministries forbidding them to release any information on social media or directly to journalists without prior approval.[22] Not only did this throw into question the procedural relationship between the Ministry of Information and the Office of the Prime Minister, but it also highlighted the broader difficulties encountered by the nascent state attempting to maintain a coherent narrative in the context of a dynamic security environment and anarchic (social) media ecology.

The importance of the Lower Shabelle conflict theatre's proximity to Mogadishu was underscored by the massive truck bomb detonated on 14 October 2017 at the busy Zoobe intersection in the heart of the capital. The attack was prepared and launched from this area and the main vehicle proceeded through checkpoints unchallenged into the city. While civilian casualties of militant attacks have always occurred, the location and magnitude of the blast – which claimed over 587 lives – was distinctive in the recent conflict history of the city.

Various dynamics of social media engagement with this attack are of relevance to this chapter's wider argument. In the aftermath of the blast extensive use was made by state and civil society actors of social media platforms to coordinate the search for the missing, and to 'crowdfund' emergency response services. Often led by diaspora Somalis or returnees, an emerging tech sector – based in Mogadishu and connected abroad – has innovated around pressing humanitarian concerns, often using open source platforms to provide new online tools. A prior example of this was the *Ushahidi*-based *Abaaraha* platform facilitating contact between humanitarian actors and victims of the drought that affected large swathes of Somalia through 2016–2017. In the context of the 14 October attack, the *Gurmad252* campaign involved fifty volunteers processing data from family members and bystanders to build an accurate picture of the destruction and to disseminate important information to injured victims and relatives (Dahir 2017). Although this constituted a 'civil society' initiative, it was promoted through government (social) media channels and became one of the most visible mechanisms through which services were coordinated. Once again, the blurring of lines between government and non-government agency became apparent with both sets of actors communicating and interacting through similar social media platforms.

The very fact that the bombing was able to take place highlighted state weakness and the continued incapacity of state security forces to secure access to the city. President Farmaajo's early post-selection 'honeymoon' period had already been thrown into question by a continued frequency of bomb attacks in the capital, while his 'nationalist' credentials were dented by his government's handling of the extradition of a senior Ogaden National Liberation Front operative to Ethiopia. The scale of the attack on 14 October necessitated a major public relations drive that, to a large extent, played out over social media and involved a bewildering cast of characters. One aspect of this mediated response involved popular blood donations and the self-publicisation of high-profile figures hooked up to the needle. These ranged from President Farmaajo himself and the British Ambassador, to Sheikh Mukhtaar Roobow – former founder member of Al Shabaab who had recently defected out of exile to the FGS. The latter individual's controversial intervention was wryly described by one Somali journalist on Twitter as *Igu sawir* 'gone too far',[23] highlighting the complexity of the discursive battlefield on which responses to violence are played out, and the multiple platforms available for individuals to insert themselves into the debate. Roobow's post-defection social media visibility was a prelude to a predicted run for government office. At the time of writing, he is standing for the presidency of the South-West Federal

State and stands a good chance of winning, assuming his path is not blocked by opposition from the FGS or Ethiopia.

Influenced by popular social media-led responses to mass terrorist violence in the West, many Somali commentators called for external signs of 'solidarity' with Mogadishu in the wake of the 14 October bombing, and lamented their general absence as a sign of the hypocrisy or racism of international media coverage. Commentators argued, with justification, that had such carnage been wrought in a Western capital then the scale and tone of coverage would have been different: why, they asked, was this not front-page news for all international outlets? Many of these same commentators have also previously critiqued the same 'mainstream' and external media for their portrayals of Somalia solely in the negative terms of violence, destruction and terrorism – a narrative that the 'Somalia rising' idea attempts to dispel with focus on many of the positive aspects of urban economic change. Recent literature highlights the potential role of social media in giving voice to 'subaltern' actors to challenge mainstream representations of contentious politics, with the Kenyan #SomeoneTellCNN campaign constituting an archetypical example (Adeiza & Howard 2016). Nonetheless, the debates around the portrayal of the 14 October destruction in Mogadishu highlighted tensions between various calls for coverage and amorphous and social-mediated 'solidarity', alongside earlier critiques of sensationalisations of violence that are equally problematic and replete with racialised undertones. This is not to suggest that objective and humane reporting cannot tread this fine line effectively. Rather, it prompts recognition that despite the recursive, potentially levelling and dialogic potentials of social/mainstream media engagement, the cumulative coverage of these overlapping media platforms is still often inadequate for the portrayal of any complex social environment – let alone the dynamic contradictions that characterise ideological and economic contestation in a city such as Mogadishu.

In this regard, a hint at the complexity of the ideological terrain of this social media environment can be found by returning to the profile of the rapper whose critical '*Igu sawir*' anthem has been referred to throughout the chapter. Ilkacase Qays's music blends hip-hop culture with ideas of diasporic-inflected transnational Somali solidarity. Its mediation through journalistic and social media networks epitomises the diverse assemblage of narratives and ideological positions that feed into debates around state reconstruction. For example, in a

YouTube-broadcast interview with (the also aforementioned) Dalsoor Media, the rapper emphasises both his amazement at Mogadishu's physical regeneration, and his desire that un-Islamic influences might be removed from the country.[24] His use here of the word *gaal* (non-believer) at this point in the interview is striking for its discursive linkage with the 'foreign', and indeed, is (mis)translated that way in the English subtitles that accompany the Somali audio. Ilkacase's recorded music and live public performance would hardly endear him to various Islamist factions active in Somali politics and the ongoing conflict. Nonetheless, his articulation of nationalist themes in the intersection of diasporic culture, and politically oriented and social media-platformed critical journalism, highlight the ways in which the new media environment facilitates a significant blurring of ideological affiliations towards a 'rising' Somalia. Reductive binary conceptions of 'Islamist' militant versus 'nationalist' state-builders are clearly inadequate here for understanding the tenor of these globalised but nationalistic debates in Somali social media.

Conclusion

This chapter has demonstrated how prior conditions of prolonged statelessness have shaped a context where state governance can be quickly challenged through an anarchic media ecology. This environment is further fragmented by the accessible interactive technologies of social media, their blurring of public/private, state/non-state distinctions, and associated practices of assemblage and remediation that both polarise and complexify the ideological tone of these debates. Moving beyond the merely discursive, the chapter also shows how those who have become part of the nascent state may lack the governmental experience that might inculcate practices of communication along lines more 'appropriate' (at least in the conventional sense) to state broadcasting and public engagement. If Donald Trump's presidency-by-Twitter can be seen to throw into question established norms of institutional communication for a powerful Western government, then one must also consider the implications of political social media engagement by power holders in a state at the extreme opposite end of the international state-capacity spectrum.

Here, the Somali state is being arduously reconstructed *in a context* of increasing digital and social media ubiquity, alongside continued armed conflict. Past repertoires of state broadcasting are limited in their effectiveness or legitimacy in this new media environment, and thus the social media communication strategies of state actors may themselves affect emergent popular understandings of what governance and state authority 'mean'. With everyone from government ministers and armed opposition members to nationalistic rappers and critical journalists hammering out debates over governance on a complex and ambiguous ideological terrain – and through the same social media platforms – what impact does this have on the privileged communicative position or the aura of prestige of the state? Whilst this question lies beyond the scope of the chapter, the analysis presented has highlighted novel problematics of state-making on the fringes of the global 'network society'. As such, the social media environment presents new dilemmas of concern to both would-be political leaders in a (post-)conflict Somalia, and to those who are attempting to understand processes of state-making and breaking in the Horn of Africa and wider continent.

Notes

1 Maxamed-Qays Cabdulqaadir Dhuubow Yare (AKA 'Ilkacase Qays')/ Aflaanta Studio '*Igu Sawir*' 2 August 2017. www.youtube.com/watch?v=Mn4kAm5-tpM (accessed 11 December 2018).

2 Harun Maruf, VOA Somali, '*Canshuuraha ay Al-Shabaab qaado*' [The taxes collected by Al Shabaab] 23 October 2018. www.voasomali.com/a/4625543.html (accessed 11 December 2018).

3 2015 Survey data from local commercial research firm Datagrid reported 97% phone ownership amongst Mogadishu residents of all 17 districts, with 56% of the sample (386) owning smartphones. Datagrid Report. www.yumpu.com/xx/document/view/39963506/telecom-survey-summary-final-email (accessed 1 November 2017).

4 Channel 4 News, 'Is the US overseeing torture in Somalia?' 9 December 2014. www.channel4.com/news/somalia-torture-united-states-cia-al-shabaab-video (accessed 15 February 2017).

5 Dalsoor Media, '*Wareysi Qaybtii 1aad: Sheekh Cali Dheere*' 5 January 2017 [Interview Part One: Sheekh Cali Dheere]. www.youtube.com/watch?v=BJwuw-Homgs (accessed 12 April 2017).

6 Caasimadda Online, 1 July 2015, '*Daawo sawirada Al Shabaab oo soo bandhigay meydadka askarii Burundi ee lagu dilay Leego*' [See pictures that Al Shabaab has published of bodies of Burundian soldiers killed in Leego]. http://caasimadda.com/daawo-sawirada-alshabaab-oo-soo-bandhigay-meydadka-askarii-burundi-ee-lagu-dilay-leego/ (accessed 28 June 2016).

7 Voice of Somalia.net, March 18, 2014, '*The Economist: Xasan Sheekh Si Musuq maasuq ah ayaa lagu soo doortay*' [*The Economist*: Xasan Sheekh was elected through corrupt practices]. https://voiceofsomalia.net/tag/xasan-gurguurte/page/5/ (accessed 1 November 2017).

8 UGUS: *Ururka Gumaadka Ummadda Soomaaliyeed* (Organisation for the slaughter of the Somali Ummah). Keydmedia, 3 May 2015, '*Warbaahinta*

oo Afka la qabtay: Ma maqli karno Magaca Al shabaab – Tuuryare' ['The media instructed: we cannot hear the name Al Shabaab – Tuuryare']. www.keydmedia.net/news/article/ warbaahinta_oo_afka_la_qabtay_ma_ maqli_karno_magaca_al_shabaab_ugus_ha/ (accessed 28 March 2019)

9 Somali National Television, 5 February 2016 *'Dilaaga Wariyaha – waa kuma Xasan Xanafi?'* [Journalist killer – who is Xasan Xanafi? www.youtube. com/watch?v=c-nGbproWkc (accessed 28 June 2016).

10 Journalists for Justice, 28 March 2016, 'Confessions of a killer'. www. youtube.com/watch?v=egKm-ibQkM8 (accessed 28 June 2016).

11 'Journalists for Justice' is distinct from the organisation of the same name in Kenya.

12 Yuusuf Garaad, personal blog, 15 July 2014, *'Saxaafadda iyo sirdoonka'* [Journalists and the intelligence agencies. http://yusuf-garaad.blogspot. co.uk/2014/07/saxaafadda-iyo-sirdoonka. html (accessed 28 June 2016)

13 Yusuf Garaad, *Xaqiiqa Times* newspaper, Mogadishu, 10 April 2015. *'Warfaafin mise sirfaafin?'* ['News broadcasting or secrets broadcasting?']

14 The #SomeoneTellMaryHarper hashtag took aim at the BBC's use of an image of the aftermath of an Al Shabaab attack to illustrate a story about Mogadishu's first 'International Book Fair'. BBC 'Debating Mogadishu Pictures', 27 August 2015. www. bbc.co.uk/news/live/world-africa-34012096?ns_mchannel=social&ns_ source=twitter&ns_campaign=bbc_ live&ns_linkname=[Debating%20 Mogadishu%20pictures%2616:10]&ns_ fee=0#post_34076461 (accessed 14 December 2018).

15 For example, the social media 'stardom' of Ugaaso Abokor, a diaspora returnee who generated significant international attention for her

Instagrammed take on life in Mogadishu: BBC, '#BBCtrending: The Somali woman who's become a global star on Instagram', 17 February 2015. www. bbc.co.uk/news/magazine-31462954 (accessed 28 June 2016).

16 BBC Somali Service, 27 July 2017, *'Maxaa keenay in erayada "Igu Sawir" iyo "Igu Dayo" ay qabsadaan baraha bulshada?'* ['What's brought the terms "*igu sawir*" and "*igu dayo*" into social media?'] www.bbc.com/somali/war-40741905 (accessed 25 October 2017).

17 @M_Farmaajo's official Twitter Feed, Tweet 22 February 2017. https://twitter.com/M_Farmaajo/ status/834613741266296834 (accessed 1 November 2017).

18 Radio Kulmiye, 25 August 2017, *'Dowladda Soomaaliya "Bariire 8 Shabaab ah ayaa ku dilnay"'*. ['Somali Government: "We killed 8 Shabaab at Bariire"'.] http://radiokulmiye.net/2017/08/25/ dowladda-soomaaliyabariire-8-shabaab-ah-ayaa-ku-dilnay-akhriso/ (accessed 27 October 2017).

19 Garowe Online, 25 August 2017, *'Wasiirka Warfaafita DF Somalia oo ka Hadlay Falkii Bariire'* ['Somali Federal Government Minister of Information speaks about Bariire incident']. www. garoweonline.com/so/news/somalia/ wasiirka-warfaafinta-df-somalia-oo-ka-hadlay-falkii-bariire (accessed 27 October 2017).

20 Various Somali online news sites featured a screengrab of the Foreign Minister's statement on this apparent confusion. See Warkii Online, 26 August 2017, *'Wasiirka Arrimaha Dibadda Soomaaliya Yuusuf Garaad oo war kasoo saaray weerarkii Bariire'*. ['Foreign Minister Yuusuf Garaad releases information about Bariire attack'.] www. warkii.com/wasiirka-arrimaha-dibadda-soomaaliya-yuusuf-garaad-oo-war-kasoo-saaray-weerarkii-bariire/ (accessed 27 October 2017).

21 Caasimada Online, 26 August 2017, '*Xasuuqa Bariire oo baraha bulshada qabsaday iyo DF oo cadaadis la kulmeysa*'. ['The Bariire massacre taken up on social media and Federal Government faces pressure'.] www.caasimada.net/xasuuqa-bariire-oo-baraha-bulshada-qabsaday-df-oo-cadaadis-la-kulmeysa/ (accessed 27 October 2017).

22 A copy of the notification letter (Somali) is available at Radio Shacab, 27 August 2017, '*Akhriso: Golaha Wasiirada oo lagu amray in ogolaansho la'aan isticmaali karin Warbaahinta*' [Read: Cabinet ordered not to use media without permission] https://radioshacab.com/articles/16490/Akhriso-Golaha-Wasiirada-oo-Lagu-Amray-in-ogolaansho-Laaan-isticmaali-Karin-Warbaahinta (accessed 26 March 2019).

23 Liban Ahmad, tweet, 16 October 2017. https://twitter.com/Libanahmad1/status/919899752329830400 (accessed 17 October 2017).

24 Dalsoor Media/Youtube '*Ilkacase Qays wareysi Muqdisho dhex wareegaya Daawo 2017*' ['Watch 2017 interview with Ilkacase Qays in Mogadishu'.] 1 November 2017. Since removed from YouTube.

References

Adam, S. M. (2001) *Gather Round the Speakers: a History of the First Quarter Century of Somali Broadcasting, 1941–1966.* London: Haan.

Adeiza, M. & Howard, P. (2016) 'Social media and soft power politics in Africa: lessons from Nigeria's #BringBackOurGirls and Kenya's #SomeoneTellCNN'. In N. Chitty, L. Ji, G. Rawnsley & C. Hayden (eds.), *The Routledge Handbook of Soft Power.* Abingdon: Routledge, pp. 219–231.

Asmolov, G. (2014) 'The Kremlin's cameras and virtual Potemkin villages: ICT and the construction of statehood'. In S. Livingston & G. Walter-Drop (eds.), *Bits and Atoms: Information and Communication Technology in Areas of Limited Statehood.* Oxford: Oxford University Press, pp. 30–46.

Banda, F., Mudhai, O.F. & Tettey, W.J. (2009) 'Introduction: New media and democracy in Africa – a critical interjection'. In F. Banda, O.F. Mudhai & W.J. Tettey (eds.), *African Media and the Digital Public Sphere.* Basingstoke: Palgrave Macmillan, pp. 1–20.

Barnes, C. & Hassan. H. (2007) 'The rise and fall of Mogadishu's Islamic Courts'. *Journal of Eastern African Studies*, 1(2): 151–160.

Bertot, J.C., Jaeger, P.T. & Grimes, J.M. (2010) 'Using ICTs to create a culture of transparency: E-government and social media as openness and anti-corruption tools for societies'. *Government Information Quarterly*, 27(3): 264–271.

Bruns, A., Highfield, T. & Burgess, J. (2013) 'The Arab spring and social media audiences: English and Arabic twitter users and their networks'. *American Behavioral Scientist*, 57(7): 871–898.

Chonka, P. (2016) 'Spies, stonework, and the suuq: Somali nationalism and the narrative politics of pro-Harakat Al Shabaab Al Mujaahidiin online propaganda'. *Journal of Eastern African Studies*, 10(2): 247–265.

Chonka, P. (2018) 'New media, performative violence, and state reconstruction in Mogadishu'. *African Affairs*, 117(468): 392–414.

Chonka, P. (2019) 'News media and political contestation in the Somali territories: defining the parameters of a transnational digital public'.

Journal of Eastern African Studies, 13(1): 140–157.

Dahir, A.L. (2017) 'How technology helped save lives right after Somalia's deadliest attack ever'. *Quartz*, 16 October 2017 https://qz.com/1103014/somalias-deadliest-ever-mogadishu-attack-was-lessened-by-technology/ (accessed 20 October 2017).

Feldman, B. (2012) 'Somalia: amidst the rubble, a vibrant telecommunications infrastructure'. *Review of African Political Economy*, 34(113): 565–572.

Gagliardone, I. (2014) 'New media and the developmental state in Ethiopia'. *African Affairs*, 113(451): 279–299.

Gruzd, A. & Roy, J. (2014) 'Investigating political polarization on Twitter: a Canadian perspective'. *Policy & Internet*, 6(1): 28–45.

Hammond, L. (2013) 'Somalia rising: things are starting to change for the world's longest failed state'. *Journal of Eastern African Studies*, 7(1), 183–193.

Hansen, S. J. (2013) *Al-Shabaab in Somalia: the History and Ideology of a Militant Islamist Group, 2005–2012*. London: Hurst.

Hess, A. (2015) 'The selfie assemblage'. *International Journal of Communication*, 9: 1629–1646.

Johnson, J.W. (1974) *Heellooy, Heelleellooy: the Development of the Genre Heello in Modern Somali Poetry*. Indiana University Publications African Series (5).

Kapteijns, L. (2010) 'Making Memories of Mogadishu in Somali poetry about the civil war'. In L. Kapteijns & A. Richters (eds.) *Mediations of Violence in Africa*. Leiden: Brill, pp. 25–74.

Kavanaugh et al. (2012) 'Social media use by government: from the routine to the critical'. *Government Information Quarterly*, 29(4): 480–491.

Lange, P.G. (2007) 'Publicly private and privately public: social networking on YouTube'. *Journal of Computer-Mediated Communication*, 13(1), 361–380.

Livingston, S. & Walter-Drop, G. (2014) 'Introduction'. In S. Livingston & G. Walter-Drop (eds.), *Bits and Atoms: Information and Communication Technology in Areas of Limited Statehood*. Oxford: Oxford University Press, pp. 1–14.

Lynch, M. (2011) 'After Egypt: the limits and promise of online challenges to the authoritarian Arab state'. *Perspectives on Politics*, 9(2): 301–310.

Mursal, M.A. (2017) 'Somali elections online: the view from Mogadishu'. *The Horn of Africa Bulletin*, 29(1): 5–8.

NUSOJ (National Union of Somali Journalists) Annual Report (2014) 'Press Freedom at Risk in Somalia: Murder, Imprisonment, Censorship and Bad Laws'. www.ifex.org/somalia/2015/01/13/somalia_annualreport_2014.pdf (accessed 20 January 2016).

Parks, L. & Mukherjee, R. (2017) 'From platform jumping to self-censorship: internet freedom, social media, and circumvention practices in Zambia'. *Communication and Critical/Cultural Studies*, 14(3): 221–237.

Phillips, J. (2006) 'Agencement/assemblage'. *Theory Culture and Society*, 23(2/3): 108–109.

Reuters (2013) 'Somalia gets first fibre-optic link to the world'. 12 November 2013. www.reuters.com/article/us-somalia-telecoms/somalia-gets-first-fiber-optic-link-to-the-world-idUSBRE9AB0SN20131112 (accessed 1 November 2017).

Roble, M.A. (2017) '"Neutral" Somalia finds itself engulfed in Saudi Arabia-Qatar dispute'. *African Arguments*, 18 August 2017. https://africanarguments.org/2017/08/16/neutral-somalia-finds-itself-engulfed-in-saudi-arabia-qatar-dispute/ (accessed 18 August 2017).

Samatar, S.S. (1982) *Oral Poetry and Somali Nationalism: the Case of Sayid Mahammad 'Abdille Hasan.* Cambridge: Cambridge University Press.

Singh, J.P. (2014) 'E-government as a means of development in India'. In S. Livingston & G. Walter-Drop (eds.), *Bits and Atoms: Information and Communication Technology in Areas of Limited Statehood.* Oxford: Oxford University Press, pp. 47–60.

Srinivasan, S. (2014) 'FrontlineSMS, Mobile-for Development, and the "Long Tail" of Governance'. In S. Livingston & G. Walter-Drop (eds.), *Bits and Atoms: Information and Communication Technology in Areas of Limited Statehood.* Oxford: Oxford University Press, pp. 1–14.

Stremlau, N., Fantini, E., & Gagliardone, I. (2015) 'Patronage, politics and performance: radio call-in programmes and the myth of accountability'. *Third World Quarterly,* 36(8): 1510–1526.

Stremlau, N., Fantini, E. & Osman, R. (2015) 'The political economy of the media in the Somali conflict'. *Review of African Political Economy,* 43(147): 43–57.

Tukefci, Z. & Wilson, C. (2012) 'Social media and the decision to participate in political protest: observations from Tahrir Square'. *Journal of Communication,* 62(2): 363–379.

United Nations Assistance Mission in Somalia/Office of the United Nations High Commissioner for Human Rights (2016) 'Report on the right to freedom of expression: striving to widen democratic space in Somalia's political transition'.

Van Dijck, J. (2013) *The Culture of Connectivity: a Critical History of Social Media.* Oxford: Oxford University Press.

Wise, J. M. (2012) 'Attention and assemblage in the clickable world'. In J. Packer & S. B. Crofts Wiley (eds.), *Communication Matters: Materialist Approaches to Media, Mobility, and Networks.* New York: Routledge, pp. 159–172.

Wodak, R., Mral, B. & Khosravinik, M. (eds.) (2013) *Right-wing Populism in Europe: Politics and Discourse.* London: A&C Black.

Wolfsfeld, G., Segev E. & Sheafer, T. (2013) 'Social media and the Arab spring: politics comes first'. *The International Journal of Press/Politics,* 18(2): 115–137.

World Bank (2016) Somalia Internet Users Dataset: https://data.worldbank.org/indicator/IT.NET.USER.ZS (accessed 1 September 2018).

3 | 'WE ARE NOT JUST VOTERS, WE ARE CITIZENS'[1]

Social media, the #ThisFlag campaign and insurgent citizenship in Zimbabwe

George Karekwaivanane and Admire Mare

Introduction

On 19 April 2016, a day after Zimbabwe's independence day commemorations, a young Zimbabwean clergyman, Pastor Evan Mawarire, posted a video on his Facebook page of his anguished monologue about the deepening economic, social and political crisis in Zimbabwe. The video quickly went viral and was soon being reported on by local and international news organisations. In the weeks that followed, Mawarire and a small team began building on the unexpected popularity of his video and created a campaign that encouraged Zimbabwean citizens to speak out against the government's mismanagement of the country. Although he was not the first individual to use social media to attempt to mobilise Zimbabweans, the #ThisFlag campaign which aimed to embolden citizens to challenge government malfeasance gained unprecedented traction across the political, ethnic, class and racial divides. Aided by the creative use of emotive videos, memes, text and audio content, the campaign used social media to produce and distribute its action[2] and consensus[3] mobilisation frames. The campaign's broad-based appeal derived in large part from the non-partisan nature of its message, as well as the identity of Mawarire as a religious figure. It elicited enthusiasm especially among Zimbabweans in the diaspora and in urban areas who were encouraged to express their dissatisfaction with the ZANU-PF government's mismanagement of the economy and abuse of authority. Such was the momentum of the campaign that, in the absence of coherent opposition by the Movement for Democratic Change (MDC), Mawarire temporarily assumed the status of Zimbabwe's 'surrogate opposition leader'.

The emergence of the #ThisFlag movement and its success in co-ordinating public acts of protest, like the 6 July national stay-away, fuelled debate within the media and scholarly circles about the role of social media in Zimbabwean politics.[4] On the one hand, some commentators optimistically asserted that the successful shutdown was evidence of the power of social media in Zimbabwe to organise people and bring about political change. On the other, sceptics downplayed the role of social media, and cast doubt on the likelihood of a social media campaign sparking a revolution in Zimbabwe. These views echo broader debates about the role of social media in politics in different parts of the world (see Shirky 2008; Morozov 2011; Gladwell 2010; Diamond 2010; Wasserman 2011; Mare 2014; Mutsvairo 2016). The case study of the #ThisFlag campaign therefore has much to offer and gain from these broader efforts to understand whether, and under what circumstances, digital social media platforms can contribute to political expression, organisation and action.

This chapter takes up this task of examining what light the #ThisFlag campaign can shed on these broader scholarly debates. It is divided into five sections. In the following section we discuss the theoretical debates in more detail and set out the insights that we draw upon in our analysis of the campaign. The next section looks at the methodological approaches and ethical considerations that inform this chapter. This is followed by a section that traces the emergence of the #Thisflag campaign and locates its roots within the broader Zimbabwean socio-economic and political context during the post-2013 period. The next section provides an overview of the key protest actions that the campaign organised, and shows the gradual movement from predominantly online actions to the mobilisation of citizens on the ground. In the last section we evaluate the political role of social media in Zimbabwe and some of the key limitations it imposed on the #ThisFlag campaign.

Social media and politics: theoretical reflections

One perspective in the debate on the socio-political impact of social media has tended to celebrate the internet and associated digital technologies as 'liberation technologies' or 'technologies of freedom' (Papacharissi 2010; Diamond 2010; Shirky 2008). The celebratory tone of this strand of literature is vividly captured by Corey Courtemanche's claim that the 'Arab Spring' showed that 'millions of fingers plucking and poking at touch screen phones, logging in, posting and meeting up can bring down a government' (Courtemanche 2011). However, there is a growing body of work that persuasively challenges the techno-determinist assumptions of this early literature, and emphasises the importance of placing the social media-inspired or co-ordinated uprisings within their proper historical context (see Mare 2014; Wasserman 2011). As Merlyna Lim correctly points out:

> to fully understand the Tahrir revolt, we need to look beyond January 2011, past the usage of Facebook and Twitter, and focus instead on how protest networks emerged, expanded, and were translated into a momentous collective action – and how the internet and social media became entangled in these processes. (Lim 2011)

It is also now increasingly evident that digital media is a double-edged sword that empowers states and enhances their surveillance capabilities, even as citizens attempt to use it to resist or challenge those same states (Morozov 2011; Lim 2012; Gladwell 2010). Over and above this, is the risk that social media activity may not translate into any social or political change. Jodi Dean cautions that networked communication technologies are not only ineffectual but 'profoundly depoliticising' as they foster 'interpassivity': 'When we are interpassive', she explains, 'something else, a fetish object, is active in our stead' (Dean 2005: 60). For Dean: '[t]he paradox of the technological fetish is that the technology acting in our stead actually enables us to remain politically passive … The "fix" lets us think that all we need is to universalize a particular technology and then we will have a democratic or reconciled social order' (Dean 2005: 63). The ultimate beneficiary of this fetishisation of technology, she points out, is not citizenry, but communicative capitalism.

In this chapter we draw on these scholarly critiques that highlight the importance of studying the deeper context in which social media co-ordinated protests are set, the double-edged nature of digital technology and the risks of fetishisation and depoliticisation that accompany it. We apply these insights in our effort to analyse the political role and impact of the #ThisFlag campaign in Zimbabwe. In doing so we also build on Mohammed Zayani's study of the evolving relationship between politics and digital media in Tunisia during the years leading up to the uprising in 2011 that ousted President Zine El Abidine Ben Ali. Zayani (2015: 12) shifts the focus away from examining the internet 'as a tool to coordinate dissent and mobilise people', or in relation to political causality. Instead, he takes as his starting point the observation that it is also a space that is embedded in a broader socio-political context, and in which people participate in specific ways. He thus foregrounds the dynamics that emerged on the internet, and in particular the emergence of digital spaces and digital cultures of contention. In talking about contentious digital culture, Zayani (2015: 12) observes that: 'Contention emerges less as overt dissidence or resistance and more as forms of assertiveness. Contention invokes a set of practices, interactions, engagements, articulations, contestations, and rejections that are not necessarily politically framed but they are political in other ways'.

The #ThisFlag campaign provides a useful window onto the emerging digital spaces and cultures of contention in Zimbabwe. We contend that by looking at the different digital media platforms on which debates around the #ThisFlag hashtag were happening, it is possible to begin to plot the co-ordinates of emerging/expanding digital spaces of contention. In exploring the ways that these spaces and cultures are constituted in the context of #ThisFlag, we focus on the circulation of 'online artefacts of engagement' (Schofield Clark 2016). We argue that these artefacts played the dual role of hailing people into these digital spaces, and acting as vehicles for a rich and layered political discourse. We further argue that these digital spaces of contention were the sites for the performance of creative forms of 'insurgent citizenship' (Holston 1998, 2007). Drawing on his ethnography in the urban peripheries of Sao Paolo, James Holston argues that in cases where inequalities are reproduced, those existing at the periphery often resort to resistance practices. These practices aim to restore human dignity and citizenship rights. Instead of conforming to characterisations such as 'active citizen' and 'passive citizen', residents organise movements of insurgent citizenship to confront the entrenched regimes of citizen inequality that the urban centres use to segregate them. Building on Holston's notion of insurgent citizenship, we show how social media platforms provided alternative spaces of participation within which members of the #ThisFlag campaign asserted themselves as citizens in a context where the ZANU-PF government actively sought to exclude dissenting voices from the public sphere. Moreover, its political discourse constructed a differentiated citizenship in the country by dividing the populace into 'patriots' who were ZANU-PF supporters and 'sell-outs' who supported the opposition (Tendi 2010).

Methodology

A central element of our research has been connective ethnography which moved between virtual and non-virtual spaces in the same way that the Zimbabwean users of social media do. (See Hine 2007; Postill & Pink 2012; Dirkesen, Huizing & Smit 2010). The virtual dimension of the ethnography involved immersing ourselves in the three most widely used social media platforms in Zimbabwe: Twitter, Facebook and WhatsApp. We monitored Pastor Evan Mawarire's Twitter and Facebook handles, as well as the #ThisFlag hashtag on Twitter, in order to gain insight into the posting behaviours and frames of mobilisation of the #ThisFlag campaign. We also engaged in textual analysis of content gathered on Twitter, Facebook and WhatsApp posted between 19 April 2016 and mid-July 2016 when Pastor Mawarire left the country for the United States of America. In order to place the #ThisFlag campaign within the wider context of citizen activism in Zimbabwe, fourteen interviews were conducted in August and September of 2017 with the activists from a number of protests campaigns such as 'OccupyAfricaUnitySquare', '16 days of Occupation', the #Tajamuka and #ThisGown.[5] These interviews provided insider perspectives that were important in interpreting the data we collected from social media platforms.

Conducting such research in an authoritarian context such as Zimbabwe inevitably throws up important and complex ethical concerns. At the heart of these is the question of how to undertake research that provides an account of forms of insurgent citizenship that challenge an authoritarian regime, without putting participants in harm's way. This ethical concern was especially important given that at the time of writing Mawarire was on trial for allegedly subverting a constitutional government, and because the government was working towards creating a new Ministry of Cyber Security, Threat Detection and Mitigation. Of particular importance in such contexts is the need to prevent a dual form of silencing that is often presided over by authoritarian regimes. Not only are citizens unable to freely express dissenting views, but the stories of those who do speak can often go untold due to the very real possibility of government victimisation of defiant citizens, which leads to an indirect form of silencing. A related challenge is that of securing informed consent, something that becomes more difficult the larger the data set becomes, and the more authoritarian the context. Linked to this is the question of which material should be considered either public or private, and why it should be considered one or the other.

In trying to deal with these ethical concerns we have taken a number of steps. We secured Mawarire's consent to use images on, and screenshots of, his social media accounts. In drawing on data from Twitter and Facebook we have also made use of material that was posted with the hashtag #ThisFlag. We took the view that material that was posted on social media with a hashtag was intended to reach a wide audience and could therefore be treated as public (Townsend and Wallace n.d.: 12). We nevertheless decided to anonymise all of those who participated in the discussions around the campaign. We have also anonymised the name of one member of the #ThisFlag team, in order to protect his identity. In discussing the interactions on semi-public forums such as WhatsApp groups we have opted not to give detailed ethnographic vignettes of the interactions in these groups so as to avoid providing any details that could be used to identify the specific subjects under discussion, or the people who were party to the discussions. We have chosen instead to provide our observations about the nature of interactions and what they can tell us about the value of social media platforms as deliberative spaces. In doing all of this we hope to balance the need to tell the story of insurgent citizenship in Zimbabwe and how it found expression via social media, while protecting the identities of the individuals who participated in it.

The emergence of the #ThisFlag campaign

The proliferation of protest campaigns such as #ThisFlag that rocked Zimbabwe's political landscape in 2016 has to be understood in the context of the country's recent political history dating back to the establishment of the Government of National Unity (GNU) in 2009. Of particular importance was the hope that characterised the GNU period, and the subsequent disillusionment that accompanied the ZANU-PF electoral 'victory' in the July 2013 elections. The tenure of the GNU witnessed the restoration of economic stability after a period of record-breaking hyper-inflation. Thanks to the abandonment of the Zimbabwean dollar, food shortages in the shops soon became a thing of the past, and real wages began to rise along with the pace of economic growth. In 2010, for example, the economy grew by 8.1 percent, a figure that was well above the 5 percent average for sub-Saharan Africa that year (Reserve Bank of Zimbabwe 2011).

This upturn in the economy inspired a great deal of optimism about the country's future, to the extent that some individuals who had left the country in search of better economic opportunities began relocating back to Zimbabwe. However, after ZANU-PF's 2013 election 'victory', the economy took a turn for the worse, and by 2015 the rate of economic growth had dropped to 1.1 percent (Reserve Bank of Zimbabwe 2016). In addition, the prospects for future growth were undermined by low investor confidence in a government that was widely seen as hostile to foreign capital, a crippling liquidity crunch and low commodity prices on the international markets. The result was a downward spiral as companies shut down or downsized, and thus exacerbated the already severe unemployment levels. The circumstances of a significant number of those who were still employed were only marginally better as both the government and private corporations were finding it increasingly difficult to pay salaries on time. In addition, the cash shortages in the banks meant that individuals were not able to access what little money they had.

The numerous uninvestigated corruption scandals within the government, such as the mis-appropriation of US$15 billion in diamond revenues, reinforced the view that the ruling elite were using political office to enrich themselves at the expense of the country. The main opposition party, led by Morgan Tsvangirai, was not seen as a credible answer to the problems when soon after the 2013 elections it was consumed by infighting and schisms. The overall impact was that, in the face of the deepening socio-economic crisis, political elites from both the ruling party and the opposition were viewed as part of the problem and not the solution. It was this loss of faith in political elites that created the space for citizen-led campaigns to rise. The earliest of these was the 'Occupy Africa Unity Square' campaign which began in 2014 and was led by the journalist Itai Dzamara.[6] The abduction of Dzamara[7] led to a lull in citizen activism. However, 2016 witnessed the emergence of several citizen-led campaigns such as the '16 Days of Occupation', and those focussed on the #Tajamuka, #BeatThePot and #ThisGown hashtags.

This broader socio-economic and political context was central in driving Evan Mawarire, Michael Moyo and Kuda Musasiwa, the members of the small team behind #ThisFlag, to launch their campaign.[8] Encouraged by the positive outlook in 2010, Musasiwa and Mawarire decided to relocate back to Zimbabwe from the United Kingdom. However, within a few years they had become disappointed and disillusioned. In the days leading up to his initial video, Mawarire had been trying, without success, to raise money for his children's pre-school fees. This situation brought home to him how desperate his circumstances had become, driving him to record his now famous video.

It is important to underscore the unexpected nature of the video's popularity as this helps to understand the development of the campaign, as well as the factors behind its subsequent decline after Mawarire went into exile in mid-July 2016. Mawarire's initial intention had simply been to share his frustrations with the people he was connected to on Facebook.[9] It was only after it went viral that he and a few friends came together to see how they could use the video to spark a wider conversation among Zimbabwean citizens. As Musasiwa noted:

> ... we never thought it would become what it became. Let's be honest. We thought we would start up a hashtag and start becoming like involved in the conversation because a lot of people have just been apathetic, and we are going to get involved and start really amplifying some of these issues through social media ...[10]

The #ThisFlag campaign was therefore not the product of long-term strategising by seasoned activists who had a clear plan and a specific goal in mind. What the team did have, however, was a set of key skills that enabled them to build a campaign that captured the imagination of thousands of Zimbabweans in the country and beyond. Mawarire, the face of the campaign, was a seasoned and charismatic orator, who had studied and worked in marketing and public relations prior to becoming a religious minister. In the past he had also experimented with making and posting serialised mobile phone videos on his Facebook page. The series of religious-themed videos, entitled '#QuickCuppaWord', provided the template which the team later built on as they established the #ThisFlag campaign. Moyo, who was tasked with the role of mobilisation and engaging government officials, had a degree in politics and government. Lastly, Musasiwa, whose role was to manage the social media side, ran a marketing company and was therefore adept at using digital platforms to raise the profile of the campaign.

In the weeks and months that followed the 19 April posting, the team launched a series of protest actions that began online, but progressively came to include the mobilisation of people on the ground. Between 19 April and 14 July, Mawarire recorded and posted some 43 videos on his Facebook page. The majority garnered around 30,000 views, along with several hundred comments, likes and shares. The most popular videos were much more widely viewed. For example, his initial video had been viewed 177,413 times on Facebook by April 2017, while his 4 July 2016 video, in which he announced the plan to hold the first national stay-away, had been viewed 150,686 times. It is worth pointing out that these Facebook statistics provide an incomplete picture of the reach of his videos and the conversations they sparked. Many of the videos were also shared via WhatsApp, Twitter and YouTube, and they provoked vibrant debates on these different platforms.

'Logging citizens back on to politics':" #ThisFlag protest actions

The team's first initiative was to invite Zimbabweans all over the world to send 'selfies' of themselves with the national flag. In a tweet on 20 April 2016, Mawarire made the following appeal which kicked off the campaign: 'Wherever you are 2day I need you to urgently take a selfie holding or wearing yo Zimflag with pride put the hashtag #ThisFlag & see what we do'.

In response, the team received hundreds of selfies, many of which were posted on Mawarire's Twitter and Facebook accounts and used in the campaign's videos. This appeal for selfies was followed by the '#ThisFlag challenge' in which citizens were challenged to carry their flags wherever they went for seven days beginning on 1 May. The team later decided to extend the challenge up to Africa Day, on 25 May. During this period Mawarire recorded daily videos that highlighted specific everyday struggles that the team felt the government should deal with. For example, in his video on 6 May Mawarire invited people to write in the comment thread of his Facebook page one thing that they would like the government to fix. The video carried the following caption: 'Day 6 of #ThisFlag. *Madhara Matikanya* [Old men you have failed us], you have failed us. So here is the truth from my generation'. By April 2017 the message had been viewed 36,111 times and it attracted 205 comments and 474 shares.

These early initiatives were politically significant because, at a time when most citizens had been forced into silence through political intimidation, the campaign was encouraging citizens to participate in relatively small actions that had important political symbolism. The act of publicly wearing the national flag signified a re-appropriation of a national symbol, and challenged a key aspect of the ruling party's political discourse. Since 2000, ZANU-PF had sought to legitimise its claim to power by pointing to its role in the anti-colonial struggle. As pointed out earlier, ZANU-PF characterised its supporters as 'patriots', while deriding opposition supporters as 'sell-outs' (Tendi 2010). The voices of young people who were born after 1980 were de-legitimised on the grounds that they were 'born-frees' who were ignorant of the history of the liberation struggle. By contrast, the #ThisFlag campaign turned this discourse on its head, presenting the ZANU-PF elites as having betrayed the promises of independence through corruption and mismanagement of the country.[12] The young people who were being encouraged to carry their flags around with them in an open performance of citizenship were re-cast as patriots. In addition, their voices and aspirations were legitimised on the grounds that they were rightful citizens of Zimbabwe.

From early June the campaign's activities began to focus more on the mobilisation of people on the ground. Although the campaign was already doing this to some degree by encouraging people to wear the national flag, meetings were not popular owing to fear of political persecution. This phase began with the efforts around the '#UndengeMustGo' petition which demanded the dismissal of the Minister of Energy, Dr Samuel Undenge, who had been implicated in the mismanagement of public funds. The team's goal was to collect a total of 10,000 signatures, after which they would present the petition to the president. By early July they had collected about 5,000 signatures.[13] However, the initiative appears to have been overtaken by events, once the team began focusing its efforts on organising the national stay-away.

The next issue the team took up was the plan by the government to introduce 'bond notes' which were supposed to ease the cash shortages.[14] However, there was widespread concern that this was an attempt to re-introduce the Zimbabwean dollar via the back door. There was fear that once the government started printing money this would ultimately lead to the return of hyper-inflation, food shortages, and general economic instability. The team therefore organised a public debate with the Governor of the Reserve Bank in order to provide a forum where ordinary citizens could voice their opinions about the plan. The debate, which was attended by around 250 people – the maximum number the venue could hold – marked the first time that the campaign was able to materialise on the ground. Significantly, the fact that 250 people were brave enough to attend the debate in a heavily guarded government building signified that what was going on should not be dismissed as mere 'slacktivism'. Furthermore, the video recordings of the forthright exchanges during the debate bear testimony to the efforts of citizens to 'speak truth to power'.

The next, and highest-profile initiative the team contributed to coordinating was the national stay-away[15] on 6 July. The success of this protest action was in large part due to the fact that the team was able to take advantage of an auspicious coincidence of events. Most important among these was the strike by civil servants that took place on 6 July. The simmering discontent about the numerous police road blocks and the associated spot fines and bribes which threatened the viability of minibus transport operators was also important. This meant that they were sympathetic to the stay-away and could be persuaded to support the protest by not providing transport into the central business district. The government's gazetting of Statutory Instrument 64 of 2016 which imposed a broad import ban also stoked further discontent as it undermined the livelihoods of cross-border traders at a time when the unemployment levels were severe. Added to all these grievances was the widely unpopular plan to introduce bond notes. Thanks to all these factors the stay-away was a success and on 6 July the central business districts of Harare and Bulawayo were virtually deserted as business owners, transport operators and members of the public heeded the call to stay away.

The plans to build on the success of the first stay-away and organise another stay-away the following week were thwarted by the arrest of Mawarire on 12 July. Ironically, although Mawarire's arrest undermined the plans for the second national stay-away, his trial on 13 July proved to be a powerful mobilising point for the campaign. On the morning of the trial, over 100 lawyers turned up at the Harare Magistrates' Court in Rotten Row to show solidarity, and assist the defence team. Outside the court hundreds of people gathered singing religious hymns and making solidarity speeches mere metres away from heavily armed riot police. By late evening when the charges against Mawarire were dismissed, there were well over 2,500 people waiting outside the courthouse. The trial was the high water mark of the campaign. After his acquittal the government sought to immediately re-arrest Mawarire, at which point he decided to go into exile. His decision triggered the decline of the campaign due to the deep sense of disappointment and disillusionment it provoked among the campaign's supporters. Although Fadzai Mahere, a lawyer, stepped in as the new face of the campaign, and made efforts to keep it going, it was ultimately not possible to reverse its decline.

#ThisFlag campaign and the emergent digital spaces of contention

On 12 July 2016, the day of Mawarire's trial, Psychology Maziwisa, a ZANU-PF Member of Parliament and former party spokesperson, sent out the following tweet: 'President #Mugabe was elected into power. He will not be tweeted out of power'. The tweet, which was meant to taunt supporters of the campaign, throws into sharp relief the question of the political efficacy of social media, especially in authoritarian contexts such as Zimbabwe. At the core of Maziwisa's critique was a view that was shared by several commentators, that the #ThisFlag campaign was largely an 'online' movement and would not have any meaningful 'offline' political impact. This critique is founded on an increasingly outdated online/offline binary conception of the way people engage with digital media. Thanks to the availability of affordable smartphones, social media apps designed for mobile phones, and data bundles that allow subscribers unlimited use of WhatsApp and Facebook for a fixed fee, social media platforms have become embedded in people's everyday lives (Hine 2015). The blurring of the line between individuals' 'online' and 'offline' lives is illustrated by the fact that many of those who turned up at the courts in solidarity with Mawarire were also providing real-time updates on social media in the form of videos, photos and text messages. Furthermore, when one examines the people who were participating in these debates on social media, it soon becomes clear how pre-existing networks were key to the growth of the campaign. Some of the networks that were drawn upon include family, religious, alumni, professional, civil society and political networks. Ultimately, what is clear is that online collectives can materialise on the ground, as was the case with the public debate on bond notes. In addition, hashtags can be embodied; the thousands gathered outside the courtroom were the physical expression of #FreePastorEvan.

A second aspect of the critique is that the kind of political impact being discussed was often an 'Arab Spring'-type of popular uprising which would topple the ZANU-PF government. This way of thinking about the political impacts of social media tends to obscure those effects that do not translate into political revolution. What is more, it projects onto the #ThisFlag campaign an objective that it never set out to achieve. Indeed, a critical problem with the campaign was that the team did not have a clearly defined objective from the outset. In this sense the campaign exhibited the central problem scholars (see Brown 2015) have noted with other instances of insurgent citizenship, viz. the lack of strategic direction and staying power to produce seismic changes in society. The team only began seriously considering the larger objective, and thinking beyond single protest actions, in the aftermath of the successful 6 July national stay-away.[16] However, Mawarire was arrested before they had managed to do much planning. Musasiwa provides valuable insight into the teams' thinking up to that point in observing that:

> … because there was no plan for an outcome, we were just so caught up in the whirlwind of this wonderful expression of us finally breaking the fear barrier and talking about stuff, that we thought that would be enough. You almost think you break the fear barrier and others will run with the politics, and others will run with the industry. But it's almost as if people are now saying 'Wow you guys have broken the fear barrier – wonderful – *saka toita sei* [what do we do now]?' And you're like, 'huh what do you mean? ...' At some point we should have been like '*haa* fuck guys let's sit down and put a strategy document together and plan this' and you know. But it's like, at this point, it's like E [Evan Mawarire] then is arrested and goes into jail and they say he's got fucking treason.[17]

When Mawarire fled into exile soon after his trial, the communication between him and the team on the ground suffered considerably.[18] In addition, his departure triggered a severe backlash as many of the campaign's supporters felt that this was a betrayal by a leader of a campaign whose slogan was 'Fed Up, and No Longer Afraid'. Consequently, not only was there no strategic planning, but the team on the ground was left struggling to hold things together in the face of deep disillusionment and declining support.

While the campaign certainly did not lead to an 'Arab Spring' style uprising, it should not be dismissed as 'slacktivism' or characterised as 'interpassivity' (Dean 2005). Rather, it helped to create, expand and enliven digital spaces of contention. By tracking the multiple online spaces and platforms where conversations about #ThisFlag were taking place, one can begin to see the expanding digital spaces of contention. And by listening in to the social media debates around #ThisFlag we can begin to see some of the key features of the nascent contentious digital culture that thrived in these spaces. However, in order to understand the way that the #ThisFlag helped to constitute this space and this culture it is important to attend to the circulation of 'online artefacts of engagement', or 'the photos, memes, quoted sayings, and original or curated commentary that evince ... people's emotional investment and participation in unfolding events' (Schofield Clark 2016: 236). These artefacts both played a role in hailing people into these spaces, and functioned as vehicles for the layered political discourse that emerged out of these spaces.

From the outset of the campaign the online interactions around the #ThisFlag were marked by the circulation of affectively charged artefacts of engagement. Mawarire's own initial video on 19 April is a powerful example. This, and the subsequent videos he posted, resonated deeply with thousands of Zimbabweans who were equally at the end of their tether as they witnessed the country sliding into its second economic tailspin within a decade, due in large part to corruption and mismanagement. Mawarire's posts therefore attracted thousands of responses as people echoed this outrage through their own artefacts of engagement, which took the form of comments, videos, gifs and images. As people responded to Mawarire's posts through comments, 'likes', 'shares' or retweets, they were circulated further and with increased velocity.

Progressively, people began producing their own videos, memes and photos which they displayed on their own Facebook timelines or posted in the comment thread below Mawarire's videos. One category of these 'popular' online artefacts invoked the words and images of famous people such as Martin Luther King Jr. and Mahatma Ghandi, urging people to act in order to challenge repression. Another category consisted of images, videos and messages that sought to make citizens aware of their collective power to bring about political change. A third category of artefacts had a distinctly religious flavour and drew on biblical passages. Given that Christianity is among the largest religions in Zimbabwe, these messages resonated, and were used to inspire, encourage and embolden citizens. One such image invoked the Old Testament story of the deliverance of the Israelites from Egypt, and depicted President Robert Mugabe as a pharaoh with the caption 'Let my people go!' boldly displayed on the image. Another image which was designed to embolden citizens again drew on the Old Testament and depicted the image of Daniel in a lion's den with an angel in the background stopping the lions from doing him any harm. Put together, these artefacts fused religion, politics and popular culture in order to convey messages of encouragement and defiance.

Between possibility and constraint: digital media and Zimbabwean politics

A closer insight into the everyday workings of these digital spaces of contention can be derived by examining the #ThisFlag WhatsApp groups. As part of its social media outreach, the campaign established around ten WhatsApp groups and began using them to pass on information, while a smaller group made up of the core team was used for planning purposes.[19] In addition to the groups that the team was running, many individuals who were not part of the team began setting up #ThisFlag WhatsApp groups, some of which were established by, and for, Zimbabweans living abroad. This proliferation of WhatsApp groups is unsurprising given the fact that WhatsApp is the most widely used social media platform in Zimbabwe, and has become embedded in people's everyday lives (The Post and Telecommunications Regulatory Authority of Zimbabwe (POTRAZ) 2015: 15). The attraction of WhatsApp also lay in its affordances, in particular, the ability to create a semi-public group of up to 256 people in which information can be shared, and discussions could take place in real time. The end-to-end encryption afforded by the platform was a further attraction, given Zimbabweans' popular concerns about government surveillance.

The #ThisFlag group in which we conducted participant observation comprised over 200 members, including Mawarire and Moyo. The bulk of the members were based in Zimbabwe, while a minority were in the diaspora. We gained membership of the group through a recommendation to the group's administrators from an existing member. About 20 percent of members participated in discussions at any given time, partly due to individuals' different daily routines. Between June and August there were often over four hundred messages posted in the group on a daily basis. However, the number progressively declined after Mawarire went into exile, and by late 2016 there were often fewer than twenty messages posted daily.

The #ThisFlag WhatsApp group enabled citizens to surmount the geographic and legal barriers that hinder citizens from coming together to deliberate about Zimbabwe's troubled social, political and economic situation. The group's interactions were typically characterised by vibrant debates, and the circulation of photographs, videos, jokes, newspaper articles and infographics related to Zimbabwe's current affairs. The forthright and irreverent tone of many of the discussions about the government and its political elite is testament to the growing assertiveness among citizens that the group fostered, underlined by the campaign's exhortation to citizens to 'Speak, Ask and Act'. This assertiveness could take many forms, ranging from ridiculing and satirising political leaders through the use of cutting humour, to angry condemnations of the government's misdeeds. The growing assertiveness that characterised these and other social media conversations inspired by #ThisFlag was not coincidental. It was one of the campaign's goals as expressed in the mantra: 'If we cannot cause the politician to change, then we will have to inspire the citizen to be bold'.

Notwithstanding the many advantages that WhatsApp presented, it is important not to overstate the platform's value as a space for citizens to engage on matters of common concern. Participant observation in the group over several weeks soon revealed a number of significant limitations of the #ThisFlag WhatsApp group as a deliberative space. Although the anonymity and encryption initially helped to cast the group as a safe space for citizens, this progressively changed as the government's efforts to clamp down on the campaign intensified. Over time, the fact that one could never really know the identity of fellow group members began to fuel growing suspicion. Allegations that the group had been infiltrated were frequently aired without any concrete evidence being offered. Disagreements about strategy were at times interpreted as evidence of infiltration by government agents who were trying to cause confusion and frustrate the campaign's efforts to organise. What is evident is that, on one hand, WhatsApp allowed for the creation of these digital spaces that were relatively outside of the government's formal ability to monitor and police. On the other, these spaces were not immune to the indirect influences of the authoritarian political climate and culture of surveillance in the country. These broader environmental factors exerted an influence that ultimately eroded the democratic potential of the space.

A significant challenge was the establishment of a shared ethos and an agreed set of rules of interaction in the group, in order to minimise conflicts and aid their resolution when they did arise. Establishing this required a leadership style and a set of skills that were not always in evidence among the group administrators. It was therefore not uncommon for the exchanges in the group to become very caustic when differences arose. Such tendencies were heightened by the 'dis-inhibition effect' that came with the anonymity that

WhatsApp afforded group members. On a number of occasions, the group's administrators entered into heated arguments with members, and these often ended with the defiant member being expelled from the group. Of particular importance here is the fact that the WhatsApp platform provided group administrators with the power to invite or expel members, thus allowing for the emergence of hierarchies and power asymmetries that could undermine open deliberation. One result of the strict control over the direction of the discussion in the group was the formation of a smaller splinter group comprised of expelled members. Another challenge was the difficulty of sustaining a consistent thread of discussion. With dozens of people participating, important discussions were often derailed or sidetracked when individuals posted memes, images or videos that were not related to the discussion at hand. As a consequence, having an exhaustive debate or building consensus around specific issues proved to be fairly difficult. This problem was exacerbated by the fact that people were active on the group at different times. The ultimate effect was that the discussion of important topics was often disjointed, which in turn made it difficult for conclusions or a way forward to be drawn up. These observations were, admittedly, limited to one group, and some of the challenges may have been related to the specific factors unique to it. However, the group dynamics do illustrate some of the limitations of WhatsApp as a platform for political engagement.

A key limitation to the political impact of the campaign was inherent in the very fact that it was using social media to reach out to and mobilise citizens. While there has been a rapid expansion in mobile internet access in Zimbabwe in recent years, this has been experienced unequally. Urbanites tend to have more access to the internet and, by extension, social media. This in turn introduced an urban bias to the campaign. Even within urban areas the access has been unevenly distributed. The rate of around US$3 for a month's access to WhatsApp is relatively affordable to those who are employed. However, in a context where the unemployment rate is, by some estimates, as high as 90 percent and is especially acute among younger people, this is quite expensive. As such, being able to participate actively on social media and consume substantial amounts of data is a marker of privilege. This is especially so when viewed in light of the vast majority of urbanites who are struggling to make ends meet through a range of increasingly precarious informal enterprises. These factors meant that there was a limit to the number of people that the campaign could reach out to via social media.

Notwithstanding the above shortcomings, it should be pointed out that a key factor which undermined the campaign and ultimately triggered its decline was the repressive response of the government. Once it became clear that simply dismissing the campaign as a non-event would not be effective, the government tried to challenge it by promoting a rival hashtag, #OurFlag, which failed to gain much traction. As the #ThisFlag campaign gained momentum in May the police were used to intimidate Mawarire – only for Mawarire to expose these attempts in one of his videos, and this provoked further outrage towards the government. POTRAZ then resorted to issuing public statements threatening legal action against those 'abusing' social media, while the government-controlled press took to labelling activists 'cyber-terrorists' (*The Herald*, 9 August 2016). On the day of the stay-away, there were numerous reports about interference with mobile internet access. The success of the stay-away ultimately led to a more aggressive approach by the government, and to the arrest of Mawarire, which had a chilling impact on the campaign team and supporters. In the weeks that followed, leading activists in the other protest movements were arrested and detained in Chikurubi maximum security prison – despite the fact that they had not yet been tried[20] – and held in the section housing dangerous criminals. The decision by the government in September 2016 to invoke Statutory Instrument 184 of 1987, and ban the production, sale and 'abuse' of the national flag, enabled it to wrest the flag from the #ThisFlag campaign. By doing so, the government effectively repossessed the national flag and criminalised its use by the #ThisFlag campaign as a potent symbol of insurgent citizenship.

Conclusion

In conclusion, we highlight the central insights that emerge from the preceding examination of the activities of the #ThisFlag campaign in Zimbabwe that can be applied to analyses of social media campaigns in different parts of Africa. In particular, we draw attention to three concepts – 'digital spaces of contention', 'online artefacts of engagement' and 'insurgent citizenship' – and the ways in which connecting them is productive when thinking about the role of social media in reshaping politics. We have argued that the campaign helped to create, expand and enliven digital spaces of contention in Zimbabwe. A central mechanism in creating these sites was the circulation of online artefacts of engagement. The exchanges on the multiple social media platforms show the inversion of official political discourse, the ridiculing of political elites and the articulation of citizens' claims on the government. What was taking place was neither 'slacktivism' nor 'interpassivity', but rather the performance of insurgent citizenship which made creative use of social media platforms and spilt over into non-virtual spaces. This involved, among other things, the appropriation of the national flag by ordinary people as a symbol of defiance and resistance, and the employment of innovative photoshopped images, memes and profile pictures to interrogate poor governance. However, as with other instances of insurgent citizenship, the #ThisFlag campaign lacked the necessary strategic planning to enable it to trigger fundamental socio-economic or political changes in Zimbabwe.

Our analysis of the #ThisFlag campaign also challenges the online/offline binary conception of the way people experience and engage with digital media. This view, we argue, is becoming increasingly outdated as social media platforms become more embedded in people's everyday lives, thanks to the availability of affordable smartphones, the social media apps designed for mobile phones, and data bundles that allow subscribers unlimited use of WhatsApp and Facebook for a (relatively) affordable fixed fee. While the claim that hashtags are transient has some validity, it requires an important qualification. From our broader analysis of the socio-political context that produced #ThisFlag, it is clear that the hashtag gave expression to deeply held sentiments among a significant section of the Zimbabwean body politic that was fed up with ZANU-PF misrule. These sentiments were encapsulated by the phrase '*hatichada & hatichatya*': 'we are fed up and no longer afraid'. Unlike hashtags, these underlying sentiments are not ephemeral, and may well find expression in other hashtags in the future. Following the 'military assisted transfer of power' in November 2017, the new president, Emmerson D. Mnangagwa, has made very little headway in arresting the socio-economic and political crisis. Despite the government's concerted efforts to manipulate public opinion through a range of social media platforms, the initial euphoria that accompanied the removal of Mugabe has all but faded. In addition, the disillusionment with Mnangagwa's 'new dispensation', and the simmering popular frustrations, are beginning to find expression through hashtags like #EDamin, which likens Mnangagwa to the Ugandan military dictator Idi Amin.

Notes

1 Mawarire interview with *The Standard*, 25 June 2016. www.thestandard.co.zw/2016/06/25/thisflag-movement-piles-pressure-fire-minister/.

2 Action mobilisation is the process by which a social movement transforms sympathisers into participants (Klandermans 1984).

3 Consensus mobilisation is the process by which a social movement tries to obtain support for its point of view (Klandermans 1984).

4 See for example Lauren E. Young, 'Did Protests in Zimbabwe really go from 'tweets to streets?' www.washingtonpost.com/news/monkey-cage/wp/2016/07/15/did-recent-protests-in-zimbabwe-really-go-from-tweets-to-streets/?noredirect=on&utm_term=.8a6eeb690da8; Blessing-Miles Tendi, 'Why a Hashtag Isn't Enough for a Revolution in Zimbabwe', https://foreignpolicy.com/2016/07/15/why-a-hashtag-isnt-enough-for-a-revolution-in-zimbabwe/; Chloe McGrath, 'What everyone's getting wrong about Zimbabwe's #ThisFlag Movement', https://foreignpolicy.com/2016/07/21/what-everyones-getting-wrong-about-zimbabwes-thisflag-movement/; and George Karekwaivanane, 'Fed up, unafraid and just getting started: what Zimbabwe's #ThisFlag must do now', https://africanarguments.org/2016/07/28/fed-up-unafraid-and-just-getting-started-what-zimbabwes-thisflag-must-do-now/.

5 These movements, which were led by various actors, sought to push Robert Mugabe out of power and highlight various social and economic problems, including the urgent need to address youth unemployment.

6 Interview with Patson Dzamara.

7 Dzamara was abducted in March 2015 and three years later it is still unclear what happened to him.

8 We have used the pseudonym Michael Moyo in order to protect the anonymity of one of the team members. Mawarire and Musasiwa gave consent to have their real names.

9 Interview with Evan Mawarire

10 Interview with Kuda Musasiwa. The unexpected nature of the roots of the movement is also made clear in Mawarire's video of 29 April 2016.

11 Interview with Mawarire.

12 For an example of Ethiopian youth similarly recasting old discourses in the #RespectTheCosntitution and #FreeZone9 bloggers campaigns, see Gagliardone and Pohjonen 2016.

13 Interview with Mawarire

14 Bond notes were a form of local currency that was going to be backed by a US$200 million loan facility from the African Export and Import Bank.

15 This is a form of protest commonly used by Zimbabwean civic and opposition activists in which citizens are encouraged to stay at home and not to go about their daily business. The stay-away serves as a way of registering popular grievances by

temporarily shutting the country down, while avoiding violent confrontations with law enforcement agencies that would result from street protests.

16 Interview with Mawarire.

17 Interview with Musasiwa.
18 Ibid.
19 Interview with Mawarire
20 Interview with Makomborero Haruzivishe.

References

Interviews

Coltart, Doug, Harare, 9 September 2017
Dzamara, Patson; Harare, 22 August 2017
Frey, Dirk, Harare; 4 September 2017
Haruzivishe, Makomborero; Harare, 8 September 2017
Manezhu, Mandowa; Harare, 5 September 2017
Manyawo, Nasper; Harare, 5 September 2017
Masarira, Linda; Harare, 28 August 2017
Mavhudzi, Donald; Harare, 29 August 2017
Mawarire, Evan; Harare, 31 August 2017
Mkwananzi, Promise; Harare, 28 August 2017
Mudehwe, Lynette; Harare, 8 September 2017
Munro, Sam; Harare, 4 September 2017
Musasiwa, Kuda; Harare, 2 September 2017
Siziba, Gift; Harare, 31 August 2017

Secondary literature

Brown, J. (2015) *South Africa's Insurgent Citizens: on Dissent and the Possibility of Politics*. London: Zed Books.
Courtemanche, C. (2011) 'Internet, the engine room of revolution'. www.smh.com.au/federal-politics/political-opinion/internet-the-engine-room-of-revolution-20110224-1b71v.html (accessed 13 November 2017).
Dean, J. (2005) 'Communicative capitalism: circulation and the foreclosure of politics'. *Cultural Politics*, 1(1): 51–74.
Diamond, L. (2010) 'Liberation technologies'. *Journal of Democracy*, 21(3): 69–83.
Dirksen, V., Huizing, A. & Smit, Bas (2010) 'Piling on layers of understanding': the use of conective ethnography for the study of (online) work practices. *New media and Society*, 12(7): 1045–1063.
Gagliardone, I. & Pohjonen, M. (2016) 'Engaging in polarized society: social media and political discourse in Ethiopia'. In B. Mutsvairo (ed.), *Digital Activisim in the Social Media Era: Critical Reflections on Emerging Trends in Sub-Saharan Africa*. London: Palgrave Macmillan, pp. 25–44.
Gladwell, M. (2010) 'Small change: why the revolution will not be tweeted'. *The New Yorker*, October 4. www.newyorker.com/reporting/2010/10/04/101004fa_fact_gladwell (accessed 18 November 2011).
The Herald (2016) 'Social media terrorists exposed'. 9 August.

Hine, C. (2007) 'Connective ethnography for the exploration of e-science'. *Journal of Computer Mediated Communication*, 12(2): 284–300.

Hine, C. (2015) *Ethnography for the Internet: Embedded, Embodied and Everyday*. London: Bloomsbury.

Holston, J. (1998) 'Spaces of insurgent citizenship'. In L. Sandercock (ed.), *Making the Invisible Visible: a Multicultural Planning History*. Berkeley: University of California Press.

Holston, J. (2007) *Insurgent Citizenship: Disjunctions of Democracy and Modernity in Brazil*, Princeton: Princeton University Press.

Klandermans, P. G. (1984) Mobilization and participation in trade union action: an expectancy-value approach. *Journal of Occupational Psychology*, 57(2): 107–120.

Lim, M. (2011) 'Tahrir Square Was a Foreseeable Surprise Tracing the history of Egyptian online activism'. www.slate.com/articles/technology/technology/2017/11/twitter_s_me_on_election_day_2016_vs_election_2017_meme_is_a_distillation.html (accessed 10 November 2017).

Lim, M. (2012) 'Clicks, cabs, and coffee houses: social media and oppositional movements in Egypt, 2004–2011. *Journal of Communication*, 62: 231–248.

Mare, A. (2014) 'Social media: the new protest drums in southern Africa?' In B. Pătruț & M. Pătruț (eds) *Social Media in Politics: Case Studies on the Political Power of Social Media: Public Administration and Information Technology*. Canton of Bern: Springer.

Morozov, E. (2011) *The Net delusion: the Dark Side of Internet Freedom*. New York: Public Affairs.

Mutsvairo B. (ed) (2016) *Digital Activisim in the Social Media Era: Critical Reflections on Emerging Trends in Sub-Saharan Africa*. London: Palgrave Macmillan.

Papacharissi, Z. (2010) *A Private Sphere: Democracy in a Digital Age*. Cambridge: Polity Press.

Postal and Telecommunications Regulatory Authority of Zimbabwe [POTRAZ] (2015) Postal and Telecommunications sector Performance Report, Fourth Quarter 2015.

Postill, J. & Pink, S. (2012) 'Social media ethnography: the digital researcher in a messy web'. *Media International Australia*, 145: 123–134.

Reserve Bank of Zimbabwe (2011) *Monetary Policy Statement*, January.

Reserve Bank of Zimbabwe (2016) *Quarterly Economic Review*, March.

Schofield Clark L. (2016) 'Participants on the margins: #BlackLivesMatter and the role the shared artifacts of engagement played among minoritized political newcomers on Snapchat, Facebook, and Twitter'. *International Journal of Communication*, 10: 235–253.

Shirky, C. (2008) *Here Comes Everybody: the Power of Organizing without Organisations*. London: Allen Lane.

Tendi, Blessing-Miles (2010) *Making History in Mugabe's Zimbabwe: Politics, Intellectuals and the Media*. London: Peter Lang.

Tendi, Blessing-Miles (2016) 'Why a Hashtag isn't enough for a revolution in Zimbabwe'. http://foreignpolicy.com/2016/07/15/why-a-hashtag-isnt-enough-for-a-revolution-in-zimbabwe/ (accessed 13 November 2017).

Townsend, L. & Wallace, C. (n.d.) 'Social Media Research: a Guide to Ethics'. www.dotrural.ac.uk/social-media-research-ethics/ (accessed 9 November 2018).

Wasserman, H. (2011) 'Mobile phones, popular media, and everyday African democracy: Transmissions and transgressions'. *Popular Communication*, 9: 146–158.

Zayani, Mohamed (2015) *Networked Publics and Digital Contention: the Politics of Everyday Life in Tunisia*. Oxford: Oxford University Press.

4 | SOCIAL MEDIA AND PROTEST MOVEMENTS IN SOUTH AFRICA

#FeesMustFall and #ZumaMustFall

Tanja Bosch

Introduction

South African social activism re-emerged in the 1990s after a brief lull following the end of apartheid and the transition to democracy. The revival of social activism emerged against the backdrop of a plethora of challenges facing the young democracy including corruption, growing social and economic inequality, unemployment and a lack of service delivery, particularly in South Africa's townships. Protests have become a daily occurrence in South Africa, as many of the poor feel excluded from the benefits of the new democracy. Although these protests are mediated in various ways, many fail to attract mainstream media attention. This chapter draws on two recent case studies to explore how citizens have used social media sites as communicative platforms for social activism. Focusing on Facebook and Twitter in particular, the chapter focuses on these cases from South Africa, which have demonstrated the potential role of social media in expanding the democratic political space via forms of hashtag activism. The two events considered here are the national student protests known as *Fees Must Fall*, which began in 2015 and continued in 2016; and the broad-based citizen-driven *Zuma Must Fall* campaign, which began in 2015 but took off in 2017 with nationwide public protest marches attended by thousands of citizens.

The increased role of the internet and social media in social protests and political uprisings has been widely documented around the world. The importance of social media came to the attention of researchers following the events of the Arab Spring, where social media played a key role in the insurgencies of Tunisia and Egypt. While the notion of these uprisings as Facebook or Twitter 'revolutions' has been widely contested, there is no doubt that social media was a key tool, providing the 'necessary scaffolding and a means of organising outside the control of the state' (Farrell 2012: 16).

Internationally, social movement activists have increasingly begun to utilise ICTs (information and communication technologies), complementing traditional forms of political participation. During protests, uprisings or periods of political instability, 'Twitter is frequently used to call networked publics into being and into action' (Papacharissi 2015: 37). Moreover, the internet has contributed to the formation of alternative public spheres, in which citizenship can be practised in different ways (Van de Donk et al. 2004). Physical protest marches and occupations of public spaces are often mediated events, with social media playing a key mobilising role in choreographing collective action, in much the same way pamphlets and other 'old' media may have in the past (Gerbaudo 2012). As Tufekci (2017) argues, social movements are empowered by their ability to use digital tools to quickly mobilise large numbers of protesters, and to connect such movements on a global scale.

However, it should also be noted that social media is not always used for progressive means or social change – terrorist and supremacist groups also often use these tools to advance their narratives and agendas (Tufekci 2017). Social media can thus also be used to spread hate speech, as was seen for example during the 2007/2008 election crisis in Kenya (Mäkinen & Wangu Kuira 2008); and also in Ethiopia (see Gagliardone 2014).

Similarly, in South Africa during the height of xenophobic conflict in 2016, a study revealed that there were 2,000 posts per day pertaining to the topic of xenophobia on various social media platforms, and that these included xenophobic posts.[1] The potential for digital media and social media to effect social change is thus highly contested in academic scholarship. Most notably, Morozov (2011) has argued that internet activism facilitates 'slacktivism', which results in a 'feel-good' factor for participants but has no impact on offline political outcomes. However, Tufekci (2017) and others counter this argument by demonstrating the role of social media in political activism despite these critiques.

This chapter explores the role of social media in contemporary political activism in South Africa, by exploring the political use of hashtags on social media sites, most notably Facebook and Twitter. The primary research questions of the present study are: 1) How do citizens in South Africa use social media platforms to engage in political affairs? 2) Focusing on specific case studies, does this participation stimulate citizen engagement and result in the broadening of the public sphere? Through an exploration of the various political hashtags (for example #FeesMustFall and #ZumaMustFall), the chapter argues that despite internet penetration issues related to the digital divide, social media is increasingly being used by citizens to engage in collective forms of networked action. These two hashtags are among the most well-known, but usually occurred alongside various other political hashtags, for example #SONA and #ANC.

The South African context

South Africa has become known as the 'protest capital of the world',[2] with a record number of social protests taking place on a daily basis. Often described as a 'rebellion of the poor' (Alexander 2010: 25), these protests arise from the persistent social inequalities of present-day South Africa, and have often been presented as service delivery protests, with citizens in townships and informal settlements protesting lack of basic services such as water, sanitation and housing. Although service delivery has become the rallying point for protests, these protests could also be seen as a manifestation of a deeper disillusionment with post-apartheid democracy. For example, Pithouse (2010) has explained the protests as a crisis of citizenship, with the vast majority of the population excluded from substantive citizenship and the dividends of democracy. A more useful description of these civil uprisings privileges the term 'community protests' to refer to a wider range of organic bottom-up uprisings, arguing that they are deeply rooted in socio-economic inequality, combined with citizens' perceptions of a non-responsive government (Wasserman, Bosch & Chuma 2018). In addition to those framed as service delivery protests, other public protests include those orchestrated by farm workers and mineworkers over wage disputes, such as the notorious Marikana strike on 16 August 2012, in which 34 striking platinum mineworkers were killed, and 78 injured by police.

Duncan (2014) critiqued early press coverage of the event, later dubbed the Marikana massacre, arguing that it was heavily biased towards official accounts, and excluded miners' voices in favour of business interests, leading to an editorial failure. In general, the mainstream media have been criticised for framing protests negatively, often focusing on violence where the majority of protests have been peaceful, in what Duncan describes as 'riot porn'.[3] In the case of the community protests for example, mainstream print media tend to predominantly subscribe to the traditional protest paradigm (Wasserman et al. 2018).

The news media are considered an important source of politics for citizens, and thus hold the potential to shape the dynamics of conflicts and the success of conflict parties (Vladišavljević 2015). Media coverage of protests could thus either amplify or silence citizen voices, particularly those on the margins of the public sphere; and in South Africa, it has predominantly presented a 'view from the suburbs' (Friedman 2011: 107), with the voices of protesters largely absent. Given this type of often one-dimensional mainstream media coverage, social movements and civil society groups often turn to nanomedia strategies, including but not necessarily limited to social media, to highlight their campaigns (Bosch, Wasserman & Chuma 2018). The term *nanomedia* (Pajnik & Downing 2008) is used to refer to a range of 'nano' – or small-scale – communicative activities. This includes demonstrations, dress, slogans, murals, songs, dance, poetry and other activities that are used by community-based movements to mobilise for political action. The term nanomedia could include traditional 'alternative media' such as radio and print, but is more encompassing to also include small-scale activities such as graffiti or street theatre, as sites or settings to practise marginalised discourses that remain outside the public sphere (Dawson 2012).

However, access to digital technologies is often limited for many working-class-based movements of the poor, though South Africa has seen the emergence of more middle-class technology-based digitally-driven protests such as the national #FeesMustFall student movement, and more recently the #ZumaMustFall citizen-driven movement, which had a large middle-class and predominantly white support base (Wasserman 2017). These protest movements (discussed in greater detail below) often become widely known in popular discourse by their hashtags, representing a type of 'hashtag activism', a term which refers to the increased role of social media as a political source, particularly its influence in placing issues on the agenda for national debate and deliberation. The use of social media in South Africa, this chapter argues, should be seen as part of the broader media ecology, including traditional media. Moreover, social media operates in tandem with offline political action, often playing the key role of coordinating physical events and disseminating protest information. There is a large history of social justice activism in South Africa, both during and after the apartheid era. Political activists of the 1970s and onwards campaigned for an end to the apartheid-era segregated racism and its associated policies and to replace the regime with a democratic government. In the post-apartheid context, a range of social movements emerged, many expressing widespread dissatisfaction with the ruling party's fiscal strategies, and with interests extending beyond the issue of state power (see, for example, Ballard, Habib & Valodia 2006; Madlingozi 2007; Robins 2008). A number of civil society organisations arose in the new dispensation, to place the issues of marginalised communities on the public agenda. These grassroots concerns included struggles over housing, land, health, education and service provision, among others. These new social movements are part of the 'marginalised and deinstitutionalised subaltern urban class in the developing world that emerged as a result of the rapid global economic restructuring of the 1990s' (Chiumbu 2015: 417), intensified by the adoption of neoliberalism macro-economic policies. These movements are increasingly combining traditional mobilisation methods with new media technologies to mobilise, create networks and lobby for social justice.

Methodology

This chapter draws primarily on data from two platforms: Twitter (Fees Must Fall) and Facebook (Zuma Must Fall). Facebook and Twitter are the most popular social networking sites in South Africa, with 16 million and 8 million users respectively. These two platforms are considered here as a proxy for social media in South Africa, even though Instagram is also rising in popularity with 3.8 million users.[4] Twitter was widely used during the student protests, and in the case of Zuma Must Fall, Facebook pages played a more central role in information sharing and activism. The chapter draws on a corpus of tweets to explore online political narratives via qualitative content analysis; as well as Facebook page data (page posts and comments) to explore the formation of online publics via social media. Benkler (2006) developed the idea of a networked public sphere that draws on online communication platforms, and Highfield and Bruns (2015) highlight how social media encourages different ways of engaging with or participating within public communication and forming ad hoc issue publics. Focusing on popular political hashtags, the chapter explores the notion of hashtag activism, i.e. discursive protest on social media united through a hashtagged word, phrase or sentence. In the case of the Twitter analysis, data was collected using the open source tool Mecodify, available on GitHub. The Fees Must Fall student protests were analysed through a content analysis of tweets, collected by searching for all tweets tagged with the hashtag #FeesMustFall during 2015 and 2016. Mecodify crawls the Twitter search page via a built-in script and extracts the tweets pulled up by search queries. It then fetches all messages and relevant information about the users who tweeted via the Twitter Application Program Interface (API).

Facebook pages were analysed using Netvizz, an open source application made available via the Digital Methods Initiative. Netvizz was developed as a data extractor that provides outputs for different sections of Facebook (pages and groups) in CSV outputs which can be analysed in Excel. Netvizz allows researchers to mine Facebook for data, bypassing manual collection or more complex programming methods (Rieder 2013). The Netvizz application was used to analyse posts and comments on the Zuma Must Fall Facebook page. The analysis included posts by the page and users. Netvizz allows for extraction of the most recent 50 posts, and in this instance these 50 posts and their comments were analysed.

This chapter uses thematic and interpretive methods of qualitative content analysis, paying attention to both the manifest content and the broader context of communication. This chapter argues for social media as 'a contemporary medium for storytelling, enabling co-creating and collaborative filtering that sustains ambient and affective engagement for the publics it interconnects' (Papacharissi 2015: 27).

Research on social media is a constantly changing field, with new methods of analysis being developed, and there are disadvantages. Digital research that relies on APIs can become platform-dependent (boyd & Crawford 2012). Moreover, Twitter is not representative of all citizens (or in this case students), and while some users post content frequently through Twitter, others participate as 'listeners' (Crawford 2009: 532). Around 40 percent of active users sign in just to listen without ever participating actively on Twitter (boyd & Crawford 2012). In the South African context, internet penetration stands slightly over 50 percent, though the growth of mobile telephony means that many more users may have internet access via mobile phones. As of 2018, there were 8 million Twitter users in South Africa, making it one of the most popular and fastest-growing social networking sites after Facebook (16 million) and YouTube (9 million),[5] in a population of

56.72 million. While not all citizens participate in social media spaces and Twitter does not represent a homogenous group of users, it contains 'an extremely diverse range of online communities' (DiGrazia, McKelvey, Bollen & Rojas 2013). As Di Grazia et al. (2013) argue, 'Empirically Twitter publics might be important because they can serve as an indicator of an otherwise difficult to observe political process'.

Researching social media also presents a range of ethical issues, most notably whether data should be considered private or public. Social media research also presents challenges in terms of obtaining informed consent as participants are rarely aware of their participation, and there is frequent potential for anonymity breaches. This study takes the approach that the use of hashtags on Twitter and posts on public pages on Facebook allows the assumption that a broad readership is assumed by these social media users; and this chapter does not cite specific tweets or posts which, through Google searches, could reveal the identities of the posters.

Fees Must Fall: #FMF and networked collective action

The Fees Must Fall student movement and the virality of the 'must fall' catchphrase began with the Rhodes Must Fall campaign, which took place at the University of Cape Town in early 2015. It began with a student activist flinging human waste at the statue of colonialist Cecil John Rhodes, which was prominently located on the campus. This quickly grew into a movement for the removal of the statue, which activists argued promoted institutional racism and a culture of exclusion on campus. This quickly grew into a broader-based movement campaigning for various issues, including the decolonisation of the university curriculum and the transformation of the faculty. The Rhodes Must Fall movement used the hashtag #RMF to set the agenda for public debate in online and offline spaces, as well as in mainstream media, with the Twitter discourse playing a key role in creating a space for debate and discussion (Bosch 2016a). Moreover, Rhodes Must Fall activists used Twitter as a space to organise offline activities and created a space for youth to become politically active.

In general, social networking sites display various affordances, which may promote participation in protest activities among youth. South African youth, in line with international trends, display high levels of political apathy and low voter turnout, or engagement in other traditional forms of political participation. Sites such as

Twitter facilitate access to large numbers of contacts, enabling social movements to reach critical mass; they promote the construction of group identities that are key features of protest behaviour; and they function as information hubs, all of which can inspire an interest in politics in young people. Valenzuela, Arriagada and Scherman (2012) argue that despite scholarly critiques from cyber-pessimists about the relationship between online activism (or slacktivism) and offline political engagement, there is a strong link between youth using online platforms (news and social media sites) and their consequent political participation and engagement.

University campuses are often seen as important spaces for enabling and facilitating student engagement with politics, as well as their wider participation in civil society (Vromen, Xenos & Loader 2015). In the South African context, university spaces and schools were often the sites of political uprising during apartheid, and students were well organised, were connected to major political movements and played a prominent role with their capacity to mobilise mass resistance (Jansen 2004). During October 2015, a wave of student uprisings spread across the country, centred around rising university fees. They became widely known as the Fees Must Fall protests, probably as a result of the widespread use of the slogan both offline and in online social media spaces, notably Facebook and Twitter. The slogan was soon reduced to the hashtag #FeesMustFall or #FMF, which circulated widely on Twitter. Despite the fact that protests took place at campuses separated by geography, socio-economics and racial composition among other factors, the students gradually built online and offline networks to coordinate a unified national movement (Molefe 2016). Online activities were thus complemented and supported by offline structures of institutional arrangements, planning and strategising. For this study, data was collected using the hashtag #FeesMustFall.

As argued previously, Twitter played a key role in the #FMF student protests as a vehicle to disseminate information and coordinate protest activities (Bosch 2016). Tweets were used to call students to protest marches, to distribute information about protest activities such as the occupation of spaces and to facilitate online discussions about what was happening on various university campuses around the country. As Papacharissi (2015: 37) argues, 'During protest, uprisings or periods of political instability, Twitter is frequently used to call networked publics into being and into action'. Many of the tweets using the chosen hashtags were thus simply intended to share information, for example about campus closures or the logistics around student protest events. During 2017, the hashtag #FMFReloaded was used in social media spaces to refer to the continuation of discussions and concerns around the costs of tertiary education, and similarly, #UKZN emerged to tag social media conversations around fee-related student protests at the University of KwaZulu Natal during 2017. Other related hashtags emerged, for example, #UCTopen and #UCTclosed, which referred to debates about whether the University of Cape Town should remain closed during the ongoing protests during 2016. Similarly, #Wits and #ReclaimWits centred around conversations taking place at the University of the Witwatersrand, but the hashtag #FeesMustFall was usually used with these other hashtags, and was key in centring and organising the online debates.

Revolutionary student movements have been a feature of transitional societies, but have also appeared with increasing frequency in Western societies (Skolnick 2010). The emergence of student protest movements in South Africa should be seen within the political and socio-economic context outlined above, and the new Fees Must Fall student protests, it could be argued, were an extension of existing social and community uprisings indicating citizen dissatisfaction with government and disillusionment with the new democracy and its failure to extend dividends to the poor. While citizen protests to this point had largely involved people taking to the streets to voice their dissent, in this instance, the disaffected made use of the digital technologies available to them via campus broadband internet access and personal devices such as smartphones. In the case of Fees Must Fall, the protests raised public awareness about the shortage of funds for higher education. A common response by university management across all campuses was to obtain interdicts against protesting students, using the law to silence voices of dissent. Many students were arrested and universities used the interdicts to justify using police and private security on campus, which many argue fuelled the violence.[6] In the instance of the University of Cape Town, university management listed several respondents in the interdict, including #FeesMustFall, for the first time obtaining an interdict against a hashtag, and potentially limiting freedom of speech, while simultaneously highlighting the importance of social media in the protests.

The role played by social media

Social media thus played a key organising role in the Fees Must Fall student protests, as a tool for the dissemination of various types of information. While conversations took place on Facebook, Twitter was central to campaign organisation, based on the number of posts per day.[7] This is primarily due to the affordances of the platform. Twitter allowed for users to easily and quickly search for protest-related information by searching for hashtags and keywords; whereas the conversations taking place on Facebook were more disjointed, and on several pages and groups, making them less easy to find and follow. The campaign for university fees to 'fall' was turned into a hashtag to facilitate its viral diffusion – representing a form of hashtag activism, in its facilitation of the formation of ad hoc issue publics. The term hashtag politics (Davis 2013) refers to the increased role of Twitter as a political source, particularly its influence in placing issues (such as FMF) on the agenda for national debate and deliberation. As a result of the viral diffusion of the campaign, it achieved some success in 2015, with the Minister of Education announcing that there would be no fee increase for the year. However, the protests flared up again during 2016 as students then began to campaign for free higher education. The debates around the feasibility and affordability of this continue to the present day, and these types of protest may become a recurring feature of the political landscape.

During the protests, social media was used to choreograph offline political activities (Gerbaudo 2012). Students used Twitter to coordinate and advertise sit-ins and occupations of physical spaces, for example, administration buildings, to organise protest marches, physical meetings and other forms of offline political activism. Twitter was used to recruit participants and to convey information about dates, times and other logistical information. Twitter also became a central source of information. Each day, students and academic staff would check social media feeds for news about protest action on campus and on whether lectures were cancelled for the day or not, as Twitter spread much more rapidly than official email notices from the university administration. In addition, it was used as a space for debate and discussion, for protest participants to form consensus about their activities, and to explain and justify protest actions.

Twitter was also used to craft alternative narratives about the protests, in opposition to mainstream media coverage. Participants used

Twitter to formulate and amplify their own narratives, to reach out to broader publics, and to organise and resist. This was often done through citizen journalism and the tweeting of photographs taken by students on the scene of protests. While mainstream news photographs have often been criticised for their visual framing of protests, in this instance students tweeted specific images, for example of police brutality, to shape counter-narratives and frame the protests from the perspective of students (Bosch and Mutsvairo 2017).

The open participation afforded by social media does not always mean equal participation, and it certainly does not imply a smooth process. Although online media tend to be much more participatory in nature, over time a few select people consistently emerge as informal but persistent spokespersons – and they tend to have large followings on social media (Tufekci 2017). Gerbaudo (2012) refers to such individuals as soft leaders or choreographers involved with setting the scene. In the case of Fees Must Fall, digital technology was used in the early stages of the campaign, to support the organisation in the absence of formal structures. This was a bottom-up protest, not driven by any one political party or student organisation. In general, digital social movements tend to focus on participation and horizontal structures, often functioning without formal hierarchies or leaders. FMF represented such a 'leaderless' decentralised and diffuse network of resistance (Juris 2012). However, as Tufekci (2017) argues, 'Once this large group is formed, however, it struggles because it has sidestepped some of the traditional tasks of organising'. This is where the FMF movement lost some of its momentum as smaller campaigns began to break out on individual campuses, and we saw the emergence of internal localised debate and discussion, more specifically online debates about whether to continue to forcibly shutdown the university or to reopen the university and resume classes without demands being met, on various campuses around the country.

#ZumaMustFall protest campaign

South Africa's transition to democracy in the mid-1990s was not marked by traditional features of violent revolution, but rising social inequality has led to ongoing community protests as citizens express disillusionment with post-apartheid democracy. The student protests are often seen as a contributor to the growing narrative of revolution and national political debate. The Zuma Must Fall national protest movement emerged during 2017, taking its name from the viral hashtag Fees Must Fall, co-opting the 'must fall' slogan which had already gone viral by the end of 2015. The two movements are similar in that they both stem from economic insecurity and dissatisfaction with ruling party policies. This was one of the largest incidences of protest action in South Africa, with thousands of South Africans taking to the streets in public marches across the country.[8]

While these protests had been simmering for a while with the early emergence of the hashtag #ZumaMustFall, the 2017 protests were sparked when President Jacob Zuma fired the Finance Minister in 2015, followed by an unpopular cabinet reshuffle in 2017, unleashing mass opposition to the African National Congress and President Zuma. The firing of the Finance Minister and uncertainty in this area caused the rand to devalue and South Africa's credit rating was reduced to junk status. Until this point, President Zuma had already come under the spotlight for various accusations of corruption, including the Nkandla scandal in which public funds were used for renovations to his private homestead. The Zuma Must Fall movement was a broad-based national campaign for the President to be recalled even though this is not constitutionally possible. There were several unsuccessful attempts for a motion of no confidence in the National Assembly.

What was particularly striking about both #Fees Must Fall and #Zuma Must Fall is that it represented protest across class and race. While most community protests in South Africa take place in the impoverished black townships, FMF took place on university campuses in urban centres, including at former white universities; while anti-Zuma marches united citizens across race and class, with unusually large numbers of white protesters leading to various critiques of it being a predominantly white protest. The peaceful marches, some of which blockaded major roads, took place in urban centres, with children present at many sites holding placards.

In this instance social media also played a key role in choreographing the protest events, through the viral nature of the hashtag #ZumaMustFall, which was also picked up by the mainstream mass media, by journalists using Twitter as part of their research. While both Twitter and Facebook were used, in addition to various disconnected WhatsApp groups, this chapter focuses primarily on Facebook, through a brief analysis of the public pages named Zuma Must Fall, and Zuma Must Fall March, liked by 81,164 and 105,316 people respectively.

For the Zuma Must Fall page, data from 1,248 posts during 2016 and 2017 was retrieved. Analysing the Zuma Must Fall March page, posts were retrieved over the same time period. The 50 most recent posts on each page were downloaded for further analysis. In most cases, posts by the page and by the user were intended for the dissemination of two types of information. Firstly, information about the protest march logistics and venues, informing people where to assemble and encouraging people to participate. In some instances, people asked questions about safety and whether they could bring children; and in others they asked about placards and other protest paraphernalia. Secondly, the majority of page posts, and in fact the posts most 'liked' and reacted to by users, were links to opinion pieces or news stories providing evidence for Zuma's poor leadership. In this instance, the Facebook pages played a key role for sharing information to support the campaign.

Photographs were 'liked' and shared more by users, rather than links, status updates or videos. The photographs most liked were usually of the various events, and those with the highest engagement score (likes, reactions, shares) showed South Africans of various races standing together or embracing at these public events. Popular photographs also showed supporters from around the world holding banners in support of the movement with a call on the page asking expatriates to come back home because they are needed here. In many instances, photos of the event were distributed (shared) and liked by people who were not present at the event. As Papacharissi (2015) has argued, platforms like Facebook have a particular storytelling infrastructure which invites observers 'to tune into events they are physically removed from by imagining what these might feel like for people directly experiencing them'.

The engagement by people located outside of South Africa is evident in the geographic locations of people who liked the page. In the case of the Zuma Must Fall page, of the 105,316 individuals who follow the page by clicking 'like', 74,216 were located in South Africa, with many others in a range of other locations, for example, 1,590 in Great Britain and 665 in the United States. This led to some internal debate and critique on the page, for example with one user asking another 'How are you a proud South African when you don't even live in SA?' (8 April 2016). Debates around citizenship and who had the 'right' to protest was one small feature of the online discussion.

However, despite the large number of followers, not all users were equally active, raising critiques of 'slacktivism' and highlighting how easy it is to follow a Facebook page by simply clicking 'like' and not engaging further. Analysing the last 50 posts on the Zuma Must Fall page revealed that there were 3,122 users liking or commenting 4,967 times. This sample did not exclude the possibility of multiple comments by single users, highlighting the potential problem of social media amplifying the voices of the most vocal users. Of the comments on these pages by users, they were overwhelmingly negative and generally took the form of users indicating their dissatisfaction with the President and venting personal frustrations, with no disagreement from other users. These included posts like: 'Put this asshole back where he belongs!! Corrupt lying cheat! He's unknowledgeable and can't even count!! Get rid of this rubbish!!!!' (29 May 2017) and:

> It's simply vile and infuriating that a fat little bald imbecile can wield so much power and intimidation over his staff. I would like to think that ANC MPs have a shred of integrity or an ounce of moral fibre. However their continued support of a cretinous criminal leaves me with only three explanations – all three of which are concerning. So ANC MPs my question is this – what is your excuse for your deplorable and despicable continued support of Zuma? (26 April 2016)

These types of comments resulted in formations of unity around these issues, with users supporting, sympathising and agreeing with each other, showing how social media can be used for the creation of issue publics and group solidarity, and how in this instance Facebook could facilitate networked community building. This also raises the role of emotions in political debate. As Cossarini (2014) argues, emotions such as anger and fear can play a key role in motivating people to engage in political action. In the case of the Zuma Must Fall campaign, the collective outrage expressed via social media played a key role in mobilising people to participate in collective gatherings. Papacharissi (2015: 70) refers to these personal contributions to emerging news streams as 'personalised action formations', arguing that in contrast to the logic of collective action, these personalised views do not necessarily lead to consensus.

Conclusion

In many contexts, social media is often a key site for the creation of protest identities (Gerbaudo & Treré 2015), and digital media can have powerful consequences for the social activities that happen in the worlds imagined by them (Weltevrede 2016). In the South African context, the catchy and viral slogan Fees Must Fall was modified by various universities as protests erupted on those campuses, for example, #WitsFeesMustFall, and later it was taken even further to indicate larger discontent with government via the mobilising hashtag #ZumaMustFall.

Both cases discussed above reflect the affordances of these communication technologies (Gerbuado & Treré 2015) and illustrate the emergence of new forms of collective identity produced via social media. The specific connective affordances of social media sites facilitate the 'in-between bond of publics, and they also enable expression and information sharing that liberate the individual and collective imaginations' (Papacharissi 2015: 9). In the case of #FMF, the outcome was immediate – a 0 percent fee increase – but the resurgence of protests has not resulted in any immediate outcomes. Similarly, the #ZumaMustFall campaign has not led to any immediate policy shifts, and President Jacob Zuma remained in office in the period immediately following the protests. While there are low barriers to entering and joining a movement online, this can often result in thin civic activity – 'thin modalities of civic engagement may not necessarily lead to action that we conventionally term impactful, but they do enable gestures that carry symbolic weight for individuals, typically by giving voice and affording visibility to issues generally marginalised' (Papacharissi 2015: 87). Papacharissi (2010) refers to this phenomenon as the emergence of 'supersurfaces', as social media extends and pluralises spaces for conversation and mobilisation organically, but without direct connection to the systemic core of civic institutions, and as a result it does not always result in the ability to effect institutional change. In this instance, #ZumaMustFall can be seen as a campaign, aimed at organising a series of one-off protest events, as opposed to a broader political movement.

Protest is considered a viable feedback mechanism for citizens in a democracy. While South Africans have a range of protest repertoires, which began during apartheid and persist to the present day, the emergence of social media tools as vehicles for the expressions of these protest activities begins to reflect the emergence of hashtag activism and its potential to amplify citizen discontent through building horizontal connections between citizens. What this examination of these two hashtag campaigns shows is the potential for social media to expand the democratic political space and broaden the public sphere. While previous research on social media and social movements has demonstrated the role played by social media in mobilising large groups of people, this discussion of #FeesMustFall and #ZumaMustFall in South Africa demonstrates the potential role for digital protests in Africa to help movements gain momentum and currency in the public domain, though that does not necessarily make them effective in driving offline political or policy change. This study also highlights the importance of social media as a tool for citizens to craft alternative narratives, alongside but also sometimes in stark opposition to mainstream media coverage.

Notes

1 www.news24.com/SouthAfrica/News/new-social-media-research-finds-xenophobia-rife-among-south-africans-20170404.

2 https://theconversation.com/south-african-protesters-echo-a-global-cry-democracy-isnt-making-peoples-lives-better-77639.

3 https://mg.co.za/article/2016-06-27-00-the-medias-anti-democratic-love-affair-with-riot-porn.

4 Data from World Wide Worx.

5 http://gullanandgullan.com/wp-content/uploads/2017/10/13907_GG-Breakthrough-infographic.pdf.

6 www.csvr.org.za/pdf/An-analysis-of-the-FeesMustFall-Movement-at-South-African-universities.pdf.

7 www.financialmail.co.za/mediaadvertising/2015/11/05/social-media-feesmustfall-tweets-rule.

8 www.news24.com/SouthAfrica/News/post-apartheid-south-africas-largest-protest-set-to-start-at-1000-20170927.

References

Alexander, P. (2010) 'Marikana, turning point in South African history'. *Review of African Political Economy*, 40(138): 605–619.

Ballard, R., Habib, A. & Valodia, I. (2006) *Voices of Protest: Social Movements in post- Apartheid South Africa*. Durham: University of KwaZulu Natal Press.

Benkler, Y. (2006) *The Wealth of Networks: How Social Production Transforms Markets and Freedom*. New Haven: Yale.

Bosch, T. (2016) 'Twitter activism and youth in South Africa: the case of #RhodesMustFall'. *Information,* *Communication and Society*, 14(6): 757–769.

Bosch, T. & Mutsvairo, B. (2017) 'Pictures, protests and politics: mapping Twitter images during South Africa's Fees Must Fall campaign'. *African Journalism Studies*, 38(2): 71–89.

Bosch, T., Wasserman, H. & Chuma, W. (2018) 'South African Activists' use of nanomedia and Digital media in democratization conflicts'. *International Journal of Communication (IJoC)*, 12. http://ijoc.org/index.php/ijoc/article/view/6419 (accessed 1 March 2018).

boyd, d. & Crawford, K. (2012) 'Critical questions for big data: provocations for a cultural, technological, and scholarly phenomenon'. *Information, communication & society*, 15(5): 662–679.

Chiumbu, S. (2016) 'Media, race and capital: a decolonial analysis of representation of miners' strikes in South Africa'. *African Studies*, 75(3): 417–435.

Cossarini, P. (2014) 'Protests, emotions and democracy: theoretical insights from the Indignados movement'. *Global Discourse*, 4(2–3): 291–304.

Crawford, K. (2009) 'Following you: disciplines of listening in social media'. *Continuum: Journal of Media & Cultural Studies*, 23(4): 525–535.

Davis, B. (2013) 'Hashtag politics: the polyphonic revolution of# Twitter'. *Pepperdine Journal of Communication Research*, 1(1): 4.

Dawson, M. (2012) 'Protest, performance and politics: the use of "nano-media" in social movement activism in South Africa'. *Research in Drama Education: the Journal of Applied Theatre and Performance*, 17(3): 321–345.

DiGrazia, J., McKelvey, K., Bollen, J. & Rojas F. (2013) 'More tweets, more votes: social media as a quantitative indicator of political behavior'. *PLoS ONE*, 8(11): e79449. https://doi.org/10.1371/journal. pone.0079449.

Duncan, J. (2014) 'South African journalism and the Marikana massacre: a case study of an editorial failure'. *The Political Economy of Communication*, 1(2).

Farrell, H. (2012) 'The consequences of the internet for politics'. *Annual Review of Political Science*, 15: 35–52.

Friedman, S. (2011) 'Whose freedom? South Africa's press, middle-class bias and the threat of control'.

Ecquid Novi: African Journalism Studies, 32(2): 106–121.

Gagliardone, I. (2014) 'Mapping and Analysing Hate Speech Online'. https://papers.ssrn.com/sol3/ papers.cfm?abstract_id=2601792 (accessed 25 February 2019).

Gerbaudo, P. (2012) *Tweets and the Streets: Social Media and Contemporary Activism*. New York: Pluto Press.

Gerbaudo, P. & Treré, E. (2015) Introduction. 'In search of the "we" in social media activism: introduction to the special issue on social media and protest identities'. *Information, Communication and Society*, 18(8): 865–871.

Highfield, T. & Bruns, A. (2015) 'Is Habermas on Twitter? social media and the public sphere'. In A. Bruns, G. Enli, E. Skogerbo, A. Larsson & C. Christensen (eds.), *The Routledge Companion to Social Media and Politics*. London and New York: Routledge, pp. 56–73.

Jansen, J. (2004) 'Changes and continuities in South Africa's higher education system, 1994–2004'. In Linda Chisholm (ed.), *Changing Class: Education and Social Change in Post-Apartheid South Africa*, Cape Town: HSRC Press, pp. 293–314.

Juris, J. (2012) 'The new digital media and activist networking within anti-corporate globalization movements'. *The Annals of the American Academy of Political and Social Science*, 597(1): 189–208.

Madlingozi, T. (2007) 'Post-apartheid social movements and the quest for the elusive "New" South Africa'. *Journal of Law and Society*, 34(1): 77–98.

Mäkinen, M. & Wangu Kuira, M. (2008) 'Social media and postelection crisis in Kenya'. *The International Journal of Press/Politics*, 13(3): 328–335.

Molefe, T. (2016) 'Oppression must fall: South Africa's revolution in theory'. *World Policy Journal*, 33(1): 30–37.

Morozov, E. (2011) *The Net Delusion: How Not to Liberate the World.* London: Penguin.

Pajnik, M. & Downing, J. (2008) 'Introduction: the challenges of nano-media'. In M. Pajnik & J. Downing (eds.), *Alternative Media and the Politics of Resistance: Perspectives and Challenges.* Ljubljana, Slovenia: Peace Institute, pp. 7–16.

Papacharissi, Z. (2010) *A Private Sphere: Democracy in a Digital Age.* Cambridge: Polity.

Papacharissi, Z. (2015) *Affective Publics: Sentiment, Technology and Politics.* Oxford, UK: Oxford University Press.

Pithouse, R. (2010) 'Politics in the slum: a view from South Africa'. *Das Argument*, 52.

Rieder, B. (2013) 'Studying Facebook via Data Extraction: the Netvizz Application'. In *Proceedings of the 5th annual ACM web science conference* (pp. 346–355). ACM. http://citeseerx.ist.psu.edu/viewdoc/download?doi=10.1.1.678.6806&rep=rep1&type=pdf (accessed 1 March 2019).

Robins, S. L. (2008) *From Revolution to Rights in South Africa: Social Movements, NGOs & Popular Politics after Apartheid.* Pietermaritzburg: Boydell & Brewer Ltd.

Skolnick, J. (2010) *The Politics of Protest.* New York: NYU Press.

Tufekci, Z. (2014) 'Big questions for social media big data: representativeness, validity and other methodological pitfalls'. In ICWSM '14: Proceedings of the 8th International AAAI Conference on Weblogs and Social Media.

Tufekci, Z. (2017) *Twitter and Tear Gas: the Power and Fragility of Networked Protest.* New Haven: Yale University Press.

Valenzuela, S., Arriagada, A. & Scherman, A. (2012) 'The social media basis of youth protest behavior: the case of Chile'. *Journal of Communication*, 62(2): 299–314.

Van de Donk, W. et al. (eds.) (2004) *Cyberprotest: New Media, Citizens and Social Movements.* London and New York: Routledge.

Vladišavljević, N. (2015) 'Media framing of political conflict: a review of the literature'. MeCoDem Working Paper. www.mecodem.eu/publications/working-papers/ (accessed 27 August 2017).

Vromen, A., Xenos, M. A. & Loader, B. (2015) 'Young people, social media and connective action: from organisational maintenance to everyday political talk'. *Journal of Youth Studies*, 18(1): 80–100.

Wasserman, H. (2018) 'The social is political: media, protest and change as a challenge to African media research'. In B. Mutsvairo (ed.), *Palgrave Handbook for Media and Communication Research in Africa.* New York: Palgrave MacMillan, pp. 213–224.

Wasserman, H., Bosch, T. & Chuma, W. (2018) 'Print media coverage of service delivery protests in South Africa: a content analysis'. *African Studies* (forthcoming).

Weltevrede, E.J.T. (2016) 'Repurposing Digital Methods: the Research affordances of platforms and engines'. Unpublished doctoral dissertation. Amsterdam University. Available online *at* https://wiki.digitalmethods.net/pub/Dmi/RepurposingDigitalMethods/Weltevrede_RepurposingDigitalMethods.pdf

5 | ENEMY COLLABORATORS

Social imaginaries, global frictions and
a gay rights music video in Kenya

Brian Ekdale

Introduction

On 15 February 2016, a Kenyan art collective named Art Attack uploaded to YouTube a remix of Macklemore and Ryan Lewis' 'Same Love', a 2012 Grammy-nominated song that criticises hyper-masculinity and homophobia in the hip hop industry. Art Attack's 'Same Love (Remix)' uses the chorus lyrics of the original – 'I can't change / Even if I tried / Even if I wanted to' – but updates the verses and the visuals to focus on discrimination against LGBTQ Africans (Art Attack 2016). The video depicts loving relationships between two same-sex couples – one gay, one lesbian – yet ends in tragedy when one of the male protagonists attempts suicide. Perhaps unsurprisingly, considering the subject matter and the video's racy depiction of gay and lesbian intimacy, the video attracted attention immediately, particularly from the nation's tabloids, conservative leaders and cosmopolitan middle class.

A week after the video's release, Ezekiel Mutua, CEO of the Kenyan Film Classification Board (KFCB), released a two-page statement condemning 'Same Love (Remix)' (Mutua 2016). According to the statement, the video 'consists of lyrics that strongly advocate for gay rights in the country, complete with graphic sexual scenes between people of the same gender as well as depiction of nudity and pornography' and it 'promotes irresponsible sexual behavior'. The statement also claims Art Attack failed to acquire a filming licence for shooting the video in Kenya. Citing both 'legal and moral considerations', the KFCB banned the video from local television and asked Google to block access to the YouTube video in Kenya. The board gave Google one week to abide by its request.

Mutua's denunciation of the video inadvertently prompted a backlash among Kenya's vocal Twitter community. After the KFCB announced the video's ban, several users turned Mutua's strong condemnation into a subversive promotional campaign. For example, one user tweeted a link to the video with the comment, 'Let me help

@infoKfcb ban this song. You guys see this song? You need to make sure you don't watch it. thanks'. Another tweeted a link to a news story about the video, adding: 'Do not @YouTube "Same Love By Art Attack" which has been banned by @InfoKfcb'. Several others sarcastically appropriated the KFCB's ban of 'Same Love (Remix)' as the *raison d'être* for sharing the video on social media.

After several weeks, Google informed the KFCB it would not block access to the video or remove it from its search engine, but Google did agree to add the following 'warning message' to the beginning of the video: 'The following content has been identified by the YouTube community as being potentially inappropriate. Viewer discretion is advised' (Lang'at 2016). Although Google's response was much softer than what the KFCB had requested, Mutua claimed victory. On 5 May 2016, Mutua tweeted 'Google flags inappropriate music video following @InfoKfcb 's sustained campaign', attaching a screenshot of a news article with the favourable headline 'Google bows to Film Board order, flags controversial gay video'. In his tweet, Mutua tagged the cabinet secretary of the Ministry of Sports, Culture and the Arts (@AreroWario) and the Media Council of Kenya (@MediaCouncilK), ensuring that his superiors and peers would notice his victory lap.

'Same Love (Remix)' by Art Attack remains on YouTube, accessible within and outside Kenya. Yet, somehow, everyone involved in the controversy surrounding 'Same Love (Remix)' appears to have achieved their original goals. Mutua used the episode to cast himself as a moral crusader who stands up to heathens and transnational behemoths (Lang'at 2016; Mukei 2016). Art Attack was able to attract national and international media attention to the plight of LGBTQ Africans (Agutu 2016; Daley 2016; Lang'at 2016; Ruvaga 2016). Kenyans on Twitter indulged in yet another opportunity to use subversive humour to mock reactionary public officials (Chambers 2016). And YouTube continues to be one of the most popular social media sites in Kenya (Alexa.com 2018). This raises the question: how is it possible that Art Attack, Mutua, Kenyans on Twitter, and Google – ostensibly enemy combatants in this cultural battle – can all claim victory? Further, what does this episode tell us about global cultural production in the digital era?

In this chapter, I attempt to answer these two questions. First, I outline a framework for studying global cultural production based on social imaginaries and global frictions. Then I discuss each of the four key social actors involved in the controversy surrounding 'Same Love (Remix)', exploring the social imaginary of each social actor and the frictions created when these divergent social imaginaries are put in contact with each other. In closing, I consider what this episode reveals about the ongoing tensions between global media giants like Twitter and YouTube and local users and regulators in Africa.

Social imaginaries and global frictions

In Ekdale (2018), I introduce an analytical framework for studying global cultural production that relies on two key concepts: social imaginaries and global frictions. Social imaginaries capture the sense of belonging people feel with those outside their direct proximity (Taylor 2004). As Benedict Anderson argued in *Imagined Communities*, the ability to construct a mental image of a community beyond one's personal experience is a prerequisite for national identity, 'because the members of even the smallest nation will never know most of their fellow-members, meet them, or even hear of them, yet in the minds of each lives the image of their communion' (1983: 6–7). Not all social imaginaries are circumscribed by national boundaries. Some social imaginaries capture a sense of unity held within a geographic region (Carpenter & Ekdale 2019; Cayla & Eckhardt 2008), while others extend to disparate parts of the world (Darling-Wolf 2015; Steger 2008). These social imaginaries help define who we are by giving us a sense of how we fit with others. Our self-identities as hybridised subjects within social imaginaries, in turn, shape our cultural practices related to media production, distribution and consumption (Ekdale 2018).

Culture is not merely the product of individualised action, nor are our practices unaffected by the worldviews of those around us. Culture production occurs within social practices involving various people shaped by divergent social imaginaries. Anthropologist Anna Tsing (2005) introduced the concept of friction as one way to make sense of the entanglements that occur between local actors shaped by global discourses. Tsing describes friction as 'the awkward, unequal, unstable, and creative qualities of interconnection across difference' (2005: 4), arguing that even when groups of people are seemingly working together, there are often significant differences in how these groups approach and make sense of their efforts. Whereas a great deal of scholarship within global media studies focuses on the flow of media and cultural products, friction provides a lens for examining what Gray (2014: 995) calls the 'multiple points of contact' that occur between cultural agents. In Ekdale (2018), I extend Tsing's work to outline a typology of frictions that occur within cultural production: collaborative frictions, which occur between groups working across difference toward a common goal; combative frictions, which occur between groups positioned in direct opposition to each other; and competitive frictions, which occur between groups with interests that change over time.

This analytical framework allows for the study of global cultural production through two entry points: the construction of social imaginaries among social actors and the frictions that occur between collaborative, combative or competing groups during the course of cultural production. In the section that follows, I first examine the social imaginaries of each of the four key participants involved in the 'Same Love (Remix)' controversy – Art Attack, Ezekiel Mutua, Kenyans on Twitter, and Google – to see how their various social imaginaries shape their social practices. I also consider the frictions that occurred between these four groups that resulted in what seems to be a mutually beneficial outcome.

Cultural producers and their social imaginaries

Art Attack

Little is known about the origins or membership of Art Attack. Art Attack's YouTube channel was created the same day 'Same Love (Remix)' was uploaded, and the music video is the only item available on the channel. The group's Twitter account (@therealartatta2), which was launched a few days after the video was released, has been dormant since May 2016. The group does not have a website, Facebook page or SoundCloud account, nor have they released any other music under the name of Art Attack. In 2014, *The Star* profiled a group of six Nairobi-based painters who worked together at a studio called Art Attack (Waweru 2014), but it is unclear if this group is the same one that released 'Same Love (Remix)'. The mystery surrounding the group is intentional. After 'Same Love (Remix)' was released, the song's writer and performer claimed that members had gone into hiding after the group received threats of arrest and attacks against their personal safety (Daley 2016). However, the song's writer/performer, who became the de facto leader and anonymous spokesman for Art Attack after the release of 'Same Love (Remix)', was interviewed by a number of national and international media outlets about the music video, as well as the larger issue of discrimination against LGBTQ Africans.

In an interview with a Nigerian podcast, the group's leader described Art Attack as 'Art-tivists', stating 'most of our stuffs are geared toward social change, and motivated mostly around what we see around the social circles in Kenya' (No Strings 2016). The song's writer/performer identifies as a cisgender, heterosexual male who said he was inspired to write 'Same Love (Remix)' after hearing LGBTQ friends discuss the daily challenges they face because of their sexual orientation (Langat 2016; No Strings 2016). According to him, 'we created this video first and foremost because we are artists and also because we were very much alive to the great challenges and tribulations that LGBTQ persons go through in Kenya and Africa as a whole' (Lim 2016). When explaining why he wrote the song, the group's leader said he wanted to raise awareness of LGBTQ discrimination both in Kenya specifically and in Africa broadly. In his interview with the Nigerian podcast, the writer/performer said most Africans are hostile toward those with non-normative sexual identities (No Strings 2016). He specifically criticised Uganda, whose parliament recently passed a bill that decreed homosexuality a crime deserving of life imprisonment. Even though the bill was later annulled by Uganda's high court, its passage indicates that LGBTQ discrimination is a political and legal as well as a social and cultural issue in Africa. Not only did Art Attack want to create a song critical of discrimination in Kenya, 'we wanted [the song] to be a pan-African song' (No Strings 2016). As the song's writer/performer told an interviewer from *OkayAfrica*, 'we wanted to bring about a change in attitude toward gay and lesbian people in Africa' (Klein 2016).

The song's lyrics share this tension of being rooted locally as a Kenyan story while also being connected broadly to the African experience. For instance, the remix opens with a dedication 'to the New Slaves, the New Blacks, the New Jews, the New Minorities for whom we need a civil rights movement, maybe a sex-rights movement, especially in Africa. Everywhere'. The first verse, then, transitions from this broad decree to a personal story of a young man who grew close to a 'male kid in school', eventually realising he was 'in love with a boy like me'. In the second verse, the protagonist comes out to his mother and father, who respond by telling him to 'pack your bags, shameless heathen, and follow the sun'. The final verse broadens again to criticise institutions like the Church and the Kenyan constitution, which criminalises homosexuality, while also condemning 'African culture' for embracing homophobia. Visually, the video focuses on two gay couples expressing their love for each other in public, in the home and in the bedroom. Yet, mixed with this narrative is stock footage of gay pride parades from around the world, images of African newspapers with headlines denouncing homosexuality, photos of famous LGBTQ Africans and clips of a prominent gay character in the American television show *Empire*. While the lyrics ground the song in Kenya and Africa, the visuals offer a transnational bricolage – depicting the struggle for freedom and acceptance in global, regional and local settings.

Thus, the producers of 'Same Love (Remix)' demonstrate a broad sense of belonging with those who seek recognition and equality regardless of one's sexual orientation or gender identity. In the social imaginary of Art Attack, the struggle against LGBTQ discrimination is most pressing in Kenya and Africa, but it is informed by the global gay rights movement. As the group's leader stated in an interview: 'Everybody has to have the freedom to do whatever they want to do, marry whoever they want to marry. So we were just trying to raise their voice, create their awareness in Africa' (Ruvaga 2016). For Art Attack, producing and releasing 'Same Love (Remix)' was an effort to confront injustice in Kenya, Africa and beyond.

Ezekiel Mutua and the KFCB

Ezekiel Mutua is no stranger to controversy. Long before the KFCB issued a statement concerning the 'Same Love (Remix)' video, Mutua had charted a path toward becoming Kenya's chief moral policeman (Wasonga 2016). A former journalist turned head of the journalists' union, Mutua entered government through the Ministry of Information, Communications and Technology and quickly rose through the ranks. In December 2015, Mutua was appointed CEO of the KFCB, a government body created in 1963 to regulate the creation and distribution of films in Kenya by issuing production licences and rating films. With the passage of the Kenya Information and Communication Act in 2013, the KFCB's mandate expanded to include the regulation of television content to ensure that no adult programming would be shown between 5 a.m. and 10 p.m. daily. For most of the KFCB's existence, very few Kenyans were familiar with the work of this government body. Under Mutua's leadership, that has changed.

Since taking over the KFCB, Mutua has waged several public battles that demonstrate a concerted effort to expand the authority of the government body and to elevate his personal profile as a guardian of traditional morality. In January 2016, a month after Mutua became the KFCB's CEO, the KFCB announced that they would be challenging Netflix's efforts to expand into the Kenyan market. In a statement citing 'this era of global terrorism', the KFCB claimed that portions of the streaming service's library represented a 'threat to our moral values and national security' (Barnes 2016; Ochieng' 2016). Mutua further added that he did not want Kenyans to be misled by Netflix's rating system because, 'the ratings are American, they are not Kenyan, they are not African' (Craig 2016). Further justifying the KFCB's stance, KFCB chairperson Jackson Kosgei said it was important that Kenya not become a 'passive recipient of foreign content that could corrupt the moral values of our children' (Kuo 2016a). Thus, from the earliest days of Mutua's leadership, the KFCB sought to define itself as a protector of Kenyan morality in the face of foreign contamination.

The KFCB's public battle with Netflix is just one of Mutua's many attempts to regulate cultural content that does not clearly reside within the KFCB's mandate. In March 2016, the KFCB shut down a Nairobi party called Project X that advertised itself with the sensational tagline 'No one goes back a virgin'. Mutua justified the KFCB's intervention with an unsubstantiated claim that the party was being organised by an 'international pornography ring', thus, making the party a site of unlicensed film production (BBC News 2016a). A year later, after posters for a 'Project X squared' party began to circulate online, the KFCB again pledged to shut down the event and punish its organisers. Mutua claimed the party was part of a wider sex syndicate run by foreign NGOs intended to recruit children into pornographic films that would be sold in foreign countries (Ambani 2017). In April 2016, the KFCB banned a Coca-Cola advertisement from airing on television during daytime hours, because the it featured a passionate kiss that lasted three seconds (BBC News 2016b). Coke later re-edited the advertisement to meet the KFCB's approval (KFCB 2016). The Mutua-led KFCB has also intervened in other matters, including commercials for alcohol and contraception, a music video he determined to be pornographic, and a sex-positive podcast hosted by two Kenyan women. In each of these cases, Mutua and the KFCB defined themselves as necessary advocates for Kenyan children and traditional moral values fighting against pernicious foreign cultural forces.

In October 2016, Mutua proposed changes to Kenyan law that would codify the KFCB's expanding mandate. The proposed Films, Stage Plays and Publications Act of 2016 would have put the KFCB in charge of regulating films, live performances, stage plays, video games, streaming television services, billboard advertisements and print publications. The language of the draft legislation was overly broad, leaving open the possibility that the KFCB could also regulate social media content, meaning all Kenyans would need a production licence and government approval before taking or posting images online (Itimu 2016). Further, the proposed revisions would have given the KFCB the authority to prevent the production, distribution and exhibition of any media 'that are not reflective of national values and aspirations of the people of Kenya' (Films, Stage Plays and Publications Act 2016). The proposed legislation was met with strong opposition, and Mutua eventually withdrew his support, even though he continues to advocate for revisions to Kenya's media laws (Openda 2016; Oduor 2016).

The seeds of Mutua's approach to the media can be found in his 2010 M.A. thesis from the School of Journalism and Media Studies at the University of Nairobi, which he completed while serving as Kenya's Director of Information and Public Communication. Mutua's thesis offers a study of how rural radio stations covered the 2008 post-election violence period in Kenya (Mutua 2010). The thesis relies heavily on Social Responsibility Theory, which argues that the press must balance their freedoms with an obligation to provide the public with accurate and comprehensive information (Mutua 2010; Siebert, Peterson & Schramm 1956). According to Social Responsibility Theory, if the press is unable to regulate itself, it may be necessary for the government to step in to enforce regulation. In his study, Mutua concludes that vernacular radio stations indeed failed their public service responsibility during Kenya's post-election period by practising 'irresponsible journalism' (Mutua 2010: 83). Mutua writes:

> The post-election crisis indicated that free and plural media were as much an answer to Kenya's democratic deficits as they are a problem. Thus, the deconstruction of the Kenyan society should be branded to include not only the re-engineering of State institutions but also other social institutions such as the media. (Mutua 2010: 16)

Social Responsibility Theory envisions an active role for government regulators when journalists fail to serve the public, and Mutua's study argues that rural radio stations during the post-election period neglected their public duties. It is therefore unsurprising that after Mutua took over as CEO of the KFCB, he fashioned the government body into an active regulator of media and cultural content in Kenya.

Banning 'Same Love (Remix)' and petitioning Google to restrict the video on YouTube is consistent with the KFCB's other actions under Mutua's leadership as well as his broader views about the relationship between media and the government. He believes government regulation of media content is a social good necessary for the protection of traditional moral values. As Mutua claims in the KFCB statement announcing the ban of 'Same Love (Remix)':

> The future of our country lies in the collective responsibility of Government institutions as well as the vigilance and support of the parents in keeping children safe online. We reiterate our commitment to work with all stakeholders to ensure the safety of our children. (Mutua 2016)

Thus, Mutua both advocates for traditional values and asserts himself as Kenya's primary cultural defender. Many Kenyans have criticised Mutua for acting as Kenya's 'moral policeman' (Madowo 2016; Mwampembwa 2016; Wasonga 2016), but Mutua has relished his moment in the spotlight. That he felt compelled to weigh in on the 'Same Love (Remix)' video demonstrates both his political and his personal agenda. In the social imaginary of Mutua, he is the guardian of traditional culture and morality, which he believes must be protected against foreign contamination. Mutua is unapologetic about his political and personal ambitions, as evidenced by a tweet he sent from his personal account on the day the KFCB banned 'Same Love (Remix)': 'KFCB is a regulator. We don't do what's popular; we do what's legal and right'. Attached to the tweet is a photo of himself.

Kenyans on Twitter

Kenyans were one of the earliest adopters of Twitter in Africa, and they continue to be among the continent's most active users (KenyanVibe 2012; Portland 2015). Twitter has been used by Kenyans to share information about acts of terrorism as well as exchange jokes about an aspirational hero (Ekdale & Tully 2014; Simon et al. 2014; Tully 2013). The social network has also been used by Kenyan public officials looking for innovative ways to engage with their constituents (Omanga 2015; Simon et al. 2014). Many Kenyans view Twitter as a site of 'playful engagement', a place where they can use 'humor and serious critique...[to] challenge inequality and push development agendas forward' (Tully & Ekdale 2014: 77). These conversations are often facilitated by hashtags, which serve as ad hoc publics that allow users to coalesce around particular topics (Rambukkana 2015). Twitter is particularly popular among Kenya's young, urban elites, those with more cosmopolitan views and aspirations (Ekdale & Tully 2014; Overney 2014). Unsurprisingly, the release of 'Same Love (Remix)' by Art Attack and the KFCB's response to the video produced a lively conversation among Kenyans on Twitter about homosexuality and free expression.

Three days after 'Same Love (Remix)' was released on YouTube, one Twitter user posted several tweets critical of the video and homosexuality, appending the hashtag #KenyanGayVideo. The hashtag quickly gained traction as a site of discussion about 'Same Love (Remix)' and the issues the video raises, attracting hundreds of tweets by the end of the day (Langat 2016). The conversation began among those who view homosexuality as immoral and ungodly, but within an hour, sex-rights advocates and fans of the video began using the hashtag to express more sympathetic views. Tweets using #KenyanGayVideo ranged from critical (for example, 'This is a disease not a right') to violent (for example, 'God, kill em, kill em all') to supportive (for example, 'As a human I totally condemn all acts of homophobia and bigotry') to defiant (for example, 'Just because gays and lesbians are silent does not mean we don't exist'). Several users also noted that the discussion on Twitter had inadvertently drawn further attention to the video (for example, 'just now I was watching the video on YouTube it was at 2k views now it 12K views- guys are really watching').

By the time the KFCB announced its ban – a little over a week after 'Same Love (Remix)' was uploaded to YouTube – the Twitter conversation using the hashtag #KenyanGayVideo had died down. The KFCB ban had the ironic effect of re-energising the discussion among Kenyans on Twitter and changing the conversation from one about homosexuality to one concerning government censorship. Several Twitter users objected to the KFCB's response, such as one user who replied to a Mutua tweet claiming the video was restricted 'on moral grounds' by saying, 'This is a joke we are a secular country. Christianity

shouldn't be a basis to gauge MORALITY. Just disband please!'
Others similarly criticised the KFCB and Mutua for intervening in a
cultural issue beyond the scope of the government body's mandate.
These tweets reflected the cynicism many Kenyans feel toward their
leaders (for example, 'Now that KFCB has banned Same Love by Art
Attack. Can we ban the government corrupt leaders') as well as the joy
many Kenyans took in watching the KFCB's ban attract more attention to the video (for example, 'The KFCB banned the song "Same
love remix" by Art Attack and now I'm more curious to listening to
the song').

For Kenyans on Twitter, the release of 'Same Love (Remix)' provided an opportunity to have a conversation about LGBTQ rights and
morality. Although many of the perspectives shared were discriminatory, they existed in a public forum where they could be challenged
by more sympathetic and accepting views. When the KFCB intervened by banning 'Same Love (Remix)' and requesting that Google
censor the video on YouTube, it prompted a backlash among those
who are wary of government censorship. For these Twitter users, open
participation and discussion using online platforms is an important element of making Kenya a more cosmopolitan and democratic society
(Ekdale & Tully 2014; Tully & Ekdale 2014). The KFCB's overreach
represented an attack on these users' values, and they responded by
appropriating the KFCB's ban to promote the video.

Google

Social media companies deliberately characterise their products as
'platforms', neutral spaces where members of the public can provide,
locate, and share information and entertainment (Gillespie 2010).
Companies like Google want to be seen as global advocates of free
expression who give the public access to open warehouses of participatory content. This discursive project obscures the role proprietary
algorithms play in shaping our experiences online, the compromises
technology companies make in pursuit of greater profit, and the fact that
companies like Google frequently alter their practices to appease powerful political and commercial entities (Gillespie 2010; Grimmelmann
2009; Seyfert & Roberge 2016). Although Google has complied with
the demands of local government gatekeepers in the past, particularly in
China (O'Rourke IV, Harris & Ogilvy 2007), doing so has been harmful to their corporate image, making people question the company's

commitment to its initial guiding principle: 'Don't be evil'. When Google receives requests to censor content, it is in its brand's interests to deny or ignore those requests; yet, it is in its financial interests to avoid lawsuits and restrictions on its business practices. Thus, when the KFCB demanded that Google restrict access to 'Same Love (Remix)' on YouTube, the company faced a dilemma: abide by the order and further damage its brand as an advocate for free expression or deny the request and possibly face legal consequences from the Kenyan government.

Interestingly, Google's initial response to the KFCB was bureaucratic. The first request sent by the KFCB was addressed to Google Kenya, Google's subsidiary in Nairobi. Google Kenya responded through a letter, sent by its lawyer, explaining that the subsidiary did not have the authority to restrict access to 'Same Love (Remix)'. The letter read, in part:

> YouTube LLC/Google Inc. and Google Kenya limited are separate legal entities. Google Kenya limited does not administer services on YouTube, nor does it have the capacity to control content that is accessible through them. We, therefore, would like to request you to submit your request electronically [to corporate headquarters]. (Business Daily Africa 2016)

In response, Mutua resubmitted his removal request to Google headquarters and said he was pleased that the review process was ongoing: 'We have not reached the point of taking [Google] to court for non-compliance but we are building a case that if we will be required to prosecute we will do so' (Murumba 2016). Meanwhile, a spokesman for Art Attack commended Google Kenya for this initial response to the KFCB:

> We obviously greatly applaud Google Kenya for choosing to have the video still stay up on YouTube all this time. We deeply appreciate that they didn't bulge [sic] and didn't give in to the government threats and orders and decided to do what is right and let people express themselves freely without having to have their rights trampled upon. (Lim 2016)

On Twitter, Kenyans continued to mock Mutua for his efforts to censor the video. After one user noted that Google had failed to abide by the KFCB's one-week ultimatum, another user replied, 'They are probably still trying to Google what a KFCB is'.

On 3 May 2016, at an event celebrating World Press Freedom Day, Mutua announced that Google had abided by the KFCB's demands. 'We are happy that the music video has been pulled down following a request we made to Google', Mutua declared (Kuo 2016c). But Google did not take down 'Same Love (Remix)'. Kenyans who visit the music video on YouTube receive a warning message that says the video is 'potentially inappropriate' and 'viewer discretion is advised', but after accepting this message, the video is viewable in its entirety. As a representative from Google Kenya acknowledged, Google's response 'doesn't mean the video isn't available for viewing in Kenya' (Kuo 2016c). While one article characterised Google's action as a 'win for Mutua' (Lang'at 2016), another labelled it a 'fail': '[Mutua] is not fooling us, everyone knows that he wanted a total ban on the video' (Kamau 2016).

Ultimately, Google succeeded in minimising its role within the cultural dispute surrounding 'Same Love (Remix)'. Google's bureaucratic response both maintained the company's preferred image as a neutral party and allowed it to delay action long enough for the controversy to subside. The contents of Google's internal discussion are unknown; the tech giant's only public statements on the matter came via a spokesperson's email to the news website *Quartz*, after the KFCB resubmitted its request:

> YouTube has clear policies that outline what content is acceptable to post and we remove videos violating these policies when flagged by our users. We review government removal requests when notified through the correct legal processes and in keeping with our company philosophy on transparency and freedom of expression. (Kuo 2016b)

At the time, Google received positive coverage for not 'cav[ing] to the Kenyan government's demands for this powerful gay rights music video to be taken down' (*Marie Claire* 2016). On Twitter, several Kenyans characterised Google as a benevolent Goliath being pestered by an overzealous and petulant David (for example, 'Google won't give a damn about an entity called KFCB. The ramifications would be much bigger if they pulled it down'). By the time Google added a warning message to the beginning of 'Same Love (Remix)', the video had been live on YouTube for nearly three months and the issue of LGBTQ discrimination in Africa had received attention from a variety of national, regional and international media. Interest in the video had plateaued, while interest in Mutua's rise as an arbiter of media and cultural content in Kenya was growing. By May 2016, the question was no longer about whether Google would abide by the KFCB's request to censor a gay rights music video but, rather, about how Kenyans should respond to a government official intent on turning himself into the nation's cultural gatekeeper (Madowo 2016).

Enemy collaborators

Months after the release of 'Same Love (Remix)', the four key players all had reason to believe they had achieved their goals. Art Attack found a sizeable audience for its art-tivist music video[1] and, more important, the group drew attention to the issue of LGBTQ discrimination in Kenya and Africa. LGBTQ Kenyans continue to struggle for acceptance at home, but the release of 'Same Love (Remix)' is now considered a landmark moment on the long road toward equality and acceptance in Kenya (Dubuis 2016). Ezekiel Mutua was able to elevate his status as a protector of traditional moral values in Kenya by getting Google to respond to his request, even if Google's response was much milder than what Mutua initially sought. By weighing in on the video, Mutua's KFCB continued to expand its jurisdiction into media and cultural issues beyond the intended scope of the government agency. Many Kenyans used Twitter to voice their opposition to or support for gay rights in Kenya as well as to satirise Mutua's efforts to block access to 'Same Love (Remix)' on YouTube. This group, consisting mostly of young, urban elites, see Twitter as an important site for expressing themselves using humour and serious critique, and they baulked at Mutua's attempt to censor content on social media. Finally, Google succeeded at fading into the background. As Google hopes to retain its dominance in global markets, the company seeks to avoid controversy. In its official response to the KFCB's request, Google managed to stay above the fray through the use of bureaucratic processes, delayed decision making and a muted response that appeared to appease all those involved.

While everyone had reason to celebrate the outcome of this episode, the long-term ramifications for participating in the controversy reveal the power differentials between the four key players. Art Attack elevated the issue of LGBTQ discrimination, but did so at great personal cost. Following the release of 'Same Love (Remix)', the artists and actors involved in the music video became victims of harassment and abuse (Daley 2016). Art Attack is yet to release another song despite the group's stated intentions at the time to continue advocating for LGBTQ rights (No Strings 2016). Mutua, on the other hand, continues to weigh in on cultural matters seemingly outside the scope of the KFCB, and he continues to receive public attention for his efforts. In September 2016, he was invited to California by Google to attend the company's Web Rangers global summit about online safety. Several journalists criticised Google's decision to invite Matua, who was characterised in the press as an 'anti-gay activist' (Thielman 2016) and 'one of Kenya's most outspoken anti-gay rights campaigners' (Kuo 2016d). In a bit of poetic justice, after Mutua used Facebook to brag that he was able to acquire a visa for the summit without following the official process, the U.S. Department of Immigration announced they would be revoking his diplomatic passport (Vidija 2016). Kenyans on Twitter took great joy in trolling Mutua for his self-inflicted wound (Maina 2016). Google, for its part, remained silent on the matter, most likely pleased to watch the issue resolve itself without having to intervene.

Tsing argues we should think of collaborations less as smooth partnerships and more as messy and often temporary unions: 'Collaborators work with the enemy in wartime. These collaborators are not positioned in equality or sameness, and their collaboration does not produce a communal good' (2005: 246). Thus, it is possible for apparent enemies to collaborate with each other in surprising and unpredictable ways. Using an analytical framework that examines the social imaginaries of those engaged in cultural production as well as the frictions that occur between these cultural producers, we can see how different groups seemingly at odds with each other can all achieve their desired outcomes. These messy interactions and unexpected collaborations are important to study because they 'serve as the building blocks of media and cultural production' (Ekdale 2018: 14). Certainly, Art Attack, Mutua, Kenyans on Twitter, and Google would not consider each other partners in cultural production, but through the collaborative frictions that occurred between these four groups, the cause of each was furthered.

Conclusion

In this chapter, I used an analytical framework for studying global cultural production through two entry points – the construction of social imaginaries and the frictions between social actors. Both of these processes occur regularly on social media. On social media, users can connect with previously distant people and ideas (Rainie & Wellman 2012; van Dijck 2013), which can expand social imaginaries as well as create moments of friction. This is evident throughout Africa where an increasingly large number of people use social media to engage with others both near and far about topics both mundane and contentious (Bosch 2017; Willems & Mano 2016). Further, social media are helping to facilitate a more democratised era of global cultural production by reducing the barriers to content production, appropriation and distribution (Burgess & Green 2018; Jenkins, Ford & Green 2013). In the case of 'Same Love (Remix)', Art Attack relied on the participatory functionality of YouTube to distribute its video to a local and international audience, while Kenyans on Twitter used the site's interactive features to engage with each other in a conversation about gay rights and internet censorship.

At the same time, this episode demonstrates the ongoing tensions between local governments and global technology companies. Even though the KFCB easily banned the video from Kenyan broadcast television, the government agency struggled to exercise jurisdictional authority over a social media site that distributes content both within and beyond national borders. Although Mutua claimed victory after Google added a warning message to the 'Same Love (Remix)' video on YouTube, he no doubt recognises his limited ability to challenge Google and other technology giants. In fact, Mutua's experience attempting to ban 'Same Love (Remix)' on YouTube parallels his experience trying to stand up to Netflix – initial threats and public denunciation quickly gave way to acquiescence and a new target (Barnes 2016; Kuo 2016a). Although many Kenyans have expressed weariness about Mutua's efforts to serve as Kenya's 'moral policeman' (Madowo 2016; Mwampembwa 2016; Wasonga 2016), they would do well also to remain sceptical of global social media companies. Had Google opted to block 'Same Love (Remix)' in Kenya, Art Attack would have been powerless to respond. Were Twitter to change its design and functionality, which it has done several times, Kenyans on Twitter would have to adapt. As long as these social media sites are able to convince users that they are neutral platforms and bastions of free expression (Gillespie 2010), they will continue to have the upper hand against local regulators and users.

Note

1 As of November 2018, the video has more than 325,000 views.

References

Agutu, N. (2016) 'Films Board Bans Art Attack's "Same Love (Remix)" for Being Immoral'. *Nairobi Star*, 23 February. www.the-star.co.ke/news/2016/02/23/films-board-bans-art-attacks-same-love-remix-for-being-immoral_c1300271 (accessed 1 February 2018).

Alexa.com (2018) *Top Sites in Kenya*. www.alexa.com/topsites/countries%3Bo/KE (accessed 1 February 2018).

Ambani, S. (2017) 'Mutua: Project X Squared "Sex Party" Won't Happen Under My Watch'. *Nairobi News*, 12 March. http://nairobinews.nation.co.ke/news/project-x-squared-film-board/ (accessed 1 February 2018).

Anderson, B. (1983) *Imagined Communities: Reflections on the Origin and Spread of Nationalism*. New York: Versa.

Art Attack. (2016) *Same Love (Remix) by Art Attack (OFFICIAL VIDEO)*. 15 February [online video]. www.youtube.com/watch?v=8EataOQvPII (accessed 1 February 2018).

Barnes, H. (2016) 'Kenya's Film Censor: Netflix a Threat to "Moral Values and National Security"'. *The Guardian*, 21 January. www.theguardian.com/film/2016/jan/21/netflix-threat-kenya-film-classification-board-censor-moral-values-terrorism (accessed 1 February 2018).

BBC News (2016a) 'Porn Ring Behind Kenya Project X "Sex Party"'. 7 March. www.bbc.com/news/world-africa-35743191 (accessed 1 February 2018).

BBC News (2016b) 'Coca-Cola Advert Banned in Kenya Over Kissing Scene'. 13 April. www.bbc.com/news/world-africa-36035210 (accessed 1 February 2018).

Bosch, T. (2017) 'Twitter activism and youth in South Africa: the case of #RhodesMustFall'. *Information, Communication & Society*, 20(2): 221–232.

Burgess, J. & Green, J. (2018) *YouTube: Online Video and Participatory Culture* (2nd ed.). Medford, MA: Polity Press.

Business Daily Africa (2016) *'We Have No Capacity to Pull Down the "Same Love" Song' Google Kenya tells KFCB*. 7 March [online video]. www.youtube.com/watch?v=7aFJUvVFopo (accessed 1 February 2018).

Carpenter, J.C. & Ekdale, B. (2019) 'Service at the Intersection of journalism, language, and the global imaginary: Indonesia's English-language press'. *Journalism Studies*, 20(1): 136–153.

Cayla, J. & Eckhardt, G. (2008) 'Asian brand and the shaping of a transnational imagined community'. *Journal of Consumer Research*, 35(2): 216–230.

Chambers, K. (2016) 'How Kenya's "Gay Love" Video Ban Backfired'. *BBC News*, 11 March. www.bbc.com/news/av/magazine-35775093/how-kenya-s-gay-love-video-ban-backfired (accessed 1 February 2018).

Craig, J. (2016) 'Netflix Off to Shaky Start with Kenyan Officials'. *Voice of America*, 22 January. www.voanews.com/a/netflix-off-to-a-shaky-start-with-kenyan-officials/3158790.html (accessed 1 February 2018).

Daley, E. (2016) 'WATCH: Kenyan Creators of Banned "Same Love" Remix are "Living in Fear"'.

The Advocate, 24 February. www. advocate.com/world/2016/2/24/ watch-kenyan-creators-banned-same-love-remix-are-living-fear (accessed 1 February 2018).

Darling-Wolf, F. (2015) *Imagining the Global: Transnational Media and Popular Culture Beyond East and West*. Ann Arbor, MI: University of Michigan Press.

Dubuis, A. (2016) 'Kenya Could Become the Next Country in Africa to Legalize Homosexuality'. *Vice News*, 9 May. https://news.vice.com/article/kenya-could-become-the-next-country-in-africa-to-legalize-homosexuality (accessed 1 February 2018).

Ekdale, B. (2018) 'Global frictions and the production of locality in Kenya's music video industry'. *Media, Culture & Society*, 40(2): 211–227.

Ekdale, B. & Tully, M. (2014) 'Makmende Amerudi: Kenya's collective reimagining as a meme of aspiration'. *Critical Studies in Media Communication*, 31(4): 283–298.

Films, Stage Plays and Publications Act (2016) Draft legislation. https://ifree. co.ke/wp-content/uploads/2016/11/ DRAFT-BILL-KFCB-21-7-Draft-10-1. pdf (accessed 1 February 2018).

Gillespie, T. (2010) 'The politics of "platforms"'. *New Media & Society*, 12(3): 347–364.

Gray, J. (2014) 'Scales of cultural influence: Malawian consumption of foreign media'. *Media, Culture & Society*, 36(7): 982–997.

Grimmelmann, J. (2009) 'The Google dilemma'. *New York Law School Law Review*, 53: 939–950.

Itimu, K. (2016) 'KFCB Wants to Regulate Social Media and People Are Not Too Happy About It'. *Techweez*, 24 March. www.techweez. com/2016/03/24/kfcb-wants-to-regulate-social-media/ (accessed 1 February 2018).

Jenkins, H., Ford, S. & Green, J. (2013) *Spreadable Media: Creating Value and Meaning in a Networked Culture*. New York: NYU Press.

Kamau, R. (2016) 'KFCB Fails in Having Kenyan Gay Music Video "Same Love" Banned on YouTube'. 5 May *Nairobi Wire*, 5 May. http:// nairobiwire.com/2016/05/kfcb-fails-in-having-kenyan-gay-music-video-same-love-banned-on-youtube.html (accessed 1 February 2018).

KenyanVibe (2012) 'Study Shows Kenya Has Second Most Active Twitter Users in Africa'. 27 January. www.kenyanvibe.com/ how-africa-tweets-study-shows-kenya-has-second-most-active-users-twitter-users-in-africa/ (accessed 1 February 2018).

KFCB (2016) *Taste the Feeling Coca-Cola Advert*. 19 April. http://kfcb.co.ke/ taste-the-feeling-coca-cola-advert/ (accessed 1 February 2018).

Klein, A. (2016) '"Same Love" in Kenya: the Cover of Macklemore's Gay Rights Anthem that Sparked a National Conversation'. *OkayAfrica*, 17 March. www.okayafrica. com/same-love-kenya-cover-macklemore-lgbt-rights/ (accessed 1 February 2018).

Kuo, L. (2016a) 'Kenya's Film Regulator is Calling Netflix a Threat to the Country's National Security'. *Quartz*, 20 January. https://qz.com/598521/ kenyas-film-regulator-is-calling-netflix-a-threat-to-the-countrys-national-security/ (accessed 1 February 2018).

Kuo, L. (2016b) 'Google Has Refused Government Demands to Take Down a Gay Music Video in Kenya'. *Quartz*, 14 March. https:// qz.com/638461/google-has-refused-government-demands-to-take-down-a-gay-music-video-in-kenya/ (accessed 1 February 2018).

Kuo, L. (2016c) 'Google Has Flagged a Kenyan Music Video Celebrating Gay Love as "Potentially Inappropriate"'. *Quartz*, 5 May. https://qz.com/676822/google-has-flagged-a-kenyan-music-video-celebrating-gay-love-as-potentially-inappropriate/ (accessed 1 February 2018).

Kuo, L. (2016d) 'Google is Hosting Kenya's Most Notorious Anti-LGBT Official at a Conference in California'. *Quartz*, 28 September. https://qz.com/793107/google-is-hosting-kenyas-most-notorious-anti-lgbt-official-ezekiel-mutua-at-a-conference-in-california/ (accessed 1 February 2018).

Langat, A. (2016) 'Ban on Sexy Music Video Raises Gay Rights Campaign Profile in Kenya'. *Reuters*, 10 March. www.reuters.com/article/kenya-gay-campaign/ban-on-sexy-music-video-raises-gay-rights-campaign-profile-in-kenya-idUSL5N16H28N (accessed 1 February 2018).

Lang'at, P. (2016) 'Win for Mutua as YouTube Flags "Gay" Kenyan Video'. *Nairobi News*, 4 May. http://nairobinews.nation.co.ke/news/youtube-flags-gay-kenyan-video/ (accessed 1 February 2018).

Lim, C.-J. (2016) 'Google Kenya Refuses to Take Down a YouTube Music Video Celebrating Same-Sex Love Despite Government Ban'. *A Plus*, 14 March. http://aplus.com/a/google-kenya-refuses-calls-to-take-down-art-attack-same-love-gay-music-video-from-youtube (accessed 1 February 2018).

Madowo, L. (2016) 'Who Will Save Us from the KFCB CEO?' *Daily Nation*, 16 April. https://webcache.googleusercontent.com/search?q=cache:eT4gUxN3JSUJ:https://www.nation.co.ke/lifestyle/dn2/957860-3166848-fk4yhoz/index.html+&cd=1&hl=en&ct=clnk&gl=us&client=firefox-b-1-d (accessed 1 February 2018).

Maina, K. (2016) 'Hilarious: KOT Troll Ezekiel Mutua After His Diplomatic Passport Was Revoked'. *Nairobi Wire*, 30 September. http://nairobiwire.com/2016/09/hilarious-kot-troll-ezekiel-mutua-after-his-diplomatic-passport-was-revoked.html (accessed 1 February 2018).

Marie Claire (2016) 'The Kenyan Govt. Couldn't get Google to Ban This Gay Rights Music Video'. 15 March. www.marieclaire.co.uk/news/watch-the-gay-rights-music-vid-kenya-couldn-t-ban-14081 (accessed 1 February 2018).

Mukei, C. (2016) 'YouTube Finally Obliges to KFCB's Request to Pull Down Gay Video'. *East African Standard*, 6 May. www.standardmedia.co.ke/evewoman/article/2000200861 (accessed 1 February 2018).

Murumba, S. (2016) 'Google Kenya Says Can't Act on Mutua Gay Video Ban'. *Business Daily Africa*, 13 March. www.businessdailyafrica.com/Corporate-News/Google-Kenya-says-can-t-act-on-Mutua-gay-video-ban/-/539550/3115542/-/item/0/-/51ttf1/-/index.html (accessed 1 February 2018).

Mutua, E. (2010) 'Media and Social Responsibility: an Investigation into Post-Election Violence Coverage by Kass and Musyi FM Stations'. Unpublished MA thesis, University of Nairobi.

Mutua, E. (2016) Statement by the Kenya Film Classification Board Chief Executive Officer Mr. Ezekiel Mutua on the YouTube Circulation of 'Same Love Remix' Music Video Issued on 23 February 2016. Official statement.

Mwampembwa, G. (2016) 'Ezekiel Mutua the Morality Police Inspector'. *Gado*, 16 October.

http://gadocartoons.com/ezekiel-mutua-moral-police-inspector/ (accessed 1 February 2018).

No Strings (Podcast) (2016) 'Let Homosexuals be! – Art Attack'. 7 March. https://nostringsng.com/podcast-let-homosexuals-be-art-attack/ (accessed 1 February 2018).

Ochieng', L. (2016) 'Board Defies CS, Says Netflix Streams Immoral Content, Threat to National Security'. *Daily Nation*, 20 January. www.nation.co.ke/business/Netflix-streams-immoral-content/996-3042086-110e8vu/index.html (accessed 1 February 2018).

Oduor, E. (2016) 'Proposed Law Rattles Kenyan Filmmakers and Media'. *The East African*, 9 December. www.theeastafrican.co.ke/news/Proposed-law-rattles-Kenyan-filmmakers--and-media/2558-3480548-3t319i/index.html (accessed 1 February 2018).

Omanga, D. (2015) '"Chieftaincy" in the social media space: community policing in a Twitter convened baraza'. *Stability: International Journal of Security and Development*, 4(1).

Openda, J. (2016) 'Journalists' Union Opposes Bill on Media Content'. *Daily Nation*, 7 November. www.nation.co.ke/news/Journalists--union-opposes-Bill-on-media-content/1056-3442988-format-xhtml-7f6r0a/index.html (accessed 1 February 2018).

O'Rourke IV, J.S., Harris, B. & Ogilvy, A. (2007) 'Google in China: government censorship and corporate reputation'. *Journal of Business Strategy*, 28(3): 12–22.

Overney, J. (2014) 'Surveying African Cities Using Twitter'. *Science Xi*, 30 April. https://phys.org/news/2014-04-surveying-african-cities-twitter.html (accessed 1 February 2018).

Portland (2015) *How Africa Tweets.* https://portland-communications.com/publications/how-africa-tweets-2015/ (accessed 1 February 2018).

Rainie, L. & Wellman, B. (2012) *Networked: The New Social Operating System.* Cambridge, MA: MIT Press.

Rambukkana, N. (ed) (2015) *Hashtag Publics: the Power and Politics of Discursive Networks.* New York: Peter Lang.

Ruvaga, L. (2016) 'Kenya Bans Music Video Saying It Promotes Gay Rights'. *Voice of America*, 18 March. www.voanews.com/a/kenya-art-attack-same-love-music-video/3243579.html (accessed 1 February 2018).

Seyfert, R. & Roberge, J. (2016) *Algorithmic Cultures: Essays on Meaning, Performance and New Technologies.* New York: Routledge.

Siebert, F.S., Peterson, T. & Schramm, W. (1956) *Four Theories of the Press: the Authoritarian, Libertarian, Social Responsibility, and Soviet Communist Concepts of What the Press Should Be and Do.* Chicago: University of Illinois Press.

Simon, T. et al. (2014) 'Twitter in the cross fire – the use of social media in the Westgate Mall terror attack in Kenya'. *Plos One*, 9(8).

Steger, M. (2008) *The Rise of the Global Imaginary: Political Ideologies from the French Revolution to the Global War on Terror.* Oxford: Oxford University Press.

Taylor, C. (2004) *Modern Social Imaginaries.* Durham, NC: Duke University Press.

Thielman, S. (2016) 'Google Invites Kenyan Anti-Gay Activist to Web Rangers Conference'. *The Guardian*, 30 September. www.theguardian.com/technology/2016/sep/30/google-invites-kenyan-anti-gay-ezekiel-mutua-web-rangers-conference (accessed 1 February 2018).

Tsing, A.L. (2005) *Friction: an Ethnography of Global Connection*. Princeton, NJ: Princeton University Press.

Tully, M. (2013) 'Microblogging and Crises: Information Needs and Online Narratives During Two "Bombing" Events in Nairobi, Kenya'. In J.E. Hayes, K. Battles & W. Hilton-Morrow (eds.), *War of the Worlds to Social Media: Mediated Communication in Times of Crisis*. New York: Peter Lang, pp. 237–256.

Tully, M. & Ekdale, B. (2014) 'Sites of Playful Engagement: Twitter Hashtags as Spaces of Leisure and Development in Kenya'. *Information Technologies & International Development*, 10(3): 67–82.

Van Dijck, J. (2013) *The Culture of Connectivity: a Critical History of Social Media*. Oxford: Oxford University Press.

Vidija, P. (2016) 'Ezekiel Mutua Ordered to Surrender Diplomatic Passport'. *The Star*, 29 September. www.the-star.co.ke/news/2016/09/29/ezekiel-mutua-ordered-to-surrender-diplomatic-passport_c1429346 (accessed 1 February 2018).

Wasonga, J. (2016) 'Ezekiel Mutua: Unmasking Kenya's Morality Police'. *East African Standard*, 15 May. www.standardmedia.co.ke/lifestyle/article/2000201806/ezekiel-mutua-unmasking-kenya-s-morality-police (accessed 1 February 2018).

Waweru, N. (2014) 'Art Attack in Kinoo'. *The Star*, 22 July. www.the-star.co.ke/sasa/2014-07-21-art-attack-in-kinoo/ (accessed: 1 February 2018).

Willems, W. & Mano, W. (eds.) (2016) *Everyday Media Culture in Africa: Audiences and Users*. New York: Routledge.

6 | BETWEEN EXCITEMENT AND SCEPTICISM

The role of WhatsApp in Sierra Leone's 2018 elections

Maggie Dwyer, Jamie Hitchen and Thomas Molony

Introduction

Sierra Leone's general elections in 2018 involved an unprecedented level of digital engagement. Traditional means of electoral information sharing, such as radio broadcasts and announcements printed in newspapers, were complemented – if not overshadowed – by messages spread online, primarily through social media platforms. For the first time, all the leading presidential candidates took part in a debate that was aired live on television and across a network of over forty radio stations. Online engagement with the debate was driven by a social media 'situation room' that created handles, hashtags and infographics in attempts to share, and subsequently monitor, the online conversation around the debate. Social media was used by political parties to engage with voters, by the National Electoral Commission (NEC) to upload PDFs of official results to be shared online, by domestic civil society organisations, and by donor-funded projects that created online platforms allowing Sierra Leoneans to report incidents of violence through social media. These examples, and more throughout the chapter, suggest that the 2018 vote can be considered Sierra Leone's first social media election.

The most recent UNDP Human Development Index (2016: 249) found Sierra Leone to have the fourth-lowest internet usage levels in the world. Between January 2017 and January 2018, however, the reported number of internet users in Sierra Leone has more than doubled (Kemp 2018). The number of people accessing social media is also on the rise. While the rates as of 2018 are still low compared to global and African averages, in the past year Sierra Leone has experienced among the highest growth rate of social media use on the continent, with a 32 percent increase (We Are Social 2018: 131). Estimates show approximately 16 percent of the population now use social media. While broad quantitative surveys can provide valuable data to get a sense of social media use, our qualitative research suggests that figures for the number of social media users in Sierra Leone often underestimate the reach of messages on social media platforms – particularly WhatsApp. In focus group discussions many participants explained that they share smartphones with family members; thus, the number of users of social media is likely considerably higher than the number of smartphone owners. Additionally, oral communication is still the dominant mode of communication throughout the country, and messages read by someone with a smartphone are quickly relayed to people without one. Freetown, Sierra Leone's capital city, is densely populated and many residents spend much time passing on news and spreading rumours while they share taxis, ride *okadas* (motorbike taxis) or spend time in other public spaces. Throughout our field research we regularly heard stories, rumours and verbal descriptions of photographs that originated on social media, told by individuals who did not have direct internet access but had heard them second-hand. Furthermore, as a civil society representative notes, 'a rumour on WhatsApp can be printed in conventional media or discussed on the radio the next morning; so it drives the news agenda, as well as being driven by the news agenda'.[1]

This chapter takes an in-depth look at the way social media shaped the electoral environment during the 2018 general elections. We do not attempt to suggest whether social media use affected the outcome of the elections, rather we explore how various election stakeholders altered their actions to incorporate a digital dimension. The study of social media during the Sierra Leone 2018 elections demonstrates how 'digital media is not disassociated from place, but rather online discursive practices are informed by, and reconfigure, local idioms, experiences and norms' (Srinivasan, Diepeveen & Karekwaivanane 2018: 8). While social media was generally a new aspect of elections in Sierra Leone in 2018, the way it was used and interpreted was closely linked to the political past. For example, variations in use of social media by political parties were related to the history of the parties and their leadership. In some circumstances social media involved fresh ways for citizens to interact with parties and government institutions, giving individuals more agency in the process. Yet, in other ways it was mediated with traditional forms of verification. For instance, an unease with the reliability of messages transmitted on social media brought about a return to digital scans of more customary forms of documentation such as 'official' letters on headed notepaper, complete with a date, signature(s) and rubber stamp.

The research also highlights the ways the social media environment in Sierra Leone is strongly influenced by socio-economic conditions. Although prices for basic smartphones and daily data packages have dropped substantially in recent years, social media use in Sierra Leone remains urban-centric, and the majority of users are male (Wittels & Maybanks 2016). Consequently, local civil society organisations in particular raised concerns about large sections of the population being excluded in the shift to digital electoral engagements. Those who do have access to a smartphone and the internet are often unable to get online consistently, and instead only purchase daily access to the internet when they have available funds. Many users consider data sizes when deciding what to download or view, skipping over photographs, videos, large files or links to webpages – all of which are data-heavy and therefore costly to access. As such, the preferred social media style of most users in Sierra Leone is simplicity. However, as further explained below, donor-funded social media applications and websites often overlook the specific ways in which users access the internet in Sierra Leone, and have created platforms that few locals use or benefit from. This highlights the necessity for a strong understanding of the unique ways in which communities and individuals use social media differently in various environments in order to better adapt efforts to meet local needs.

Researching social media in Sierra Leone

The research for this chapter involved four months in Sierra Leone, with a first round conducted in 2016 (at the height of government discussions about regulating social media) and a second in 2018 (leading up to and during the elections). Comparison across time is enabled here since one of the members of the research team (Dwyer) was also present during the 2012 election cycle. The 2016–2018 research took place in Freetown, Kambia, Kono and Makeni. Ten focus groups were held to better understand the views of 'average' social media users. These were complemented by a wide range of interviews with key individuals representing: the Ministry of Information and Communication; the Sierra Leone Police Media Team; the National Telecommunications Commission (NATCOM); the Independent Media Commission; the All People's Congress (APC); the Sierra Leone People's Party (SLPP); the National Grand Coalition (NGC); the NEC; over a dozen different civil society organisations; six media outlets; academics from Fourah

Bay College; four foreign donor agencies within Sierra Leone; and the administrators of two popular WhatsApp groups. This wide range of interviewees demonstrates the complex web of online interactions and initiatives that developed over the course of the elections. Additionally, throughout the course of the research we were invited to join WhatsApp groups related to election discussions. In these groups we identified ourselves to the members as researchers and no objections were raised. Still, while recognising that WhatsApp is a closed network we did not collect direct content from the groups. Instead, the value of being a part of the groups was to understand the types of information shared as well as ways information flowed within and between groups through WhatsApp users.

Our research, along with other findings from survey data, found that WhatsApp is by far the most popular social media platform in Sierra Leone (as it is among the US-based diaspora when communicating with family and friends back home (Onigbanjo Williams et al. 2018: 373). For this reason, WhatsApp is the main focus of this chapter. The platform's dominance can be explained by several factors. It is cheap to use, which allows data packages to last for a longer period of time, particularly if users choose to conserve data by not downloading videos and photos. Voice messaging functions along with emoticons allow people with limited literacy to engage in debates. This makes WhatsApp a more participatory platform, as 'you don't need to be able to type text to participate', as one WhatsApp group administrator put it.[2] Finally, there is a perception – though not necessarily a reality – that what is discussed on WhatsApp is more private and secure than on other social media platforms. As another informant explained, 'on Facebook people are still defined by their regional and ethnic identity, as on your profile you have to provide a name and a place of birth – which in Sierra Leone are indicators of your likely political affinity and will shape people's perceptions of how you talk about politics'.[3] A telephone number is all that is required to join a WhatsApp group.

Information is shared, or 'culled' (the term used within Sierra Leone) by individual users through a myriad of WhatsApp groups. The lingua franca for these discussions is typically 'Kringlish'; a mixture of Krio and English. WhatsApp groups, which currently can be comprised of up to 256 members, often replicate offline societal structures. They can be centred around friendship groups, alumni networks, church or professional associations; open to residents of specific districts or chiefdoms; established with specific goals or actions in mind; or created to provide a particular service. There are WhatsApp groups that share newspaper front pages every morning, or in which members can ask for advice on the best route to navigate Freetown's heavy traffic. In the political realm, there are few groups that could be defined as 'politically neutral', but there are also no groups or WhatsApp channels[4] that are officially linked to political parties in Sierra Leone. There are many groups that are clear in their political affiliation, and groups may even contain current or aspiring political figures, in addition to party supporters; but they are not seen to speak on behalf of the party. This means that the myriad groups through which information is shared – combined with the more closed nature of the platform – makes it very difficult to establish the source of a piece of information, and hence its validity. Sections below further evaluate how individuals attempt to navigate rumours and fake news on WhatsApp, and elaborate on why – despite its popularity – this platform has been viewed by government agencies as problematic.

Elections and social media use

The 2018 elections were the fourth general elections since the end of Sierra Leone's civil war (1991–2002). These elections have been won by three different presidents,[5] and have now led to two transitions between political parties.[6] This series of elections and transitions of power through the ballot box is a significant change from the turbulent politics of the 1960s to 1990s, a period that was marred with manipulated polls, a series of military coups and a one-party state (from 1978 to 1992). Sierra Leoneans have not taken their relatively new democratic freedoms for granted. With voter turnout rates consistently over 80 percent, after Guinea Bissau the country has the second-highest voter turnout in West Africa (Institute for Democracy and Electoral Assistance). A vibrant political environment has developed post-war, but the country remains in need of sustained development. Adult literacy was 48.1 percent and life expectancy 51.3 years in 2016 (United Nations Human Development Programme 2016).

While much progress has been made in ensuring political freedoms in this post-war era, the transition to democracy has not been without its problems. The first two post-war elections were tarnished by widespread allegations of corruption and regional election-related violence (Bangura & Söderberg Kovacs 2018; Christensen & Utas 2008; Harris 2014). However, the 2012 election saw a significant reduction in cases of election-related violence, and Ernest Koroma won with a decisive victory in the first round for a peaceful vote that the Carter Center (2012: 2) deemed 'remarkably transparent and well-managed'. Still, in 2016 rumours persisted that President Koroma was seeking 'more time' beyond the constitutionally provided two-terms due to the debilitating impact of the Ebola epidemic, leading to concerns ahead of the 2018 vote about the fragility of the electoral process. The constitutional validity of a delay in the vote until March 2018 was questioned, but in the end Koroma did not appear on the ticket.

It was long anticipated that the 2018 elections would be highly competitive. The APC's candidate, Dr Samura Kamara, was being challenged by Brigadier (Rtd) Julius Maada Bio of the SLPP, who had contested and lost in 2012, while a 'third way' was also offered by the NGC's Kandeh Yumkella. Bio led Kamara by just 0.6 percent of votes after the first round with neither reaching the required 55 percent threshold. Bio was able to maintain this advantage in the second round, in which he secured 51.8 percent of the vote to be elected president. Although the SLPP won control of the executive, for the first time in Sierra Leone's history the party of the President does not now control the legislature.

While this chapter explores how, in 2018, social media became a key aspect of Sierra Leonean election dynamics for the first time, the government has for many years expressed concerns about social media use. In 2016, a series of meetings were held between NATCOM, lawmakers and state security personnel to propose legislation that would govern 'irresponsible use' of social media (Clottey 2 February 2017). In terms of what exactly the legislation would regulate, the Director of Consumer and Corporate Affairs at NATCOM stated that 'we are talking about incitement. We are talking about immorality and all of it' (Cham 7 October 2016). With reference to the 2009 shutdown of Facebook in China, the Deputy Information Minister reiterated the seriousness of the Government of Sierra Leone's approach by explaining that 'if it causes us to use the China way, we will use it' (Cham 7 October 2016).

In the midst of these ongoing discussions, Theresa Mbomaya, 20, was arrested for forwarding a message in a student WhatsApp group that, while promoting a forthcoming demonstration against the removal of fuel subsidies, implied that any vehicle trying to disrupt it could be set on fire (Thomas 21 November 2016). She was charged with incitement under the 1965 Public Order Act, and detained for five days. Students then protested around the courthouse to call for Ms Mbomaya's release, local and international media criticised the government response, and a volunteer coalition of thirty-two lawyers successfully argued for her right to freedom of expression set out in Sierra Leone's 1991 constitution. After this incident, the government reconsidered its plans for legislating against social media use. In an interview shortly after Ms Mbomaya's arrest, a senior official from the Ministry of Information and Communication cited the importance of donors and external relations in the plans for legislation, adding that 'we do not want the international community coming in and saying we are harassing people'.[7] Local resistance to the proposed legislation, and a lack of resources to implement it, are further disincentives that likely influenced the government's decision not to act in a heavy-handed manner.

While the Government of Sierra Leone is yet to pass any legislation to limit social media content or use, a wariness of the platforms still remains. The government has applied a variety of less-legalised methods to attempt to monitor or control social media content. For example, it has tried to discredit individuals who it deems to have used social media to share information it regards as 'unsuitable', and there are widespread rumours of a team within the Criminal Investigations Department that is tasked with monitoring social media content. During the 2018 elections, a twelve-hour countrywide internet blackout, which began just as the votes for the second round were being counted, was regarded with much suspicion and widely blamed on the ruling APC. Overall, the government strategy under President Koroma was less about engaging in a discussion as to how to improve the material being shared through social media, and more about ways of controlling the space in which it exists. It is yet to be seen if President Bio will reignite earlier attempts to regulate or monitor social media, or whether he will take a different approach that seeks to improve digital literacy and citizen-led monitoring mechanisms for social media use.

Political parties and campaigning on social media

Sierra Leone's political history has been dominated by two political parties: the APC and the SLPP. These two parties have ethno-regional bases. The APC is associated with the northern and western regions and their ethnic groups, primarily the Limba and Temne. The SLPP is most popular in the southern and eastern regions, and generally associated with the Mende ethnic group. There are some variations to the pattern; for example, Kono and Western Area can be considered 'swing' districts (Bangura & Söderberg Kovacs 2018). While there are many other smaller parties – in 2018 a total of seventeen parties put forward candidates – no other party has ever won the presidency or gained a significant number of seats in parliament. In the run-up to the 2018 elections, there was a widespread expectation that either the APC or SLPP would win the presidency, but there were also high hopes that a more sustained challenge would be posed to the two dominant parties, especially in parliament. In particular, the NGC – established five months before the election following a split in the SLPP – received much attention, within and outside Sierra Leone, for its attempt to reach across regional and ethnic lines by providing voters with the 'third way'. The presidential candidate went on to win less than 7 percent in the first round, although they did win four parliamentary seats.

The campaigns of all the major parties drew on social media, principally through messages urging people to vote for their candidates. The messages were posted on official Facebook and Twitter pages, but the prevalence of WhatsApp meant that the parties were also reliant on a network of supporters to act as online information distributors. While traditional media had previously been the primary avenue for sharing party news, the SLPP's media strategist stated that in this election the party 'issued [its] press releases through social media first' believing it 'to be the most effective way of reaching the most people'.[8] This shift meant that social media became a driving force for mainstream media, with news often circulating online first before being printed in the newspapers or aired on the radio.

While social media was a tool used by all parties, interviews with party officials from the APC, NGC and SLPP demonstrated differing views on the importance of social media in gaining votes. The APC expressed some scepticism over the value of social media in campaigning, and instead spent much more of their campaign money on more conventional media such as large billboards and paid endorsements by popular musicians. The SLPP and NGC took a more varied approach, with social media as an integral part of their engagement strategy. Both parties shared a belief that social media platforms, and WhatsApp in particular, had given them greater access to citizens at a much reduced cost. As an SLPP media strategist explained, 'social media is a very effective and affordable way of reaching out. At times using the mainstream media is expensive and less effective'.[9] The view that social media is a 'cheap' way to campaign is a key reason why SLPP and NGC were more enthusiastic about the platforms. The APC, the ruling party at the time, had more funding and easier access to state resources. The SLPP and especially the NGC were seen to have less funds, and thus for them inexpensive alternatives to posters and large rallies were even more important.

For the NGC, the appeal of social media as a campaigning tool went beyond its relatively low cost, as it was also linked to one of their target audiences. An NGC spokesperson explained:

> The NGC's social media strategy was designed to win over new voters – as a party we had only been in existence for five months, so we did not have an existing support base – and to encourage people to go out and vote, and [to explain] how they could do that.[10]

The NGC was especially keen to try to gain support among young voters, with the idea that the youth may be less invested in the traditional parties and so more open to a new alternative. Social media platforms, often associated with more tech-savvy youth, thus became a strategic way to reach out to potentially undecided voters. Conversely, APC's nonchalant attitude towards social media likely reflected a (over) confidence in their ability to attract loyal voters who had long been dedicated to the party.

While all political parties drew on social media for political campaigning, its use by parties is still in its infancy. All parties simply reposted their standard press releases on social media, without much attempt to tailor these to social media audiences. There were some attempts to develop more technologically advanced messages, but these often fell flat. For example, the SLPP created a thirty-minute documentary on the life of its presidential candidate, Julius Maada Bio, and sought to share it on social media. Yet this was far too data-heavy for most people to download, watch or share. The NGC, by contrast, was far more strategic and creative in their use of social media. By hiring three young Sierra Leoneans to manage the day-to-day operation of their Twitter, Facebook and Instagram platforms, they were the only party to employ a 'professional' social media team to assist their online messaging. They used more advanced features of the platforms by broadcasting rallies on Facebook Live, and intended to – though ultimately did not – have a Facebook Live chat with their candidate Kandeh Yumkella to allow for greater citizen interaction. However, there was criticism levelled at the NGC that their advanced social media tactics spoke more to Sierra Leoneans abroad who, although influential in some ways, were ultimately not able to vote.

An APC media spokesperson cited the NGCs poor electoral performance in the first round, versus its impressive social media campaign, as evidence that the online and offline campaigns had different levels of impact:

> It is a very different war on social media than in the offline political realm between the political parties ... the NGC did lots and had a big presence on social media, but what percentage of votes did it win in the first round? 6.9 percent.[11]

While the NGC's percentage of votes was small compared to the two dominant parties, their progress at the constituency level can be considered commendable for a new party – especially in a system where in the last election no parliamentary seats were won by a third party. Nevertheless, it is difficult to make assessments about the influence of parties' use of social media on how people voted. No political party sought in any meaningful way to track the reach and impact of their posts and other social media engagements. The case suggests that social media may be especially advantageous to newer parties or those with limited funds, and that the platforms may play a part in diversifying the political landscape moving forward; allowing, potentially, for alternative parties to have a wider reach.

Party supporters on social media

The interactive nature of social media was a key appeal to all parties, and the platforms contributed to an overall shift in the way in which the parties campaigned. Election campaigns in Sierra Leone, as in much of Africa, are often synonymous with large party rallies. These rallies attempt to attract mass audiences through a party-like atmosphere with loud speakers playing popular music, dancing by party supporters or sub-groups (often hired women's groups) and, occasionally, appearances by celebrities or well-known public figures. Rallies generally follow a 'bigger-is-better' strategy, and pictures of seas of people wearing party colours at these events are later used to publicise a party's popularity. Although the rallies attempt to provide a dynamic atmosphere, the role of the audience is typically passive, since they primarily listen to top-level members of the party speak.

However, in this election, recognition that attendance at political rallies did not always translate into political support saw all parties gradually move towards different electioneering tactics that were more citizen-focused and less expensive.

While large-scale rallies were held across the country in the first round of voting, more attention was placed on '*ose-to-ose*' ('house-to-house' in Krio) engagement with voters in the second round as parties questioned the translation of big rally crowds, often at high costs to the party, into votes. More localised campaigning did allow for citizens to have a greater degree of engagement with party officials and candidates, and offered them the chance to ask questions about what those running for office intended to do to improve their everyday realities. Social media engagement complemented this more intimate approach to campaigning by giving individual supporters more agency.

During the 2018 elections social media was a dynamic space where individuals without any official party position took it upon themselves to share political messages with their contacts, often expanding participation and facilitating mobilisation for ordinary citizens. As has been the case for a number of years in other countries (Piata 2016; Ross & Rivers 2017), many individuals also created visuals and memes to support their favoured candidate. Visuals were widely shared and often more accessible to those with lower literacy levels. This marks a shift in individual engagement from past elections when visual campaign material, usually in the form of posters that generally required professional production, printing and distribution, tended to be only created by the parties themselves. However, the flexibility of social media has created new avenues for individuals to engage in the creation and sharing of photographs, cartoons and digitally produced party graphics. Whether intentional or not, by generating messages and distributing images within their existing networks, these individuals have become more than mere 'clicktivists' (Endong 2018; Halupka 2014; Morozov 2013) but politically participative 'communications activists' (Bolt 2012: 195). In small and often very personal ways, the creation of political images that are then circulated more widely among Sierra Leoneans is a localised example of the worldwide emergence of what Karolina Koc-Michalska and Darren Lilleker (2017: 2) describe as the 'porosity between the online and offline environments' that holds the potential to redefine the terms of democratic engagement. Yet while visuals were a popular mode of communication, there were also many cases of manipulated images, which threatened the legitimacy of electoral institutions, as later examples will demonstrate.

The more individualistic involvement in the campaigns as seen through social media potentially allowed party supporters' messages to reach wider audiences. However, this was not without challenges as it also meant that parties had limited control over messages spread about their candidates. All the political parties attempted to monitor social media for messages and images that could damage their campaign. Here too they often relied on direct engagement with supporters, and the assistance of party members. For example, an NGC spokesperson explains: 'We empowered NGC members to monitor WhatsApp for us, to report back when they saw information that was being shared that was false and we then took a decision to either respond or not, depending on the severity of the allegations'.[12] The SLPP noted a similar strategy:

> If [an allegation] was viewed as a fairly minor issue, it was often left to individual party members, operating in their personal capacity, to respond appropriately. But when the allegations were more serious, a SLPP Media Committee was convened to provide a party response, most often in the form of a press release.[13]

While individual users alerted party leadership about potentially damaging messages online, the verification of information to substantiate counter-narratives was done through existing party structures. If reports of violence in a particular district were being circulated, political parties would draw on their local party base in the area and ask them to provide evidence – ideally with images – before formulating a response.

Parties had a clear strategy to respond to 'fake news' that could discredit their candidates, but little was done if the false stories could offer an advantage. For example, the SLPP did not attempt to counter a widely shared online story – that may or may not have been started by their supporters – that Maada Bio was going to win the first-round vote by 56.3 percent. At the time of the rumour only 25 percent of votes, which were being released proportionally, remained to be counted, making it almost mathematically impossible to win by the figure circulating in the online story. The SLPP were not alone in seeking to eke out every advantage to them in what was the country's closest postwar election to date. This example lends support to the view of one respondent who believed that 'social media's impacts in Sierra Leone's elections are more damaging than positive; it is a platform used more by people to abuse political opponents than to promote their own party's values and promises'.[14] This view was shared by another respondent who argued that 'you hardly see political party supporters using social media to promote their own candidate and his manifesto promises, instead they use it to attack opponents and criticise their ideas'.[15]

However, political party representatives disagreed. They believe that by allowing information to flow more freely 'WhatsApp has got more people talking about policy issues and ideas'.[16] Still, an SLPP representative acknowledged the often contradictory approaches used on social media, both by the party and its supporters, noting:

> We wanted to have an element of our online presence which was about presenting, positively, what the party would do in office. But it is not just about keeping your support base, we want to win others over and sometimes you have to play dirty to do that.[17]

A similar approach – employed offline and online – was adopted by the APC when they sought to promote the integrity of their candidate and the party's track record of service delivery, at the same time as highlighting allegations of corruption against the SLPP's candidate and his party's history of failing to deliver on its promises while in office. While social media provided some new avenues for individual engagement with the political issues, parties and candidates, these interactions were not necessarily more positive. Many messages fell back on traditional narratives, particularly those relating to regional and ethnic divides.[18] These observations in Sierra Leone resonate with other cases, such as social media use during the 2015 elections in Nigeria, which demonstrate the way the platforms often perpetuate ethno-regional divides (Mustapha 2017: 315).

Activism and education

Political parties and their supporters were not alone in their view of the strategic advantages of social media; civil society and activists also turned to the platforms. The limited cost associated with social media was a key aspect for civil society groups, which often operate on limited budgets. For many organisations, WhatsApp was viewed as 'a cheap and effective programme management tool'.[19] National Elections Watch, a domestic observer group, had observers covering all the 10,000-plus polling stations. They used a series of WhatsApp groups to coordinate activities and share information, from the local to the national and vice-versa. In areas where there was no internet network coverage, members of groups that did have access were responsible for contacting colleagues, often by telephone, to ensure that they were regularly updated, and to gather information. Similar approaches were used by other civil society organisations and networks to coordinate their activities and to gather real-time campaign information to help shape and inform public responses.

In addition to using social media for internal coordination, civil society saw the platforms as a way to better connect voters with politicians, and to advocate for a more transparent election process. As a civil society leader explained: 'WhatsApp can help democratise information, and it is up to us to find ways of doing so in a way that engages citizens and politicians alike'.[20] One example of this was that social media platforms, along with conventional media, were used to gather citizens' questions for the televised presidential debate. This allowed individuals countrywide, many of whom would not otherwise have direct access to political leadership, to pose questions to candidates.

The 2018 election also saw civil society groups use social media to draw attention to potential electoral irregularities and pressure the government to respond. For instance, when there was a delay in announcing the date on which the election was to be held, civil society groups and activists forced a government response after they took to popular platforms to raise awareness of this issue among citizens and media. Even though the legality of the 7 March date remained in question (as it was a week after President Koroma's mandate constitutionally expired), the way in which social media was used by civil society to place pressure on the government to release funds allocated to the NEC showed how online platforms could be used as an effective advocacy tool.

Local civil society organisations also turned to social media to promote voter education initiatives. These were especially important given that, with a large youth population, around 35 percent of the electorate in this election would be first time-voters. Graphics were created and shared on social media to help voters prepare for casting their ballots, something that was particularly necessary since voters had to cast four different ballots during the general elections. These online messages were complemented by other offline youth-tailored approaches, many of which were organised under a civil society collaboration called the 'Standing Together for Democracy Consortia'. For example, popular musician Emerson, along with other local musicians, produced the song '*Mi Vote Na Mi Life*' ('My Vote is My Life' in Krio) and traversed the country to explain, at well-attended sessions, what to consider when selecting who to vote for on the ballots.

Fake news and wariness of social media

While there was excitement about the way in which social media could be used strategically by various election stakeholders, there was also wariness about potential manipulation of the platforms, especially WhatsApp. The NEC, for example, expressed a reluctance to use WhatsApp. It provided information about voting, updates about the electoral process, and results on multiple forms of media, typically announcing first on the radio, before uploading the information to their website. They operated a well-organised and regularly updated website which catalogued all press releases and details of vote tabulations down to the district levels for the various categories of voting.[21] Yet the NEC were cautious about sharing information directly on social media platforms, and preferred to instead link readers back to their website where the files could be downloaded.

The NEC's scepticism of social media was explained by an official of the organisation who stated that 'we want to put social media aside [particularly WhatsApp] because it is open to manipulation'.[22] They feared that text or graphics could be altered, which could cause tension or confusion. Ultimately the NEC believed that if it could remain absent from WhatsApp and communicate to citizens through other media, they would not be sharing results on this platform and could therefore avoid any involvement in fake news. This strategy worked to an extent, and the mantra that 'the only credible results are those announced by NEC' was one that many Sierra Leoneans adopted. However, there was little to stop rumours circulating about the voting results figures that the NEC might announce. During the run-off vote, and in response to baseless accusations against the Commission, the NEC felt compelled to break their WhatsApp non-engagement to issue several press releases to counter social media rumours. For example, a photograph of an election official reviewing ballot papers was widely circulated on social media by both APC and SLPP with claims that she was altering ballots cast. In fact, the official was doing her job correctly, and was simply carrying out a standardised cross-checking exercise. In this example, countering fake news was not only an issue of providing accurate information, but was linked to maintaining the integrity of the institution and the election overall. Despite accusations from both sides that it had acted partially, and notwithstanding that the APC decided to contest the results announced in court, the NEC was able to deliver credible results under immense political pressure.

Many examples of fake news were shared widely on social media, but users also had a sense of frustration with the difficulty of deciphering the accuracy of information. For example, one interviewee explained that 'for political propaganda WhatsApp is very useful. But as a citizen, how can you use the information being shared to make an informed decision in an environment that is very adversarial both on- and offline?'[23] Some organisations, both local and international, attempted to provide advice to voters on how to identify false stories. For example, BBC Media Action Sierra Leone (2018) developed a graphic with the title 'How to spot fake news', which they posted online. However, most of their advice required a willingness for the user to browse additional websites, and digital literacy. The guidance tells social media users to 'click away from the story to investigate the site and author', and to 'cross-check other credible news outlets'. As noted earlier, many social media users in Sierra Leone are not on unlimited plans that allow for such online forays. Users constantly adapt their usage to consume the least amount of data, and so fact verification through cross-checking other websites is a financial decision. Besides, with news spread on WhatsApp, where assessing the origin of a message is difficult, it is often impossible to 'click away … to investigate the site and author' (BBC Media Action Sierra Leone 2018). The literature on fake news and politics has also yet to appreciate these realities for social media users in countries such as Sierra Leone.

Rather than cross-checking multiple websites to verify online content, during the election period Sierra Leoneans employed more localised informal norms to attempt to confirm election data on social media. While Facebook and Twitter do provide some avenues for verification of accounts with large followings, the same does not hold for WhatsApp. As a result, the format in which messages were disseminated became important. A gradually accepted truth among WhatsApp users in Freetown was that 'official' statements were only really official so long as they were shared as a PDF, and if the scanned letter had been written on party headed notepaper, signed, dated and stamped. This approach was adopted by political parties, the NEC and civil society alike in an effort to prevent others pretending to speak for them. In several instances this helped voters to decipher whether information was indeed genuine. For example, shortly before the run-off presidential election, a PDF purportedly from Sam Sumana's Coalition for Change (C4C) was shared on WhatsApp in which he encouraged supporters to vote for the APC candidate.[24] Although a forged signature had been used, the letter was not stamped and it was quickly – and correctly – discredited as being a fake. However, this was an election where people 'learned from experience, to better look for, and deal with, fake news';[25] and so, in other cases, fake press releases proved to be quite effective (especially earlier in the electoral process). Still, this type of verification style, as well as mass amounts of data on the NEC website, was not always accessed by end-users – simply because it was too expensive to download the attachments.

While many social media users saw benefits to the 'new' features afforded on social media, their trust in the data reverted to a trust in more familiar, 'traditional' official documentation. In Sierra Leone as elsewhere, any user of WhatsApp quickly learns how easy it is for a message to be created in another person's name and then forwarded with no trace of its true origins. Faking hard-copy official documents, on the other hand, takes the deception to a slightly more sophisticated level that involves forgery and/or unauthorised use of headed notepaper, a signature and a stamp. For the average citizen with a mobile phone, an official letter is less easy to fabricate than a plain text WhatsApp message. The opposite is true for verification: assessing the veracity of plain script on the screen of a mobile phone is more difficult than authenticating a (scanned) hard-copy official document. The PDF representing the scanned document is very clearly a facsimile of a more recognisable artefact that can be scrutinised for the correct signature(s), font, rubber stamp(s) and so on, in exactly the same way that people are accustomed to do so with its 'original' physical counterpart. The hard-copy document could of course be faked – as in the C4C example above – but it is the involvement of each individual verifier in the process of determining the document's authenticity that adds to its veracity. This is not particular to Sierra Leone. Anthropological and other social research on understandings of documents and materiality in many other settings show that paper-mediated documentation in particular can represent familiar bureaucratic rules, ideologies, knowledge, relationships and practices (Gordillo 2006; Hull 2012; Kelly 2006) that many of the less tangible silicon alternatives are yet to achieve. So too can we see in the use of social media during the Sierra Leone elections that people are still more likely to trust a letter – or a scanned image of a letter – because, in contrast to unverified plain text, it closely represents a recognised and more verifiable 'official' document.

Donor interest and engagement

The most popular and widely used forms of social media engagement were localised; messages spread between contacts in Sierra Leone, using simple formats which conserved data and were often written in variations of local dialects or adapted formats suitable for those with lower literacy. However, there were also many attempts made by foreign donors to use the digital realm in an attempt to ensure a peaceful and transparent election. These efforts were often funded and instigated externally, but involved local civil society in their implementation. Yet a lack of coordination between the various programmes led to overlapping efforts and likely weakened their overall impact. For example, three different initiatives – the Women's Situation Room, the Sierra Leone Open Election Data Platform, and SierraLeoneDecides.com – all sought to capture and share similar data on violent incidents. All also had multiple forms of social media presence (primarily Twitter and Facebook) and encouraged Sierra Leonean voters to share incidents of violence through social media channels. The goal was to then locate these incidents on an interactive online map, adapted from the Ushahidi platform, which was first developed in response to the Kenyan post-election violence of 2007–8. In at least the case of the Women's Situation Room, this information was then planned to be connected to local community leaders and security services, enabling faster responses to violent incidents.

Fortunately, there were limited incidents of violence during the elections. The Sierra Leone Open Election Data Platform documented five cases, while the interactive map on the SierraLeoneDecides.com website shows none. This is not to say that there were only five incidents of violence; rather, that very few Sierra Leoneans engaged with these platforms. It also suggests that these largely donor-driven initiatives placed an over-emphasis on the potential for countrywide violence. Violence in past elections has been mostly limited to particular regions, and more targeted attention on these areas with links to local security forces would have been more appropriate in the Sierra Leone context.

These websites and their related social media connections also included data about candidates, locations of polling stations, and voting results. The Sierra Leone Open Data Initiative and the SierraLeoneDecides websites each attempted to create an interactive digital environment where users could participate in polls, download documents and upload pictures from the election (which then linked to photo-sharing sites such as Flikr). However, a closer look at the platforms indicate limited local engagement with these tools. For example, some two months after the elections, the polls on SierraLeoneDecides only counted thirty votes. Both sites are very data-heavy, with some pages including multiple embedded videos, along with dozens of pictures. As such they are less suited to the data-light engagement preferred by most local users of social media in Sierra Leone.

The disconnect between the more advanced online platforms funded by donors and localised uses of social media in the country indicated a familiar 'design reality gap' (Heeks 2002) often seen in Information and Communications Technologies for Development (ICT4D) initiatives (Burrell & Oreglia 2015; Wyche & Steinfield 2016). This is demonstrated by the high use of WhatsApp during the elections, in contrast to the lack of engagement with the interactive mapping platforms. A review of such platforms would be welcome ahead of the next round of elections to ensure that foreign donors' efforts better meet the needs of Sierra Leonean voters.

By contrast, local civil society organisations appeared more in tune with the reality of social media use in Sierra Leone, and often rejected or at least tempered more techno-optimistic views. Several of these groups expressed concern that an over-emphasis on social media would isolate those that they work closely with, particularly rural populations, those with lower literacy and women. Socio-economic and demographic data for Sierra Leone demonstrate that these are very real concerns, and should be given greater consideration when designing ICT4D initiatives aimed at Sierra Leone.

Conclusion

The study of social media use during the Sierra Leonean elections of 2018 demonstrates the importance of 'the unique terrain in which the technology is deployed' (Nyabola 2018: 38). While research on social media during elections in other parts of Africa have largely focused on Facebook and Twitter engagement, in Sierra Leone WhatsApp was the key space for the sharing of news – fake or otherwise – and a forum for wide-ranging political discussion. The reasons for the popularity of the platform include that it is relatively inexpensive, especially as it allows users to choose whether or not to download data-heavy – and therefore costly – content. This suits both cash-strapped voters and newer political parties with limited funds, who were able to engage in election-related communication using the increasingly affordable ever-popular smartphone. The sharing of these devices, and the centrality of oral communication in Sierra Leonean society, helped spread the political and civil society messages to those priced out of the emerging 'WhatsApp marketplace' – a space for all manner of discussion, from high politics to the saltier gossip of everyday electoral intrigue. Another significant advantage of WhatsApp in Sierra Leone is that it is relatively simple to use, especially for those with low levels of literacy, who, like many other users, enjoyed the visuality that the platform can provide.

The 2018 elections saw the emergence of localised communications activists, oftentimes with no official party position, who used social media to spread their message. The research presented here identifies a marked shift from previous party-centric electoral campaigning to an era where more individual initiatives entered the fray and engaged their contacts – and undoubtedly some new citizens when appealing messages were then forwarded to new WhatsApp groups – through visual images in the forms of photographs, self-created memes and home-made cartoons. Manipulated images continued to circulate though, and voters and high-profile election stakeholders alike were wary of 'fake' content. For all the technologically progressive talk of the latest round of general elections, 2018 also saw a return to (scanned images of) familiar 'official' documents that appeared to offer more trustworthy assurances of their authenticity. This offers a small contribution from Sierra Leone to the global debate about fake news. At present, however, the focus of the academic literature about the phenomenon still tends to be northern and still often views fake news mostly through the lens of Facebook and Twitter (for example, Guess et al. 2018; Jankowski 2018; Tandoc et al. 2018).

Similarly, there is sparse literature on methodological considerations concerning study of WhatsApp. In the (otherwise excellent) 680-page *SAGE Handbook of Social Media Research Methods* (Sloan & Quan-Haase 2017), for example, only two passing references are made to WhatsApp. The centrality of WhatsApp to the elections in Sierra Leone, as well as to everyday communication outside the 'hot' ballot-casting period of electoral contestation in much of sub-Saharan Africa – raises the importance of understanding the hugely popular social media platform as a serious research site. This is not without its challenges though, especially in terms of online (i.e. not face-to-face) qualitative and quantitative data collection. One difficulty WhatsApp poses for researchers is that the information on the platform is not publicly available. As suggested in this chapter, it is also challenging to trace the original source of information on WhatsApp, and it is very hard to assess its reach and impact. Additionally, the predominance of graphics, emoticons and voice recordings on WhatsApp, in addition to photographs and other images (Hand 2017: 216), challenges researchers' ability to catalogue and interpret these forms of data. And as with other social media platforms (McKenna et al. 2017: 89–90; Ruths & Pfeffer 2014; SMRG 2016: 14; Vitak 2016), research on WhatsApp raises questions about the representativeness of the online groups, as well as concerns about voices that are excluded from these platforms. As this chapter has shown, civil society groups in Sierra Leone are well aware of this, and are concerned that the shifting of political engagement towards social media risks further marginalising some sectors of society. There are signs from 2018 that local solutions to the constraints of communicating online are emerging, but well-meaning donors are still lagging behind.

Notes

1 Interview with civil society representative, 5 March 2018.

2 Interview with WhatsApp Group Admin, 5 March 2018.

3 Interview with civil society representative, 14 March 2018.

4 This function allows for the sending of bulk messages, usually for marketing purposes.

5 Post-war elections have taken place in 2002, 2007, 2012, and 2018. Post-war presidents include Ahmad Tejan Kabbah (1998–2007), Ernest Koroma (2007–2018), and Julius Maada Bio (2018–present).

6 The SLPP held the presidency from 1998 to 2007; there was then a transition to APC from 2007 to 2018, and the SLPP returned to power in 2018.

7 Interview with representative of Ministry of Information and Communication, 25 November 2016.

8 Interview with Abu Bakar Joe Sesay, Sierra Leone People's Party, 14 March 2018.

9 Interview with Abu Bakar Joe Sesay, Sierra Leone People's Party, 14 March 2018.

10 Interview with Anthony Kamara, National Grand Coalition, 6 March 2018.

11 Interview with Abdulai Bayraytay, All People's Congress, 21 March 2018.

12 Interview with Anthony Kamara, National Grand Coalition, 6 March 2018.

13 Interview with Abu Bakar Joe Sesay, Sierra Leone People's Party, 14 March 2018.

14 Interview with civil society representative, 16 March 2018.

15 Interview with civil society representative, 14 March 2018.

16 Interview with Anthony Kamara, National Grand Coalition, 6 March 2018.

17 Interview with Abu Bakar Joe Sesay, Sierra Leone People's Party, 14 March 2018.

18 For example, the APC fell back on tribal narratives online by encouraging supporters to 'come back to [their] roots'.

19 Interview with civil society representative, 12 March 2018.

20 Interview with civil society representative, 21 March 2018.

21 The 2018 general elections involved votes for president, parliament and local council representatives.

22 Interview with official from the National Electoral Commission, 20 March 2018.

23 Interview with civil society representative, 12 March 2018.

24 The C4C was another party that ran in the elections, winning 3.5 percent in the presidential election first round. It won eight parliamentary seats, all in Kono district.

25 Interview with international donor representative, 26 March 2018.

References

Bangura, I. & Söderberg Kovacs, M. (2018) 'Competition, uncertainty and violence in Sierra Leone's swing district'. In M. Söderberg Kovacs & J. Bjarnesen (eds.), *Violence in African Elections*. London: Zed Books, pp. 129–150.

BBC Media Action Sierra Leone (2018) 'How to spot fake news'. 2 January 2018. www.facebook.com/bbcmediaactionSL/photos/a.4901 96074345765.115465.48243478512 1894/1802449173120442/?type=3 (accessed 6 January 2018).

Bolt, N. (2012) *The Violent Image: Insurgent Propaganda and the New Revolutionaries*. London: Hurst.

Burrell, J. & Oreglia, E. (2015) 'The myth of market price information: mobile phones and the application of economic knowledge in ICTD'. *Economy and Society*, 44(2): 271–292.

Carter Center (2012) 'Observing Sierra Leone's November 2012 General Elections: Final Report'. Atlanta, GA: The Carter Center,.

Cham, K. (2016) 'Sierra Leone moves ahead with controversial plan to "control" social media'. 7 October 2016. http://politicosl.com/

articles/sierra-leone-moves-ahead-controversial-plan-control-social-media (accessed 7 June 2018).

Christensen, M.M. & Utas, M. (2008) 'Mercenaries of democracy: the "Politricks" of remobilized combatants in the 2007 general elections, Sierra Leone'. *African Affairs*, 107(429): 515–539.

Clottey, P. 2 February (2017) Sierra Leone Expresses Concern About Social Media Misuse. www.voanews.com/a/sierra-leone-expresses-concern-about-social-media-misuse/3704517.html (accessed 7 June 2018).

Endong, F.P. (2018) 'Hashtag activism and the transnationalization of Nigerian-born movements against terrorism: a critical appraisal of the #BringBackOurGirls Campaign'. In F.P. Endong (ed.), *Exploring the Role of Social Media in Transnational Advocacy*. Hershey, PA: IGI Global, pp. 36–54.

Gordillo, G. (2006) 'The crucible of citizenship: ID-paper fetishism in the Argentinean Chaco'. *American Ethnologist*, 33(2): 162–176.

Guess, A. et al. (2018) Selective exposure to misinformation: evidence from the consumption of fake news during the 2016 U.S. presidential campaign. www.dartmouth.edu/~nyhan/fake-news-2016.pdf (accessed 18 February 2018).

Halupka, M. (2014) 'Clicktivism: a Systematic Heuristic'. *Policy & Internet*, 6(2): 115–132.

Hand, M. (2017) 'Visuality in social media: researching images, circulations and practices'. In L. Sloan & A. Quan-Haase (eds.), *The SAGE Handbook of Social Media Research Methods*. London: SAGE.

Harris, D. (2014) *Sierra Leone: a Political History*. New York, NY: Oxford University Press.

Heeks, R. (2002) 'Failure, Success and Improvisation of Information Systems Projects in Developing Countries'. Development Informatics Working Paper 11, University of Manchester, IDPM.

Hull, M.S. (2012) 'Documents and Bureaucracy'. *Annual Review of Anthropology*, 41: 251–267.

Institute for Democracy and Electoral Assistance. Voter Turnout Database (updated regularly). (www)idea.int/data-tools/data/voter-turnout (accessed 7 June 2018).

Jankowski, N.W. (2018) 'Researching fake news: a selective examination of empirical studies'. *Javnost – The Public: Journal of the European Institute for Communication and Culture*, 25(1–2): 248–255.

Kelly, T. (2006) 'Documented lives: fear and the uncertainties of law during the Second Palestinian Intifada'. *Journal of the Royal Anthropological Institute*, 11(1): 89–107.

Kemp, S. (2018) 'Digital in 2018: world's internet users pass the 4 billion mark'. https://wearesocial.com/blog/2018/01/global-digital-report-2018 (accessed 4 May 2018).

Koc-Michalska, K. & Lilleker, D. (2017) 'Digital politics: mobilization, engagement, and participation'. *Political Communication*, 34(1): 1–5.

McKenna, B. et al. (2017) 'Social media in qualitative research: challenges and recommendations'. *Information and Organization*, 27(2): 87–99.

Morozov, E. (2013) *To Save Everything, Click Here: the Folly of Technological Solutionism*. New York: Public Affairs.

Mustapha, M. (2017) 'The 2015 general elections in Nigeria: new media, party politics and the political economy of voting'. *Review of African Political Economy*, 44(152): 312–321.

Nyabola, N. (2018) *Digital Democracy, Analogue Politics: How the Internet Era is Transforming Politics in Kenya*. London: Zed Books.

Onigbanjo Williams, A., et al. (2018) 'Critical communications: a retrospective look at the use of social media among American Sierra Leoneans during the Ebola outbreak'. *The Journal of Social Media in Society Spring*, 7(1); 366–380.

Piata, A. (2016) 'When metaphor becomes a joke: metaphor journeys from political ads to internet memes'. *Journal of Pragmatics*, 106 (December): 39–56.

Ross, A.S. & Rivers, D.J. (2017) 'Digital cultures of political participation: Internet memes and the discursive delegitimization of the 2016 U.S Presidential candidates'. *Discourse, Context and Media*, 16 (April): 1–11.

Ruths, D. & Pfeffer, J. (2014) 'Social media for large studies of behavior'. *Science*, 346(6213): 1063–1064.

Sloan, L. & Quan-Haase, A. (eds.) (2017) *The SAGE Handbook of Social Media Research Methods*. London: SAGE.

SMRG (2016) 'Using social media for social research: an introduction'. Social Media Research Group Report. London: HMSO.

Srinivasan, S., Diepeveen, S. & Karekwaivanane, G. (2018) 'Rethinking publics in Africa in a digital age'. *Journal of Eastern African Studies* (advanced access).

Tandoc, E.C., et al. (2018) 'Defining "Fake News"'. *Digital Journalism*, 6(2): 137–153.

Thomas, A.R. (2016) 'Female student in Sierra Leone arrested and detained for sharing WhatsApp message'. 21 November 2016. www.thesierraleonetelegraph.com/female-student-in-sierra-leone-arrested-and-detained-for-sharing-watsapp-message/ (accessed 7 June 2018).

United Nations Human Development Programme (2016) 'Human Development Report 2016' United Nations Human Development Programme, New York: United National Development Programme.

Vitak, J. (2016) 'Challenges and Opportunities of Doing Research with Social Media Data; Access and Collection: Social Media Data ≠ All People'. http://socialmediadata.org/2016/challenges-and-opportunities-of-doing-research-with-social-media-data/ (accessed 6 June 2018).

We Are Social (2018) 'Digital in 2018 in Western Africa Part 1 – West www.slideshare.net/wearesocial/digital-in-2018-in-western-africa-part-1-west-86865478 (accessed 15 March 2018).

Wittels, A. & Maybanks, N. (2016) 'Communication in Sierra Leone: an Analysis of Media and Mobile Audiences'. Research Report, BBC Media Action, London.

Wyche, S. & Steinfield, C. (2016) 'Why don't farmers use cell phones to access market prices? Technology affordances and barriers to market information services adoption in rural Kenya'. *Information Technology for Development*, 22(2): 320–333.

7 | CHAOS AND COMEDY

Social media, activism and democracy in Senegal

Emily Riley

Introduction

'To *sathie* (steal) or not to *sathie* (steal), that is the question #ThisCountryIsAJoke' reads a Shakespeare-inspired tweet by Maïmouna Dembelé, a journalist, activist and aspiring political candidate. Her comical jab was aimed towards the political coalition led by Senegalese President Macky Sall, who was publicly accused of creating confusion in preparation for the 2017 parliamentary elections. People like Maïmouna brought attention to efforts to steal votes or suppress voter turnout for opposition parties. The political season of 2017 was chaotic and contentious as additional corruption stories plagued the state, from rampant cheating in the countrywide high-school exit exams and accusations of a negligent Ministry of Education, to increasing electricity blackouts by the state-run electric company *Senelec* at crucial moments, including the night before election day. These were the kinds of laughably calculated or infuriatingly systemic occurrences that became fodder for jokes and humoristic commentary by the public. Because it was election season, the issues of state impropriety were accentuated, and permeated daily conversations. Maïmouna's reference to the country as a joke expresses a disgruntlement with the state of affairs and a feeling that the state was making an open mockery of the needs of the population and the democratic electoral system. For Maïmouna and other journalists I spoke with, the invocation of language such as teasing (#ThisCountryIsAJoke), or *toñ* in Wolof, blamed political elites for not taking them or their relevance seriously, in a communicative style, joking cousins or joking kinship, very familiar to most Senegalese. Her borrowing of Shakespeare's famous quote from his play *Hamlet* offers a comedic take that seems to tease the state in an act of powerful agency, or what Obadare (2009) calls 'getting even with the powerful elite'. Social media, it seems, is a particularly apt modality through which citizens such as Maïmouna openly deliberate topics in the purview of otherwise inaccessible state institutions. For example, Maïmouna and a few of her close childhood friends would have lunch together most Wednesday afternoons. She a journalist, another friend a radio personality, and a friend who worked as Macky Sall's communications director, would joke about a host of topics, politics especially. They often poked fun at their friend, Patrice, who worked for Macky Sall, jokingly pleading with him to put in a good word with the boss or teasingly shaming him for policies and political moves made by Macky Sall's administration that they did not agree with. Although they saw one another quite often, Maïmouna and her group would tag Patrice and Macky Sall on tweets regarding discussions they had among friends, effectively bringing it out into the open. This tactic allowed their mockery to be broadcast and amplified to new networks, while also remaining an inside joke.

Chapter layout

This chapter is a discussion of the creative ways Senegalese, and particularly cyber activists, as they call themselves, use social media to 'talk back' to their institutions as a way of participating in democratic processes. I will first explore the political engagement of a select few cyber activists during the 2017 parliamentary election in Senegal, and consider the landscape of social media use in Senegal and the role social media has played in new forms of public discourse among journalists and state actors. I then briefly address the growing efforts to do ethnographies in multi-dimensional environments, or polymedia (Madianou 2015), weaving the participatory observations and interviews of classic ethnography with digital forms of community with new types of 'communicative grammar' and communicative communities (Treré 2015). By engaging with social media content analysis, field observations and interviews, I will focus on one activist in particular and the association he works with. Papa Ismaila Dieng is a member of the social media and cyber security association called Africtivistes: the African League of Bloggers and Cyber Activists. Africtivistes joins together young men and women from across the continent who are passionate about changing the political landscape and participation in their countries by engaging in training on digital activism. They learn about cyber security and the power of social media and its symbols to create political momentum. In the context of the 2017 election, I will especially discuss some of the most important hashtags, #*Tuvotesavecquoi*, Whatareyouvotingwith? and #*SunuDepute*2017 and #OurRepresentative2017, among others made popular by Africtivistes members and used by many Senegalese social media users. These hashtags question state transparency and parody candidates and their parties, using ridicule to develop counternarratives to state power. They also reveal a complex kind of democratic engagement that is both shrouded in frustration, yet demonstrates a deep civic pride and confidence they can make a difference. This chapter seeks to contextualise the growing presence of social media activists in an African context and the creative ways they seek legitimacy and attempt to shift public debate on political participation.

The likes of Maïmouna and her journalist and activist friends have engaged with social media in dynamic ways both through everyday use and during consequential times such as the 2017 parliamentary elections. As professionals, they see cellphones and social media as their pad and paper, their medium to communicate with their audience. This chapter examines Senegalese activists' use of social media as a democratic tool generally; more specifically, it considers particular ways that activists and everyday citizens in Senegal engage with democratic institutions and events such as elections through social media platforms in new and creative ways. Secondly, I am particularly interested in how humour and teasing – central components to Senegalese and regional social interaction – are used in the virtual world of social media to express frustrations with and aspirations for a democratic process that reflects and serves them. I discuss certain elements of the syncretic institution of joking kinship (Galvan 2006) within social media rhetoric as modes of engaging with politics, and the concept of #hashtag activism as a way of collectively and directedly mobilising these frustrations into agent action. In what Cornwall and Coelho (2007) call 'new democratic spaces', social media have become a space for many Senegalese to widen their 'participatory sphere' and to find new ways of interacting with one another and with state institutions, and to circulate information. Critique of the state that is both directed at the politician via tagging and yet indirect due to the virtual reality of the relationships allows young people to express themselves in a society where public discourse is overwhelmingly dominated by elders writ large. Even in the 'on-place' (Augé 2009) of Twitter and Facebook, regular citizens can become activists in their own right by being part of specific hashtag movements (Gerbaudo 2012; Yang 2016) to varying degrees. In order to discuss these topics, I depend on my interactions with Papa Ismaila Dieng, as well as many of his and others' Twitter tweets and Facebook posts that take on issues of political corruption and election disorder, and offer social commentary through humour. I focus on several of Papa Ismaila's tweets that poke fun at different party campaign posters, as well as specific hashtags that became popular during the election. They are in reaction to state mishandling of the administration of new voting cards, and other perceived injustices having to do with the voting process. Although he is one of thirteen million Senegalese, it is clear from the amount of commentary on his posts and his relative fame that his online interactions represent the discontent that many young and educated Senegalese feel towards the democratic process, their perceived lack of real traction in it, and their efforts to change this situation. Despite following the suggested path of pursuing a higher-education degree for future prospects, Papa Ismaila's generation continues to struggle for steady and meaningful employment. I explore how social media offers a site for constructing counternarratives (Bonilla & Rosa 2015) that contest the postcolonial state's efforts to banalise power (Mbembe 2006) through new symbols such as hashtags, and new forms of old institutions such as joking kinship relationships.

The 2017 parliamentary elections in Senegal were often described as chaotic, fraudulent and frustrating. There were a record number of parties and coalitions as well as the issue of administering new voting ID cards sanctioned by the Economic Community of West African State (ECOWAS). On social media, in daily conversations and in print media, many Senegalese expressed a feeling that the government and those seeking office were 'teasing' them, or not taking the population seriously. At the same time, many social media activists used Twitter and Facebook to comment, critique and diffuse important voting information and, in many ways, 'tease' back by posting campaign posters or memes of the candidates with comedic commentary.

'Everything is all mixed up (*jaxasoo*),' Papa Ismaila tells me. 'Not since before the 1993 election, has it been like this,' he said, referring to the 2017 parliamentary elections and chaos within the electoral commission processing the voting cards. The government had embarked on new voting cards sanctioned by ECOWAS that would replace old identification, but failed to produce and distribute all cards ahead of the July 2017 elections. The company chosen to produce the 'state of the art' biometric eID cards had promised a four-month turn around following the six-month registration period (IRIS 2016). Had all gone to plan, the cards would have been printed and distributed to the population a month before the election in 2017.

Instead, many people had not registered, did not have their cards, and did not know where to vote since the new cards could mean a change in voting district. City Halls and the Ministry of the Interior as well as the *Commission Electorale Nationale Autonome* (CENA, the Independent National Election Commission), were scrambling up to the day of the election to print cards, leaving many unsure of where to vote and how. 'Since we passed the electoral code of '93, at least people knew how to vote and where to vote, but not now,' Papa Ismaila noted. Papa Ismaila Dieng is a young freelance journalist, blogger and social media activist. His quick wit and humour are unmistakable as he laughs at his own jokes, even when they touch on political matters that should not be amusing. He is as funny virtually as he is in person. Papa Ismaila was one of the first members of the small yet active group of web activists, Africtivistes. Comprised largely of journalists and civil society activists from across much of West Africa, members function in multiple languages and stay connected through Twitter and Facebook. Unlike mainstream journalists who rarely rely on social media as a means of reporting the news (Lemke & Chala 2016), Papa Ismaila used his personal Facebook and Twitter accounts for reporting. As Africtivistes' membership has picked up, they have begun holding workshops on cyber security that rotate through different countries in the region such as Niger and The Gambia. One of their taglines reads 'strengthening democracy through the digital' (Africtivistes n.d.), and their workshops range from topics of political stability and peace, democracy and the use of digital resources as platforms for members of civil society to circulate, inform and speak out against everyday injustices. Although much of the communication strikes a serious and journalistic tone, bloggers employ humour as a way to lighten the mood – and also, as Papa Ismaila puts it, to push his audience to 'reflect on what's going on'.

I argue in this chapter that the role of joking and teasing are employed in imaginative ways through the use of social media and how these platforms can be spaces for innovative expressions of new kinds of kinship among newly formed cyber communities; and also rethink what the role of joking cousins is in an institution, such as the Africtivistes association. I am also interested in exploring how the use of social media and practices of teasing demonstrated in this chapter might be spaces and opportunities for youth to democratise the political process, while also considering Achille Mbembe and Bakhtin's understanding of ridicule both as a form of resistance and the use of such an institution as joking to mean a sign of the power relationship between the state and its subjects. Are these sites simply 'transient sites of fleeting engagement' (Bonilla & Rosa 2015: 4–17) or sophisticated networks creating new forms of kinship? Online communities are at once spatially dislocated while existing in the online space, with a specific type of kinship that expresses shared notions of national identity and national struggle.

In the case of a social media community in Senegal, the hashtag #kebetu – meaning Twitter in Wolof – demarcates any topic having to do with Senegalese life. It is as though users are an 'imagined community' (Anderson 2006) that engages in dialogue even if they have not physically met. Papa Ismaila shared an anecdote of meeting a stranger on the street with whom he had corresponded via tweets a hundred times but had never met in person. Much of the content in tweets and posts with the hashtag #kebetu turns to humour as a way to make a statement or respond to a tweet. Therefore, in this chapter I interpret whether social media is a democratising force (Sunstein 2018) that is a predominantly youth-oriented platform in a society such as Senegal, where youth defer to their elders, and investigate if the institution of teasing is a particularly effective mode of communication in digital spaces.

Anthropologists have long written about the prominent role of joking kinship relations, and the joking cousins figure in African societies (Fouéré 2004; Irvine 1973; Irvine 1992; Labouret 1929; Paulme 1939; Radcliffe-Brown 1940; Smith 2004). It has been described as a somewhat fictive relationship between people of similar origins or ethnic cousins expressed through mutual insulting and teasing at which neither party can take offence (de Jong 2005). Marie-Aude Fouéré (2004) argues that despite the multi-faceted role joking relationships play in many African societies, ethnographers have long painted its prominence with a large brush as one based solely on peacekeeping and diplomatic relations between and among ethnic groups. Historically they were also used as an expression of power dynamics and in reinforcing social status as jokes referenced themes of subordination such as slavery or hierarchy (Galvan 2006). De Jong (2005) argues joking relations based on ethnic categories were canonised as a colonial governmentality and later by the Senegalese state as a 'tradition' for national unity. De Jong writes that with respect to conflict resolution in the Casamance region of Senegal, the state capitalised on folk tales of relations between the Jola and Sereer ethnic groups in order to create policy to solve complex divisions spurring ongoing conflict in this region. Galvan (2006) argues that in fact, joking kinship relations are examples of institutional syncretism, a continuous reconfiguration of institutional elements in creative ways, and extend into realms beyond *official* and *practical* kinship (Bourdieu 1977). Similarly, Mbembe argues the postcolony is effective in controlling its subjects because it constructs a world of familiarity, a shared and unified nation. He also notes that friction arises from the chaotically pluralistic postcolonial state 'constantly shifting and reshaping the meanings of signs', which he adds is as much a project of the ruled as the rulers. Ridicule is therefore as much about exposing the misgivings of the state as it is levelling the playing field. Despite new considerations of the flexible form of joking kinships and their historical exploitation by states eager to create a narrative of national identity and consolidate power, little attention has been given to how regular citizens, particularly youth, also mobilise the use of joking and kinship, as they understand it, to engage with and move the state. This also necessitates examining whether new online communities such as Africtivistes are signs of new conceptions of kinship that have different forms of power and relating. Also, given the closeness a tweet and tagged participant affords, what kind of new kinships develop between ruler and ruled?

My contribution to this topic of social media and democracy in Africa is ethnographic. It is to provide a small, yet intimate, glimpse of personal experiences in the virtual worlds of social media and its intersections with physical reality. The project of ethnography has traditionally been that of a human ethnographer interacting with other humans in the field by way of observation, documentation of stories and informal conversations, as well as interviews. The interpersonal aspect of ethnography has always seemed to be the most authentic, and yet as people move to online sources for connection and kinship has this really changed? Caliandro (2018: 553) argues that the distinction between online and offline realities has blurred to the point that it is increasingly possible to 'study the everyday practices of social actors and the cultural forms naturally emerging from them, in and throughout the Internet'. In other words, we must take seriously the value of tweets and posts as primary sources and a piece of the ethnographic puzzle. The realm of hashtag ethnography is a newer pursuit for the ethnographer, who must balance an analysis of human experience and subjectivity between the 'real' and 'virtual' worlds. In many respects, treating the internet and social media not as an object to study, rather as a source of new language to help us understand communities that use it (Caliandro 2018). My own process for this study included such a balance; observing the work of journalists during the election campaigns as well as parsing through their online activities. I was fortunate to have sufficiently good access to Pape Ismaila that I was able to reference his tweets during our discussions and gain insight into his process. Much like notes from hours of participant observation, I identified patterns of language used in tweets and posts as well as the semiotic categorisation of hashtags. I encountered journalists and bloggers like Papa Ismaila during press conferences and rallies for the various political campaigns I was following, and became fascinated by their methods and contributions to political debate. Maïmouna allowed me to sit in on her coalition's meetings in the early stages of their formation, giving me not only significant insight into the political process, but access to fellow journalists, such as Papa Ismaila and the Africtivistes.

Social media and the election: introducing Africtivistes and Papa Ismaila Dieng

Senegal's electoral system is mixed, with a 165-member parliament, 90 of whom represent the 35 national departments across the country, along with 15 newly added representatives of those living in the diaspora. Sixty seats are based on a national proportional vote using a largest remainder system (Kelly 2013). Each coalition or party proposes two lists, one with representatives nominated in each department and another for the 'national list' that ranks the candidates hoping to benefit from the proportional votes in order. For every 55,174 national votes secured by the coalition a member was elected, starting with the *tête de liste*, or coalition frontman or woman. Less significant candidates vie for the closest spot to the leader, in the hope that the coalition receives enough for each person on the list. This rule contributes to the splitting of parties into coalitions, as many politicians feel they have a better chance to win their seat if they are the *tête de liste* as opposed to further down the list of someone else's party.

The three largest coalitions were *Bennoo Bokk Yakaar*, headed by the Prime Minister, Mahammad Dionne (and governed by Macky Sall); *Mankoo Taxawu Senegal* ('Stand United') led by the mayor of Dakar, who was imprisoned in March of 2017 on charges of corruption, which many believed to be trumped-up charges to prevent him from presenting his candidacy; and *Mankoo Wattu Senegal* ('Unite to Heal the Divide'), a coalition largely comprised of politicians from the former administration and led by the 91-year-old former President Abdoulaye Wade. Much of the intensity leading up to and during the campaigns encompassed several components: rumours of whether Abdoulaye Wade would return to Senegal having lived in France since losing in 2012; protests to liberate Khalifa Sall (or at least allow him to vote); and confusion and lack of transparency regarding the transition to ECOWAS-sanctioned identification cards used for voting. It was rumoured that of the forty-seven coalitions and parties, Macky Sall, the incumbent, had helped finance several smaller parties; especially women-led coalitions that had minimal resources but were established in an attempt to dilute the competition by taking votes away from the main coalitions. Papa Ismaila pointed out that 'the fee for registering your party was 15 million CFA [$30,000] and when you think about where those parties are getting that money, it's clear they won't win any seats, so the administration [Macky Sall's government] sponsored them'.

Social media was an important factor to political campaigns as they toured around the country. Select campaigns were documented by the state television company *Radio Télévision Sénégalais* (RTS) during legs of the journey before switching to another campaign. Parties and coalitions had friends or professionals film and post live videos of rallies and the parade of cars throughout urban and rural spaces to the official party Facebook page and Twitter accounts. Music blasted in the background as the master of ceremonies, with microphone in hand, looked straight into the camera and encouraged online supporters, and those present, to vote for their primary candidate. Cellphones captured shots of the candidate sitting atop the roof of their car as they drove slowly through busy neighbourhoods and small villages with sandy roads. They posted and tweeted about the progress of the campaign and wrote positive messages about the candidate and notes of thanks to the populations they encountered along the way. Lesser-known parties and candidates taped video selfies in front of their party poster aligning themselves with the recognisable leader and working within a tight budget. The party posters and their many iterations were the inspiration for Papa Ismaila's tweets mocking the campaigns and candidates.

Journalists and activists covering the campaign also relied heavily on social media for receiving and conveying information. In the case of Papa Ismaila, the network has served also as a way to share information, support the political struggles of regional colleagues and disseminate news locally. For example, while the repressive former President Yaya Jammeh contested the results of the Gambian elections of 2016, several Gambian activists operating underground at home and in Senegal sent information to Papa Ismaila and other Africtivistes members to publish in the Senegalese newspapers. On behalf of the Africtivistes and using the hashtag, #GambiaHasDecided, Papa Ismaila published a blog post on his website with the official association statement that Jammeh should respect the will of the people and step down (Dieng 2017). Gambians abroad also published their opinions on social media in the hope that it would make it to those able to access the sites in Senegal. More recently, the group has held training sessions in Niamey, Niger, as well as Dakar to discuss the issue of cyber security and the theme of 'Digital Democracy' (Africtivistes 2018), a collaborative initiative to explore ways the digital can bridge cooperative gaps between state governments and civil societies. The goal was to train members across West Africa on the theory and practice of cyber security for professional journalists and social media actors.

Papa Ismaila was one of the earliest members of the Africtivistes group after its founding in 2014. He grew up in Dakar and was trained as a journalist at the *Institut Supérieur des Sciences de l'Information et de la Communication* (ISSIC) in Dakar and later started working for online newspapers such as *Xalima*. He manages his own blog where he writes articles about politics, a topic that has always fascinated him, and he is a student of Senegalese political history. In fact, he comes from somewhat of a political family, with a father who was a founding member of Cheikh Anta Diop's pan-African party. He became more publicly known for his coverage of the Hissène Habré trial, the former President of Chad who had sought refuge in Senegal after being ousted following years of dictatorship. The trial was a first on the continent, a collaboration between the African Union, Senegal and other international organisations to create a special African court housed in Dakar, beginning more than twenty years after Habré first sought asylum in Senegal, accused of torture and mass murder, among other offences. Before this event, Papa Ismaila had mostly been writing spotlight articles for online newspapers, but at the beginning of the trial he gained access to the courtroom. Phones and computers were prohibited except for journalists with specific badges, and so Papa Ismaila started tweeting and posting on Facebook about events as they unfolded. He feels the Habré trial has changed the perception of social media as a tool for serious journalism. In fact, he said he sees more news programmes quoting tweets from private journalists like him who often serve as field reporters: 'TV morning news has started referencing our tweets when speaking about a certain event' he said. He gained popularity as people liked what he was writing and preferred the short and real-time updates via tweets and Facebook posts to the longer articles that took time to publish and read.

In the last decade, the number of internet users has grown exponentially in Senegal, and more recently social media sites have become commonly used as modes of communication. Companies such as Facebook made the decision to offer the site free of charge so that users in many countries, including Senegal, could connect to Facebook without using their data, drastically increasing the number and frequency of users (Shearlaw 2016). Other social media platforms such as WhatsApp became more popular means of communication due to their use of internet rather than phone credits, especially for those making international calls to friends and family members living abroad. So, it is unsurprising that with the boom in cellphone and internet use, social media has also become a popular form of expression, especially as a political tool. Conglomerate phone companies operating in Senegal such as Orange, Tigo and Espresso offered increasingly sleek portable Wi-Fi connectors, allowing users to connect their devices wherever they wish. According to Papa Ismaila, social media sites such as Twitter and Facebook gained popularity in Senegal around 2008 when he first created his accounts. From 2008 to 2013 the number of internet users doubled (from 10.6 to 20.9 out of 100 people) (Lemke & Chala 2016). More recently it has been a virtual space for users to talk politics, organise, and gain an intimacy with state leaders by engaging with their tweets and posts, especially during election seasons. In many cases to directly criticise. In the next section I explore the creative ways in which Papa Ismaila and others use social media as a way to engage with the political elite and their campaigns. They do so by hybrid uses of French and Wolof hashtags, and linguistic and cultural play with popular sayings and mockery.

Campaign publicity: posters, billboards, and mockery

Campaign signage was paramount to the visibility of parties and their leaders. In the form of photo collages or personal photos superimposed on party colours with a sample *bulletin*, or ballots voters would choose at the voting booth. Posters were plastered on cars, put up on billboards lining main thoroughfares, wrapped around poles and circulated online. The majority of posters, some more professional than others as Papa Ismaila would point out, had a photo of the party leader, and a variation of taglines in Wolof or a list of candidates from the party. Papa Ismaila chose to take the campaign posters of various parties or coalitions and poke fun at them on Facebook and Twitter by displaying the digital poster and providing a short commentary.

One campaign poster tweeted by him showed a miniature figure of Abdoulaye Wade – former President and parliamentary candidate – waving to the larger images of three relatively unknown members of his party's list. Intended to show Wade waving to supporters, Papa Ismaila imagines him, instead, as a father waving goodbye to his children: '*Children, you are leaving?*' says Wade. 'Yeah dad, we are going' they reply. 'Say hello to Senegal for me' he says, followed by the tags *#kebetu #SunuDepute2017*, #OurRepresentative2017. This tweet mocks the leadership of the *Parti Démocratique Sénégalais*' continued dependence on Wade, and his own need for the party, even after he retreated to France following his defeat to Macky Sall in 2012 and his age of 91 years. Since then, the party has been mostly incapable of organising and choosing a successor.

Papa Ismaila mentioned he asked most party leaders for their campaign posters, so he could write about them and circulate their information to his followers, assuming a more diplomatic take. After being ignored, he found a different way to get his hands on them and took the liberty of mocking them. Other Twitter users began following suit. They commented on slapdash graphics, mocked the layout of photos they imagined illustrated comedic scenarios, and alluded to connections between poster designs and popular consumer products. The two main hashtags used were #kebetu, a way of cataloguing references to Senegalese matters, and *#SunuDepute2017*, specifically indexing tweets and posts to do with the 2017 election. Both hashtags were created by Africtivistes founders such as Demba Gueye (@dembagueye) and Cheikh Fall (@cypher007) (Ba 2016) who continue to be the forces behind the association and work closely with Papa Ismaila. The use of hashtags was clerical and semiotic indexing while also serving as a performative frame (Bonilla & Rosa 2015) in the context of mostly urban, Wolof-speaking users. During the 2012 presidential elections when social media was truly becoming a force in Senegal, the hashtag *#SunuDepute2012* emerged and has consequently evolved as the major demarcation for elections. These hashtags serve many purposes and during the campaigns they allow people to talk about the candidates and make certain pleas, while during the election they serve as a rapid crowdsourcing of information about events, voting station locations and irregularities regarding voting, as well as general commentary about Senegal or the election in particular.

Beyond *#kebetu* and *#SunuDepute2017*, users' tweets and posts referenced popular culture about themes of cooking spices or feminine beauty products, particular political realities, and cultural phenomena. For example, one post featured the poster for the Prime Minister, Mahammad Dionne, in the foreground of the official party symbol of BBY with a washed-out complexion next to a previous photo with much darker skin. Papa Ismaila's post writes '*Before and after le passage de Boun Abdallah à Elles Sont Toutes Belles #kebetu #SunuDepute2017*' ('Before and after the appearance of Boun Abdallah on *They're So Pretty*'). The reference to his complexion and appearance on a popular women's modelling show remarks on the popularity of skin whitening in Senegal as a visual symbol of new-found wealth, and his transition to be the frontman of the President's party as symbolic of his own transformation into a rich man. Much of Twitter had made fun of the fact that as Prime Minister he went by the name Mahammad Dionne, switching to his full name, Mahammad Boun Abdallah Dionne, which some felt was a political manoeuvre to play up the religious significance of his name in a country with a majority of devout Muslims. Sambaa Bokoom, a Twitter follower of Papa Ismaila, shared a post of the same campaign poster of the Prime Minister with the tagline '*Kouleu Mackyllagé kouleu done phaaaré kouleu ko tiapal eupneu ... . #DionePoudeur #PubMulticafé #BennoBokkDégué*'. The comment reads 'whoever did your makeup' with the use of the President's name Macky, which sounds similar to '*maqui*' of the word '*maquillage*' or make-up in French. It continues: '*whoever was supporting you, it's too much*'; criticising the obvious signs of the wealth this position has brought him. The various hashtags refer to the poster as an advertisement for a powdered coffee and milk mix (*#PubMulticafé*) that matches his skin tone, echoing a popular way of describing a person of mixed race as having a coffee with cream complexion, '*café au lait*'. He also takes a shot at the integrity of the President's party – Bennoo Bokk Yakaar (Together for an Emergent Senegal) – as *#BennoBokkDégué*, 'Let's All Tell the Truth'. *Bennoo* meaning 'of one/unit', *bokk*, 'to share', *yakaar*, 'hope', and *dégué* or *dëgg*, 'the truth'. The tweet and post are packed with critique of political and religious posturing, feelings of political promises never kept and societal obsessions with certain kinds of beauty as markers for success and the overtly and ridiculously obvious showing of that success. There had also been frustration voiced on social media that the parliamentary elections had become a referendum on Macky Sall's presidency, questioning the seriousness of the separation of powers between the presidency and the legislative branch. The comment about telling the truth is then an unveiled critique of state corruption and lack of real candour and transparency, even as the signs are obvious (Mbembe 2006). The use of irony and joking were ways of criticising unequal relationships in a context of uncertainty (Devlieger 2018) and ridicule is often a means through which ordinary people make meaning out of a reality that has become surreal or absurd (Obadare 2009; Goldstein 2003).

Another poster commented on by Papa Ismaila and Sambaa takes aim at the message a party was trying to give that they view as comically unprofessional. In a mix of French and Wolof, the party's subtitle read: '*Votez Assemblée Bi Ñu Bëgg! Députe yi ñu bëgg au service de la Nation*' 'Vote for The Assembly We Want! Representatives we want in service of the Nation'. Eight members of the party are lined up, alternating men and women – possibly speaking to the gender parity law mandating party lists respect equal gender representation – standing in front of a deep purple background. Sambaa jokes they are the *#CoalitionBissap* – 'Hibiscus Coalition', referring to the treasured hibiscus drink of a similar shade of purple. They both comment on the elegant outfits the members are wearing, as though they were going to a baptismal ceremony or dressing for the well-watched 'Night of Bazin', a fashion show of popular fabrics and the latest clothing trends. Papa Ismaila asks, '*Wa yenn soiree kou key teugg? Kougn ko ndeyale? Gnata lagne fay battrer? #kebetu*' – 'Hey, at your party, who was the griot, who was the maiden of honour, and how much did you pay the drummer?' referring to their expensive clothing and the phenomenon of ceremonies as flaunting wealth that the average Senegalese does not have. This echoes a popular criticism of politics as being too steeped in folkloric practices such as the presence of griots at official meetings, mimicking ceremony. Politicians are frequently cited as the reason for inflated family ceremonies, which are highly expensive, monetised and unsustainable for many families, as they have been spaces for campaigning and political posturing (Riley 2016; Diouf 1990). This critique also speaks to the frustrations of many that politicians are only interested in buying supporters, not helping their long-term welfare.

Papa Ismaila's mockery of campaign posters and slogans was also laced with historical and cultural references to political figures and their dynamics, as well as allusion to kinship rules and criticisms of individuals pretending to be important religious leaders. Generally, he was poking fun at the sheer volume of parties and the lack of seriousness from many that was reflected in the amateur nature of the posters themselves. In his derision of poster designs and identification of the reckless political process, Papa Ismaila voiced the mockery he felt many politicians were making of the political foundation of Senegal itself. In addition, he lamented the loss of civil discourse and a generation of trained politicians. Gone were the days when politicians displayed an argumentative rhetoric or style of debate that was engaging and civil. Now, he felt insults flew in the face of opponents and politicians, and their followers, who were mainly young kids looking to create havoc. Civil political debate steeped in the art of playing up kinship relations with one's adversary had turned to ineffectual and hollow insults.

This, in part, was why he began posting various election campaign signs and fliers while poking fun at their slogans, photos and graphics. He aimed to expose what he saw as their lack of sincerity as well as to use joking to diffuse tensions as reflected in the exchange of insults. He also wished to lighten the mood of a campaign that was tense even before it officially began with new coalitions, the jumbling of political parties and candidates vying for coveted seats in parliament, a stadium collapse which prompted a day of mourning that suspended campaigning, and bouts of violence on the campaign trail. He hoped more people would get involved in the political process, and take more of an interest in the election and politics in general, if it was more light-hearted. Papa Ismaila said most people were disillusioned with politics, arguing that aspirations for political office were about money and that the offices were diluted by the mere fact that '*ñeppa bëgga nekk député*'– 'everyone wanted to be a politician' despite a lack of training or real experience in leadership roles. In another sense his mockery of campaign paraphernalia, including clothing patterned with party symbols, was also a way of talking back to what many felt was the state and politicians' 'teasing' or 'making a mockery of' voters. Just as Maïmouna posted, 'This Country is a Joke' while referring to poor infrastructure, and the inability of the state to clean the streets, among other things, Twitter and Facebook were spaces to express certain grievances with the government or the state of affairs with the police whether through unmasked frustration or humour.

#TuVotesAvecQuoi: talking back to the state

In addition to social media being a way for users to satirise the state of affairs, public platforms such as Twitter also offered a space for informed citizens such as Papa Ismaila to hold a mirror up to those in power. Take for example the Twitter exchange between Papa Ismaila and the Senegalese President, Macky Sall, in late June of 2017. Upon winning an award for citizenship engagement in honour of a fellow activist just a few months before the election, the President tweeted a note of congratulations to Papa Ismaila's Twitter handle @aliamsi, citing his engagement in responsible activism and strengthening democracy in Africa. Although Papa Ismaila and other Africtivistes tweeted back in appreciation, he took advantage of the public occasion to remind Macky Sall that democracy was allowing people to vote, writing: 'Mr. President, I hope you will keep your promise of democracy', hinting at the rumours of voter suppression that had plagued the campaign for months. He joked about the large number of coalitions campaigning, 'doubling every time each election, rising to 47 this year and potentially double that next time around', before quickly turning to the more urgent issue of the stability of democracy in Senegal: the fact that, five days before the election, most Senegalese still did not know where and how they would vote. More disparaging was the looming feeling that voting would be irregular because people decided it was not worth it to vote, or rather there were increasing suspicions of ballot tampering. In addition, many criticised the government for spending 50 billion CFA on the new voting ID cards, only to fail to have them ready on time. Papa Ismaila mentioned that many people, including himself, were making several trips to their local office to retrieve their cards and even queuing the day of the election only to find they still were not ready.

Despite having more than a year to produce new voting cards it became evident close to election day that the government was not going to deliver, as it cited issues with the printing schedule. Twitter users decried the disorganisation they found when trying to obtain their new card or when they discovered it was not yet ready. As the election approached and the state felt mounting pressure to address the issue – thanks in part to activists like Papa Ismaila making noise – the President made the executive decision to allow an extension on existing voting cards. Citizens who had not yet received their new card could vote with an older ID card. This, of course, excluded newly registering voters or new ID card holders. In addition, the voting commission altered the election procedures to require voters to take a minimum of five party ballots into the voting booth – they would otherwise have had to take one for all 47 registered parties – claiming that the measure was being introduced to save time. President Sall tweeted a photo of the signed law from the commission and Papa Ismaila tagged him in response, taking issue with the fact that the President forced the Constitutional Council into a corner, problematising the constitutional order and the electoral rules that had been in place since 1993. Papa Ismaila tweeted: '*L'avis du Conseil Constitutionnel signifie que tout ce qui a été fait depuis octobre 2016 et qui nous coute 50 milliards (cfa), diarouko wone. #kebetu*' – 'The ruling of the constitutional council demonstrates all that has been done since October of 2016, costing us 50 billion cfa [$100,000] wasn't worth it/ didn't matter, #kebetu'. Most anticipated this move, just three days ahead of election day, but still took the opportunity to make fun of it on Twitter and Facebook with the hashtag #TuVotesAvecQuoi #*WhatAreYouVotingWith*. The official Constitutional Council statement outlined the types of identification accepted in order to vote. Acceptable forms included existing voting cards, passports, government issued IDs, drivers' licences, or receipts of newly enrolled voters. Following Papa Ismaila's tweet of the full document, others began posting pictures of identification cards from universities, their judo clubs, or their membership cards pledging support to their particular marabout or football club followed by the hashtag. Pictures circulated of government workers for the National Commission for Elections dealing with cards spread out on the floor of what looks like their own homes. Online commentators criticised workers' unprofessionalism and lack of discretion and care. Others tweeted photos of voting cards in trash bins, or dug-out holes outside city hall buildings in various parts of the city, or screenshots of video stills showing cards in disarray on tables in what seems to be city hall offices or party headquarters.

#TuVotesAvecQuoi provided an abundance of creative opportunities for users to mock the entire card fiasco and the decision by the President to change the rules at the last minute. Many online commentators felt these efforts to create chaos by the administration were symptomatic of a larger issue; that the government was more concerned with preserving a sense of control than taking the population seriously. Several users posted a photo of a young Macky Sall on his University Athletics Union member card, with taunts that he should try to vote with that card in an attempt to bring him to their level, asking he be held to the same standards imposed upon them. Others posted a photo of him holding his own ECOWAS card, part of the first batch to come out and a publicity stunt to advertise the new programme that so fatefully led them to the current state of affairs. 'You have yours but where is mine?' a user wrote using the hashtag. By trivialising the process, and even tagging Macky Sall to get his attention, users took advantage of the way Twitter particularly (due to its public nature) is a space that creates a collective identity (Treré 2015) catalogued by a targeted topic to articulate and protest state hypocrisy and voice frustrations of being left out of the process altogether (Bonilla & Rosa 2015). Tagging those concerned forces a topic into public conversation. And yet this was a new way for people who 'have never participated in politics', as Papa Ismaila said, to feel 'closer' to politicians by posting directly to the President's tweets, for good and bad. In the case of #TuVotesAvecQuoi, there is a dual sense of the mockery of the voting cards process and a palpable frustration with not only the negligence or perhaps intent on the part of the state to hinder voting, but one's weariness and inability to do much about it. It expresses being in a constant state of what Caroline Melly (2017) calls *embouteillage*, or bottleneck, a kind of dispossession one feels as bureaucracy is slow (stuck, often) and democratic possibilities seem uncertain due to the lack of movement – for example an enforced voting ID requirement yet inability to vote without access to a card – or moving target of where to vote. These realities are common symptoms in countries like Senegal which have endured structural adjustment programmes and other major economic instabilities, rendering the state ineffectual and chaotic. Ridicule is not just a way of 'getting even with the state' but navigating the endless improvisation required of the postcolonial subject in reaction to the improvisational state (Obadare 2009).

The elections: chaos, comedy, social media activists taking charge

By the time election day came around, the mood was cautiously optimistic, with a large number of people still without voting cards and an air of suspicion about how the day would unfold. It had rained so hard on election eve that debris blocked small roads and flooding impaired driving and mobility throughout Dakar. People complained that although the weather had impacted the electricity, they doubted that the state-run *Senelec* would be in any hurry to get it back up and running. Many turned to Twitter to express a commonly used gag, turning the power company's name, *Senelec* into *Senelekk*, referring to the Wolof word *lekk*, to eat, a complaint that the company often charges consumers even when the power goes out, effectively 'eating their money'. This harkens to Bayart's (2009) 'politics of the belly', referring to the unequal relationship of politicians as patrons and citizens as clients that becomes visualised by symbols of eating and well-fed bellies. Everyone seemed anxious that an already vacillating electorate would be further discouraged to get out and vote due to the weather and general discontent with the government and the election process. There were whispers at the polling stations that Macky Sall had visited a mystic to make it rain or that God was punishing the very advent of voting in fraudulent elections. On the surface it was obvious that Macky Sall's coalition *Benno Bokk Yakaar* had the means to out-compete the competition in advertising and the ability to move about the country, making visits to the far corners of Senegal. This, however, did not quell fears that they would also use their influence to change the results, stuff the ballot boxes or implement last-minute rules to create further confusion and frustration among many, or even dissuade them from voting altogether.

On election day, all parties had state-registered volunteers to make the rounds of voting stations in certain neighbourhoods, to be vigilant for signs of misconduct and to advocate for their party interests if a dispute was to occur. They had their work cut out for them, often running or taking taxis from one voting station to the next to ensure there were no issues. Papa Ismaila and his colleagues used social media to amplify their work with a new and very efficient form of surveillance of voting that could reach more people and serve as a public record of events. All day, I was glued to my Twitter and Facebook feeds watching as Papa Ismaila and other Africtivistes members sent virtual messages about the status of different stations, some of which they made public. He had traded in his posts mocking campaign posters for a serious tone designed to help facilitate the voting process. They reported that some stations had been affected by flooding, 'Hann Bel-Air Elhadj Doudou Mbathie school is under water, no sign of voting', and answered comments from followers looking for information on where to vote or to report vote tampering or disorganisation. Papa Ismaila gave status updates of various Dakar neighbourhoods and cities across Senegal saying, 'Mbour Voting Station Chateau d'Eau Nord: at 3pm, only 2 of 11 [booths] have started voting', or 'Liberté 5 school: voting taking place, no issues reported'.

One post from Papa Ismaila, which had a slew of responses, gave information for voting stations where members or friends were currently voting, and captured people's frustration with the process. 'Liberté 6A school: Voting has not started at 9:15. Not all voting material is complete' says Papa. In the comment feed, a follower writes '9:30 and voting also hasn't started at Ibrahima Koita in Dieuppeul'. 'If the problem of material is this bad in Dakar, it must be a nightmare in the rest of the country' another follower writes, followed by a photo of a friend's inked finger indicating they had voted. In fact, photos of pink-dyed fingers were all over Facebook and Twitter with prideful commentary of accomplishing a civic duty, despite many feeling that the system was rigged. Maïmouna, who was featured at the beginning of this article as saying '#ThisCountryIsAJoke', posted a photo of herself and her ten-year-old son who she brought along to observe the process, saying 'I want to make him into a model citizen'. At the same time that critiques flow freely, so too do expressions of civic duty and love of country.

Towards the end of the day, Papa Ismaila posted pictures of the official results for several voting stations, breaking them down by the number of people registered, those who voted and a summary of votes for each party. His followers expressed their shock at the stark difference between those registered and those who voted in a particular station. 'The number of those who didn't vote is crazy' one follower said, to which Papa Ismaila responded 'low voting participation is good for the large parties', hinting that the voting card fiasco was part of voter-suppression efforts by the state. Many followers asked for clarifications and thanked him for his help in navigating the voting process and results as they came out.

Conclusion

Papa Ismaila and members of the Africtivistes group have begun using social media platforms to assert themselves as democratic actors in creative and innovative ways. Hashtag activism (Bonilla & Rosa 2015) allows for creative acts of reinterpretation and an opportunity to reframe daily frustrations into articulated visuals that may not have been possible offline. In fact, social media is a space where any technically capable users with a phone or computer and the internet can contribute, allowing for new expressions of political participation and activism that are both local and pan-African. Up for debate is certainly the question of whether these tools can serve as democratising spaces if the very medium to participate is contingent upon having access to these tools and the level of education to be able to read and engage with them. Through an ethnographic look at activism online and off, in this chapter I have attempted to demonstrate the new and creative ways young Senegalese journalists and activists utilise social media to form new types of kinship. Their use of humour on public platforms such as Twitter and semi-private ones, including Facebook, serve several purposes, including to incite political participation and diffuse real conflict, and to criticise moves by the state to cut out their full participation. Ridicule and joking serve an important role in disrupting the banality of power (Mbembe 2006) and the hegemony of everyday state bureaucracy by exposing its chaotic yet calculated actions. Part of the democratising force of social media and ridicule in this case is to expose the uses and abuses of state power in order to 'level the playing field' and to impose the voices of an often times marginalised youth. Capturing the mishandling of voting cards on city hall property and making the image go viral on social media with captions mocking the state workers is a uniquely rapid way of sharing information and inserting themselves as formidable participants in national political discussions. Hashtags ensure their messages will be seen by a specific group of people who are then free to comment directly to the sender or to tag the person in the photo all the way up to the President. The example of Papa Ismaila's tweeted comment directly to Macky Sall and his administration was a bold attempt to expose his inconsistences. Maïmouna's posts about the country being a joke and her tagging and teasing of her childhood friend working closely with the President are archives of a constant frustration and yet willingness to participate in political debates through innovative and familiar means.

References

Africtivistes (2018) 'Africtivistes – La Ligue Des Cyber-Activistes Africains Pour La Démocratie' (n.d.) www.africtivistes.org/!/ (accessed 27 March 2018).

Africtivistes (n.d.) 'De la Démocratie numérique en Afriqu : quel mécanisme de collaboration entre gouvernement et acteurs de la société civile?'2éme Sommet Africtivistes: Africtivistes. www.africtivistes.org.

Anderson, Benedict (2006) *Imagined Communities: Reflections on the Origin and Spread of Nationalism*. Revised. New York: Verso.

Augé, Marc (2009) *Non-Places: an Introduction to Supermodernity.* Translated by John Howe, second edition. London: New York: Verso.

Ba, Mehdi (2016) 'Sénégal: les 9 stars du #kebetu'. JeuneAfrique.com. December 19. www.jeuneafrique.com/mag/379507/societe/senegal-9-stars-kebetu/.

Bayart, Jean-François (2009) *The State in Africa: the Politics of the Belly*. London: Polity.

Bonilla, Yarimar & Rosa, Jonathan (2015) '#Ferguson: digital protest, hashtag ethnography, and the racial politics of social media in the United States'. *American Ethnologist* 42(1): 4–17. https://doi.org/10.1111/amet.12112.

Bourdieu, Pierre (1977) *Outline of a Theory of Practice.* Cambridge UK: Cambridge University Press.

Caliandro, Alessandro (2018) 'Digital methods for ethnography: analytical concepts for ethnographers exploring social media environments'. *Journal of Contemporary Ethnography.* 47(5): 551–578.

Cornwall, Andrea & Schatten Coelho, Vera (2007) *Spaces for Change? The Politics of Citizen Participation in New Democratic Arenas.* New York: Zed Books.

de Jong, Ferdinand (2005) 'A joking nation: conflict resolution in Senegal'. *Canadian Journal of African Studies* 39(2): 391–415. https://doi.org/10.1080/00083968.2005.10751322.

Devlieger, Clara (2018) 'Rome and the Romains: laughter on the border between Kinshasa and Brazzaville'. *Africa* 88(1): 160–182. https://doi.org/10.1017/S0001972017000614.

Dieng, Papa Ismaila (2017) 'Africtivistes – le choix du peuple gambien doit être respecté pour préserver la paix'. Wordpress. Aliamsi, 16 January. https://aliamsi.wordpress.com/2017/01/16/africtivistes-le-choix-du-peuple-gambien-doit-etre-respecte-pour-preserver-la-paix/.

Diouf, Mamadou (1990) 'Le Clientélisme, la "technocratie" et après?' In Momar-Coumba Diop (ed.) *Sénégal: Trajectoires d'un État*. Dakar: Codesria.

Fouéré, M.-A. (2004) 'L'objet ethnologique des "relations à plaisanteries" dans l'espace est-africain (Tanzanie): de la construction savante d'une coutume à la restitution des situations sociales de l'utani'. Thèse de doctorat (Paris: EHESS).

Galvan, Dennis (2006) 'Joking kinship as a syncretic institution'. *Cahiers d'études Africaines*, no. 184 (December): 809–834. www.cairn.info/resume.php?ID_ARTICLE=CEA_184_0809.

Gerbaudo, Paolo (2012) *Tweets and the Streets: Social Media and Contemporary Activism*. London: Pluto Press. http://ebookcentral.proquest.com/lib/ku/detail.action?docID=3386687.

Goldstein, Donna M. (2003) *Laughter Out of Place: Race, Class, Violence, and Sexuality in a Rio Shantytown*. Berkeley: University of California Press.

IRIS (2016) 'Senegal Selects IRIS to Implement First ECOWAS Biometric eID with Voter Card for its Citizens'. 4 October. www.iris.com.my/media_20161004_senegallaunch.html.

Irvine, Judith T. (1973) 'Caste and Communication in a Wolof Village: a Dissertation in Anthropology'. Ann Arbor, Mich.: University Microfilms International.

Irvine, Judith T. (1992) 'Insult and responsibility: verbal abuse in a Wolof village'. In Jane H. Hill & Judith T. Irvine (eds.), *Responsibility and Evidence in Oral Discourse*. Cambridge: Cambridge University Press, pp. 104–134.

Kelly, Catherine Lena (2013) 'The 2012 legislative election in Senegal'. *Electoral Studies*, 32: 905–908.

Labouret, M.H. (1929) 'La parenté à plaisanterie en Afrique occidentale'. *Africa*, 2: 244–254.

Lemke, Jeslyn & Chala, Endalk (2016) 'Tweeting democracy: an ethnographic content analysis of social media use in the differing politics of Senegal and Ethiopia's newspapers'. *Journal of African Media Studies*, 8(2): 167–185.

Madianou, Mirca (2015) 'Polymedia and ethnography: understanding the social in social media'. *Social Media and Society*, 1(1): 1–3.

Mbembe, Achille (2006) 'The banality of power and the aesthetics of vulgarity in the postcolony'. In Aradhana Sharma & Akhil Gupta (eds.), *The Anthropology of the State: a Reader*. Blackwell Readers in Anthropology 9. Malden, MA and Oxford: Blackwell Pub.

Melly, Caroline (2017) *Bottleneck: Moving, Building, and Belonging in an African City*. Chicago: University of Chicago Press.

Obadare, Ebenezer (2009) 'The uses of ridicule: humour, "infrapolitics" and civil society in Nigeria'. *African Affairs*, 108(431): 241–261. https://doi.org/10.1093/afraf/adn086.

Paulme, D. (1939) 'Parenté à plaisanterie et alliance par le sang en Afrique occidentale'. Africa, 12(4): 433–444.

Radcliffe-Brown, A.R. (1940) 'On joking relationships'. *Africa*, 13(3): 195–210. https://doi.org/10.2307/1156093.

Riley, Emily (2016) 'Terànga and the art of hospitality: engendering the nation, politics, and religion in Dakar, Senegal – ProQuest'. https://search.proquest.com/openview/4ddb7b515c2f39f3a7c7e8ca057c837f/1?pq-origsite=gscholar&cbl=18750&diss=y (accessed 27 March 2018).

Shearlaw, Maeve (2016) 'Facebook lures Africa with free internet – but what is the hidden cost?' *The Guardian*, 1 August. www.theguardian.com/world/2016/aug/01/facebook-free-basics-internet-africa-mark-zuckerberg.

Smith, E. (2004) 'Les cousinages de plaisanterie en Afrique de l'Ouest, entre particularismes et universalismes'. *Raisons politiques*, 13: 157–169.

Sunstein, Cass R. (2018) *#Republic: Divided Democracy in the Age of Social Media*. Princeton NJ: Princeton University Press.

Treré, Emiliano (2015) 'Reclaiming, proclaiming, and maintaining collective identity in the #YoSoy132 movement in Mexico: an examination of digital frontstage and backstage activism through social media and instant messaging platforms'. *Information, Communication, and Society*, 18(8): 901–915.

Yang, Guobin (2016) 'Narrative agency in hashtag activism: the case of #BlackLivesMatter'. *Media and Communication*, January: 13–17.

8 | SOCIAL MEDIA AND ELECTIONS IN NIGERIA

Digital influence on election observation, campaigns and administration

Nkwachukwu Orji

Introduction

The question of the influence of social media on the democratic process remains a subject of lively debate (Boulianne 2015; Murthy 2015; Couldry 2015; Gil de Zuniga, Molyneux & Zheng 2014; Bode, Vraga, Borah & Shah 2014; Valenzuela 2013; Bode 2012). This is much more so in developing countries where democracy is emerging and the effect of social media has the potential to be quite distinct (Lim 2013, 2012: Tufekci & Wilson 2012). This chapter contributes to the ongoing debate on the political effect of social media by examining the ways it has influenced elections in Nigeria. The chapter focuses on Nigeria's 2011 and 2015 general elections, looking at how social media has shaped three critical aspects of the electoral process: election observation, election campaigns and election administration. The focus on Nigeria is understandable considering that prior to the country's 2011 general elections, the electoral process in the country was severely discredited by poor organisation, lack of transparency, allegations of irregularities and disputes over results (Suberu 2007; Orji 2014). The need to improve the integrity of elections in Nigeria led election stakeholders to seek solutions in digital technologies in general and social media in particular. This chapter examines the extent to which social media has contributed to improving the credibility of elections in Nigeria, and helped improve the country's electoral process by broadening access to information and encouraging greater communication and networking, as well as improving the efficiency of mobilisation. To appropriately situate the chapter in the Nigerian context, the following sections will explore the challenges of organising elections in Nigeria, lay out the social media landscape in the country, and review the political effect of social media, before looking at the role of social media in Nigeria's electoral process.

A brief review of elections in Nigeria

The evolution of electoral democracy in Nigeria has been protracted and difficult. Since Nigeria's independence in 1960, the country has organised nine general elections and numerous regional, state and local elections. Of these elections, the 1979, 1993 and 1999 polls were conducted by military regimes to allow for transition to civilian rule, while the other elections were conducted by incumbent civilian regimes to consolidate democratic rule. Elections organised by incumbent civilian regimes have been the most problematic (Agbaje & Adejumobi 2006). With the exception of the 2011 and 2015 elections, these elections have been characterised by attempts by the ruling parties to contrive and monopolise the electoral space and deliberately steer the process in their favour.

This pattern was reflected in the 'simulated' landslide victories recorded by the ruling parties in the 1964, 1983, 2003 and 2007 elections (Ibeanu 2007). The United Progressive Grand Alliance (UPGA), which was a coalition of predominantly Southern parties, contested the 1964 federal election against the Nigerian National Alliance (NNA), whose base of support was in Northern Nigeria. The Northern Peoples' Congress (NPC) and its allies in the NNA took advantage of their control of the federal government to achieve a controversial victory (Dudley 1973). The 1983 general elections were also manipulated by the incumbent National Party of Nigeria (NPN), which won the presidency and gubernatorial elections in seven out of the nineteen states in 1979, and thereafter attempted to extend its political power throughout the federation. The allegations of vote manipulation in the 1983 elections triggered violent protests in some parts of Nigeria (Hart 1993). The 2003 and 2007 general elections were also allegedly flawed due to poor organisation and vote rigging (Lewis 2003; Suberu 2007).

The outcome of the 2007 elections, in particular, severely dented Nigeria's democratic credentials due to the national and international condemnation it elicited. One major problem with the 2007 elections was a lack of transparency from the Electoral Commission. Many election observation groups that monitored the elections reported a general lack of openness by the Electoral Commission in its work. For instance, the COG (2007: 25) claimed that 'several of our observers encountered a lack of openness regarding information and basic electoral arrangements', such as detailed figures for voter registration at all levels, and decisions and instructions from the Independent

National Electoral Commission (INEC). The mission noted that lack of transparency led to 'a diminution of confidence in the process' (Commonwealth Election Observer Group 2007: 44).

On a positive note, however, the 2007 elections led to a great deal of soul-searching among the Nigerian leadership. The President at the time, Umaru Musa Yar'Adua, publicly acknowledged that the election, which brought him to power, was fundamentally flawed. He therefore established the Electoral Reform Committee (ERC) to suggest measures that could improve the conduct of elections, restore electoral integrity and strengthen democracy in Nigeria. Some of the ERC's recommendations were reviewed and adopted as amendments to the Constitution and Electoral Act in 2010. The government also attempted to restore the integrity of elections in the country by appointing credible leadership to the INEC. For its part, INEC adopted a series of internal measures aimed at restoring public confidence in the electoral process, including a communication policy, which accorded a strong role to social media (Kuris 2012). Furthermore, civil society organisations that run election observation missions sought to improve their capacity to gather and transmit real-time information about elections through social media. Before looking at how social media has shaped the electoral process in Nigeria, it is pertinent to map the social media landscape in Nigeria.

The social media landscape in Nigeria

Due to the low availability of personal computers, mobile phones have become the primary medium of internet access in Nigeria. Mobile phone ownership has grown massively in Nigeria in the past decade, as Table 8.1 demonstrates. According to the Nigerian Communications Commission, the number of active mobile phone lines as of December 2017 stood at 144 million.[1] Increase in mobile phone usage has been followed by a corresponding growth in internet use. Internet use statistics released by Internet World Stats for June 2017 show that about 92 million Nigerians now use the internet – an internet penetration rate of 47.7 percent. Though internet penetration in Nigeria is still relatively low, the current figures represent a dramatic increase from the 200,000 internet users in 2000.[2]

A report by Alexa.com, an internet traffic monitoring website which tracks the most popular websites among users in a particular country on a monthly basis, shows that Google.com, Google.com.ng, YouTube.com and Facebook.com are the top four most popular websites in

Table 8.1 Mobile subscription rates, 2007–2017

Active Lines	2017	2014	2012	2011	2010	2009	2008	2007
Mobile (GSM)	144,631,543	136,772,475	109,829,223	90,566,238	81,195,684	65,533,875	56,935,985	40,011,296
Mobile (CDMA)	217,566	2,187,845	2,948,562	4,601,070	6,102,105	7,565,435	6,052,507	384,315
Fixed Wired/ Wireless	139,344	183,290	418,166	719,406	1,050,237	1,418,954	1,307,625	1,579,664
Total	144,988,453	139,143,610	113,195,951	95,886,714	88,348,026	74,518,264	64,296,117	41,975,275

Source: Author's calculations based on Nigerian Communications Commission (NCC), Annual Subscriber Data. www.ncc.gov.ng/stakeholder/statistics-reports/subscriber-data#annual-subscriber-technology-data.

Nigeria as at February 2018. Facebook ranks tops among the social networking sites, with over 15 million monthly active users in Nigeria as of 30 June 2015 (Strydom 2015).

The relevance of social media as a news source has continued to grow among both journalists and their audience. In Nigeria, around one in seven of all news stories originates from social media (Africapractice 2014: 8). The growth of social media has encouraged the rise of alternative news sites with a crowd-sourcing approach to news gathering. One study found that as of 2009 there were about 120 news gathering and distribution websites based on Nigerian content and largely controlled by Nigerian citizens at home and in the diaspora (Dare 2011: 21). Founded in 2006, Sahara Reporters is widely regarded as Nigeria's leading online news site, and describes itself in the following terms: 'Using photos, text, and video dynamically, the site informs and prompts concerned citizens and other human rights activists to act, denouncing officially-sanctioned corruption'.[3] Other online news websites using the citizen journalism approach include iReports, PointBlankNews and Elendu Reports.

While alternative news sites are expanding, audiences in Nigeria still seek verified news from newspapers. This has encouraged the mainstream news media to migrate online. In the past decade, use of social networking tools by mainstream media has been on the rise. Leading national newspapers such as *Vanguard* and *Punch* have revamped their websites to incorporate User Generated Content (UGC). The *Vanguard*, in particular, has garnered large numbers of Facebook and Twitter followers over a short period, because of its embrace of digital technology.[4] The newspaper has incorporated posts and tweets into its electronic platforms and created avenues for reader interactivity, comments, and discussions. Vanguard has a well-packaged community site where user content features on the newspaper's home page. The increasing engagement of the mainstream media with social media has helped transform Nigeria's media environment. According to Africapractice:

> the traditional lines between professional journalism and what is often termed participatory (citizen) journalism or grassroots media are becoming increasingly blurred as more journalists operate blogs and Twitter accounts and more non-journalists, bloggers and Twitterati become increasingly professional in their news reporting and commentary. (Africapractice 2014: 9)

The professional journalist now shares 'the journalistic sphere with tweeters, bloggers, citizen journalists, and social media users' (Ward 2014).

Blogging is becoming increasingly popular in Nigeria. Available data indicate that there were at least 885 Nigerian blogs in July 2011 (Akoh, Jagun, Odufuwa & Akanni 2012: 36). Blogging is still in its infancy in Nigeria though, and this explains some of its features. As observed by Akoh et al. (2012: 38), many blogs in Nigeria are personalised. They tend to be focused on the blogger rather than on users, their content is often poorly presented and organised, and they tend to suffer from severe design constraints and are generally visually tedious while – save for a few cases – user activity is limited and the frequency of updates is sparse. Some blogs also suffer from intermittent downtime. Notwithstanding these drawbacks, Nigerian blogs are creatively specialised and focused on serving a specific audience. Their content is gradually improving in quality, they are diversifying across a wide variety of issues including those that would generally be considered controversial by traditional media, and many utilise the speed of the internet to share breaking news, strengthening the role of social media as a news source (Akoh et al. 2012: 38).

Blogs are complemented by online forums where Nigerians write, comment and report on different issues ranging from politics, society, human rights, disasters, family and entertainment. Nairaland.com, with more than 1.4 million members, is the most popular online forum in Nigeria. Founded in March 2005, the site features large chat rooms where Nigerians interact on a wide range of issues including news, romance, politics and entertainment. Alexa.com claims that the users of the site are mainly low-income and single but well-educated young males.[5] Other popular online forums include nigerianbestforum.com, naij.com, odili.net and naijapals.com.

Political effects of social media

The literature underscores three potential political effects of the use of digital technologies, especially social media. The first is the role of social media in improving access to and the use of information. One reason why social media might bolster citizen political engagement is its ability to lower the cost of information gathering, processing and transmission. Through social media, vast amounts of information about politics and government are accessible in the public domain like never before (Dimitrova & Bystrom 2013; Valenzuela 2013). A recent study suggests that approximately half of Facebook users obtain their news through the network, and that a majority of Facebook users are exposed to news incidentally through social network ties formed on Facebook (DeSilver 2014). Social media use, undoubtedly, facilitates exposure to political news and information – exposure to political information is positively related to the development of citizens' knowledge of political issues and effective participation in the political process (McLeod et al. 1996).

While social media makes a difference in terms of expanding information sources, there are questions about the authenticity of available information. Given the vast number of information sources, how do people know which ones to trust? One simple solution is to filter out information, but that can create a further problem, especially if people simply avoid engaging with politics altogether. A related question regarding the role of social media in expanding information sources touches on the need to transform information to knowledge. As Noveck (2000: 23) notes, 'it is not information *per se* which is useful to the democrat but knowledge, information which has been distilled and contextualized so that it can impart meaning'. Although social media increases information availability, this may not alter the cognitive capacity for processing information. In fact, Polat (2005) acknowledges that there is an increase in the amount and sources of information, but argues that the range and diversity of arguments, or the depth of thematic aspects, remains limited. As Bimber (1998) suggests, 'it is not simply the availability of information that structures engagement; it is human interest and capacity to understand many complex issues'. Increased availability of information must combine with strong civil society mobilisation to produce socio-political transformation.

The above underscores the instrumental role of the media, including social media. Stremlau and Price (2009: 26–29) point to the role of the media as an enabler and an amplifier. As an enabler, the media promotes specific ideals, such as nation and state-building, national identity and a national vision. The media can equally be used negatively, for instance, to disseminate fake news as well as hate and dangerous messages. As an amplifier, the media can help to project voices and views of citizens (and the government). What the media amplifies and how wide it can resonate depends on how well it is used.

The second political effect of social media is stimulation of communication and networking. A major strength of social media is that it offers convenient, cheap and innovative means of communication between large numbers of people across time and geographical boundaries. This makes it easier for individuals to identify other people with common political interests, and to create online networks. Unlike the telephone, which enables 'one-to-one' conversation, and print and broadcast (radio and television) media, which allow 'one-to-many' broadcasting, social media supports all these forms of communication as well as 'many-to-many' communication (Polat 2005). Social media also supports four major forms of communication, namely: conversation, information aggregation, broadcast and group dialogue (Weare 2002).

Social media can stimulate communication and networking in several ways. Some scholars suggest that it increases exposure to mobilising information (Gil de Zuniga, Jung & Valenzuela 2012; Tang & Lee 2013), or maintain that it strengthens ties to political or activist organisations (Bode et al. 2014, Tang & Lee 2013) and aids the formation and sustenance of online groups (Conroy, Feezell & Guerrero 2012; Valenzuela, Park & Kee 2009). Others suggest that social media might have some peer learning and/or contagion effect – for example, observing Facebook friends express their views online might motivate other users to engage in political activity on Facebook (Vitak et al. 2011). Papacharissi (2002: 13) argues that digital technologies facilitate communication and networking by providing access to otherwise unavailable information and by promoting personal expression; in her words, 'making it possible for little-known individuals and groups to reach out to citizens directly and restructure public affairs'. In a later study she claims that the communication and network effects of social media have resulted in a collapse of the boundaries between the private sphere and the political public sphere, such that the private sphere becomes the realm of the political (Papacharissi 2010).

Clay Shirky locates the communication and network effects of social media in the concepts of freedom and shared awareness. He contends that the political use of social media ultimately enhances freedom: 'To speak online is to publish, and to publish online is to connect with others. With the arrival of globally accessible publishing, freedom of speech is now freedom of the press and freedom of the press is freedom of assembly' (Shirky 2008: 171). The result of the new freedom, according to Shirky, is a fundamental social change: 'Our social tools are dramatically improving our ability to share, co-operate, and act together. As everyone from working biologists to angry air passengers adopts those tools, it is leading to an epochal change' (Shirky 2008: 304). Shirky argues that another communication and networking effect of social media is 'shared awareness' – the ability of each member of a group to not only understand the situation at hand but also understand that everyone else does, too. To him, shared awareness is essential in initiating collective action and in finding solutions to collective problems, and social media increases shared awareness by propagating messages through social networks.

The 'two-step flow of communication' thesis developed by Lazarsfeld, Berelson and Gaudet (1948) provides further insight to the communication and networking effect of social media. The thesis is based on an observation that the flow of mass communications may be less direct than was commonly assumed – 'influences stemming from the mass media first reach "opinion leaders" who, in turn, pass on what they read and hear to those of their every-day associates for whom they are influential' (Katz 1957: 61). This implies that one's social network, including family members, friends and colleagues, are crucial agents of political opinion formation. As recent studies demonstrate, by engendering social networks and a two-step flow of communication, social media – which has not only transformed media consumption but media production as well – retains a strong role in political opinion formation (Choi 2014; Norris & Curtice 2008).

Although it appears that social media has several positive communication and network effects, some scholars doubt the ability of social media to stimulate strong social ties, considering that online networks lack robust personal connections and may be unlikely to boost the levels of personal trust, which is necessary for direct political action (Gladwell 2010). Others argue that virtual or mediated forms of communication are an inadequate substitute for traditional forms of communication, especially face-to-face interaction (Putnam 2000).

The third political effect of social media is that it offers organisations and political activists a platform for more efficient political mobilisation. Political mobilisation is 'the process by which candidates, parties, activists, and groups induce other people to participate' in politics in order 'to win elections, to pass bills, to modify rulings, [and] to influence policies' (Rosenstone & Hansen 1993: 25, 30). Studies show that social media platforms enable otherwise disengaged citizens to join political and social causes, increasing their likelihood of being further mobilised, either by direct exposure to messages and profiles of social movements, NGOs and other interest groups, or indirectly through incidental exposure (Xenos & Moy 2007). The convenience of social media use and increased access to information may entice a broader section of the population to politics and bridge knowledge deficiencies blamed for disengagement. Sebastian Valenzuela (2013) suggests that more than other types of media, social media provides apt avenues for encountering different forms of mobilising information, including identificational, locational and tactical information. The appeal of social media to younger people, in particular, creates the possibility of recruiting a new generation of activists and active participants in political activities (Ward, Gibson & Lusoli 2003), supporting an earlier suggestion that innovative methods of digital participation may attract more young people to politics (Coleman & Hall 2001). Finally, by lowering the costs of accessing political information and offering more convenient ways of engaging in political life, social media could improve the efficiency of mobilisation for activists and organisations and activate those individuals who are already predisposed to or interested in politics (Xenos & Moy 2007).

The supposed effects of social media on citizen mobilisation are, however, debatable. A major argument against online political mobilisation is that it amounts to 'preaching to the converted', because social media facilitates engagement among like-minded citizens and technology alone is unlikely to stimulate citizen interest in politics if none existed previously (Ward et al. 2003). In her theory of virtuous circle, Norris (2001) exemplifies how the media, in general, serve to activate existing 'converts' rather than mobilising new participants in the political process. In other words, opportunities offered by social media may be attractive mainly to those people who are interested, knowledgeable and already engaged in the political process. The following section will assess the use of social media in Nigerian elections touching on the key ideas examined in this review, namely that social media is a source of information, a platform for communication and networking, and an enabler of political mobilisation.

Use of social media in Nigerian elections

Social media has been used to share information, facilitate communication and networking, and mobilise the public politically in three critical areas of the electoral process in Nigeria, namely, election observation, electoral campaigns and election administration.

Election observation

In social media, ordinary Nigerians have found an effective means of watching the polls. Civil society organisations (CSOs), politicians, political parties and the electorate use social media as a messaging tool to network, communicate and mobilise. Social media platforms enable groups and organisations to mobilise the public to serve as 'citizen journalists' or 'citizen observers' during elections. Citizen journalists or observers are individuals that actively participate in observing, documenting and reporting major events in the society such as elections. Social media supports individuals with little or no training in journalism to cover and share their election experiences through audio, text, photographs and video. Sometimes, the traditional media recruit these citizen journalists as eyewitnesses, while political parties and civil society organisations have engaged them as key informants.

Several CSOs in Nigeria have established social media platforms through which they share information, engage with the electorate and observe the electoral process. One major innovation by the CSOs during the 2011 elections was the creation of crowd-sourcing platforms that allow users to share information on the election using social media messaging tools. They use these platforms as a novel instrument to collect and disseminate observer reports about issues such as the timely distribution of election materials, the prompt commencement of voting, the conduct of election officials, incidents of violence and the overall administration of the polling stations. In a country with over 70 million registered voters and 120,000 polling units, social media improves the efficiency of election observation by increasing coverage and reporting while minimising costs.

The outbreak of violence in the aftermath of the 2007 Kenyan elections led to the development of Ushahidi as an accessible and free platform to monitor elections. Ushahidi, which means 'testimony' or 'evidence' in Swahili, is a website developed to map reports of post-election violence in Kenya. Ushahidi uses crisis-mapping software to collect eyewitness reports of violence sent by email and text message, and inputs them on a Google Map. The software further aggregates and organises the data into a timeline. During the 2011 elections, the Community Life Project in Lagos set up the Reclaim Naija platform as an election incident reporting system built on the Ushahidi model.

The Reclaim Naija platform allowed Nigerians to report incidents of violence and electoral malpractices through text messages. The messages received were then plotted on an interactive map. Between the National Assembly election of 9 April 2011 and the presidential election of 16 April 2011, citizen observers submitted 6,000 incident reports to the platform. The Reclaim Naija platform was also used to report incidents and progress during the voter registration exercise in January 2011. The reports sent through Reclaim Naija were collated in real time and fed back to INEC. This assisted INEC in troubleshooting in many locations across the country. The information was also useful to the media in monitoring and publishing stories on the voter registration exercise, thereby helping to amplify the voice of the people. In addition, the Reclaim Naija website, with its interactive features, served as a one-stop online resource for information on the 2011 elections. It featured all the polling units, electoral constituencies, the Nigerian Constitution, information on candidates, the 2010 Electoral Act, the election timetable, electoral guidelines, certified voters' registration figures and a range of voter education modules.

Besides the Reclaim Naija project, a coalition of internet-savvy Nigerians known as Enough is Enough (EiE) initiated a number of projects to mobilise young Nigerians through electronic platforms to demand credible elections. The core of EiE's activity was the Register, Select, Vote and Protect (RSVP) campaign, which was designed to encourage young people to participate in the 2011 elections by using tweets and Facebook messages to stir interest and increase registration and turnout (Harwood & Campbell 2010). The RSVP campaign involved mobilising voters by organising civic enlightenment rallies in Abuja and Lagos using social media channels and working with celebrities in conducting voter education. Among the key supporters of the RSVP campaign is the famous novelist Chimamanda Adichie. In an article in the UK *Guardian* newspaper, Adichie (2011) praised its work, noting that 'a coalition of groups worked to register young voters, using Facebook, Twitter and texts' and 'At voter registration venues, which were sometimes chaotic, young people brought food and water to make sure the staff did their jobs well'.

EiE also built an interactive mobile phone application for election mapping known as Revoda. Revoda made it possible for users to register their phone numbers with a particular polling unit, so that reports made about the polling unit could easily be authenticated and followed up by INEC (Asuni & Farris 2011: 2). By June 2012, Revoda recorded over 10,000 downloads. This application made it possible to document deficiencies observed during the 2011 elections. The EiE coalition further worked with INEC to set up Facebook and Twitter accounts that allowed for the open exchange of information, ideas and comments between INEC and other election stakeholders including the public. EiE established a YouTube channel where videos of important events were publicly shared.

Another example of civil society efforts to access and disseminate election-related information is the IAmLagos Project. The goal of the IAmLagos Project was to collect and report election results from polling units in Lagos State within the period of the elections. The project systematically contacted voters in all the wards throughout Lagos State who could post election results to a reporting platform. The significance of the project lies in the fact that counting and collation of results are known to be a problematic aspect of the electoral process in Nigeria due to lack of transparency and the potential for manipulation. Citizens were mobilised to participate in the IAmLagos Project through messages shared on various social media platforms, including the project website, Facebook page and Twitter account, as well as by contacting its call centre. The Social Media Tracking Centre considers the IAmLagos Project to have been 'very effective in improving social media coverage of polling units in Lagos with 80% coverage achieved during the gubernatorial elections' (Asuni & Farris 2011: 11).

The IAmLagos Project mirrors the Project Swift Count, a country-wide initiative aimed at using information and communication technology to monitor and report elections. Project Swift Count was executed by a coalition of four CSOs, including the Federation of Muslim Women's Associations in Nigeria (FOMWAN), Justice, Development and Peace/Caritas Nigeria (JDPC), the Nigeria Bar Association (NBA) and the Transition Monitoring Group (TMG), with the technical assistance of the National Democratic Institute (NDI). The goal of Project Swift Count was to obtain and share with the public both qualitative and quantitative data and analysis regarding elections in real time using SMS text messaging (Project Swift Count 2011). This information makes it possible to verify the accuracy of the results announced by INEC based on a statistical sampling of polling units across Nigeria.

The extensive use of social media during the 2011 and 2015 general elections forced the traditional media in Nigeria to review their strategy and diversify their information-gathering and dissemination methods. Many traditional media houses enlisted the services of citizen journalists to expand their team of reporters covering these elections. In addition, reporters who were full-time employees of these media institutions used electronic messaging tools to share their reports and facilitate their work. In order to reach out to various election stakeholders, traditional media houses adopted an innovative means of interacting with the public through social media. For example, Channels Television now delivers daily news updates through an online application that can be downloaded on Androids, Blackberries, iPads and iPhones from their website. The *Daily Trust* newspaper, which has been on Facebook since June 2010, delivered news updates (with links to its website) to an estimated 89,000 Facebook followers in 2011 (Asuni & Farris 2011: 10). There is also provision for the traditional media houses to receive online comments and feedback from the public. The use of social media for election observation in Nigeria has led to greater scrutiny of the electoral process, and this has helped to improve the transparency and credibility of the process.

Election campaigns

Just like CSOs, political parties and their candidates are using social media to carry out electoral activities. During the 2011 and 2015 general elections, politicians, their parties and their supporters used social media channels to canvass for votes. Many candidates that contested the elections had Facebook and Twitter accounts. The then President, Goodluck Jonathan, was among the first candidates to use social media as a campaign tool. President Jonathan made a remarkable move by announcing his intention to run for re-election on Facebook. Bearing in mind the intense arguments that characterised the debate on whether President Jonathan should contest in 2011 or not, this announcement attracted a stream of messages on his Facebook page. By December 2010, he had nearly 300,000 Facebook followers (Ekine 2010).

During the 2015 general elections, candidates for political office and their supporters used Twitter as one of their main political messaging tools, employing hashtags such as #GEJ_WINS and #CHANGE. To show that they were in tune with the times, the front-running political parties in the 2015 elections (that is the All Progressives Congress (APC) and Peoples' Democratic Party (PDP)) staged Google Hangouts. The APC's Vice Presidential Candidate, Yemi Osinbajo, and the then Lagos State Governor, Babatunde Fashola, used the platform to address the youth. The PDP's Google Hangout session was staged for its Lagos governorship candidate, Jimi Agbaje.

Parties and their candidates designed and set up several interactive websites and apps to reach supporters. Websites such as Forwardnigeria.ng and Apcgmbpyo.org were affiliated with the PDP and APC presidential candidates, respectively. Candidate-specific apps such as the APC Situation Room for the APC presidential candidate were also established. Individuals and CSOs played a critical role in the campaigns by driving conversation via social media. EiE established a website, eie.ng, that provided information on candidates vying for political office. Sterling and Greenback, a Lagos-based enterprise, created a sentiment machine that measured the level of support for different parties. Sponsored posts were placed on various websites to catch the attention of the public. Social media brand promoters were also part of online advertising strategies.

The APC made some of the most innovative use of social media during the 2015 election campaign. The party tried to crowd-source funds for their campaign by employing means ranging from ringtones, premium SMS and e-transactions to get supporters to contribute financially. The NCC later banned the APC's mobile crowdfunding short-code, but a Federal High Court sitting in Lagos overturned the decision. The court also directed the NCC and the telecommunication service provider involved in the deal to pay 500 million Naira in damages to the party. Gbosa Technology Ltd established a broad-based fundraising platform, SpeaksForUS, to help organisations with crowd-sourced fundraising. The website had a category for political donations where the public could contribute by buying political posters, bags and other party branded items.

Individuals and media houses used social media as platforms for online polls. Online media organisation Sahara Reporters, the social media aide to President Goodluck Jonathan, Reno Omokri and African Independent Television (AIT), ran the most popular polls. Organisers of the polls created various tools and applications to stir public interest and facilitate participation. Nigeria Decide 2015 and NaijaPolls were some of the notable apps designed to allow the public to vote for their preferred candidates. However, online polls were marked by controversies. There were accusations of double voting and biased umpires. Whatever the case may be, it was clear that parties involved in the elections did not want to look like they were falling behind in the digital popularity race.

Election administration

Some of the criticisms against INEC's handling of the 2007 elections was that the Commission could not sufficiently engage with other stakeholders in the electoral process (COG 2007). INEC's inability to receive and respond to concerns raised by candidates, voters and election observers attracted specific criticism (Jinadu 2011, Ibrahim & Garuba 2008). To ensure that this flaw did not recur in subsequent elections, the Commission strengthened existing channels of communication between it and other election stakeholders and established new ones. One major action that the Commission took was to revamp its website and make it more interactive. In 2010, volunteers from various CSOs worked with INEC staff to establish a social media structure that included setting up Facebook, Twitter and YouTube profiles. INEC also established a situation room, equipped with direct telephone lines and social media platforms, to enable people to provide feedback to the Commission during elections. These social media channels have changed the way the Commission communicates with election stakeholders since 2011. Through its enhanced communication channels, INEC could receive reports from various parts of the country and provide responses on issues within a reasonable time. In the three days before, during and after the 2011 presidential election, more than 70,000 people were able to directly contact the Commission – the Commission received about 4,000 tweets and 25 million hits on its website (Asuni & Farris 2011: 10, 18). During the 2015 elections, INEC expanded the use of social media through the establishment of an INEC Citizens Contact Centre (ICCC). The ICCC provided direct, real-time reception of feedback from citizens. The ICCC was designed as a modified situation room to work as a channel of continuous communication and exchange of information between the Electoral Commission and the public (INEC 2014). Members of the public could contact the ICCC with questions or complaints and receive rapid responses from the INEC officials.

Conclusion

This chapter has examined the use of social media in Nigerian elections. Drawing from the literature on the political effects of social media, the chapter notes that social media has helped to bridge information gaps in Nigeria's electoral process, leading to increased communication, transparency and citizen involvement. Furthermore, the chapter shows that social media has shaped three critical aspects of the electoral process: election observation, election campaigns and election administration. The analyses in this chapter indicate that information gathering and dissemination occurred in the areas of voter education and mobilisation, election logistics and operations, and election observation; enabling election stakeholders to transmit peace messages, track operational failures and violence, and combat electoral irregularities.

Nigeria's experience with the use of social media in the 2011 and 2015 elections suggests that the tool will play a prominent role in future elections in the country. Two major factors make this prognosis likely. The first is the tendency of Nigerians to follow global trends in the use of social media, and to adapt to innovations in information communication technology. With a predominantly young population, Nigeria has the prospect of keeping pace with the latest developments in information and communication technology, as well as being a driver of innovation in digital media technology. This means that there are enormous opportunities for more extensive use of social media in future elections in Nigeria. Secondly, the gains made by politicians, political parties, CSOs and INEC in the use of social media will likely spur further experiment and innovation in the use of communication technology in election campaigning, election observation and election administration.

Notwithstanding the many positive sides of the use of social media in elections, there are, however, many aspects of social media that weaken its value and call for caution in its use. Many questions have emerged about the reliability of the information collected and shared through social media. The crowd-sourcing technique used by many activists often relies on information provided by individuals in local communities, who are sometimes anonymous reporters. Bearing in mind that some of these 'citizen journalists' might be people with partisan interests and biases, it is difficult to affirm the accuracy of the reports they provide without first subjecting them to a systematic verification process. Reliability may improve if independent verification checks are built into the system – for example, if a random sample of reports are vetted by a trusted and independent agency, or if reports from multiple sources are compared and found to contain similar information.

The ease of anonymity in social media messages, which in itself is a major appeal of this tool, may also be its main drawback. During the 2011 and 2015 election campaigns, social media was occasionally misused as a vehicle for inciting violence. Regrettably, there is an absence of a clear strategy on how to deal with this problem in future elections. Yet, there is a good opportunity for key election stakeholders such as INEC, political parties and CSOs to intervene by liaising with the Nigerian Communication Commission to develop modalities for preventing and managing abuse of social media in elections.

Notes

1 Nigerian Communications Commission, Subscriber Statistics. www.ncc.gov.ng/ stakeholder/statistics-reports/ subscriber-data#monthly-subscriber-technology-data.

2 Internet World Stats, Usage and Population Statistics. www.internetworldstats.com/stats1.htm.

3 http://saharareporters.com/about.

4 Vanguard's Facebook followers increased from 11,943 in February 2011 to 1,516,788 in October 2015. www.facebook.com/vanguardngr/. Its followers on Twitter equally increased from 3,384 in 2011 to 901,044 in October 2015 https://twitter.com/vanguardngrnews.

5 www.alexa.com/siteinfo/nairaland.com.

References

Adichie, Chimamanda (2011) 'A Nigerian revolution: the political awakening of my country's young people could transform Nigeria's rotten democracy'. *The Guardian* [London], 16 March. www.guardian.co.uk/commentisfree/2011/mar/16/nigerian-revolution-young-people-democracy.

Africapractice (2014) 'The social media landscape in Nigeria: the Who, the What and the Know'. www.africapractice.com/wp-content/uploads/2014/04/Africa-Practice-Social-Media-Landscape-Vol-1.pdf.

Agbaje, Adigun & Adejumobi, Said (2006) 'Do votes count? The travails of electoral politics in Nigeria'. *Africa Development*, 31(3): 25–44.

Akoh, Ben, Jagun, Abiodun, Odufuwa, Fola & Akanni, Akintunde (2012) *Mapping Digital Media in Nigeria: a Report by the Open Society Foundations*. London: Open Society Foundations.

Asuni, Judith B. & Farris, Jacqueline (2011) *Tracking Social Media: the Social Media Tracking Centre and the 2011 Nigerian Elections*. Abuja: Shehu Musa Yar'Adua Foundation.

Bimber, Bruce (1998) 'The internet and political mobilization: research note on the 1996 election season'. *Social Science Computer Review*, 16(4): 391–401.

Bode, Leticia (2012) 'Facebooking it to the polls: a study in social networking, social capital, and political behavior'. *Journal of Information Technology and Politics*, 9(4): 352–369.

Bode, Leticia, Vraga, Emily K., Borah, Porismita & Shah, Dhavan V. (2014) 'A new space for political behavior: political social networking and its democratic consequences'. *Journal of Computer-Mediated Communication*, 19: 414–429.

Boulianne, Shelley (2015) 'Social media use and participation: a meta-analysis of current research'. *Information, Communication & Society*, 18(5): 524–538.

Choi, Sujin (2014) 'The two-step flow of communication in Twitter-based public forums'. *Social Science Computer Review*, 33(6): 696–711.

COG (Commonwealth Observer Group) (2007) Report of the Commonwealth Observer Group, Nigeria State and Federal Elections, 14 and 21 April 2007. London: COG.

Coleman, Stephen & Hall, Nicola (2001) 'Spinning on the web: e-campaigning and beyond'. In Stephan Coleman (ed.), *Cyber Space Odyssey: the Internet in the UK Election*. London: Hansard Society.

Conroy, Meredith, Feezell, Jessica T. & Guerrero, Mario (2012) 'Facebook and political engagement: a study of online political group membership and offline political engagement'. *Computers in Human Behavior*, 28(5): 1535–1546.

Couldry, Nick (2015) 'The myth of "us": digital networks, political change and the production of collectivity'. *Information, Communication & Society*, 18(6): 608–626.

Dare, Sunday (2011) *The Rise of Citizen Journalism in Nigeria – a Case Study of Sahara Reporters*. Reuters Institute Fellowship Paper, University of Oxford.

DeSilver, Drew (2014) 'Facebook is a news source for many, but only incidentally'. Pew Research Center. www.pewresearch. org/fact-tank/2014/02/04/ facebook-is-a-news-source-for-many-but-only-incidentally/.

Dimitrova, Daniela V. & Bystrom, Dianne (2013) 'The effects of social media on political participation and candidate image evaluations in the 2012 Iowa caucuses'. *American Behavioral Scientist*, XX(X): 1–16.

Dudley, Billy (1973) *Instability and Political Order: Politics and Crisis in Nigeria*. Ibadan: Ibadan University Press.

Ekine, Sokari (2010) 'Use and abuse of social media in Nigerian elections'. www.newint.org/ blog/majority/2010/10/21/ use-and-abuse-of-social-media-in-nigerian-elections/.

Gil de Zuniga, Homero, Jung, Nakwon & Valenzuela, Sebastian (2012) 'Social media use for news and individuals' social capital, civic engagement and political participation'. *Journal of Computer-Mediated Communication*, 17: 319–336.

Gil de Zuniga, Homero, Molyneux, Logan & Zheng, Pei (2014) 'Social media, political expression, and political participation: panel analysis of lagged and concurrent relationships'. *Journal of Communication*, 64(4): 612–634.

Gladwell, Malcolm (2010) 'Small change: why the revolution will not be tweeted'. *New Yorker*. www.newyorker.com/ magazine/2010/10/04/small-change-malcolm-gladwell.

Hart, Christopher (1993) 'The Nigerian elections of 1983'. *Africa*, 63(3): 397–418.

Harwood, Asch & Campbell, John (2010) 'Opinion: text messaging as a weapon in Nigeria'. *Global Post*, September 22. www.globalpost. com/dispatch/africa/100916/ text-messaging-weapon-northern-nigeria.

Ibeanu, Okechukwu (2007) 'Simulating landslides: primitive accumulation of votes and the popular mandate in Nigeria'. In: Isaac O. Albert, Derrick Marco & Victor Adetula (eds.), *Perspectives on the 2003 Elections in Nigeria*. Abuja: IDASA-Nigeria.

Ibrahim, Jibrin & Garuba, Dauda (2008) *Governance and Institution-Building in Nigeria: a Study of the Independent*

National Electoral Commission (INEC). Dakar: CODESRIA.

INEC (Independent National Electoral Commission) (2014) INEC Activity Report 2011–2014. Abuja: INEC.

Jinadu, Adele L. (2011) 'Nigeria'. In: Ismaila M. Fall, Mathias Hounkpe, Adele L. Jinadu & Pascal Kambale (eds.), *Election Management Bodies in West Africa: a Comparative Study of the Contribution of Electoral Commissions to the Strengthening of Democracy*. Johannesburg: Open Society Foundations.

Katz, Elihu (1957) 'The two-step flow of communication: an up-to-date report on an hypothesis'. *Public Opinion Quarterly*, 21(1): 61–78.

Kuris, Gabriel (2012) 'Rebooting the system: technological reforms in Nigerian elections, 2010–2011'. Innovations for Successful Societies, Princeton University. https://successfulsocieties.princeton.edu/sites/successfulsocieties/files/Policy_Note_ID190.pdf.

Lazarsfeld, Paul F., Berelson, Bernard & Gaudet, Hazel (1948) *The People's Choice: How the Voter Makes Up His Mind in a Presidential Campaign*. New York: Columbia University Press.

Lewis, Peter (2003) 'Nigeria: elections in a fragile regime'. *Journal of Democracy*, 14(3): 131–144.

Lim, Merlyna (2012) 'Clicks, cabs, and coffee houses: social media and oppositional movements in Egypt, 2004–2011'. *Journal of Communication*, 62(2): 231–248.

Lim, Merlyna (2013) 'Many clicks but little sticks: social media activism in Indonesia'. *Journal of Contemporary Asia*, 43(4): 636–657.

McLeod, Jack M. et al. (1996) 'Community integration, local media use, and democratic processes'. *Communication Research*, 23(2): 179–209.

Murthy, Dhiraj (2015) 'Twitter and elections: are tweets, predictive, reactive, or a form of buzz?' *Information, Communication & Society*, 18(7): 816–831.

Norris, Pippa (2001) *Digital Divide: Civic Engagement, Information Poverty, and the Internet Worldwide*. Cambridge: Cambridge University Press.

Norris, Pippa & Curtice, John K. (2008) 'Getting the message out: a two-step model of the role of the internet in campaign communication flows during the 2005 British general election'. *Journal of Information Technology and Politics*, 4(4): 3–13.

Noveck, Beth S. (2000) 'Paradoxical partners: electronic communication and electronic democracy'. *Democratization*, 7(1): 18–35.

Orji, Nkwachukwu (2014) 'Nigeria's 2015 election in perspective'. *Africa Spectrum*, 49(3): 121–133.

Papacharissi, Zizi (2002) 'The virtual sphere: the internet as a public sphere'. *New Media & Society*, 4(1): 9–27.

Papacharissi, Zizi (2010) *A Private Sphere: Democracy in a Digital Age*. Cambridge: Polity Press.

Polat, Rabia K. (2005) 'The internet and political participation: exploring the explanatory links'. *European Journal of Communication*, 20(4): 435–459.

Project Swift Count (2011) *Project 2011 Swift Count's Final Report on Nigeria's April 2011 General Elections*. Abuja: Project Swift Count.

Putnam, Robert D. (2000) *Bowling Alone: the Collapse and Revival of American Community*. New York: Simon & Schuster.

Rosenstone, Steven J. & Hansen, John M. (1993) *Mobilization, Participation, and Democracy in America*. New York: Macmillan.

Shirky, Clay. (2008) *Here Comes Everybody: the Power of Organizing without Organizations.* London: Penguin.

Stremlau, Nicole & Price, Monroe E. (2009) *Media, Elections and Political Violence in Eastern Africa: towards a Comparative Framework.* London: University of Oxford Center for Global Communication Studies and Annenberg School for Communication, University of Pennsylvania.

Strydom, T.J. (2015) 'Facebook rakes in users in Nigeria and Kenya, eyes rest of Africa'. *Reuters,* 10 September. www.reuters.com/article/2015/09/10/us-facebook-africa-idUSKCN0RA17L20150910.

Suberu, Rotimi (2007) 'Nigeria's muddled elections'. *Journal of Democracy,* 18(4): 95–110.

Tang, Gary & Lee, Francis L.F. (2013) 'Facebook use and political participation: the impact of exposure to shared political information, connections with public political actors, and network structural heterogeneity'. *Social Science Computer Review,* 31(6): 763–773.

Tufekci, Zeynep & Wilson, Christopher (2012) 'Social media and the decision to participate in political protest: observations from Tahrir Square'. *Journal of Communication,* 62(2): 363–379.

Valenzuela, Sebastian (2013) 'Unpacking the use of social media for protest behavior: the roles of information, opinion expression, and activism'. *American Behavioral Scientist,* 57(7): 920–942.

Valenzuela, Sebastian, Park, Namsu & Kee, Kerk F. (2009) 'Is there social capital in a social network site?: Facebook use and college students' life satisfaction, trust, and participation'. *Journal of Computer-Mediated Communication,* 14: 875–901.

Vitak, Jessica et al. (2011) 'It's complicated: Facebook users' political participation in the 2008 election'. *Cyberpsychology, Behavior, and Social Networking,* 14(3): 107–114.

Ward, Stephen (2014) *Digital Media Ethics.* University of Wisconsin Centre for Journalism Ethics. https://ethics.journalism.wisc.edu/resources/digital-media-ethics/.

Ward, Stephen, Gibson, Rachel & Lusoli, Wainer (2003) 'Online participation and mobilisation in Britain: hype, hope and reality'. *Parliamentary Affairs,* 56: 652–668.

Weare, Christopher (2002) 'The internet and democracy: the causal links between technology and politics'. *International Journal of Public Administration,* 25(5), 659–691.

Xenos, Michael & Moy, Patricia (2007) 'Direct and differential effects of the internet on political and civic engagement'. *Journal of Communication,* 57(4): 704–718.

9 | FROM FM RADIO STATIONS TO INTERNET 2.0 OVERNIGHT

Information, participation and social media in post-failed coup Burundi

Jean-Benoît Falisse and Hugues Nkengurutse[1]

Introduction

The failed coup of 13 May 2015 led, overnight, to the quasi-destruction of independent media in Burundi. Ordinary citizens, journalists and politicians were left with few other options than turning to social media to gather information, voice their opinion and try and influence public life. In 24 hours, the battlefield of the information war between the regime of President Nkurunziza and the Burundian opposition and civil society switched from FM radios to social media (Vircoulon 2016). This paper considers this fast transition, the way citizens, journalists and politicians have navigated it, and the sort of public space it has contributed to building. In line with the literature on social media, it is argued that a new public space was, somewhat forcibly, opened (Mossberger, Tolbert & McNeal 2008). However, we also contend that this space is not necessarily more inclusive of ordinary citizens than the space available to citizens during the 'golden era' of Burundian FM radio stations (2005–2013). Although some platforms, in particular WhatsApp, are vital for the circulation of underground information and can act as an alert system, social media seems, overall, to be controlled by a minority of 'brokers' who partially overlap with the ruling regime.

This chapter contributes to the growing literature on social media in Burundi (Manirakiza 2015; Dimitrakopoulou & Boukala 2017; Frère 2017) and more generally in Africa (e.g. Mudhai, Tettey & Banda 2009; Paterson 2013) and in contexts of social and political instability (e.g. Howard et al., 2011; Kyriakopoulou 2011; Mäkinen & Kuira 2008) in two different ways. Firstly, where most previous studies discuss the general category of social media or one platform in particular, we develop a comparative approach to the three main platforms – WhatsApp, Facebook, and Twitter – and show how differences in the nature of the platform affect their use in a context marked by suspicion and limited political rights. This is especially important in a global context marked by what Miller et al. (2016) – who do not study African contexts – call 'polymedia': most people use a range of social media platforms for a range of purposes. Secondly, we analyse social media in relation to the evolution of traditional media. Contrary to previous studies, our aim is not to understand the evolution of journalism as a profession in Burundi (Frère 2016) but rather to explore the changing spaces where public opinion is expressed.

While we certainly agree with Karlsen (2015) that the main characteristic of social media is its network structure, we were also influenced by the seminal work of Katz & Lazarsfeld (1955) on the theory of the two-step flow of communication in mass media. The idea of 'opinion leaders' as central points in the functioning of communication flows, interpreting and relaying messages to members of their sphere of influence, seems particularly relevant in the case of Burundi. Beyond 'communities of interests', we approach social media as a battlefield, in which categories such as subscribers or followers must be treated with care (Castells 2015).

(Political) Social media is a question of collective action, and this paper is an attempt to map it. The analysis rests on a combination of different research methods. Being based in Burundi, one of the co-authors has observed and documented the mutation of Burundian media as it was happening. He also carried out a manual review of posts coming out of influential Twitter and Facebook accounts between July and December 2015. This first analysis was limited in scope but revealed hypotheses which we explored with three complementary approaches. Firstly, interviews; secondly, a review of secondary data on the use of social media such as the International Telecommunication Union (ITU), the Internet World Stats (IWS), and the World Bank; and thirdly, our own quantitative analysis of Twitter using MeCodify, an open-source code that is part of the Media Conflict and Democratization Project.[2] The choice of Twitter was guided by convenience: it is harder to generate the same type of analysis with Facebook, which has more privacy settings, and impossible with WhatsApp. To document practices on these two platforms, we relied on: (1) analysis of discussions on eight WhatsApp groups to which the Burundian co-author gained membership (four sympathetic to the ruling party and four to the opposition); (2) interviews with 32 members of such groups; and (3) analysis of the Facebook activity of nine Burundian public figures from the opposition, ruling party and civil society.

The rest of the chapter is structured as follows: the next section considers the events surrounding the sudden switch to social media and includes discussion of the spread of social media in Burundi. We then show how the ruling party quickly became one of the strongest players on Twitter and Facebook. Next, we continue with the exploration of how Twitter, Facebook and WhatsApp each constitute a different 'public' space. The last section reflects on the filtering of social media information by ordinary citizens.

The forced and rapid re-configuration of media in Burundi

In 2000, in Arusha, Tanzania, the Tutsi-dominated regime in place in Bujumbura signed a peace agreement with different Hutu rebel factions. It sought to bring an end to half a century of ethnic and regional tensions marked by coups (1966, 1976, 1989, 1996), massacres (1972, 1988, 1993), and an authoritarian monopolisation of power and resources by a small Tutsi elite. The tensions in the country had culminated into a bloody civil war that would only stop in 2008, after the main Hutu faction, the National Council for the Defence of Democracy – Forces for the Defence of Democracy (CNDD-FDD), won the 2005 election and the last rebel group, the Palipehutu-FNL, finally laid down their arms (Lemarchand 2009; Uvin 2009). The Arusha agreement contained provisions to increase freedom of press and expression in the country (Palmans 2005, 2006; Frère 2011, 2015b; Kane & Bizimana 2016). In stark contrast with the preceding decades, Burundi would soon become acclaimed in Africa and beyond as a model of peacebuilding and press freedom (Curtis 2012; Frère 2016). The mid-2000s saw the development of a high-quality media which worked at bringing the different ethnic and political groups together and prepared the population for socio-political changes such as the reintegration of the former rebels into the army and police corps. Authors such as Frère (2015a) and Tayeebwa (2017) argue that the media managed to 'de-ethnicise' interpersonal relationships around the country. In particular, FM radio stations set the pace of public life in a country where the electrification rate is still below 5 percent (Frère 2016). The RPA, *Radio Publique Africaine*, founded by soon-to-be opposition politician Alexis Sinduhije with the support of soon-to-be United States ambassador to the United Nations Samantha Power, exemplified a fresh and dynamic freedom of speech with radio shows giving ordinary people a chance to be heard and to discuss their opinions and experiences. RPA, and the independent FM radio stations in general, soon acquired the nickname 'the voice of the voiceless' (in French: *la voix des sans voix*). Until the events of May 2015, the most listened-to radio shows were, by a very large margin, news bulletins (INMAR 2014: 24). The reputation of RPA and Burundian media spread beyond the country, with Sinduhije featuring in the 2009 edition of the *Time* magazine annual list of the top 100 most influential people in the world.

By early 2015, as the country was preparing for its third post-civil war general election, the civil space had shrunk. A series of laws curbing individual and press freedoms were passed in 2013, including a piece of legislation forcing journalists to disclose their sources and forbidding news stories that could 'undermine national security' (Nshimirimana and Gatavu 2017). The relationship between the ruling party, the CNDD-FDD and the media had never been comfortable (Deslaurier 2007) but tensions had clearly picked up after the 2010 elections, which the opposition boycotted, and the International Crisis Group later called 'a logistical success but a political failure' (Vircoulon 2015). A CNDD-FDD Member of Parliament captured the mood of his party in those years when, in 2014, he called journalists 'nothing else than politicians' (MP Kekenwa, cited by *Iwacu* newspaper, 21 July 2014). Nevertheless, radio stations and, increasingly, TV stations, were still very popular and still broadcasting. Alongside the RTNB, *Radio-Television Nationale du Burundi*, eighteen local private radio stations and four local private TV channels were operating in Burundi by 2014. The same year, an estimated 96 percent of the population were regularly listening to the radio (INMAR 2014) and that figure was possibly growing, owing to the presence of FM receivers in the increasingly popular mobile (non-smart)phones. As Frère (2016: 144) points out, the situation in early 2015 was that two profoundly incompatible systems had evolved in parallel: while the media was becoming 'more independent, pluralist, and aware of their political function', the state was progressively turning into a military-dominated one-party system (see also Vandeginste 2015; Bouka 2017).

Access to the internet was still limited. Journalists used ICT in their work (Frère 2009) but the online presence – including on social media – of the mainstream media was minimal, with the notable exception of the website of the *Iwacu* weekly newspaper (a long-standing French-language publication with an in-print circulation that never exceeded 2,500 copies). Social media was limited to a small part of the population:

mostly the urban youth in a country that is the second least urban-ised in the world (The United Nations Population Division's World Urbanization Prospects 2016).[3] As of 31 December 2012, there were 41,900 Facebook users in Burundi for a population of around 10,395,000 (IWS). Neighbouring Rwanda, by contrast, with a pop-ulation only slightly larger, had almost five times more Facebook subscribers. In 2014, the World Bank estimated the penetration rate of the internet in Burundi to be at a mere 1.4 percent. Meanwhile, neighbouring Rwanda was at 10.6 percent (also see Figure 9.1 below). Manirakiza (2015) argues that, as they were experiencing a noticeable restriction of the public space, Burundians, especially those residing in the urban centres, nevertheless turned to social media in late 2014 and early 2015. This is consistent with our findings that the politicisation of social media was underway prior to the May 2015 unrest. However, it does not mean that there was a large change in terms of the amount of political activity on social media. In fact, Figure 9.1 below shows that, as far as Twitter is concerned, discussion of Burundi grew in the weeks rather than in the months before the 13 May coup attempt (which is the peak of over 6,000 tweets and retweets). Of course, this Twitter activity also includes global interest in a current event, but what is interesting is what has happened since, as a higher average level of Twitter activity has persisted.

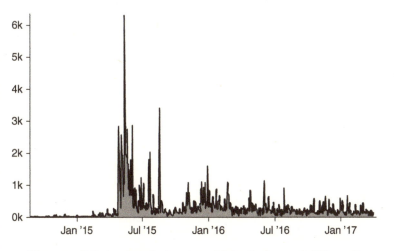

Figure 9.1 Daily tweets and retweets containing the keywords (#)Burundi [generated using MeCodify 3.10 (+ HighCharts.com)]

The foiled coup and its aftermath

On 25 April 2015, the CNDD-FDD national congress announced that the incumbent President of the Republic, Pierre Nkurunziza, had been designated as its candidate for the presidential election. Contesting the legality of a possible third mandate for Nkurunzia, protesters took to the streets of Bujumbura. In an attempt to prevent unrest from spreading farther, the regime shut down the RPA and some FM transmitters in the countryside and forbade the media from covering the demonstrations. On 13 May 2015, elements of the Burundian army rebelled against President Nkurunziza and staged a coup. They took control of Bujumbura city centre, and a crowd gathered in front of the RPA office. Armed clashes concentrated around media compounds: the coup plotters besieged the RTNB and burned down the privately owned and pro-government radio station Rema FM while unidentified individuals fired grenades into the offices of *Bonesha* FM, *Renaissance* Radio and Television, Radio *Isanganiro* and the RPA. These four radio stations had been more critical of the government and had relayed the civil society and opposition 'stop the third mandate' (*halte au troisième mandat*) campaign. The rebels never captured the RTNB and surrendered within a few hours. Nkurunziza went on to secure a third mandate in an election boycotted by most opposition parties, and which the international community refused to recognise as free and fair.[4]

At the time of writing this chapter, most independent Burundian TV and radio stations had not recovered from the events surrounding the failed coup. The regime initially closed all the radio stations damaged during the coup attempt, arguing that they had supported the coup plotters. On 19 February 2016, *Rema FM* and *Isanganiro* were authorised to reopen after signing an agreement with the government intended to 'prevent them from committing the same mistake that led the government to close them' (RPA 2016). With this agreement and a significant number of its former journalists in exile, *Isanganiro* lost its critical voice. The other three major independent broadcasters – RPA, *Bonesha* and *Renaissance* – remain closed as of 2018. Smaller radio stations still exist, but they have become cautious, focussing on entertainment and religion. In 2017, when a relatively unknown business-oriented radio station, CCIB FM+, ran a short segment on the massacre of Burundian refugees in DR Congo, the government closed it for three months. According to Amnesty International

(2015), the government remains hostile to journalists. They have to register with local authorities and work with a designated fixer when they leave Bujumbura. Some journalists have disappeared, and others have reportedly been harassed and blacklisted. As a consequence, as Frère points out in a recent article, 'Burundian journalists have lost self-confidence and trust in their ability to perform their professional ethos and the role they believe they should play in society'. They have moved from 'being powerful to being powerless' (Frère 2017: 3).

Against the background of a country that is becoming a de facto one-party state, the public RTNB has established a de facto quasi-monopoly on TV and radio broadcasting. Its senior management assumes an editorial line whose objective is to support the actions of the government. It gives a preponderant place to spokespersons of the regime. An inside source explained to us, in late 2015, that:

> the RTNB rarely reports evidence of insecurity; it only talks about illegal weapons 'seized' by the police and in most cases the population contests that the weapons were there in the first place. [...] When the population reports police violence to RTNB journalists, it never makes the news.

Migrating to the Internet and social media

As in other contexts of social unrest, such as Kenya during and shortly after the 2007 elections (Mäkinen & Kuira 2008) or Arab countries during the Arab Spring (Howard et al. 2011), the internet – and social media in particular – has become a refuge for the independent media and citizens of Burundi. It is a space that is a priori harder for the regime to control: Parks and Mukherjee (2017), who work on Zambia, explain how different tactics such as jumping between platforms and anonymity are used by journalists and citizens alike to continue to engage with sensitive topics. However, with a poorly educated population, the online written press was not very popular in Burundi in 2014. That year's INMAR survey estimated that only 39 percent of the population had read an article in a written medium in the previous year, and over 90 percent of the respondents were finding the written press too hard to understand. Social media, however, offers the possibility of more interactive channels. Journalists from the RPA and *Bonesha* FM exiled in Kigali have set up two web-radios: *Humura Burundi* and *Inzamba*. They collaborate with a third platform, *SOS*

Media Burundi, whose Burundi-based journalists are anonymous. The audio clips of *Humura Burundi* and *SOS Media Burundi* are shared via Facebook and Twitter accounts, and further circulated through WhatsApp. *Izamba* has had a dedicated website since 14 July 2015 but its Facebook page is also popular. An analysis of Google searches shows that the web-radios are now much more popular than the websites of the original radio stations. This forced 'migration' to social media has also meant a change of the sources of information that both journalists and citizens use. Journalists working for *Humura, Inzamba* and *SOS Media* acknowledge that, without access to the field, social media accounts have become their primary source of information. This is also the case for international media and researchers such as the *Armed Conflict Location & Event Data Project* (ACLED), probably the world's most ambitious attempt to collect micro-level data on violence, whose reporting on Burundi has become gradually more reliant on social media. At the level of citizens, the next section will show how the key providers of information in post-failed coup Burundi are now a set of social media influencers who are not necessarily coming from the traditional media.

As in other contexts, this 'migration' to social media replicates the greater exclusion from information of the many citizens who do not have access to the internet – 95 percent of the Burundi population in 2016 according to the ITU – and are often disproportionately rural and older. Whether the closure of independent media prompted people to seek access to the internet is a complicated question. Between the end of 2014 and the end of 2015, there was a remarkable growth in the number of internet users, from 1.38 to 4.87 percent of the population (ITU); mobile phone ownership increased from 0.32 to 0.49 per inhabitant (ITU); and the number of Facebook users rose from 0.66 percent of the population in 2012 to 5.97 by 15 November 2015 (IWS). Compared to other years, those relative changes are phenomenal and much higher than in the rest of the region. However, in terms of the more general evolution over the period 2009–2016, Burundi follows the regional trend and is not a regional leader. By 2016, the percentage of its inhabitants who had access to the internet remained a quarter of Rwanda's and a third of Tanzania's. As in other countries, the infrastructure has developed considerably, including since 2015, and the cost of accessing the internet has dropped as affordable plans allow unlimited 30-day use of WhatsApp and Facebook for US$ 1.87. In the words of the journalist and writer Roland Rugero (cited by Manirakiza 2015): 'with BIF 1,000 [US$ 0.67 at the time], the most loquacious of the Burundians can stay in contact with his friends during three full days [...]. Of course, one must "thank" Chinese manufacturers and their cheap handsets'. In fact, even the emergence of web-radios, or at least the use of digital devices to listen to radios, must be understood as part of a broader trend in Africa, including in contexts not marked by crises (Chiumbu & Ligaga 2013).

It is worth noting that the regime has so far tried to control, rather than shut down, social media. There are technical, economic and strategic explanations for this. Firstly, shutting down social media is not necessarily a very effective approach: when the government blocked WhatsApp in the early hours of the insurrection, a reportedly high number of people turned to virtual private networks (VPN) and carried on using WhatsApp. Secondly, and perhaps more importantly, even a short shut-down of the internet can have significant economic consequences, and especially so when telecom companies constitute a significant taxpayer in a gloomy economic context (see Howard, Agarwal and Hussain (2011) for an example from Egypt). Finally, and as we argue below, the regime is also trying to win the war of public opinion, domestically and abroad, and has learned to use social media for its own advantage – including to identify opponents and increase surveillance. Recent legal changes have made this surveillance easier. A law passed on 26 May 2015 imposes a 'single gateway for all incoming and outgoing telecom traffic from Burundi' (CIPESA 2016) and another law passed on 17 March 2016 prevents people from owning more than two SIM cards from the same operator and facilitates the government's access to data held by providers.

Towards a *less* inclusive and *less* democratic (social) media?

This section shows that, in Burundi, the 'migration' to social media has not necessarily meant the development of a more inclusive and participatory public space, contrary to what has been observed and theorised in other contexts (Ellison & Hardey 2014; Iosifidis & Wheeler 2016). We first consider the presence on Facebook and Twitter of traditional key actors of public life – politicians, journalists and activists – before turning to the use of Twitter, Facebook and WhatsApp in more detail.

The first key players in Burundian politics to invest in social media were journalists such as Antoine Kaburahe and civil society activists such as Pacifique Nininahazwe. This is not surprising given their international outlook and the increasing difficulties they were facing in accessing the physical public space in the early 2010s. What is perhaps more surprising is to find that the CNDD-FDD and President Nkurunziza already had their Twitter accounts created in early 2012, before most opposition politicians and journalists. Indeed, Rugero (2015) reports that, until 2014, it was common for the ruling party to demean journalists calling them *journaleux* (a pejorative term for a journalist) *de Facebook* or to tell them that 'votes are on the hills deep inside Burundi, not on the internet'. Willy Niyamitwe was probably instrumental in orchestrating the CNDD-FDD and the President's early adoption of social media. A brother of the Minister of Home Affairs and a former director at the pro-regime privately owned radio station *Rema FM*, he was a rebel during the civil war; and like the President, his father was killed during the 1972 massacres. He is the most vindictive face of the regime on social media and is suspected to have recruited an entire task force to work with him. Looking at his Twitter account (and the account of the presidency), Dimitrakopoulou and Boukala (2017) characterised his approach as an hegemonic struggle to legitimise and defend the regime. In fact, Niyamitwe's many Facebook and Twitter feuds with opposition politicians and activists may have motivated the unknown attackers who attempted to assassinate him in December 2016. A few months later, he was granted the title of ambassador (without being accredited to a specific country).

Judging by the number of subscribers and followers, the ruling party is a fundamental force on social media that is, even more so than at the beginning of the crisis, able to counter-attack, launch offensives and divert the debate when needed. The different institutions in Burundi now make full use of Twitter and Facebook. Nowadays, information usually goes to the official government accounts before being broadcast on national radio. Even the National Police gives its version of the facts in real time, further altering the balance of power between journalists and sources (Broersma & Graham 2012).

Twitter: a global discussion between a select few

Among the social media used in Burundi, Twitter is the most elitist. Its *lingua francae* are French – an official language which is spoken fluently by no more than 12 percent of the population[5] – and English, rather than the national language, Kirundi. Twitter's primary usage appears to be to directly address people and institutions outside of Burundi, including the diaspora, without intermediaries.

However, not every voice is heard the same way on Twitter. Looking at tweets using a series of Burundi-related keywords and hashtags[6] in the period May 2016 to May 2017, the activity seems concentrated in the hands of a few Twitter accounts. While more than 43,000 different Twitter accounts had used at least one of the keywords and hashtags, nearly 25 percent of the 268,387 tweets came from only twenty Twitter accounts – unsurprisingly, all appeared to be institutional accounts that are maintained by a team and are, therefore, able to produce a higher volume. The case of retweets, which give more indications about the quality of tweets and the attention they receive, is even clearer: of the close to 717,000 retweets, nearly 39 percent came from only twenty Twitter accounts. Seventy percent of the users who tweeted about Burundi never got retweeted, and almost one quarter were retweeted fewer than five times.

The rankings of the top-10 most retweeted and quoted Twitter users appears to have stabilised as the crisis became protracted. While between April and July 2015 Westerners topped the list, they disappeared in the May 2016 to May 2017 period. What is also clear, is that, with the exception of civil society activist Pacifique Nininahazwe, none of the current top influencers was a major public figure in Burundi before the crisis (Figure 9.2).

The influencers belong to different categories: (1) people or institutions closely associated with the ruling party – it is interesting to note that no opposition politician is in the top 20; (2) media outlets and journalists, including *SOS Media*, *Iwacu* newspaper and a journalist form RTNB; and (3) activists and bloggers who mostly seem to support the opposition. Opposition sympathisers often identify as *sindumuja* ('I am not a slave' in Kirundi) and are often based outside Burundi. They engage in Twitter wars with the supporters of the ruling party who usually identify as *imbonerakure* ('those who see far' in Kirundi), the youth wing of the ruling party.

The Burundian Twittersphere can be analysed as a series of campaigns largely addressed to the international community. #1212massacres raised awareness of the clashes between youth and the police on 21 December 2015 and the massacres that ensued; #freeourkids followed the imprisonment of schoolchildren accused of defacing the photo of President Nkurunziza in their schoolbooks,

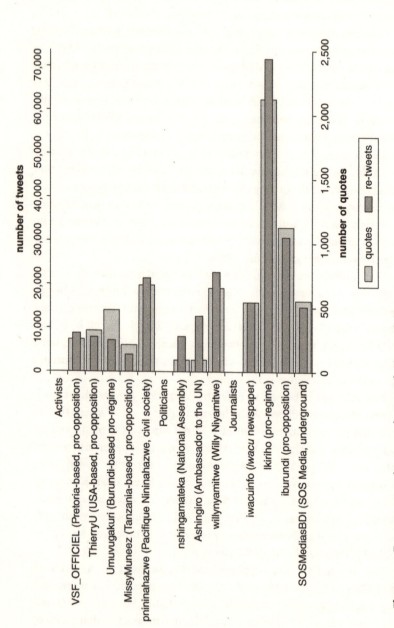

Figure 9.2 Top 10 tweeters (quotes and retweets), May 2016–May 2017

[data collected using MeCodify 3-10]

and even drew the attention of Nobel Peace Prize laureate Malala Yousafzai; #bringbackoursoldiers aimed to end Burundian involvement in peace missions (those missions are seen as a cash cow for the regime); and #ndondeza ('help me find') started in May 2016 and is used to bring international attention to cases of missing persons.

#burundigenocide is a good example of the dynamics of such Twitter campaigns. It started shortly after 3 November 2015, which is the day the President of the Senate was caught, off microphone, assuring Bujumbura local representatives that the police would 'work' in pro-opposition neighbourhoods. The vocabulary, bearing similarities to that used by Rwandan genocidaires (Kinyarwanda and Kirundi are part of the same dialect continuum), alarmed the International Federation for Human Rights, a Paris-based NGO. Together with an anti-regime Burundian news outlet (officially based in Harare), they started a long Twitter feud with Willy Nyamitwe and a news outlet which is generally favourable to the regime. These four accounts gathered over 25 percent of the retweets on the topic. Niyamitwe's attempt to counter-attack with the hashtag #thisismygenocide, in reference to the 1972 Hutu genocide, was not successful. The campaign, and especially the intense Twitter activity on chosen days, was clearly coordinated, seeking to influence the international community before important meetings. It may well have been successful, because the United Nations adopted a set of three resolutions condemning Burundi on 12 November 2015, 1 April 2016 and 29 July 2016 (United Nations Security Council 2015, 2016, 2016).

Facebook: encouraging extremisms?

Before the crisis, Facebook was perceived to be mostly for interacting with family and friends, including members of the diaspora. While informants described Twitter as a challenging exercise of communication, partly because of the language and the concise form, Facebook is seen as more popular and 'less intellectual', opening the possibility of longer political interventions in Kirundi.

The civil unrest in Bujumbura in early 2015 was a crucial moment in the politicisation of Burundian Facebook. The platform was reportedly used to mobilise the population to move from (the virtual) discussion to the physical occupation of the streets in defiance of the authorities. Rather than a purely spontaneous or contagious process, political mobilisation can be analysed as a 'communication strategy' to channel forces for joint action (Chazel & Touraine 1993; cited by Manirakiza, 2015). A process of identification of allies and stigmatisation of opponents prepared the descent from virtual space into the streets. For instance, the opponents of Nkrurunziza's third term defined themselves as the 'defenders of democracy', using the above-mentioned nickname, '*sindumuja*'. They are addressed as '*imijeri*' ('puny wandering dogs', a serious insult in Kirundi) by the pro-Nkurunziza camp, who portray themselves as the genuine guarantors of democracy.

As with other social media, Facebook is used as a vehicle for political manipulation through spreading rumours, fake documents and doctored photos. Tactics inspired by Burundian politics, such as the 'nyakurisation' – dividing of the opposition by creating 'truer' (Kirundi: *nyakuru*) splinter parties (Hirschy & Lafont 2015) – are also found on Facebook, where multiple and conflicting accounts of the same person or party are found. The curation of public profiles is also obvious: for instance, a new profile was created on 18 July 2017 for Agathon Rwasa, the leader of the FNL party who eventually joined the government. It contains no criticisms of the ruling party.

On Facebook, which is a less public space than Twitter, insidious strategies are developed that would not be tolerated in the traditional media. They include the revision of history or attempts to 'ethnicise' the crisis, such as portraying all opponents as Tutsi who want to usurp the power in the hands of the Hutu majority. The level of hatred and violence displayed on some Facebook pages, especially anonymous ones, is staggering and has repeatedly been denounced by Western countries and the United Nations (United Nations 2016). This may be due to the structure of Facebook, which 'allows multiple threads to continue in parallel and go unnoticed; creating longer lasting spaces where certain individuals and groups are offended, ridiculed and discriminated' (Gagliardone, Gal, Alves & Martinez 2015: 14). One possible explanation is that Facebook has become the new favourite venue of various extremists who, until recently, had mostly confined themselves to relatively obscure micro-blogging sites that Turner (2008: 1161) described as 'communities where [people] can express the unspeakable and float opinions that would never be acceptable in the political field'.

WhatsApp: people's battlefield?

Our informants suggest that WhatsApp is the most widespread social media in Burundi. It is both the primary source of 'raw' information and the main channel for circulating information, curated or not. Its popularity builds on its privacy features but also on its financial accessibility – it works on the most recent 'basic' phones – and the possibility to easily share pictures, videos, and especially sounds. These are fundamental in the context of a low command of written French, English and even Kirundi across the country.

As opinion makers on Facebook, Twitter and blogs recognise, it is on WhatsApp that much new information is found. In line with what Miller et al. (2016) describe in other contexts, in Burundi, WhatsApp is probably the platform where most social change occurs and most offline movements are prepared. During the insurrection in Bujumbura, WhatsApp was a key channel through which the inhabitants of the *quartiers contestataires* (the dissenting neighbourhoods) transmitted information about the movements of the police, the location of gunfire, and arrests, as well as images of those killed and injured. As in neighbouring DR Congo, WhatsApp was, and still is, used as an 'informal security network' (Tkach & Williams 2017). The keyword *tabariza tabariza* ('alert alert') is used to share urgent security-related information and pass it on to human rights groups. As one anonymous informant, who was arrested in the *quartier contestataire* of Musaga, explained:

> When I was arrested, a neighbour saw the plate of the police vehicle and recognised the officer who directed the operation. He even took the risk of taking a picture with his phone. WhatsApp groups relayed the information, and in a few hours, my family was contacted by human rights defenders. When I was with the intelligence services, the police complained about the coverage I was receiving on social media and that human rights defenders had details of my arrest and insisted on seeing me. I was eventually released. A policeman told me later that it would have been worse for me without this alert. (2 June 2016 (our translation from Kirundi))

The regime fully understands the importance of WhatsApp. The CIPESA 'State of Internet Freedom in Burundi 2016' report provides examples of arrests of citizens on the basis of belonging to a WhatsApp group that had spread 'rumours' and 'misleading information'. The regime seems to be monitoring users of some groups through informers, or at least it has been able to propagate that idea (CIPESA 2016). It is not uncommon to see the police, who are known across Burundi for their poor level of literacy among the rank and file, search through people's WhatsApp. Police spokesman Pierre Nkurikiye declared that WhatsApp newsgroups are often responsible for spreading fake news:

> This crime has been a source of chaos in the country, especially at the time of the insurgency. Many Burundians fled rumours and the false information that had been spread by these groups and also by some media. In reality, there was nothing. (RFI 2016 (our translation from French))

In the tense period of June to December 2015, on several occasions, all shops in the city centre of Bujumbura closed in the middle of the day following simple rumours circulated via WhatsApp. For instance, on 23 June 2015, a rumour circulated that elements of the army had come to town to capture the Army Headquarters and that they had asked people to empty their houses in anticipation of combat. In less than an hour, the city centre was empty. The attack never took place. It is hard to assess the exact source and intent of those rumours, but a possibility is that, in some cases, the rumour can help probe the reaction in case the event were true. After the assassination of Burundi's head of intelligence services, Adolphe Nshimirimana, on the morning of 2 August 2015, a rumour spread that veteran civil society activist Pierre Claver Mbonimpa had been assassinated in retaliation. Mbonimpa held a press conference denying his assassination. Two hours later, he barely survived a gun attack as he was returning home.

The crackdown on WhatsApp groups can also be understood as an attempt to further silence media that is critical of the regime. The news bulletins of *SOS Media*, *Inzamba* and *Humura* web-radios are primarily transmitted from group to group every night, as opposed to being directly sourced by people who are reluctant to take the risk of being caught accessing the web-based content of illegal radio stations. This may explain the relatively low number of official Facebook subscribers to *Humura Burundi* (63,490 by 1 February 2018) or *SOS Media Burundi* (45,585). Innocent Muhozi, the president of the NGO Burundian Press Observatory, contends that the police are not after rumours or defamatory remarks – they are after the listeners of the good quality web-radios – which are seen as more dangerous, claiming that 'there are hundreds of thousands of people who, every day, still find information through WhatsApp' (RFI 2016; our translation from French).

Finally, it is important to note that WhatsApp is also used by ruling party sympathisers to gather resources. Various groups use the platform when publicly donating money to the regime. For instance, on 6 November 2017 the group *Les Patriotes Abateramyi* donated BIF 417,000 (around US$237) towards the organisation of the 2020 elections.

Overall, the capture of Twitter by a few key players and the hate speech on Facebook suggest that the 'migration' to social media has not opened up a more inclusive public space. On the contrary, the type of (relatively) open public discussion that was taking place on radio, and which sometimes included the participation of ordinary citizens, was apparently pushed towards more private spaces. Such spaces, including WhatsApp, are occasionally infiltrated and not always considered safe enough to allow 'free' forms of speech.

Filtering information?

Tweets and posts on Facebook and WhatsApp blur the boundaries between facts, analysis, outright 'fake news' and opinions. The authenticity of information is hard to research beyond individual case studies, and it is, therefore, impossible to assess the net social benefit or nuisance of social media in Burundi: some posts are clear hate speech while others may save lives.

The sudden shutdown of the traditional independent media did cause an initial period of disarray characterised by intense rumours. As Turner (2005) points out in a pre-crisis article on rumour in Burundi, conspiracy theories and rumours may reinforce the ruling power, for they suggest that it has a 'hidden supplement' (2005: 37). The situation has, however, evolved and patterns of social media consumption have become established. Informants suggested to us that they have educated themselves to distinguish between credible sources and a lower class of information akin to a rumour. Repeated experiences are crucial parts of this process, but there are also some external signals that are used, such as the presence of photo or video. The most popular sources of information on Twitter and Facebook (judging by followers and shares) almost all have a physical or institutional face. They signal who has curated the information. Over time, anonymous accounts have gone out of the list of top tweeters.

As shown in the Twitter analysis, a large proportion of the key sources are not journalists; they are opinion makers who use social media to construct public opinion. They make a careful choice of facts and retain only those that are able to fix the attention of their audience. They, rather than the actual source or witness of the information, are the true 'citizen-journalists', for they are hugely influential in deciding what will become visible. Meanwhile, the job of the Burundian journalists, in exile or not, has changed from analysing primary material gathered in the field, often with first-hand knowledge of what the facts are, to perusing social media and assessing the authenticity of facts reported by sources they do not know personally.

The idea of 'impartial' news in public life has, mostly, been lost. The media regulator of Burundi sees its function as supporting the government, and independent news outlets that have gone under-ground or are located outside the country are a priori hostile towards the government. The idea of 'ethical news' is also under attack, on two levels. Firstly, numerous pictures and videos, including of violence and dead bodies, circulate without any concern for consent. Secondly, the partisan viewpoint of many news outlets has also meant that, often, the presumption of innocence is absent from news reporting.

Conclusion

In Burundi, the destruction of the independent media during and after the failed coup attempt of 13 May 2015 has come with an increase in the use of social media. Social media has been a refuge for independent media and has allowed civil society activists and oppo-sition politicians to continue to exist in the public space. However, contrary to what some of the literature on social media had hoped for (for example, Kyriakopoulou 2011), there is no evidence that social media has led to them initiating a dialogue with the regime. Nor has a space more inclusive of ordinary citizens been created: we found that Facebook and especially Twitter are dominated by a small number of actors – including a few journalists and spokespersons – who act as brokers or 'notaries of citizenship', as described by Manirakiza (2015). By sharing and tagging, commenting or posting to social networks, they influence and construct opinions and decide whose voices will be heard. What seems to be emerging and will need to be confirmed by further research is that only 'a minority of users can bridge the structural holes in the network' (González-Bailón & Wang 2016, p. 102). This is valid in the case of making one's tweet visible or in the case of linking different groups on Facebook and WhatsApp. It raises questions about the contacts and identity of social media users (Rane & Salem 2012) that this study could not explore in depth. Social media has become the main source of information for most, but it neither means that anybody can meaningfully and safely join, nor that facts are readily available for all in the public space. The chapter also suggests a 'polymedia' specific to the fragile context of Burundi. The dynamics of WhatsApp, Facebook and Twitter are quite different. WhatsApp in particular is less dominated by 'bosses' and is used as a warning mechanism and the prime channel for sharing – including to those with low levels of literacy – audio-form news segments from web-radios opposed to the regime.

As other authors before us, we also suggest that social media can be an escalating force (Meyer, Baden & Frère 2017), which narrows perspectives rather than widening viewpoints, and comes with a risk of versing into radicalism (Moyo 2012). Looking at cross-country data, Warren (2015) argues that, as opposed to traditional media, social media can substantially increase the risk of conflict because there are no 'economies of scale in the marketplace of ideas' (p. 298). This mechanism might be at play in Burundi where the intermediation of quality FM radio stations in generating a constructive debate has been lost. What is more, the shift to social media seems to have allowed radical elements to re-enter popular media.

More research is needed to fully comprehend the evolution of social media in Burundi and spaces of restricted freedom of press and expression. In particular, the network structure of the Burundian WhatsApp, which is the main platform, is still poorly understood. There is also a need for the exact influence and engagement of the diaspora and the refugee population to be explored further.

Notes

1 Both authors contributed equally to writing this chapter. Nkengurutse collected the qualitative data. Falisse collected the quantitative data.

2 http://mecodem.eu

3 Official statistics on their website https://population.un.org/wup/ (accessed 29 March 2019).

4 Frère (2016) provides a more comprehensive account of the coup attempt and its direct effect on Burundian media.

5 Burundi Census, 2008.

6 These included 'Burundi', 'burundicrisis', '1212massacres', 'burundigenocide', 'imbonerakure', 'ndondeza', 'sindumuja' and 'Nkurunziza', all of which were used with and without hashtags.

References

Amnesty International (2015) *Burundi: media clampdown intensifies after coup attempt.* www.amnesty. org/en/latest/news/2015/06/ burundi-media-clampdown- intensifies-after-coup-attempt/ (accessed 28 March 2019).

Bouka, Y. (2017) 'Burundi: between war and negative peace' In G.M. Khadiagala (ed.), *War and Peace in Africa's Great Lakes Region.* London: Palgrave Macmillan, pp. 17–31.

Broersma, M. & Graham, T. (2012) 'Social media as beat: tweets as a news source during the 2010 British and Dutch elections'. *Journalism Practice*, 6(3): 403–419.

Castells, M. (2015) *Networks of outrage and hope: social movements in the internet age.* Oxford: John Wiley & Sons.

Chazel, F. & Touraine, A. (1993) *Action collective et mouvements sociaux.* Paris: Presses Universitaires de France.

Chiumbu, S.H. & Ligaga, D. (2013) '"Communities of strangerhoods?": internet, mobile phones and the changing nature of radio cultures in South Africa'. *Telematics and Informatics*, 30(3): 242–251.

CIPESA (2016) *State of Internet Freedom in Burundi 2016: Charting Patterns in the Strategies African Governments Use to Stifle Citizens' Digital Rights.* Kampala: CIPESA - Open Net Initiative.

Curtis, D. (2012) 'The contested politics of peacebuilding in Africa'. In D. Curtis & G.A. Dzinesa (eds), *Peacebuilding, Power and Politics in Africa.* Athens: Ohio University Press, pp. 20–57.

Deslaurier, C. (2007) '"Et booooum!" Provocations médiatiques et commotions politiques au Burundi'. *Politique africaine*, 107(3): 167–187.

Dimitrakopoulou, D. & Boukala, S. (2017) 'Exploring democracy and violence in Burundi: a multi-methodical analysis of hegemonic discourses on Twitter'. *Media, War & Conflict*, 11(1): 125–148.

Ellison, N. & Hardey, M. (2014) 'Social media and local government: citizenship, consumption and democracy'. *Local Government Studies*, 40(1): 21–40.

Frère, M.-S. (2009) 'News media use of icts amidst war, violence, and political turmoil in the Central African Great Lakes'. In O. Mudhai, W. Tettey & F. Banda (eds), *African Media and the Digital Public Spheres.* New York: Palgrave Macmillan.

Frère, M.-S. (2011) 'Covering post-conflict elections: challenges for the media in Central Africa'. *Africa Spectrum*, 46(1): 3–32.

Frère, M.-S. (2015a) 'After the hate media'. *Global Media and Communication*, 5(3): 327–352.

Frère, M.-S. (2015b) 'Les médias, "chiens de garde" des élections au Burundi et en RDC?' *Afrique contemporaine*, 256(4): 119–138.

Frère, M.-S. (2016) 'Silencing the voice of the voiceless: the destruction of the independent broadcasting sector in Burundi'. *African Journalism Studies*, 37(1): 137–146.

Frère, M.-S. (2017) '"I wish I could be the journalist I was, but I currently cannot": experiencing the impossibility of journalism in burundi'. *Media, War and Conflict*, 10(1): 3–24.

Gagliardone, I., Gal, D., Alves, T. & Martinez, G. (2015) *Countering online hate speech.* Paris: Unesco Publishing.

González-Bailón, S. & Wang, N. (2016) 'Networked discontent: the anatomy of protest campaigns in social media'. *Social Networks*, 44: 95–104.

Hirschy, J. & Lafont, C. (2015) 'Esprit d'Arusha, es-tu là? La démocratie burundaise au risque des élections de 2015'. *Politique africaine*, 137(1): 169–189.

Howard, P.N., Agarwal, S.D. & Hussain, M.M. (2011) 'When do states disconnect their digital networks? Regime responses to the political uses of social media'. *Communication Review*, 14(3): 216–232.

Howard, P.N. et al. (2011) 'What was the role of social media during the Arab Spring ?', *Project on Information Technology and Political Islam* (Working Paper 2011.1), pp. 1–30.

INMAR (2014) *Etude d'auditoire au Burundi*. Bujumbura, Burundi.

Iosifidis, P. & Wheeler, M. (2016) *Public Spheres and Mediated Social Networks in the Western Context and Beyond*. Berlin: Springer, p. 296.

Kane, O. & Bizimana, A.J. (2016) 'Media-state relations in Burundi: overview of a post-traumatic media ecology'. *Communicatio*, 42(2): 155–169.

Karlsen, R. (2015) 'Followers are opinion leaders: the role of people in the flow of political communication on and beyond social networking sites'. *European Journal of Communication*, 30(3): 301–318.

Katz, E. & Lazarsfeld, P.F. (1955) *Personal Influence: the Part Played by People in the Flow of Mass Communications*. New York: Transaction Publisher.

Kyriakopoulou, K. (2011) 'Authoritarian states and internet social media: instruments of democratisation or instruments of control?' *Human Affairs*, 21(1): 18–26.

Lemarchand, R. (2009) *The Dynamics of Violence in Central Africa (National and Ethnic Conflict in the 21st Century)*. Phildelphia, PA: University of Pennsylvania Press.

Mäkinen, M. & Kuira, M.W. (2008) 'Social media and postelection crisis in Kenya'. *International Journal of Press/Politics*, 13(3): 328–335.

Manirakiza, D. (2015) 'Les nouveaux espaces de la contestation: Facebook, opinion publique et communication politique au Burundi'. Paper presented at the 2015 ECAS Conference.

Meyer, C.O., Baden, C. & Frère, M.-S. (2018) 'Navigating the complexities of media roles in conflict : the INFOCORE approach'. *Media, War & Conflict*, 11(1): 3–21.

Miller, D. et al. (2016) *How the World Changed Social Media*. London: UCL Press.

Mossberger, K., Tolbert, C. & McNeal, S. (2008) *Digital Citizenship: the Internet, Society and Participation*. Cambridge, MA: MIT Press.

Moyo, L. (2012) 'Blogging down a dictatorship: human rights, citizen journalists and the right to communicate in Zimbabwe'. *Journalism*, 12: 745–760.

Mudhai, O., Tettey, W. & Banda, F. (2009) *African Media and the Digital Public Sphere*. New York: Palgrave Macmillan.

Nshimirimana, V. & Gatavu, A. (2017) 'Freedom of assembly in Burundi: assessment of peaceful protests April–June 2015'. *International Journal of Not-for-Profit Law*, 12(19): 243–258.

Palmans, E. (2005) 'Les médias face au traumatisme électoral au Burundi'. *Politique africaine*, 91(1): 66–81.

Palmans, E. (2006) 'L'évolution de la societe civile au Burundi'. In F. Reyntjens & F. Marysse, *L'Afrique des Grands*

Lacs Annuaire 2005–2006. Paris: L'Harmattan, pp. 209–231.

Parks, L. & Mukherjee, R. (2017) From platform jumping to self-censorship: internet freedom, social media, and circumvention practices in Zambia. *Communication and Critical/ Cultural Studies*, 14(3): 221–237.

Paterson, C. (2013) 'Journalism and social media in the African context'. *Ecquid Novi: African Journalism Studies*, 54 (December): 37–41.

Rane, H. & Salem, S. (2012) 'Social media, social movements and the diffusion of ideas in the Arab uprisings'. *Journal of International Communication*, 18(1): 97–111.

RFI (2016) *Burundi: arrestation des membres d'un groupe de discussion WhatsApp.* www.rfi.fr/ afrique/20160824-burundi-arrestation-groupe-whatsapp-communication (accessed 28 March 2019).

RPA (2016) *Deux radios parmi lescinq détruites ont été réouvertes moyennant un acte d'engagement.* http://rpa.bi/index.php/2011-08-15-07-10-58/societe/item/2100- (accessed 28 March 2019).

Rugero, R. (2015) 'Burundi: comment on s'apprête à compaoriser Nkurunziza' *Iwacu*, 9 March.

Tayeebwa, W. (2017) 'From conventional towards new frames of peace journalism: the cases of Uganda and Burundi'. In Lumumba-Kasongo and Gahama, J. (eds.), *Peace, Security and Post-conflict Reconstruction in the Great Lakes Region of Africa.* Dakar: CODESIRA, pp. 209–236.

Tkach, B. & Williams, A.A. (2017) 'Mobile (in)security? Exploring the realities of mobile phone use in conflict areas'. *Information Communication and Society*, 21(11): 1639–1654.

Turner, S. (2005) '"The Tutsi are afraid we will discover their secrets" – On secrecy and sovereign power in Burundi'. *Social Identities*, 11(1): 37–54.

Turner, S. (2008) 'Cyberwars of words: expressing the unspeakable in Burundi's Diaspora'. *Journal of Ethnic and Migration Studies*, 34(7): 1161–1180.

United Nations (2016) *Burundi : un responsable de l'ONU appelle à mettre fin aux discours incendiaires.* www.un.org/apps/newsFr/storyF.asp?NewsID=37917#.WnxC1Oco82y (accessed 28 March 2019).

United Nations Security Council (2015) *Resolution 2248 (12 November 2015),* S/RES/2248.

United Nations Security Council (2016) *Resolution 2279 (1 April 2016),* S/RES/2279.

United Nations Security Council (2016) *Resolution 2303 (29 July 2016),* S/RES/2303.

Uvin, P. (2009) *Life after Violence: a People's Story of Burundi.* London: Zed Books.

Vandeginste, S. (2015) 'Briefing: Burundi's electoral crisis – back to power-sharing politics as –usual?' *African Affairs*, 114(457): 624–636.

Vircoulon, T. (2015) Burundi: How to Deconstruct Peace, IPI Global Observatory. http:// theglobalobservatory.org/2015/11/burundi-nkurunziza-peacebuilding-united-nations-rwanda-genocide/ (accessed 28 March 2019).

Vircoulon, T. (2016) 'Burundi turns to whatsapp as political turmoil brings media blackout'. *The Guardian* 14 June. www.theguardian.com/global-development/2016/jun/14/burundi-turns-to-whatsapp-as-political-turmoil-brings-media-blackout (accessed 28 March 2019).

Warren, T.C. (2015) 'Explosive connections? Mass media, social media, and the geography of collective violence in African states'. *Journal of Peace Research*, 52(3): 297–311.

10 | CYBERCRIME AND THE POLICING OF POLITICS IN TANZANIA

Charlotte Cross

Introduction

In many African countries, increased use of social media in party political campaigning, organisation of protest and the dissemination of news has been met with attempts to police digital communication. Often justified as necessary to ensure peace and security and to prevent the dissemination of 'false' information, governments have employed a range of measures to restrict access to social media and what can be shared online. In some countries, including Cameroon, Ethiopia, The Gambia and Uganda in 2016 and 2017, mobile phone operators have been ordered to block access to the entire internet or to specific social media platforms at politically sensitive periods, such as during elections or periods of prolonged protest. Elsewhere the arrest of journalists and others for 'misuse' of social media platforms, and new legislation that creates restrictions on what can be shared online, have generated concerns about freedom of expression.[1]

This chapter draws on interviews with police officers and local government officials conducted in Dar es Salaam and Mwanza (September 2016–January 2018) alongside media sources to explore the policing of social media in Tanzania. It argues that understanding the impact of increased social media use on politics in Africa requires consideration of the ways in which policing and politics are connected. Policing of social media use and content can be seen as part of a long history of police involvement in politics in Tanzania and elsewhere in the region. The relationship between African police forces and political change has received less attention than that of African militaries, whose interventions have often taken the more dramatic form of military coups. However, the police exercise significant influence over political life and who can participate in it, as they may be given authority to regulate political activities such as meetings, protests and campaigns, and they exercise discretion over using their powers of arrest and detention (Hills 1996: 273).

Policing can be understood as the implementation of techniques intended to ensure security to subjects (Johnston 1999). Whilst this may include protecting citizens from violence and other threats, a dual definition of security takes into account both this 'demand side', whereby security is an entitlement of citizens, and a 'supply side'. From this perspective, security is also 'a process of political and social ordering, maintained through authoritative discourses and practices of power' (Luckham & Kirk 2012: 10). Thus, the privileged claims police make to determine what constitutes security and threats to it are political actions that shape and are shaped by the wider political landscape. In Tanzania, as in many other post-colonial African contexts, the police have historically been valued more by leaders for this latter role as enforcers of political decisions and maintainers of a particular order, than for providing an effective public service (Hills 2007: 407).

As social media use increases, police forces across Africa are grappling with how to police online spaces. Whilst there are significant challenges related to protecting citizens from new threats such as online theft, in many contexts, including Tanzania, interpretations of what constitutes 'cybercrime' have been influenced by political calculations. The consequences of this in the Tanzanian case are explored below. However, the chapter concludes by considering the difficulties of applying to social media the politically partisan policing practices that characterise offline policing. Limited police capacity, difficulties in regulating communication that transcends national borders, and the way in which social media enables influential users to undermine police narratives and challenge police engagement in politics are potentially significant obstacles for police and governments seeking to restrict political debate and control access to information.

Policing politics in Tanzania

Partisan policing of political debate and other political activities, affecting opposition parties and supporters, civil society organisations and media outlets, has underpinned the electoral dominance of Tanzania's ruling party, *Chama Cha Mapinduzi* (CCM), since the 1960s. The Tanzania Police Force (TPF), like other sectors of the administration, was closely tied to the ruling party during Tanzania's twenty-six years as a one-party state. The retention of colonial legislation enabled the police to play a role in suppressing potential opposition to CCM and police were used to violently uphold public order and ensure implementation of government policy (CHRI 2006; Ingle 1972: 202–203; Shivji 1990, 2001).

Tanzania's return to multiparty politics in 1992 did not lead to significant changes to legislation or other regulations governing the operation of the TPF. The Inspector General of Police is a presidential appointee, as are Regional Commissioners, who are empowered to order police to arrest individuals deemed 'likely to commit a breach of the peace or disturb the public tranquillity' (Regional Administration Act 1997). During general and local elections since the reintroduction of multiparty competition in 1992, election laws have been enforced in a discriminatory manner favouring the ruling party (Ewald 2011; Ewald & Wohlgemuth 2012; Hoffman & Robinson 2009; LHRC & ZLSC 2017). Police permits, required for any public assembly, are often denied to opposition parties at very short notice, with little explanation or with only reference to confidential 'intelligence reports' claiming a threat to peace (LHRC n.d.). Policing of political meetings, demonstrations and voting is often violent, particularly in Zanzibar where opposition to CCM has historically been stronger (FIDH and LHRC 2001). On the mainland, as opposition parties have gained greater support in recent years, arbitrary use of force by police during protests and political rallies has resulted in fatalities (LHRC and ZLSC 2013, 2014). Journalists are vulnerable to harassment and arrest by police (LHRC and ZLSC 2014).

In October 2015, CCM's candidate, John Pombe Magufuli, won the most recent presidential election and CCM retained a parliamentary majority. The contest was the closest in Tanzania's electoral history, with the former Prime Minister, Edward Lowassa, winning 40 per cent of the vote for the opposition coalition, Ukawa.[2] The apparent threat to CCM's dominance precipitated a shift to more overt forms of political repression (Paget 2017). Attempts to police how opposition parties communicate with voters intensified, underpinned, firstly, by claims that security is at risk. The police exercise a privileged role in determining what constitutes a threat to security and deciding upon a subsequent course of action. In the words of Tanzania's Attorney General, '...once the police force says something related to security issues, everyone should comply' (quoted in Lamtey 2016). Thus, in addition to preventing gatherings on security grounds, numerous charges of sedition have been levelled against politicians and journalists. Secondly, claims that information is 'false' have been evoked to legitimise closing media outlets and prosecuting politicians and other dissenting voices. Whilst these claims are also linked to fears for Tanzania's record of relative peace in the region, criminal defamation laws and legislative restrictions on use of 'abusive language' enable police to justify action taken against those who make 'false' critical statements against the government.

Compounding previous restrictions on political assemblies, a police ban on all political rallies was imposed in June 2016 on security grounds. Two months later, following opposition plans to hold mass demonstrations under the slogan UKUTA (*Umoja wa Kumpanbana na Udikteta*, Alliance to Combat Dictatorship), this prohibition was extended to include internal political party meetings. UKUTA protests were cancelled amidst fears of clashes with security forces, and the ban was subsequently relaxed to permit internal meetings and enable Members of Parliament (MPs) to hold and attend rallies in their own constituencies only.

Arrests of opposition politicians proliferated in 2016–2018. At least twenty-three MPs affiliated to the largest opposition party, Chadema, and the leader of a smaller party, ACT Wazalendo, were arrested during this period – some on multiple occasions. Chadema-affiliated elected representatives at lower levels and volunteers and party officials have also been seized by police. The majority of these cases constitute attempts to control how politicians communicate with the electorate and what they say, including accusations that they have held unlawful assemblies or participated in political meetings outside of their constituencies, and charges of sedition or use of 'abusive language' including, in the case of one Chadema MP, 'insulting' the President in a manner likely to cause a breach of peace (Kapama 2017). MP and Chadema's chief legal advisor Tundu Lissu alone faced five sedition cases during this period, including one charge related to allegedly referring to Magufuli as a petty dictator (*The Citizen* 2016).[3] Some arrests of MPs and local politicians were ordered by Regional and District Commissioners, who appear to be using their powers to order police seizures more frequently under the Magufuli regime to target both elected politicians and underperforming government staff.[4] Police have also intervened in the policing of parliament, by arresting and delivering MPs to the parliament building to appear before its own ethics committee over statements they have made criticising the Speaker, which have been deemed false, offensive or likely to incite hostility against the government (Kiango 2017).

Many arrests of opposition MPs and others do not result in prosecution. Arrests are to some extent an end in themselves, whereby the purpose is not to enforce the law, but to harass the opposition and frustrate their activities. Being arrested is time consuming, particularly when those detained are denied bail and must remain in remand prison for long periods, and expensive, even when charges are not brought (Ewald and Wohlgemuth 2012). This poses particular difficulties for smaller parties and elected politicians or party officials at lower levels of government.

Media legislation gives ministers and police considerable discretion in determining what can be reported, what may threaten national security and what is 'true'. The Media Services Act (2016), for example, prohibits publication of 'any false statement, rumour or report which is likely to cause fear and alarm'. Government controls on the media are enforced through suspensions of major newspapers and radio stations. In the period between August 2016 and November 2017, eleven newspapers, radio stations and television stations were suspended, for periods of up to two years, as a result of publishing content that was either deemed likely to incite hostility against the government or contained false or misleading statistical information, even when this was subsequently corrected. When commenting on media reporting of 'inflammatory' material (*mambo ya uchochezi*), the President noted 'I am telling owners of media outlets, be careful, watch it, if you think you have that kind of freedom: not to that extent'[5] (quoted in Voice of America 2017). Public access to political information was further reduced by the government decision in February 2016 to halt live broadcasting of parliament.

Policing politics online

Although internet users remain a minority in Tanzania (Research ICT Africa 2017), social media has emerged as a new front in the policing of politics. Indeed, 'the majority of complaints [the Tanzania Communications Regulatory Authority (TCRA)] receive[s] about cybercrime come from politicians'.[6] This section explores government and police attempts to extend existing strategies for controlling political debate into online spaces, by criminalising online dissent and content that challenges government narratives about Tanzanian development, whilst encouraging self-censorship through threats to social media users and introducing expensive registration procedures for those who wish to share online content. Tanzania is not unique in Africa or beyond in trying to minimise the potential for new modes of communication to bolster the political opposition. Similar strategies to those adopted in Tanzania have been pursued in countries including the Democratic Republic of Congo, Kenya, Uganda and Zambia (CIPESA 2018). Indeed, developments in Tanzania could be seen as part of a global rise in 'digital authoritarianism' (Shahbaz 2018) and increasing evidence that expansion of internet access is not necessarily a threat to authoritarian regimes (Kalathil and Boas 2003).

It is clear that widespread social media use does pose difficult security dilemmas for African governments. Rumours and hate speech which are spread over social media are reportedly fuelling ongoing conflict in the region in Burundi and South Sudan (LeRiche 2016; Vircoulon 2016), and Kenya's 2017 elections have illustrated the political importance of 'fake news' (Portland 2017). Al Shabaab has an active online presence (see Menkhaus 2014), leading to concerns about the group's use of social media for communication and recruitment in eastern Africa (IGAD 2016). Cybercrime has grown alongside the expansion of information and communications technologies in the region, costing Tanzania an estimated $85 million in 2016 (Serianu 2016). However, police engagement with social media to date suggests that cyber security strategies are more closely informed by Luckham and Kirk's (2012) 'supply side' understanding of security as part of processes of political and social ordering, as the designation of some social media use as cybercrime has been informed by a desire to preserve existing political power structures.

Social media use has the potential to disrupt and undermine existing restrictions on communication between politicians and the electorate and on the dissemination of information that is not authorised by the government. As elsewhere in the region, a range of social media platforms have been enthusiastically embraced by political parties, major established news outlets and alternatives such as blogs, and by individuals. The impact of increased social media use on political campaigning and political journalism was apparent during general elections held in 2015. WhatsApp, due to its appeal across demographic groups and accessibility, being pre-installed on many phones, was particularly important to political parties in reaching supporters and potential voters. As many users are members of multiple large WhatsApp groups, messages, often containing negative information about rival candidates, spread rapidly (Mohammed 2015). Party youth wings, which have in the past provided security at rallies, are now also deployed online to defend their parties' reputations (Kolumbia 2016).

Outside of election periods, politicians are making use of and monitoring social media. For example, opposition MP Zitto Kabwe, an early adopter of Twitter among Tanzanian parliamentarians, credits the platform with increasing pressure on the government to respond to a motion of no confidence he had tabled against the Prime Minister in 2012, who subsequently resigned whilst eight other ministers were sacked (Kabwe 2012). More recently, Chadema MPs have taken videos on their phones from within parliament to be disseminated by WhatsApp, in order to subvert the restrictions on live coverage of parliamentary procedure noted above, and alleged bias in the edited highlights produced by the national broadcaster, Tanzania Broadcasting Corporation. In addition to planning nationwide demonstrations, party youth wings can threaten major social media campaigns, as Chadema's did, for example, in 2017 in response to perceived police inaction over corruption allegations (Lamtey 2017). Social media also facilitates whistleblowing, and several major corruption scandals have come to light through Tanzania's largest online discussion site, Jamii Forums. In a growing number of cases, content posted online has provoked government into taking action to protect citizens' rights (see Buguzi 2016).

However, content shared on social media has also been subject to similar measures to those applied offline that appear to threaten freedom of expression. Existing legislation that outlaws sedition and sharing 'false' information has been applied to social media communication, including the Electronic and Postal Communications Act (2010) and the new Media Services Act (2016). In 2015, two new pieces of legislation were introduced, which extend the powers of the police to regulate what is said online. A Cybercrimes Act (2015), was signed into law by President Magufuli's predecessor, Jakaya Kikwete. The Act contains provisions addressing significant challenges such as child pornography, cyber bullying and computer fraud. However, the implementation of the law to date appears to vindicate concerns voiced by journalists, opposition MPs, human rights advocates and aid donors that the legislation would be used to limit freedom of expression.[7] For example, the Act prohibits the dissemination of information that is 'false, deceptive, misleading or inaccurate' or with intent to 'defame, threaten, abuse, insult', imposing a significant fine or a prison term of at least six months, with no maximum limit. It also gives police powers to seize electronic equipment without a court warrant. Similarly, the Statistics Act, also introduced in 2015, prohibits publication of 'false' statistical information and sharing of official statistical information in a way that may lead to the 'distortion of facts', imposing unlimited penalties with a minimum of three years' imprisonment or a fine of ten million Tanzanian shillings (4,451 USD).

Both pre-existing legislation and that pertaining specifically to online communication have been used to charge those who criticise the government on social media, including on public forums such as YouTube, in messages to WhatsApp groups, and in personal Facebook posts. At least seventeen people have been arrested over critical comments made about the President, including a musician and producer who posted a music video for their song '*Dikteta Uchwara*' ('Petty Dictator') on YouTube, and others who shared memes showing doctored images of Magufuli within WhatsApp groups. 'Insulting' or 'mocking' the police and the TCRA has also resulted in charges being brought. The penalties for those convicted are very severe. One man convicted of insulting President Magufuli was sentenced to two years in jail without the option of a fine and others have been denied bail on grounds of possible injury to the 'victim' of their posts and the risk they will tamper with evidence, resulting in long periods of time in remand prison before their case is tried (*Guardian* reporter 2017). Echoing the President's warning to media owners that they should not overestimate their freedom, Zanzibar's Deputy Director of Criminal Investigation has warned, 'It is unfortunate that some people think that freedom of expression includes using abusive language against leaders' (quoted in Yussuf 2016).

'Insulting' leaders is of concern to police in part because of its perceived potential to catalyse collective mobilisation against the government. Online criticism of leaders is often represented as having the potential to incite protest or inflame tensions between Tanzanians, meaning, as a senior police officer in Mwanza Region explained, 'If you insult the President, it is a matter of security' (interview, January 2018). Thus, attempts to limit dissent on social media are justified with reference to the importance of preserving security, as is the case when the TPF prevent meetings and demonstrations. Tanzania retains colonial-era sedition offences, which are susceptible to very wide interpretation (LHRC and ZSLC 2017). Charges of incitement of hostility against the government or to violence have frequently been levelled against opposition politicians over criticism of the government they have voiced both off- and online. In August 2016, for example, when the opposition coalition planned major nationwide demonstrations to protest against what they described as moves towards dictatorship in Tanzania, charges were brought against Chadema officials, supporters and one MP, Godbless Lema, for incitement on social media after they encouraged people to protest. The Regional Police Commissioner for Singida reportedly discussed with the TCRA whether it was possible to close all of local MP Tundu Lissu's social media accounts to prevent him from sharing 'inflammatory' statements (*uchochezi*) (Dar 24 2016), and the leader of opposition party ACT Wazalendo, Zitto Kabwe, was threatened by the Speaker with a ban from parliament over his contin-ued allegedly inflammatory use of social media (Mwangonde 2017).

Allegations of sharing 'fake news' (*habari za uzushi* or *taarifa za uongo*) have also been levelled to preserve government control of politi-cal debate, enabled by the false and misleading information clauses in the Media Services, Cybercrime and Statistics Acts.[8] Those arrested on this basis include thirty-six staff and volunteers working for the Tanzania Civil Society Consortium on Election Observation who were accused of publishing false information during the 2015 general elec-tion count when they were monitoring the election process, as well as volunteers for Chadema who shared provisional results over WhatsApp (CIPESA 2016: 4). In November 2017, Zitto Kabwe was charged under the Statistics and Cybercrimes Acts for querying buoyant offi-cial national economic growth figures in analysis of other government financial statistics he shared on his Facebook page. Local police in Mwanza also reported receiving false statements over the phone, 'espe-cially during the periods when they are having political rallies'.[9] It is not only national elections that provoke contestation over the truth of mate-rial disseminated electronically to the electorate. One local government chairperson representing CCM who successfully defended his post in a 2015 local election, for example, recounted that a defeated competitor from an opposition party had sent a mass SMS to local residents accus-ing him of adultery. The chairperson pursued a criminal case in court and the perpetrator was subsequently sentenced to spend six months in prison or pay a fine of 150,000 Tanzanian Shillings (67 USD).[10]

Whilst these prosecutions for content shared on social media relate to use of the major global platforms WhatsApp and Facebook, perhaps the site that most preoccupies the TPF is Tanzanian site Jamii Forums, the country's most popular online discussion forum, with over 418,000 members, who post under anonymous user profiles, and over 2,800,000 followers on Facebook. The site has been instrumental in revealing several major corruption scandals affecting the upper echelons of government as it is sometimes used as an arena for whistleblowing. In an attempt to prevent anonymous posting, the site's founders were charged under the Cybercrimes Act for refusing to reveal the identity of those users who are accused by police of committing cybercrime. The government has also sought to extend regulation of media outlets to incorporate individual social media users through the introduction of a registration system for 'bloggers' with an extortionate annual fee (Electronic and Postal Communications Act (Online Content) Regulations, 2017). Similar legislation has been introduced in the Democratic Republic of Congo and Zambia (CIPESA 2018) as well as countries including Russia, Egypt and Cambodia (Shahbaz 2018).

Public statements made by police and awareness campaigns run by the TCRA suggest that the main threat posed by cybercrime to Tanzanian citizens is not that they may become a *victim* of such crime, but that they may become a perpetrator. In introducing a TCRA campaign, for example, the Acting Director General noted, 'The Campaign has come at a time when the Cybercrimes Act 2015 is operational yet many people are still unaware of how to avoid getting into the trap' (quoted in Zacharia and Tesha 2016). Indeed, in government-owned media, the word 'victim' is used to describe those who have been prosecuted for committing cybercrime.[11] The objective of educating people about cybercrime is thus to reduce offences committed, rather than to enable citizens to protect themselves online.

To some extent, the increased use of social media within Tanzanian politics enables police to identify and act upon political dissent over a wider geographic area and offers access to new spheres of political activity, beyond formal meetings, rallies and election campaigns. Individuals who are not directly connected to political parties are much more likely to be affected as their everyday communications about politics are more visible when shared online. Offline, TPF capacity to detect criminal activity and respond to reported crime is constrained by severe shortages of resources and personnel. This is not only the case in rural areas distant from important economic and political sites, but also in the sprawling informal settlements that make up the majority of the country's largest cities. The ability to conduct 'online patrols' of sites that are publicly available, such as Instagram and Jamii Forums,[12] however, offers a relatively easy and cost-effective way to monitor political activities and demonstrate 'success' in dealing with cybercrime.

In much of Tanzania, neighbourhood crime, including alleged defamation or other disputes, is largely delegated to community policing groups organised by local government committees, and citizens often require a letter of introduction from their local government chair before reporting crime to the police (Cross 2014, 2016). Policing social media enables police to take a more proactive approach and to use their discretion to pursue alleged offenders even where no complaint has been made about their actions. Frequent threats to this effect are made to social media users, warning of police surveillance and cultivating a sense of uncertainty around the technological capacity of police to view online communications and identify internet users. Regarding a rumour that suggested police involvement in the shooting of an opposition politician, Tundu Lissu, in September 2017, for example, a police spokesperson warned, 'If you know that you posted any comment about this come yourself [to the Criminal Investigation Department] before you are sought out. We have our ways of being able to find [those who posted]' (quoted in Edward & Adrian 2017).[13] The Cybercrimes Act provides for the use of electronic evidence in prosecutions, which also expands the timeframe over which police can pursue critics of the government. Another police spokesperson, for example, warned those who 'misuse' the internet, 'Whoever is involved in these criminal acts should not think that they are safe; we will arrest them even if they committed offences years back... the long arm of the law will soon catch up with them' (quoted by *Daily News* reporter 2015).

Challenges of policing social media

This chapter has outlined attempts by the TPF to extend the partisan policing of politics, which has a long history in Tanzania, into digital spaces of political communication. However, policing social media poses some particular challenges for law enforcement, and it is not always straightforward to translate strategies that are used offline into an online environment.

Firstly, although internet users are a minority of Tanzanians, monitoring all social media communications, even just those that are publicly available, is a significant task that is likely currently beyond the capacity of the TPF. Officers acknowledge that police resources are limited and that they require additional technical support and equipment, including computers, to deal with cybercrime.[14]

It is difficult to establish the extent of digital surveillance in Tanzania. It is clear that technology obtained from China as well as European and Israeli firms has been employed by African governments, and most comprehensively by Ethiopia, to monitor political opponents (Marczak et al. 2017; Gagliardone, Stremlau & Aynekulu 2018), and the Tanzanian security services reportedly do use Israeli technology to conduct targeted surveillance of individuals (Quintal 2018). However, police concerns about 'cybercrime' extend beyond high-profile individuals to 'ordinary' social media users and very localised dynamics of political competition. Measures such as compulsory registration for bloggers and threats made to social media users collectively and individually may encourage self-censorship to some extent. However, the Tanzanian government has not established a comprehensive system of social media surveillance and censorship, such as that operating in China, where material that is deemed problematic is rapidly identified and removed (King, Pan & Roberts 2013), and does not engage in routine internet filtering as is the case in Ethiopia (Human Rights Watch 2014). This means that police are obliged to identify and react to specific examples of social media 'misuse' and to arrest and prosecute individuals.

When 'illegal' content is published in offline print media or disseminated over radio, total suspensions of the media outlet concerned are ordered. However, blocking Facebook or WhatsApp would require the cooperation of mobile phone operators, would be likely to attract significant international attention, and may in any case be ineffective as virtual private networks (VPNs) have been used in other countries in the region to subvert government-imposed shutdowns. When problematic material is posted on social media, therefore, individuals must be pursued, which is time consuming and also difficult in cases when social media communication is shared within closed groups and cannot be accessed through online patrols. Successful prosecutions have been brought over messages sent to groups via WhatsApp; however, identifying offences on platforms like this depends upon a police officer being a member of a group to which messages are sent or another member reporting misconduct. Although police have warned administrators of

WhatsApp groups that they are responsible for reporting 'crimes' that are committed by other members (Edward 2017), it is not clear that this will have any impact on crime-reporting behaviour. Thus, when policing cybercrime, as in other areas of police work in Tanzania and elsewhere in Africa, relatively 'informal' modes of everyday surveillance dependent upon inter-personal relationships remain important (Göpfert 2016; Purdeková 2016).

Secondly, the transnational nature of social media communication can make behaviour that is defined as cybercrime in Tanzania difficult to address for national police forces. As major social media platforms such as Facebook are run by large corporations based elsewhere, obtaining their assistance in enforcing Tanzanian law can be difficult. As a senior officer in the Criminal Investigation Department explained:

> It's difficult to get information particularly as they are based in the United States, so if you go to them and say we need to investigate this illegal activity, somebody has posted something or somebody has insulted the President, they say that this is not illegal in their understanding, so it is difficult. (Interview, September 2017)

Facebook's own reporting indicates that during 2016 no requests from Tanzania for user data were granted (CIPESA 2017). Some of the government's most daring critics are also based outside of the country, such as Mange Kimambi who shares vitriolic criticism of the President and government and political gossip on Instagram, along with anonymised WhatsApp messages from Tanzanians complaining of poor service delivery or reporting corruption. The TPF issued a warrant for Kimambi's arrest should she return to the country, according to a leaked image of the document she posted on her Instagram page. However, whilst the TPF's Cyber Crime Unit has threatened to trace offenders outside of the country with the cooperation of Interpol (Rugonzibwa 2017), it is not clear that the international policing body would collaborate in tracking those who are accused of the very specific politically informed interpretation of cybercrime that has shaped social media policing in Tanzania.

Finally, social media also enables those who are the subject of social media policing to share in real time what is happening to them and potentially undermine police statements about their cases. In Tanzania, for example, several MPs have tweeted prior to or following arrests, and sometimes highlight breaches of police procedure. As

Paget (2017: 161) observes, experiences of repression are treated by the Tanzanian opposition as 'important pieces of political theatre'. Social media can amplify these practices and gives opposition politicians an opportunity to articulate an alternative narrative of events. Thus, whilst currently politicised policing might affect the extent to which social media can be used to bring about political change, new forms of communication may also enable a broader contestation of the relationship between policing and politics in Tanzania in the future.

Conclusion

This chapter has argued that attempts to assess the transformative potential of social media for politics in Africa must take account of existing relationships between politics and policing. In Tanzania allegations of cybercrime have been used to limit freedom of expression online, individuals have paid a heavy price for expressing criticism of the government, and surveillance of social media platforms may encourage self-censorship. Similar measures taken in countries across the continent as well as internet shut-downs and evidence of social media surveillance have attracted considerable international attention, but there is limited literature that explores how law enforcers understand and enact these strategies and the implications of locally specific policing practices for the relationship between social media and politics. This chapter makes a contribution towards greater understanding in this area, but also demonstrates the dynamic and contested relationship between policing, politics and social media in Africa. The role courts might play in upholding internet freedoms, the influence of African governments' international partners, and particularly China, in sharing strategies and technology for control of online spaces, and how the plural nature of policing provision in Africa shapes understanding of and approaches to cyber security, are likely to be influential in shaping the policing of politics online in the future.

Notes

1 Of course, such measures are not only being employed in Africa. See, for example, West (2016) on internet shutdowns globally in 2015–2016.

2 Ukawa, which stands for *Umoja wa Katiba ya Wananchi* (Coalition of Defenders of the People's Constitution), brought together four opposition parties, which fielded a single presidential candidate, former CCM member and Prime Minister Edward Lowassa.

3 Lissu was shot multiple times outside his home in Dodoma on 7 September 2017 by assailants unknown at the time of writing. He survived the attack,

which Chadema blamed on state security institutions (*Citizen* reporter 2017).

4 They may be empowered, or indeed scared, into action by Magufuli's '*hapa kazi tu*' (only work here) slogan and his summary dismissals of senior public servants perceived to not be doing their job correctly. Indeed, he instructed a new cohort of District Commissioners and Regional Commissioners in March 2016, 'you have authority to incarcerate people for up to 48 hours so that they will know you need to be respected' (quoted in Hamis 2016).

5 Translated by the author from Swahili: '*Nawaambia Wamliki wa vyombo vya habari*, be careful, watch it, *kama mnafikiri mna freedom ya namna hiyo*, not to that extent'.

6 TCRA official, interview, January 2018.

7 See Article 19 (2015) for further analysis.

8 Much like 'inflammatory' statements, which are prosecuted using provisions introduced by the colonial administration, 'fake news' is not a new concern in Tanzania. First President Julius Nyerere, for example, reportedly established an undercover 'rumour-busting squad' to quash false reports circulating in the aftermath of the 1964 army mutiny (Bjerk 2015: 3).

9 Officer Commanding Station E, interview, September 2016.

10 Interview, January 2018.

11 See for example *Daily News* (2015); Kapama (2015).

12 Virtually all posts on Jamii Forums are visible to all visitors to the site, even if they do not register themselves.

13 Author's translation from Swahili: '*Kama unajijua uli-comment chochote kuhusu taarifa hiyo njoo mwenyewe kabla hujatafutwa, tuna njia zetu tunaweza kuwafikia*'.

14 Interviews Criminal Investigation Department, Dar es Salaam and Mwanza, September 2017.

References

Article 19 (2015) *Tanzania Cybercrime Act*. Article 19 Legal Analysis, May 2015.

Bjerk, P. (2015) *Building a Peaceful Nation: Julius Nyerere and the Establishment of Sovereignty in Tanzania, 1960–1964*. Rochester, NY: University of Rochester Press.

Buguzi, S. (2016) 'How social media is shaking up Govt'. *The Citizen*, 9 October. www.thecitizen.co.tz/News/How-Social-media-is-shaking-up-Govt/1840340-3410148-dpr4yf/index.html (accessed 1 April 2019).

CHRI (Commonwealth Human Rights Initiative) (2006) *The Police, the People, the Politics: Police Accountability in Tanzania*. New Delhi: CHRI.

CIPESA (Collaboration on International ICT Policy for East and Southern Africa) (2016) *State of Internet Freedom in Tanzania 2016: Charting Patterns in the Strategies African Governments Use to Stifle Citizens' Digital Rights*. Kampala: CIPESA. https://cipesa.org/?wpfb_dl=229 (accessed 1 April 2019).

CIPESA (Collaboration on International ICT Policy for East and Southern Africa) (2017) 'The growing trend for African governments' requests for user information and content removal from internet and telecom companies'. CIPESA Policy Brief July 2017.

CIPESA (Collaboration on International ICT Policy for East and Southern Africa) (2018) *State of Internet Freedom in Africa 2018*. Kampala: CIPESA.

The Citizen (2016) 'Opposition leader Tundu Lissu to spend night in cell over Magufuli insult'. *The Citizen*, 29 June. http://mobile.thecitizen.co.tz/news/Opposition-leader-Tundu-Lissu-to-spend-night-in-cell-/2304482-3273256-format-xhtml-e1jb9pz/index.html (accessed 1 April 2019).

Citizen reporter (2017) 'Lissu escapes jaws of death'. *The Citizen*, 23 September. www.thecitizen.co.tz/News/Lissu-escapes-jaws-of-death/1840340-4108572-xiancj/index.html (accessed 1 April 2019).

Cross, C. (2014) 'Community policing and the politics of local development in Tanzania'. *Journal of Modern African Studies*, 52(4): 517–540.

Cross, C. (2016) '*Ulinzi shirikishi*: popular experiences of hybrid security governance in Tanzania'. *Development and Change*, 47(5): 1102–1124.

Daily News (2015) 'One more cyber-crime victim arraigned in court'. *Daily News*, 26 October 2015.

Daily News reporter (2015) 'TCRA, Police Warn Against Cyber Crime'. *Daily News*, 18 November. www.dailynews.co.tz/index.php/home-news/44296-tcra-police-warn-against-cyber-crime (accessed 6 October 2016).

Dar 24 (2016) '*Polisi wajipanga kumzuia Lissu kutumia mitandao ya kijamii*'. 20 March [Online]. www.dar24.com/polisi-wajipanga-kumzuia-lissu-kutumia-mitandao-ya-kijamii/ (accessed 1 April 2019.

Edward, E. (2017) '*Viongozi wa makundi ya* What's App (sic) *waonywa*'. *Mwananchi*, 13 October. www.mwananchi.co.tz/habari/Viongozi-makundi-What-s--App--kitanzini/1597578-4137734-cgj8fc/index.html (accessed 13 October 2017).

Edward, E. & Adrian, P. (2017) '*Waliotoa maoni picha ya kachero watakiwa kujisalimisha kwa DCI*'. *Mwananchi*, 12 September. www.mwananchi.co.tz/habari/Waliotoa-maoni-picha-ya-kachero-watakiwa-kujisalimisha-kwa-DCI/1597578-4092776-lnnbjj/index.html (accessed 15 September 2017).

Ewald, J. (2011) *Challenges for the Democratisation Process in Tanzania: Moving Towards Consolidation 50 Years After Independence?* Gothenburg: University of Gothenburg.

Ewald, J. & Wohlgemuth, L. (2012) 'Challenges for the opposition and democratisation in Tanzania: a view from the opposition'. *Africa Development*, XXXVII (2): 63–95.

FIDH (International Federation for Human Rights) & LHRC (Legal and Human Rights Center) (2001) 'Zanzibar: wave of violence; a fact finding report on police brutality and election mismanagement in Zanzibar'. www.fidh.org/IMG//pdf/zanzio501.pdf (accessed 1 April 2019).

Gagliardone, I., Stremlau, N. & Aynekulu, G. (2018) 'A tale of two publics? Online politics in Ethiopia's elections'. *Journal of Eastern African Studies* [Online]. DOI: 10.1080/17531055.2018.1548208 (accessed 1 April 2019).

Göpfert, M. (2016) 'Surveillance in Niger: gendarmes and the problem of "seeing things"'. *African Studies Review*, 59(2): 39–57.

Guardian reporter (2017) 'Mbeya resident charged with insulting President Magufuli'. *The Guardian*, 10 February. http://ippmedia.com/en/news/mbeya-resident-charged-insulting-president-magufuli (accessed 20 November 2017).

Hamis, I. (2016) 'Kurejesha nidhamu sawa, lakini siyo kwa kutumia nguvu'. *Mwananchi*, 26 October [Online]. www.mwananchi.co.tz/Makala/Kurejesha-nidhamu-sawa--lakini-siyo-kwa-kutumia-nguvu/1597592-3430602-15fa9q5/index.html (accessed 1 April 2019).

Hills, A. (1996) 'Towards a critique of policing and national development in Africa'. *The Journal of Modern African Studies*, 34(2): 271–291.

Hills, A. (2007) 'Police commissioners, presidents and the governance of security'. *The Journal of Modern African Studies*, 45(3): 403–423.

Hoffman, B. & Robinson, L. (2009) 'Tanzania's missing opposition'. *Journal of Democracy*, 20(4): 123–136

Human Rights Watch (2014) *'They know everything we do': Telecom and internet surveillance in Ethiopia*. New York: Human Rights Watch.

IGAD (Inter-Governmental Authority on Development) (2016) *Al-Shabaab as a Transnational Security Threat*. Djibouti: IGAD Security Sector Programme and Sahan Foundation.

Ingle, C.R. (1972) *From Village to State in Tanzania: the Politics of Rural Development*. Ithaca, NY: Cornell University Press.

Johnston, L. (1999) 'Private Policing in Context'. *European Journal on Criminal Policy and Research*, 7: 175–196.

Kabwe, Z. (2012) 'Comment on the use of social media and politics in #Tanzania #GermanAfricaInitiative'. *Zitto na Demokrasia* blog. Transcript and video of Kabwe's participation in panel debate 11 December, Berlin. https://zittokabwe.wordpress.com/2012/12/13/comment-on-the-use-of-social-media-and-politics-in-tanzania-germanafricainitiative/ (accessed 1 April 2019).

Kalathil, S. & Boas, T.C. (2003) *Open Networks, Closed Regimes: the Impact of the Internet on Authoritarian Rule*. Washington DC: Carnegie Endowment for International Peace.

Kapama, F. (2015) 'Student becomes first cyber crime victim'. *Daily News*, 10 October 2015.

Kapama, F. (2017) 'Mdee arraigned in court over inflammatory utterance'. *Daily News* 12 October. http://dailynews.co.tz/index.php/home-news/53523-mdee-arraigned-in-court-over-inflammatory-utterance (accessed 16 October 2017).

Kiango, B. (2017) '*Zitto asafirishwa chini ya ulinzi wa polisi*'. Mwananchi, 21 September. www.mwananchi.co.tz/habari/Zitto-asafirishwa-chini-ya-ulinzi-wa-polisi/1597578-4105380-p9of1cz/index.html (accessed 21 September 2017).

King, G., Pan, J. & Roberts, M.E. (2013) 'How censorship in China allows government criticism but silences collective expression'. *American Political Science Review*, 107(2): 326–343.

Kolumbia, L. (2016) 'Social media, where the battle has shifted a gear'. *The Citizen*, 28 September. www.thecitizen.co.tz/magazine/politicalreforms/Social-media--where-the-battle-has-shifted-a-gear/1843776-3397646-14i69l7/index.html (accessed 29 September 2016).

Lamtey, G. (2016) 'Bavicha considers countrywide demonstrations'. *The Citizen*, 2 September. www.thecitizen.co.tz/News/Bavicha-considers-countrywide-demonstrations/1840340-4080276-x57m8i/index.html (accessed 4 September 2017).

LeRiche, M. (2016) 'Facebook and social media fanning the flames of war in South Sudan'. Centre for Security Governance, 12 July. http://secgovcentre.org/2016/07/facebook-and-social-media-fanning-the-flames-of-war-in-south-sudan/ (accessed 1 April 2019).

LHRC (Legal and Human Rights Centre) (n.d.) *Freedom of Assembly: Freedom of Assembly is a Civil Right*. Thematic Brief II.

LHRC (Legal and Human Rights Centre) & ZLSC (Zanzibar Legal Services Centre) (2013) *Tanzania Human Rights Report 2012*. Dar es Salaam and Zanzibar: LHRC and SLSC.

LHRC (Legal and Human Rights Centre) & ZLSC (Zanzibar Legal Services Centre) (2014) *Tanzania Human Rights Report 2013*. Dar es Salaam and Zanzibar: LHRC and SLSC.

LHRC (Legal and Human Rights Centre) & ZLSC (Zanzibar Legal Services Centre) (2017) *Tanzania Human Rights Report 2016*. Dar es Salaam and Zanzibar: LHRC and SLSC.

Luckham, R. & Kirk, T. (2012) 'Security in Hybrid Political Contexts: an End-User Approach'. Justice and Security Research Programme Paper, London School of Economics.

Marczak, B. et al. (2017) 'Champing at the cyberbit: Ethiopian dissidents targeted with new commercial spyware'. *The Citizen Lab*, 6 December. https://citizenlab. ca/2017/12/champing-cyberbit-ethiopian-dissidents-targeted-commercial-spyware/ (accessed 1 April 2019).

Menkhaus, K. (2014) 'Al-Shabaab and social media: a double-edged sword'. *Brown Journal of World Affairs*, XX(11): 309–327.

Mohammed, O. (2015) 'WhatsApp is now the primary platform for political trash talk in Tanzania's election campaign'. *Quartz*, 27 September [Online]. https://qz.com/africa/510899/ whatsapp-is-now-the-primary-platform-for-political-trash-talk-in-tanzanias-election-campaign/ (accessed 1 April 2019).

Mwangonde, H. (2017) 'Ndugai now threatens to ban Zitto Kabwe from parliament until 2020'. *The Guardian*, 14 September. www.ippmedia.com/en/news/ ndugai-now-threatens-ban-zitto-kabwe-parliament-until-2020 (accessed 16 November 2017).

Paget, D. (2017) 'Tanzania: shrinking space and opposition protest'. *Journal of Democracy*, 28(3): 153–167.

Portland (2017) *The Reality of Fake News in Kenya*. https://portland-communications.com/publications/ reality-fake-news-kenya/ (accessed 1 April 2019).

Purdeková, A. (2016) '"Mundane sights" of power: the history of social monitoring and its subversion in Rwanda'. *African Studies Review*, 58(2): 59–86.

Quintal, A. (2018) 'My nasty encounter with Tanzanian repression'. *Daily Maverick*, 13 November. www. dailymaverick.co.za/article/2018-11-13-my-nasty-encounter-with-tanzanian-repression/ (accessed 1 April 2019).

Research ICT Africa (RIA) (2017) 'Cost of smartphones continues the digital divide in Tanzania'. Policy Brief, 4 August 2017.

Rugonzibwa, P. (2017) 'Police alert, vow arrest on cybercrime everywhere'. *Daily News*, 10 November. http:// dailynews.co.tz/index.php/ home-news/54148-police-alert-vow-arrest-on-cybercrime-everywhere (accessed 14 November 2017).

Serianu (2016) *Tanzania Cyber Security Report: Achieving Cyber Security Resilience: Enhancing Visibility and Increasing Awareness*. www.serianu.com/downloads/ TanzaniaCyberSecurityReport2016. pdf (accessed 1 April 2019).

Shahbaz, A. (2018) *Freedom on the Net 2018: the Rise of Digital Authoritarianism*. Washington DC: Freedom House.

Shivji, I. (1990) *State Coercion and Freedom in Tanzania*. Roma: National University of Lesotho.

Shivji, I. (2001) 'A study of police powers and political expression'. Research and Education for Democracy in Tanzania (REDET) Framework Paper.

Vircoulon, T. (2016) 'Burundi turns to WhatsApp as political turmoil brings media blackout'. *The Guardian* 14 June. www.theguardian.com/global-development/2016/jun/14/burundi-turns-to-whatsapp-as-political-turmoil-brings-media-blackout (accessed 1 April 2019).

Voice of America (2017) '*RAis Magufuli aonya uhuru wa vyombo vya habari unakikomo*'. Voice of America Swahili, 25 March. www.voaswahili.com/a/rais-avikemea-vyombo-vya-habari/3781459.html (accessed 1 April 2019).

West, D.M. (2016) 'Internet Shutdowns Cost Countries $2.4 Billion Last Year'. Brookings Institute Center for Technology and Innovation. www.brookings.edu/wp-content/uploads/2016/10/intenet-shutdowns-v-3.pdf (accessed 1 April 2019).

Yussuf, I. (2016) 'Police arrest one for incitement'. *Daily News*, 28 February. www.dailynews.co.tz/index.php/home-news/47403-police-arrest-one-for-incitemen (accessed 3 October 2016).

Zacharia, A. & Tesha, A. (2016) 'Regulator worried about cybercrimes'. *The Citizen*, 18 August, p. 28.

Legislation cited

Cybercrimes Act (2015)
Electronic and Postal Communications Act (2010)
Electronic and Postal Communications (Online Content) Regulations (2017)
Media Services Act (2016)
Regional Administration Act (1997)
Statistics Act (2015)

11 | A FAMILIAR REFRAIN

Political discourse and Facebook use in
Mombasa, Kenya

Stephanie Diepeveen

Introduction

This chapter looks at the juncture of two emerging dynamics in Kenya: the increasing animation and diversity of public information flows on social media, and the potential for continuity and change in the divisive discourses through which politics are being interpreted. Increasing social media use appears to generate more variation and greater scope both in who contributes and in the sheer amount of information circulating publicly about Kenyan politics. By interrogating how the logic and affordances of Facebook intersect with new contributors to public information flows, this chapter questions this apparent openness. It asks: to what extent, if at all, does Facebook use present an opportunity for alternative voices and ideas to inform public debate? To do this, it examines public information on Facebook concerning the County of Mombasa during a period of heightened insecurity and public controversy in February 2014. By looking at how Facebook was used, and the debates that unfolded, it argues the affordances of Facebook communication may well expand who contributes to public information, but this does not necessarily challenge the terms of debate. It reveals Facebook is diversifying who informs public information flows in Mombasa, particularly when official channels are closed, slow to report or perceived as unreliable. Equally, it finds that the way in which Facebook connects people – through personalised interfaces and familiar networks – is reinforcing attention on dominant personalities and familiar narratives.

Reframing debate away from questions of access and participation

Scholarship paints an ambiguous picture about how social media use affects public information flows. On one side, social media seems to provide greater opportunities for anyone to contribute to and access public information (Goldstein & Rotich 2008; Ifukor, 2010). Facebook, specifically, enables any user to share information that could in theory be read across the platform. With cost- and distance-based barriers to information lowered, there is evidence of a growing diversity of voices contributing to public information within Africa and a rising number of people with access to that information (Goldstein & Rotich 2008; Mäkinen & Kuira 2008). Scholars argue that more information, produced by and accessible to more people, provides the means for citizens to mobilise and challenge dominant discourses and authorities (Howard & Hussain 2011: 35–36; Ekine 2010; Moyo 2009: 67). Social media's potential as an alternative source of public information appears to heighten in times of insecurity or increased repression of the media (Papacharissi & Oliveira 2012: 268). As face-to-face communications and mainstream media become more difficult to access and more unreliable, more people seem to look to social media for public information (Howard & Parks 2012: 360).

At the same time, scholars emphasise that what unfolds through social media is not necessarily driven by the citizen. Corporate and state authorities retain control and oversight over networked activity. The Ethiopian and Sudanese governments show this in an extreme, through distinct but explicit efforts to shape and monitor internet infrastructure (Gagliardone 2016; Lamoureaux & Sureau 2019). More widely, governments across the continent have engaged in internet or social media shutdown, usually in the context of elections or political unrest. Outside of the state, corporate oversight is visible in projects justified by the rhetoric of expanding internet access, in which corporations from Google to Facebook become potential gatekeepers to such access through, for example, Facebook and Airtel's Free Basic Services (Facebook 2015). At the same time, the nature of engagement through online channels is argued by some to be weak (Gladwell 2010), and separate from and even challenging to offline political action (Dean 2009; Morozov 2011).

Different views on the political possibilities of social media as a tool for communication invoke different arguments about how technology is political (Winner 1980), with some tending to a view that technology has political affordances tied to its design (either popular politics, for example, Osborn 2008 and Nyamnjoh 2005, or state control, Gagliardone 2016), and others emphasising how technology acquires meaning as it is used (for example, Larkin 2008). Rather than assume one view over the other, this chapter is open to either and both premises: that Facebook has affordances that intersect with forms of power in unequal ways, and that it is also malleable and underdefined, constituted in its context and use. With this, it avoids a strict dichotomy of digitally mediated information flows as utopian or dystopian, taking a similar position to that of Aouragh & Alexander (2011), who argue that networks produced through capitalist logics do not preclude their concurrent use to resist these logics. Deeper understanding of the politics of digitally mediated information flows requires attention to the intersection of greater openness and new forms of control and surveillance, in context and in convergence with offline and broadcast media. From this open approach, this chapter asks: how do the affordances of Facebook communications intersect with the nature and possibilities of political discourses in Kenya?

To answer this question, this chapter focuses on Facebook use in Mombasa County. It examines three active spaces for public information on Facebook: (1) elected politicians' Facebook pages, specifically then-Governor of Mombasa, Ali Hassan Joho, then-elected senator of Mombasa, Hassan Omar Hassan, and Abdulswamad Nassir, Member of Parliament for Mvita Constituency; (2) a self-proclaimed citizen journalist, Mombasa County Government Watch (MCGW); and (3) a political discussion group, Mombasa Youth Senate (MYS). A more in-depth case study of MYS on the political significance of the Facebook discussion as a 'public' or 'public sphere' is found in Diepeveen (2019).

This chapter draws on observations and interviews conducted on the ground in Mombasa and online between August 2013 and June 2015. This included 162 semi-structured face-to-face interviews and 39 informal interviews with participants in political discussion-based gatherings on the ground and online, and members of civil society, political parties and the county and national governments. I regularly created PDFs of public Facebook groups and pages over the course of fieldwork. I used this PDF archive to identify and analyse the effect of changes made to the Facebook interface, or by users to their groups, pages and profiles. User names have been removed from quotations or pseudonyms used, except in cases in which a user profile was already anonymised, or where someone presented themselves as a public figure (for example as an elected representative).[1]

Dominant refrains in political discourse in Mombasa

Contemporary ideas of political belonging and difference in Mombasa have been shaped through waves of trade, migration and colonial rule, including Portuguese occupation in the sixteenth century, Arab rule from 1735 onwards, and the establishment of a British Protectorate in 1895 (Mathews 2013: 140; McIntosh 2009: 50). While group identities began to crystallise as Swahili, Arab and African in the seventeenth century, there arguably remained some permeability between identities (Mathews 2013). This flexibility of identity became increasingly rigid in relation to the British colonial administration, which sought to order people and territory through racial hierarchies that placed 'natives' in the lowest position vis-à-vis the law, political and military authority, and control of material resources (Constantin 1989).

A sense of marginalisation along regional and ethnic lines was fed throughout the post-independence period (Kanyinga 1998: 57). In the early 1990s, legal space for public discussion expanded as multi-party competition was reintroduced and some formal restrictions on public expression and association were relaxed. This allowed for the re-emergence of latent feelings of discontent among coastal communities in Kenya, reflecting a sense of past disadvantage vis-à-vis national politics (Haynes 2006; Oded 2000: 149–150).

The period since the early 2000s has been marked by ambivalence between expanding opportunities for public discussion in Kenya, and popular frustration with personalised, corrupt and elite politics. Such ambivalence has sustained rather than mitigated divisive identities and competing views of marginalisation in Mombasa. The 2002 general elections were an exciting moment, indicating the potential for substantive change in government in Kenya. Forty years of KANU rule ended as the National Rainbow Coalition (NARC) was elected on a platform of change. This indicated a more open space for public discussion, supported by the introduction of the first vernacular radio station in 2004. Widespread optimism at the outcome of the elections was quickly challenged in the months and years that followed. The openness of Kenyan politics became questionable as fractures emerged within individual alliances in NARC and there were delays in fulfilling campaign promises (Berman, Cottrell & Ghai 2009). Subsequent elections further revealed a polarising political environment. Post-election violence in 2007–2008 brought divisive ideas about advantage and marginalisation in citizen–state relations to the fore, showcasing controversies over corruption, inequality and personalised and ethnic politicking (KNCHR 2008: 22).

While this unrest created space for the promulgation of a new constitution on 27 August 2010, constitutional change has not led to the dissipation of divisive ideas about the distribution of political power and advantage. Both the 2013 and 2017 general elections manifested in a sharp national divide between two party coalitions, led by Uhuru Kenyatta and Raila Odinga. In Mombasa, both elections saw the clear dominance of Odinga's party, the Orange Democratic Movement (ODM). ODM's party dominance masked unresolved differences about the distribution of benefit and disadvantage in relation to the national and county governments. On one side, public discourses advocating coastal secession persist, indicating a shared identity among some as *wapwani* (people of the Coast) (Willis & Chome 2014; Willis & Gona 2013). The Kenyan government's participation in a global 'war on terrorism' (Prestholdt 2011) and its offensive in Somalia since 2011 have fed a perceived political disadvantage tied to being Muslim in Kenya (Horowitz & MUHURI 2013). On the other side, ethnographic research in 2013 and 2014 by the author revealed a competing reoccurring narrative that those from upcountry tended to be marginalised within county politics. Reinforced repeatedly through observations and interviews with politicians and campaign strategists as well as in existing scholarship (Mwakimako & Willis 2014; Willis & Chome 2014; Willis & Gona 2013), ethnic, religious and regional forms of identity in Mombasa remain points of contention, shaping people's real and perceived relations to the government and to individual national and county leaders.

Facebook as a space for public debate

With a relatively open regulatory environment, contention over the terms and distribution of political benefit is expressed in public debate in the streets, markets, local drinking establishments, *matatu* (minibuses) and bus stages, and broadcast and print media. In the past decade, social media has become part of this array of public communication channels. Nationally, Kenya stands out on the continent, contrasting with a continental average of 28.3 percent internet penetration and a total of 146.6 million Facebook subscribers. Kenya's internet penetration is projected to be 81.8 percent (31 March 2017), with 5.5 million Facebook subscribers recorded in 2016 (as of 30

June 2016).[2] A new community of citizen journalists, bloggers and commentators has emerged around Twitter. Discussion coalesces around often satirical and playful hashtags (Tully & Ekdale 2014) and key personalities, who have become an alternative voice to mainstream media and the government (Ogola 2015, 2019).

Facebook is particularly accessible and popular. The number of people actively using Facebook in Kenya appears to outstrip other social media sites (Kenya ICT Board 2010; Ndavula, Mberia & Mwangi 2015). Each social media site operates through a particular logic and design. As this chapter aims to unpack, the logic and design of a technology forms a crucial piece in shaping how it becomes used and experienced, thereby affecting terms of public discourse. Facebook is a corporation that accumulates value by building connections among users. Each user becomes observable to others through the content they share. This begins with the creation of a user profile. Facebook offers a range of features through which an individual can curate their appearance, through images, titles, descriptors and so on, something which will be considered in the context of Mombasa below. Upon creating a Facebook profile, users become part of a wider network on Facebook through connections that extend from familiar acquaintances. Facebook's design prompts a user to connect to others, usually based on a similar interest, place or organisational affiliation (boyd & Ellison 2007: 212). People build and extend their networks by joining groups, creating and joining notices for events, engaging with different applications (for example, games and quizzes), and liking pages for organisations, celebrities or campaigns. Facebook is constantly creating new and evolving ways for people to connect with others, and to access and contribute to circulating information.

There has been a growing number of Facebook groups and pages discussing Mombasa politics and current affairs since the 2013 general elections. The office of the Governor of Mombasa County began to regularly post updates on his activity on both Facebook and Twitter. A few other locally based elected leaders also began to use Facebook as one way to publicise their activity to the wider electorate, with some, although less frequent, updates on Twitter. New 'citizen journalists' have also entered the scene, creating Facebook pages and Twitter handles to share information.

By early 2014, networked communication appeared to have become increasingly important to public information access in Mombasa amidst growing insecurity. Tensions between different groups of citizens, and the national and county governments, had been growing over the previous months, much of this tied to radicalisation and counter-radicalisation activity in the city. In October 2013, a prominent radical sheikh was shot and killed in public, adding to a growing list of targeted killings of Muslim leadership. Throughout November and December, some male Muslim youth attempted several takeovers of four mosques in the city. Face-to-face communication became increasingly difficult as confrontations and protests erupted on the streets between Muslim youth and Kenyan security forces around these events. Separately, conflict between the county government and hawkers, who had been removed from the streets of the Central Business District, also contributed to protests on the ground in the centre of town. Tensions culminated on 2 February 2014 when government security forces raided a prominent mosque in central Mombasa, then known as Masjid Musa, where a meeting claiming to teach youth about jihad was taking place. On the day, more than 100 arrests were made and violence spread from the mosque into the streets (Al Jazeera 2014).

Even before it took place, information pertaining to the event at the mosque was publicised in the form of a public advertisement circulated on Facebook, announcing: '*Kongamano Masjid Musa ijumapili* [sic] 2/2/2014: *Umoja wa vijana wa jihad*' ('Meeting at Masjid Musa on Sunday, 2 February 2014: Unity of the youth of jihad'). During the unrest, social media provided a ready space for leaders and citizens to shape public dialogue, mediated by the social media technology as opposed to the media sector. Activity by politicians, citizen journalists and group forums spiked in the immediate aftermath of the unrest.

Information flows in mainstream media

When violence broke out, the streets emptied, shops closed and people retreated to private locations. Local and national media outlets were active in reporting on the events, its controversies and who was involved. National media houses and local radio stations reported through websites, TV and radio stations, Facebook pages and Twitter handles. This section reviews content in the three national daily newspapers in Kenya: *The Standard, The Daily Nation* and *The Star*, published through February and March 2014. At first, print media simply attempted to stay apace with events, reporting on immediate violence, for example the deaths of a General Service Unit (GSU) officer and at least one youth. There were also a few speculative mentions of links to religious radicalisation (Onsarigo & Otieno 2014). As the immediate violence subsided, newspapers turned their attention to prominent political and religious leaders, and their reactions. The printed press discussed the aftermath of the raid by referring to the actions and statements of already prominent local political and religious leaders. Their focus shifted away from the events at the mosque, and towards the debate on the balance between the threat of 'radicalisation' and the justifiable use of force (Mghenyi 2014b).

Similar to what Patel (this volume) finds in relation to print coverage of the government's counterterrorism initiative, Operation Usalama Watch, newspapers predominantly covered the responses of political leaders. In this case, their focus was on elected and nominated government representatives based in Mombasa, presenting them as treading between two distinct concerns: careful to show seriousness towards radicalisation, and support for residents of Mombasa against the force used by the security forces. Government officials were quoted defending the police actions and affirming concerns about radicalisation (*Nation* reporter 2014). A concern for local residents manifested in reports of a personal interest in the case of one youth who disappeared in the midst of the raid. The newspapers relayed statements and actions made by Mr Omar Hassan and Mr Nassir, which presented them as critical of police actions; Mr Nassir also questioned the activity of the Kenyan National Intelligence Service (Obbayi 2014; Murage 2014; Otieno 2014). Governor Joho, who was away at the time of the raid, garnered greater attention in the press on his return to the city a week later (Mghenyi 2014a). Like Mr Hassan Omar and Mr Nassir, Mr Joho was reported expressing concern about the raid, though this was accompanied by an expression of concern about youth radicalisation and avoided direct criticism of police and security forces' actions (Mosoku 2014).

The newspapers also reported on religious leaders' perspectives and activities, suggesting they too occupied an ambivalent perspective. Islamic umbrella organisations were presented as being caught between appeasing the government and appeasing the Muslim community. Reports showed them affirming support for Muslims in Mombasa, and making statements that expressed concern about the severity of police action (Mosoku 2014). Their reported statements also attempted to defend Muslim teachings and the Muslim community to non-Muslims (Lornah 2014). Equally, they outlined the efforts they were making to address radicalisation within their communities (Mghenyi 2014c; *Nation* team 2014).

By mid-February, the raid and its aftermath featured less prominently in the printed press. Still, religious divisions and insecurity re-emerged in subsequent months, reignited by an attack on a church in Likoni constituency, Mombasa on 23 March, and the shooting and killing of a radical and prominent sheikh, Abubakar 'Makaburi' Shariff, on 2 April. The national government and security forces responded increasingly harshly to these events. On 30 March, a shoot-to-kill policy was introduced in Mombasa targeting the attackers on the church, and in April, a new security effort, called Operation Usalama Watch, was launched nationally (Human Rights Watch 2015). These events kept issues around insecurity (see Patel, this volume) and political and religious tensions in Mombasa in the printed press.

The image of the attentive politician on Facebook

In addition to mainstream media, social media was an easily accessible platform for other actors – both public figures and private citizens – to post updates on events, and position themselves in relation to the unrest. Facebook did not replace offline political action, but did provide a means to continue public discussion within an uncertain and unstable physical environment. Prominent local politicians published their own press statements, and posted videos and statements on their public Facebook pages. While the politicians examined here also had Twitter accounts at the time, their activity, and responses to their activity, were much higher on Facebook. By sharing through Facebook, political leaders projected an image of communicating directly to their electorate, unmediated by the press. At the time, Governor Joho's official public Facebook page had more followers than any other county politician. By August 2014, 82,526 users 'liked' the page (recorded 18 August 2014 at 17:44 BST); Mr Omar Hassan also garnered a substantial following, with 51,453 likes for his public page (recorded 26 July 2014 at 10:44 BST). Public Facebook pages, managed by individuals or their teams, and not the mainstream press, allowed an opportunity for politicians to shape their public image in ways that differed from the media.

Mr Joho was initially slow to respond; at the time of the Masjid Musa raid he was travelling internationally. He published his first press statement on the event on his public Facebook page three days later, while still abroad. Facebook became a means for him to give direct input into public information prior to returning to the city. His initial post recognising the event echoed the press' interpretation of the Governor's standpoint. He took a cautious tone, avoiding a strong association with either the security forces or the youth: 'I will therefore give a comprehensive statement after meeting government officials, local leaders, religious leaders, youth and women'. There was an immediate interest in his contribution, evident in the number of likes, comments and shares. At the time, Facebook 'likes' simply indicated a user's awareness and interest in a post or comment. 'Comments' were nested underneath a post; they allowed for more substantive engagement as users could react by sharing text, images and/or videos, suggesting the potential for a discussion to form around a post. Facebook 'shares' involved a user forwarding the post to another group, private message, page or user profile, indicating its on-going circulation. This particular post was shared at least 84 times and acquired 520 comments. Mr Joho continued to provide a commentary on the event while absent from the city through his official Facebook page in the following days. On 6 February, he shared ten photos of released minors who had been arrested, and on 8 February he posted photos of his brother and his lawyer, hosting a lunch for them. The subsequent two posts were directed to the residents of Mombasa, indicating personal concern and support for the arrested minors. Such posts continued to engender interest. The former was commented on 60 times and shared 18 times, and the latter was commented on 126 times and shared 29 times.

Mr Omar Hassan and Mr Nassir provided more vocal, immediate and critical commentaries on the raid through their public Facebook pages, again seeming to direct their comments to their constituents. They used the site to reinforce an image of individual concern for the city's residents. Unlike Mr Joho, both published statements on their public Facebook pages on the same day as the raid. Mr Omar Hassan described the attack as unjustifiable, positioning himself on the side of the residents of Mombasa by stating 'I have asserted time and again that I represent every citizen of Mombasa' (recorded 28 March 2017 at 09:40 GMT). Like Mr Joho's, this post affirming concern for the youth attracted attention; it was shared 64 times and commented on 315 times. Mr Nassir presented a similar image as a concerned representative. He immediately criticised the raid as another chaotic blunder by the police,[3] (recorded 27 March 2017 at 09:15 GMT), and explained his stance on the events in following posts, including re-posts of press statements, all defending the residents of Mombasa.

Expressions of concern for Mombasa residents, specifically youth, attracted immediate attention in the context of this initial violent and local event. Users appeared interested in reading about the views and actions of these local elected leaders. Attention dwindled as the event became more distant. After these initial few posts, the number of comments, shares and likes was more varied and indicated an overall decline in interest. It was in the immediacy of local unrest that these three local leaders were able to use public Facebook pages to attract attention and project a public self-image to constituents that reaffirmed their individual concern. Both the content of their posts and the very act of posting through individual pages were conducive to this image of the individual caring leader. In this way, Facebook's design of the individual page, while theoretically open to being used by anyone or any organisation to garner attention, proved to be highly compatible with a personalised view of the political leader. Therefore, Facebook posts seemed to reinforce the messages already being conveyed in the printed press, which, by printing local leaders' statements, was already emphasising these individuals' concerns and agency. Thus, the content on politicians' public Facebook pages, and their act of posting, did not necessarily diversify the content of public information but rather reinforced an existing emphasis on the individual in authority, and the individual leader's concern (or lack thereof) and responsibility. Activity around politicians' public profiles might have diversified the voices directly reporting on events, but by reinforcing a pre-existing emphasis on the individual politician.

Citizen Journalism on Facebook

The message delivered through the political leaders' Facebook pages emphasised a particular image of the elected leader already present in the printed press: conveying an individual care for one's constituents and expressing concern about excessive use of force by security forces against youth. This narrative invoked questions about the events that took place and whether security forces were justified in their actions, or if this event was a further example of national government repression directed against those who identified as Muslim, coastal and male. Locally created Facebook pages and groups became spaces for Mombasa residents to discuss these questions, while also expressing concerns and sharing information that drew from their particular perspective on the ground.

The raid in early 2014 occurred when public and political discussion about Mombasa politics was beginning to grow and diversify. At that time, pages and groups to discuss and debate local issues and events in Mombasa were still limited in number. My fieldwork in 2014 followed the rising activity and diversification of these spaces in the months after the raid, which continued as the country progressed towards the 2017 elections. However, back in February 2014, one page, MCGW, stood out as one of the only citizen-convened spaces on Facebook that was readily positioned to report and comment on the raid. As one of the first Facebook pages to be created by ordinary, in this case anonymous, citizens in Mombasa, MCGW was launched on 16 April 2013 by two politically active individuals who had campaigned for an unsuccessful gubernatorial candidate. They created MCGW as an online anonymous news source, 'to keep an eye on how things are going', as expressed in an interview in March 2014.[4] The format of MCGW's Facebook page mirrored those of the press and the politicians: only the conveners could post, while followers could comment on and share posts. The content of posts took several consistent forms. MCGW copied and pasted text from the mainstream media (inconsistently providing the source of the content), and copied and pasted text from civil society groups' and politicians' pages. It also shared posts that claimed to be the perspective of a 'concerned citizen'; these usually posed a question, critique or opinion of a member of the county executive or assembly.

During the raid on Masjid Musa, MCGW was able to occupy a unique position, contributing information quickly and offering a commentary that challenged some of the press and politicians' public messages. MCGW used photos and videos to support its posts. These posts generated immediate interest and attention, corresponding to a sudden and profound increase in the number of followers of the page. In the first two weeks of February, the number of followers of MCGW rose by more than 3,500, which was a greater number of new followers in those two weeks alone than in the subsequent six months combined. During these same two weeks, which followed the attack on the mosque, three posts between 2 and 6 February stood out in terms of the number of shares and comments they generated (155 shares and 151 comments combined): a news report on the police and youth stand-off published on the day of the raid; a press statement by Mr Nassir; and a news account questioning if one of the youth was the child of a well-known controversial sheikh, Aboud Rogo, who had been shot and killed two years before. MCGW continued to post about topics related to the raid throughout February. In the month after the raid, 16 percent of posts (20 out of 124 posts) were about Masjid Musa and its aftermath (recorded between 2 February and 2 March 2014). While they continued to generate some attention, as with the politicians' pages, this was to a lesser degree than the initial three posts. Still, 43 percent of the fourteen posts commented on or shared more than twenty times during this period were about the raid.

The three posts noted above, as well as subsequent posts about the raid that attracted attention, shared common features in their content and in the sorts of comments they generated. First, similar to the politicians' pages, content about politicians' actions and reactions created interest. Users tended to engage with posts that shared how politicians were defending the arrested youths. For instance, the post shared by the most users (77 times) in the month after the raid was a video of Mr Nassir making a statement about the raid in the Kenyan parliament. Second, users commented on and shared posts that invoked emotion and raised issues of personal concern and security. Online discussion was not disassociated from what was happening on the ground. Residents of Mombasa would use MCGW to learn about and interpret local events. The emotional and personal nature of comments indicated connections between place, local politics and online discussion. Comments in the immediate aftermath of the raid were predominantly made from the perspective of Muslims residing in Mombasa. Their content and tone identified a connection to the youth who were arrested. Users expressed scepticism about the justifiability of government action and raised suspicions that different narratives about the events being circulated from both official and informal sources were unreliable. Their comments weighed and debated the reliability of different sources of information, comparing YouTube videos, photo evidence and official statements.

The burst of activity on MCGW in the aftermath of the raid suggests a particular role for citizen journalists on Facebook in times of insecurity. The authors of MCGW presented themselves as anonymous on Facebook but, by sharing local, emotive and timely information, their page attracted attention even given the ambiguous source of the posts. With their voice, the political nature of Facebook arguably becomes multiple and conflicting: its technical design directed attention to personalised leadership, as shown above, but it also allowed for new and anonymous voices to claim public attention. Local controversy surrounding the Masjid Musa raid empowered MCGW's anonymous administrators to become sources of public information and conveners of debate. Nonetheless, at the same time, while providing a challenging view of political leadership, their posts did not challenge a concern for the role and responses of key political leaders in discussions about the events. While the perspective on leaders differed from the mainstream printed press and politicians' pages, MCGW retained a focus on political leadership. The content of their posts therefore continued to direct attention to prominent local political figures and their actions in the aftermath of the raid.

Open public discussion and the Facebook group

In addition to adding new sources of information through the Facebook page, Facebook brought new opportunities for public discussion through the format of the Facebook group. Facebook groups allow for discussion of issues of common concern to a subset of users. Any member of a public Facebook group can post and initiate a discussion in a group. Group administrators control the extent to which they maintain oversight over posts and comments. Groups can be open, in which administrators allow any Facebook user to view and join the group. Others have some restrictions, such as administrator approval for new members or pre-approval of posts before they are publicly visible. Some are fully private or secret, and are searchable and visible only to their members.

The way in which the Facebook group was used, and acquired meaning, in Mombasa added another dimension to the way in which Facebook was political. When the raid took place, groups convened to discuss Mombasa politics were uncommon, with most Mombasa-based Facebook activity based around organisations, causes or individuals. Arguably the first group to evolve into an animated space for open discussion of local political issues, MYS was created on Facebook a few days prior to the raid on Masjid Musa. In an unstructured interview with the author, its conveners conveyed that they created the group from the perspective that the reasoned citizen could and should interpret public affairs and shape public debate.[5] Building from Facebook's connective structure, linking users as 'friends', the group was first formed when its founders invited approximately 200 users from among their Facebook friend networks to join. Since, it has consistently grown in number, as the public group enables anyone to request to join and any member of the group to add other users.

MYS did not immediately result in animated debate about local political issues and events. Initial members were not explicitly told of the group's intention, but arbitrarily added by its founders. As a result, discussion in early February around the Masjid Musa raid was unfocused and disjointed. Posts ranged from motivational quotes, to stories on health and medicine, to opinions on local and national politics. They also generated little discussion; the number of posts vastly outnumbered comments. By the end of February, 172 posts had been made but only 25 comments, and only once was a post shared beyond the group.

Coherent political discussion only manifested after the group obtained a sufficient number of active users who were familiar with the group's intent and interested in reading and contributing political and local content. The group's potential in relation to public discourse was clarified as individuals navigated the group interface and invested it with meaning through their accumulating contributions. By early March, greater consistency in content appeared among posts and comments, which were increasingly focused on current affairs and local politics. With this, like MCGW, the group indicated the potential for citizens to convene active discussion about local issues. A few individuals became responsible for most of the posts that sparked discussion; these same users also tended to regularly comment on others' posts. Familiarity between members, both on Facebook and offline, supported a sustained discussion by partially tempering hostilities, resulting in some restraint and even humour around contrary opinions.

In the group's early days, it was noticeable that the nature of public discussion was shaped by strong ties which developed around a few individuals, as opposed to being dictated by a wide array of weak linkages between many individuals. Restraint associated with a degree of familiarity among active members became visible in discussions in the months following the Masjid Musa raid, specifically in response to the attack on the church in the Likoni area of Mombasa and the speech by controversial the Sheikh Abubakar Makaburi Shariff. Both generated active discussions in MYS. As discussion unfolded through comments on two posts, new perspectives and new points of contention were raised. Initial comments expressed concern and shock, similar to the emotive sentiments that immediately followed MCGW's posts after the Masjid Musa raid. This time, sentiments were sympathetic to Christians living in a Muslim-dominated county. While the object of concern differed, like MCGW, activity was in response to emotional and personal issues, interpreted through a religious lens. By this point, the group seemed to surpass a collectivity that could be imagined to be fully known by any one member, having reached between 300 and 400 members. Still, coherent debates about religion, the actions of religious leaders and the role of NGOs unfolded, with indications of some familiarity, friendliness and humour among those who commented.

The influence of familiar connections on the tone of discussion has diminished as the group has grown in members and the frequency of contributions has increased. In discussions with the author in January 2014, prior to the group's formation, the founders expressed their interest in creating a discursive space free from individual bias and control; the public nature of the Facebook group supported this because comments and posts were not moderated prior to becoming public.[6] Facebook user profiles also enabled individuals to continually alter their public appearance, in ways potentially quite different from who they were on the ground. This furthered the sense of openness and unpredictability about what might be said. Taking advantage of the flexibility of user identities on Facebook, some participants in MYS claimed full anonymity, while others created titles and descriptors that were different from how they were recognised outside of Facebook, such as *Mheshimiwa* ('Honourable'), Prince, *Mzee* ('respected elder') or Governor.

While the public group and flexible user profile gave the discussion a dynamic and elusive quality, this did not necessarily diversify people's perspectives. Instead, uncertainty compelled users to return to familiar narratives about political divisions and elite-driven politics when responding to others' comments. Conversely, by bringing uncertainty to users' experiences, Facebook's flexible and distributed platform ended up focusing users' attention on well-known public figures and familiar narratives. Comments reacting to others' contributions repeatedly voiced pre-existing and dominant ideas of difference and political advantage. If a user expressed support for a politician in MYS, they could be accused of having a personal connection to that politician or of having received some material benefit in the form of employment, scholarship or cash. The group conveners themselves raised such suspicions.[7] This is illustrated in a response to a post made on 13 July 2014. A conversation about the Mombasa County Commissioner and the Governor of Mombasa digressed into personal allegations between users. One individual was accused of having been paid by specific politicians to make biased statements.

A group administrator commented: [name] is a driver to Mwembe Tayari ward rep and @Jb we understand u sold ua fb acc [your Facebook account] @1k to a ward rep to insult this pg [page]. u wont make it (recorded 24 August 2015 at 23:39 EAT).

Group administrators have also been the source of suspicions. Periodically, they have made some effort to limit accusatory and insulting language. While usually preferring to limit discussion through appeals to members to voluntarily self-censor, at times they have exercised administrative controls by blocking users from the group and deleting comments and posts. For example, on 11 March 2014, one administrator threatened to delete any further comments in a conversation in which the participants had begun to criticise each other's English language skills.[8] These actions provoked allegations by other members that they were motivated by political bias and intolerance of opposing views.

MYS differs from both the politicians' pages and MCGW in that it was intentionally made to be open for any citizen to initiate and direct discussion. With this, new contributions to public information were possible, and were visible in the varied and incoherent early discussions when the group was formed. Technologically, the public group brought greater flexibility to how the platform might be used to support different political interests and raise different voices. However, what people expected and how they interpreted others' comments reveals a similar refrain: one that tended to suspect those they disagree with of being influenced by personal political preferences and by patronage and partisan networks. As the group became more open and less bound by familiar connections, its openness was met with a tendency by users to return to familiar and dominant divisions to interpret others' contributions. Again, key political figures entered into the narrative as they were imagined to be infiltrating and shaping discussion, working through personal and network connections with users.

Conclusion

By exploring how the Facebook page and group structures were used for public discussion in Mombasa at a moment of insecurity, this chapter shows how the combination of its technological design and use ended up reinforcing dominant political narratives and power relations. The Masjid Musa raid was a critical point in heightening tensions about the relationship between residents of Mombasa and the national government. National security forces responded increasingly harshly to indications of religious radicalisation, resulting in a public confrontation that unfurled in the streets. It resulted in a few months of rising concern and tension around religion and radicalisation in the coastal region. The local and controversial nature of this event and its aftermath seemed to provide the context for more varied and participatory public information flows. Interest in new and unverified sources of information through Facebook immediately rose.

Analysis of public discourse around this event reveal the multiple and conflicting ways that Facebook is political. On one side, Facebook easily provided opportunities for more people to contribute to publicly circulating information, beyond the established press, as they took advantage of its flexible design and capacity to facilitate open and networked information flows. Diverse individuals, both local politicians and lesser-known residents, made use of Facebook to shape public information, and to attract attention. Through the Facebook page, local political leaders spoke directly to their constituents, emphasising a personal concern for them as their representative. Also through the Facebook page, MCGW, an anonymous self-defined citizen journalist, generated interest based on the local and immediate content of what they shared, posting information from the perspective of someone affected from within the local community. Through the Facebook group, a more open discussion about the events was possible, as any user could introduce topics.

Yet, on the other side, the combination of what attracted attention, and both the familiar and uncertain dimensions of Facebook presence and connections, reproduced familiar refrains about political difference and advantage. The printed press already tended to focus on the actions and commentary of the individual leader (see also Patel, this volume), publishing their expressed concern to address insecurity and maintain the support of the people of Mombasa. Similarly, on Facebook, pages and groups that generated interest around the Masjid Musa raid also gave attention to individual leaders and familiar narratives. Through direct and also surprising ways, Facebook's technological design showed an affinity for pre-existing and individualised forms of power. In the context of a networked and personalised view of politics, Facebook's structures reinforced rather than challenged existing dynamics. The individual page enabled an individual political leader or celebrity to speak to followers, who then read, commented and shared. The malleable user profile generated uncertainty about users' identities and intentions, making users unwilling to take others at face value and instead causing them to return to familiar narratives to interpret what was shared.

The political possibilities of Facebook-mediated communications thus emerge at the intersection of its design and affordances, and users' experiences. Around the Masjid Musa raid, the ways that Facebook groups and pages structured communications ended up limiting diversity in the content attracting attention. Facebook's scope and accessibility might suggest it will result in open and diverse information flows, as anyone with a Facebook account could share information with a potentially global audience. Yet in Mombasa, when insecurity on the ground was increasing and Facebook was used as an immediate source of information about local events, it did not seem to challenge dominant political discourses in any widespread way. This chapter adds to understanding about how Facebook relates to opportunities for citizen journalism and voice by differentiating between changes in the scope of who participates in providing information, and changes in the content and terms of debate. This helps to clarify how Facebook can simultaneously expand participation and reinforce existing power dynamics, through the combination of its design and use. In Mombasa, it has shown that even as the diversity of who contributes increased, the content of contributions attracting attention did not necessarily diversify. As people experienced and made use of Facebook's networked infrastructure for public discussion, the content that people were interested in and the logic through which they interpreted information did not seem to be disrupted.

Notes

1 Ethical approval was obtained from the Ethics Committee for the School of the Humanities and Social Sciences, University of Cambridge, on 7 August 2013.

2 http://www.internetworldstats.com/stats1.htm (accessed 25 August 2017).

3 This was followed by 53 comments, 16 shares and 58 likes.

4 Interview, MCGW administrator, 5 March 2014.

5 Interview by the author with two founders of MYS and a civil society coordinator, 31 January 2014.

6 Interview by the author with two founders of MYS and a civil society coordinator, 31 January 2014.

7 For example, a post to MYS, 31 October 2014, recorded 2 November 2014 at 14:13 EAT; and a post to MYS, 1 February 2015, recorded 2 February 2015 at 16:28 EAT.

8 Recorded on 12 March 2014 by refreshing and monitoring the page. Deleted comments were estimated to have been written between 23:44 EAT on 11 March 2014 and 8:54 EAT on 12 March 2014.

References

Al Jazeera (2014) 'Deadly clashes after police raid Kenya mosque'. *Al Jazeera* (online) 2 February. www. aljazeera.com/news/africa/2014/02/ clashes-after-police-storm-kenya-mosque-20142213377444840.html (accessed 2 February 2016).

Aouragh, M. & Alexander, A. (2011) 'The Arab Spring: the Egyptian experience: sense and nonsense of the Internet Revolution'. *International Journal of Communication*, 5: 1344–1358.

Berman, B. J., Cottrell, J. & Ghai, Y. (2009) 'Patrons, clients, and constitutions: ethnic politics and political reform in Kenya'. *Canadian Journal of African Studies/La Revue canadienne des études africaines*, 43(3): 462–506.

boyd, d. m. & Ellison, N. (2007) 'Social network sites: definition, history and scholarship'. *Journal of Computer-Mediated Communication*, 13(1): 210–230.

Constantin, F. (1989) 'Stratification on the Swahili coast: from race to class?' *Africa*, 59(2): 145–160.

Dean, J. (2009) *Democracy and Other Neoliberal Fantasies: Communicative Capitalism and Left Politics*. London: Duke University Press.

Diepeveen, Stephanie (2019) 'The limits of publicity: Facebook and transformations of a public realm in Mombasa, Kenya'. *Journal of Eastern African Studies*, 13(1), 158–174 DOI: 10.1080/17531055.2018.1547251

Ekine, S. (ed.) (2010) *SMS Uprising: Mobile activism in Africa*. Oxford: Pambazuka Press.

Facebook (2015) 'Airtel Africa and Facebook launch free basic services in 17 African countries'. *Facebook* (online) 19 November. www. facebook.com/notes/airtel-kenya/ airtel-africa-and-facebook-launch-free-basic-services-in-17-african-countries/989548301108621/ (accessed 6 March 2018).

Gagliardone, I. (2016) *The Politics of Technology in Africa: Communication, Development, and Nation-Building in Ethiopia*. Cambridge: Cambridge University Press.

Gladwell, M. (2010) 'Small change: why the revolution will not be tweeted'. *The New Yorker*, 4 October.

Goldstein, J. & Rotich, J. (2008) *Digitally Networked Technology in Kenya's 2007–2008 Post-Election Crisis (2008–09)*. Cambridge: Berkman Center for Internet and Society at Harvard University.

Haynes, J. (2006) 'Islam and democracy in East Africa'. *Democratization*, 13(3): 490–507.

Horowitz, J. & MUHURI (2013) *We're Tired of Taking You to the Court: Human Rights Abuses by Kenya's Anti-Terrorism Police Unit*. New York: Open Society Foundations.

Howard, P. & Hussain, M.M. (2011) 'The role of digital media'. *Journal of Democracy*, 22(3): 35–48.

Howard, P. & Parks, M. (2012) 'Social media and political change: capacity, constraint, and consequence'. *Journal of Communication*, 62(2): 359–362.

Human Rights Watch (2015) 'Kenya: counterterrorism operations undermine rights', *Human Rights Watch*, 29 January. www. hrw.org/news/2015/01/29/ kenya-counterterrorism-operations-undermine-rights (accessed 29 January 2016).

Ifukor, P. (2010) '"Elections" or "selections"? Blogging and Twittering the Nigerian 2007 general elections. *Bulletin of Science, Technology and Society*, 30(6): 398–414.

Kanyinga, K. (1998) 'Politics and struggles for access to land: "Grants from above" and "squatters" in coastal Kenya'. *European Journal of Development*, 10(2): 50–69.

Kenya ICT Board (2010) *Digital Kenya: a study to understand the on-line life of Kenyans: Key findings.*

KNCHR, Kenya National Commission on Human Rights (2008) *On the Brink of the Precipice: a Human Rights Account of Kenya's Post-2007 Election Violence* (Preliminary Edition). Nairobi: KNCHR.

Lamoureaux, S. & Sureau, T. (2019) 'Knowledge and legitimacy: the fragility of digital mobilization in Sudan'. *Journal of Eastern African Studies*, 13(1): 35–53.

Larkin, B. (2008) *Signal and Noise: Media, Infrastructure and Urban Culture in Nigeria.* Durham and London: Duke University Press.

Lornah, K. (2014) 'Jihad is about peace, says Muslim cleric'. *The Star* (online) 5 February. https://allafrica.com/stories/201402050723.html (paid subscription necessary.

Mäkinen, M. & Kuira, M. W. (2008) 'Social media and postelection crisis in Kenya'. *The International Journal of Press/Politics*, 13(3): 328–335.

Mathews, N. (2013) 'Imagining Arab communities: colonialism, Islamic reform, and Arab identity in Mombasa, Kenya, 1897–1933'. *Islamic Africa*, 4(2): 135–163.

McIntosh, J. (2009) *The Edge of Islam: Power, Personhood, and Ethnoreligious Boundaries on the Kenya Coast.* Durham and London: Duke University Press.

Mghenyi, C. (2014a) 'Joho to meet leaders over Sunday chaos at Masjid Musa in Mombasa'. *The Star* (online) 7 February.

www.the-star.co.ke/news/article-154249/joho-meet-leaders-over-sunday-chaos-masjid-musa-mombasa (accessed 15 February 2014).

Mghenyi, C. (2014b) 'Marwa asks Muslim heads to stop battles'. *The Star* (online) 10 February. https://allafrica.com/stories/201402101955.html.

Mghenyi, C. (2014c) 'Muslim leaders learn extremism'. *The Star* (online) 10 February. https://allafrica.com/stories/201402110342.html.

Morozov, E. (2011) *The Net Delusion: How Not to Liberate the World.* London: Allen Lane.

Mosoku, G. (2014) 'Governor Hassan Joho to unveil anti-radicalisation roadmap for Mombasa youth'. *Standard Media* (online) 12 February. www.standardmedia.co.ke/article/2000104485/governor-hassan-joho-to-unveil-anti-radicalisation-roadmap-for-mombasa-youth (accessed 15 February 2014).

Moyo, L. (2009) 'Repression, propaganda, and digital resistance: new media and democracy in Zimbabwe'. In O. F. Mudhai, W. J. Tetty & F. Banda (eds.), *African Media and the Digital Public Sphere.* New York: Palgrave Macmillan, pp. 57–72.

Murage, G. (2014) 'Police face suit for mosque raid'. *The Star* (online) 12 February. https://allafrica.com/stories/201402120387.html.

Mwakimako, H. & Willis, J. (2014) *Islam, politics, and violence on the Kenyan Coast* (4). Observatoire des enjeux politiques et sécuritaires dans la corne de l'Afrique Note. www.lam.sciencespobordeaux.fr/sites/lam/files/note4_observatoire.pdf

Nation reporter (2014) 'Lenku defends police in Masjid Musa

raid'. *The Daily Nation* (online) 6 March. www.nation.co.ke/news/Joseph-ole-Lenku-defends-police-in-Masjid-Musa-raid/1056-2234170-47a8abz/index.html (accessed 18 October 2017).

Nation team (2014) 'Muslim leaders blamed for youth radicalisation'. *The Daily Nation*, (online) 9 February. www.nation.co.ke/news/Muslim-clerics-blamed-for-Mombasa-violence/-/1056/2198362/-/rr7dbfz/-/index.html (accessed 18 October 2017).

Ndavula, J.O., Mberia, H.K. & Mwangi, M.K. (2015) 'Online campaign in Kenya: implementing the Facebook campaign in the 2013 general elections'. *International Journal of Education and Research*, 3(7): 255–266. http://erepository.uonbi.ac.ke/bitstream/handle/11295/91976/Ndavula_Online%20campaign%20in%20Kenya.pdf?sequence=1 (accessed 26 September 2017).

Nyamnjoh, F.B. (2005) *Africa's Media: Democracy and the Politics of Belonging*. London: Zed Books.

Obbayi, K. (2014) 'Mombasa senator asks president to intervene in "missing" youth case'. *The Star* (online) 20 February. https://allafrica.com/stories/201402210196.html.

Oded, A. (2000) *Islam and Politics in Kenya*. London: Lynne Rienner Publishers.

Ogola, G. (2015) 'Social media as a heteroglossic discursive space and Kenya's emergent alternative/citizen experiment'. *African Journalism Studies*, 36(4): 66–81.

Ogola, G. (2019) '#Whatwouldmagufulido? Kenya's digital "practices" and "individuation" as a (non)political act'. *Journal of Eastern African Studies*, 13(1): 124–139. DOI: 10.1080/17531055.2018.1547263.

Onsarigo, C. & Otieno, B. (2014) 'Kenya: two killed in Mombasa Masjid Musa fighting'. *The Star* (online) 3 February. http://allafrica.com/stories/201402040198.html (accessed 28 March 2017).

Osborn, M. (2008) 'Fuelling the flames: rumour and politics in Kibera'. *Journal of Eastern African Studies*, 2(2): 315–327.

Otieno, B. (2014) 'Nassir plea for peace'. *The Star* (online) 13 February. www.africanewshub.com/news/1042556-nassir-plea-for-peace (accessed 15 February 2014).

Papacharissi, Z & Oliveira, M.F. (2012) 'Affective news and networked publics: the rhythms of news storytelling on #Egypt'. *Journal of Communication*, 62(2): 266–282.

Prestholdt, J. (2011) 'Kenya, the United States, and counterterrorism'. *Africa Today*, 57(4): 2–27.

Tully, M. & Ekdale, B. (2014) 'Sites of playful engagement: Twitter hashtags as spaces of leisure and development in Kenya'. *Information Technologies & International Development*, 10(3): 67–82.

Willis, J. & Chome, N. (2014) 'Marginalization and political participation on the Kenya Coast: the 2013 elections'. *Journal of Eastern African Studies*, 8(1): 115–134.

Willis, J. & Gona, G. (2013) '*Pwani c Kenya*? Memory, documents and secessionist politics in coastal Kenya'. *African Affairs*, 112(446): 48–71.

Winner, L. (1980) 'Do artefacts have politics?' *Daedalus*, 109(1): 121–136.

12 | INSIDE THE #OPERATIONUSALAMAWATCH ECHO CHAMBER

Twitter as site of disruption or elite conversation?

Alisha Patel

Introduction

No longer universally perceived as a 'liberation technology', the relationship between information and communication technology (ICT) and democracy has become increasingly complex and contested. For some, 'big data' has morphed into 'big brother' as governments resort to surveillance technologies to monitor the actions of their citizens. For others, social media has played an important role in increasing transparency and accountability of governments, exposing human rights abuses and democratic deficits. In a more radical fashion, others still have turned to 'hacktivism' and other disruptive technologies to expose the dark underbelly of the internet.

The significant and rapid change in communication facilitated by the internet, and specifically social media technologies, has been borne out in sub-Saharan Africa, catalysed by the interplay of more widespread access to mobile phones and increased network penetration. This is only set to increase over the coming decades alongside demographic changes. Kenya is a key site of technological innovation and dynamism, and is one of the most active communities on the continent. Often identifying as #KOT (Kenyans on Twitter), Twitter has become a platform for a self-identifying digital community.

Yet, while these technologies have engaged ordinary citizens, they have also been employed by elites, including by the government and traditional print media (Keane 2013). Both have played contentious roles in conflicts along Kenya's path of democratisation, particularly during elections. During the 2007 general elections and post-electoral violence that followed, both media and politicians stood accused – and were charged with – communicating messages of hate to citizens. These messages prompted ethnic clashes, which resulted in hundreds being killed and many thousands displaced (Abdi Ismail and Deane 2008; Somerville 2011). During the 2013 elections, mindful of the violence that came before, journalists were too quick to overlook serious democratic deficits for the sake of 'peaceocracy' (Stremlau & Gagliardone 2015; Gustafsson 2016). Since then, President Uhuru Kenyatta (2013–present) has taken increasingly authoritarian measures to co-opt the media and stifle freedom of expression. This has been demonstrated by threats against journalists and decisions to strip media houses of their licences. In January 2016, Denis Galava (see Chapter 13, this volume), an esteemed Kenyan journalist and editor at Nation Media Group, was sacked after publishing a critical editorial against the president. A few months later, the government stopped advertising in commercial media, a move widely seen as an attempt to punish the media and starve them of critical advertising revenue. This repression has intensified following the 2017 elections and presidential election re-run, with Kenyatta shutting down the country's three biggest TV stations to stop coverage of the mock swearing-in ceremony of opposition leader Raila Odinga (Ogola 2018). Given these concerning trends, the migration of political and media elites to online spaces and their interaction with a growing online community is an important, although overlooked, area of study.

Through a quantitative and qualitative study, this chapter analyses the interaction between traditional print and social media platform Twitter during one of the key democratisation conflicts in Kenya's recent history: the government's 'war on terror' stemming from the threat posed by militant group Al Shabaab. The Somali community has long been stigmatised by Kenya's political and media elite, but following the uptick in attacks claimed by Al Shabaab during 2014, the framing of the Somali community as 'terrorists' became increasingly pronounced. In response, security forces undertook crackdowns in Somali neighbourhoods of Nairobi, particularly in the neighbourhood of Eastleigh. The chapter looks at one such crackdown, part of the government's 'Operation Usalama Watch', and analyses whether alternative and subversive narratives of the conflict were advanced on Twitter, and, if so, which voices gained prominence. In doing so, the chapter aims to interrogate the role of Twitter as an important platform for democratic contestation and representation of alternative and challenging viewpoints.

This chapter begins with an overview of Kenya's media ecology, highlighting that the interests of government and major media houses are heavily intertwined because of government ownership of key outlets, and the importance of securing lucrative state advertising contracts. Next, the chapter outlines the connection between social media and democracy. It then analyses the print media and Twitter responses to Operation Usalama Watch, comparing the dominant narratives and key actors that participated in these debates. Ultimately, the findings highlight that there was a high degree of polarisation in commentary both in print media and on Twitter, with two distinct narratives emerging from the conflict. One spoke to the importance of preserving national security at all costs, while the other rallied against the government's approach, criticising the unjust profiling of Somalis. Analysis also highlights that the voices of established, elite actors – including government and media voices – gained the most influence. This is somewhat unsurprising given the resources available to the government and media. Yet, it also calls into question theories that advance the inherently democratic credentials of social media. Instead, many of the power structures prevalent in the Kenyan political landscape are replicated online.

Control and co-option: the intertwined interests of government and media houses in Kenya

Kenya's media landscape remains among the most vibrant and diverse on the continent, but is heavily intertwined with the historical, political and economic context in which it has evolved. Key to understanding the role and influence of the media in Kenya is the high level of media concentration and government control and co-option in constraining, enabling and generally shaping Kenya's media ecology (Ogola 2011). More specifically, Kenya's current media landscape is reflective of patterns of clientelism and patronage, asymmetric power held by the executive branch of government, a winner-takes-all style of political competition, and the politicisation of ethnicity.

Historical factors are therefore of critical importance when analysing contemporary Kenyan media. Through his 'ideology of order' (Atieno-Odhiambo 1987), President Jomo Kenyatta's (1964–1978) state-building project utilised the state's machinery, including the media, for propaganda purposes and to alienate political rivals in what ultimately led to the co-option of the mainstream news media (Ogola 2011). These patterns were replicated and extended under President Daniel arap Moi (1979–2002), where independent and critical publications were banned outright (Ogola 2011). During this time, the government also restricted and limited political freedoms, especially press freedoms and freedom of expression. However, the advent of multi-party politics in 1992, to some extent, brought with it liberalisation and expansion of the media space. Media outlets, and in particular radio stations, proliferated. Alongside this, ownership bases expanded and content became bolder and more critical, with the media increasingly acting as a check on government power.

However, while journalistic freedoms have increased over the decades, Kenyan media remains only 'partly free' (Freedom House 2018). This is to some extent explained by structural factors, which have historically meant that government and media are closely connected. While Kenya has over 60 TV stations, more than 130 radio stations and several newspaper titles, the industry remains dominated by three major players: the Nation Media Group, Standard Media Group and Royal Media Services (Ogola 2018). Political economy analysis of Kenya's media highlights patterns of both concentration and co-option, facilitated by government ownership and influence of media outlets, as well as the indirect influence afforded by government advertising. Ultimately, this has resulted in a 'problematic relationship between the news media and a powerful parallel political infrastructure' (Ogola 2011: 77), without whose support most news media would have difficulty surviving.

Ownership of the major newspapers has significantly compromised the independence of private media houses and their ability to be unbiased and critical, and provide adequate oversight and accountability of the government's actions. This can be in both direct and indirect ways: key political actors continue to hold stakes in media groups, and the owners of media houses themselves retain close connections to the political elite. Among the key stakeholders of the Standard Group, which not only owns the Standard newspapers – Kenya's second most popular daily and weekly newspapers – but also Kenya Television Network (KTN), are former President Daniel arap Moi, his son Gideon, as well as former Moi aide Joshua Kulei. The Nation Media Group is the largest media conglomerate in East and Central Africa and its founder and principal shareholder is the Aga Khan, who himself has continued to hold strong ties with presidents, partly to safeguard business interests (Cheeseman et al. 2016; Ogola 2011). These connections have led to criticism of media houses being constrained in their ability to hold the government to account. This issue is widespread, and continues despite transfers of political power. To further consolidate his power, President Uhuru Kenyatta has invested heavily in MediaMax, his family media company, which owns several radio stations, a television station and a national newspaper (Ogola 2018). Following his inauguration in 2013, top editors and journalists were called to State House and the invitation was soon repaid with sympathetic media coverage, and a few high-level journalists were offered lucrative jobs in government (Ogola 2018). However, those who refused to be co-opted were summoned routinely to State House, with Kenyatta even warning on World Freedom Day in 2014 that journalists did not have absolute freedom on what to publish or broadcast.

Moreover, the commercial interests of media houses cannot be underestimated, specifically the importance of securing lucrative advertising contracts. Media revenue from advertising has steadily increased over the past decade. Mindful not to lose this important source of funding, it is not uncommon for media owners to interfere with editorial decisions to protect lucrative sources of advertising income. Principal among these sources is the government. Through withdrawal of advertising, the government is able to effectively punish those critical of its policies, ultimately contributing to a culture of self-censorship and undermining the democratic function of the media. In February 2017, the government announced that it would no longer be advertising in local commercial media, with state departments and agencies instructed to advertise in government publications and the MyGov online portal. This decision was widely seen as punitive action against critical voices; a means not only to starve them of a vital revenue source, but to undermine freedom of expression as a form of indirect state control (Ogola 2017).

Taken together, selective advertising, ownership and co-option of media, and successive attempts to restrict media freedoms over decades, have created an exceptionally concentrated yet prolific media oligopoly, which is often heavily tied to government interests. Although these media coexist with forms of a vibrant citizen activism, the vast resources held by the media – as well as their established base, reputation and vast readership – have also enabled them to embrace technological innovation and become key players within the online space.

Social media: democratic platform or elite echo chamber?

Social media in sub-Saharan Africa has become an increasingly prevalent mode of communication, largely a result of the advent of cheap smartphones and better internet network penetration. Indeed, according to Pew Research Center (2018), technology usage in Kenya (measured as a percentage of adults who use the internet at least occasionally or own a smartphone) remained close to 40% between 2013 and 2017. Access and participation continue to grow at a rapid pace. Described as a 'liberation technology', Diamond (Diamond & Plattner 2012: ix) notes, 'these electronic tools have provided new, breathtakingly dynamic, and radically decentralised means for people and organisations to communicate and cooperate with one another for political and civic ends'. More specifically, social media's flat and decentralised structure has been seen to have reconfigured the practice of participatory democracy and it has established itself as a key site to bridge the gap between political elites and the citizens they represent. Popular sites serve as indispensable platforms for reformers, revolutionaries and contemporary democracy movements, allowing for the collective expressions of dissent, dissemination of information and action (Youmans & York 2012). Users can function as 'citizen journalists' and 'opinion leaders', competing with established media sources to provide political commentary and challenge the prevailing discourse (Bennett & Segerberg 2012). Crucially, unlike print and broadcast media, social media has facilitated a two- and even multi-way form of communication. Not only are users able to situate themselves in new 'digital communities', but they are also able to forge new connections and maintain existing ties in the consumption and exchange of information and opinions. Critically, these ties can transcend traditional hierarchies of age, region, ethnic or socio-economic identity, and act as a check on state power (Aday and Livingston 2008). Platforms such as Twitter have allowed users to reach thousands of 'followers', instantly informing, entertaining and mobilising them for a particular (political) cause.

However, while new social media affords opportunities for democratic consolidation, arguments put forward that they will be realised rely on a number of assumptions. Firstly, they assume that political elites have democratic tendencies and that communication environments are facilitative. Unfortunately, in too many cases governments have exercised their own logics, and instead new technologies have enabled them to better monitor and neutralise pro-democracy or anti-government movements and dissidents, often using a veiled pretence of curbing hate speech or terrorist activities to protect their citizens. As Voltmer and Sorensen (2016: 7) argue, 'the result is a more centralised, manipulated and elite-driven process of public communication'. In this way, 'the logic of the traditional media blends with interactive modes of communications' (Mazzoleni 2014: 44) in what has been characterised as 'hybrid logics' (Chadwick 2013; Klinger & Svensson 2015). These logics interplay with those of social media sites themselves, with the architectural design of new media platforms reflecting their own growth and profit ambitions – ultimately affecting the scope of surveillance, as well as who communicates with whom and which voices gain prominence (Howard & Parks 2012; Youmans & York 2012).

Secondly, the arguments assume that there is a level playing field on the online space, where each ordinary citizen-user can battle for influence with established journalists, politicians and celebrities. Social and digital architecture precludes this, as both on- and offline users are overwhelmingly more likely to seek out views from those with high economic, cultural or symbolic capital (Bourdieu 2005; Phillips 2010) – whose opinions they respect or simply want to hear and challenge. In the online space, these figures will easily outcompete ordinary users through the number of 'followers', 'likes' and/or 'retweets' they have. Therefore, it is this elite group that often frame news events. In particular, journalists have also engaged and adapted to evolving digital modalities. Yet, research has shown that despite the highly interactive and participatory format, they have gradually aligned their online engagement with old norms and practices, citing their host news organisation or mainstream media and often seeking to remain gatekeepers (Lasarosa, Lewis & Holton 2012; Singer 2005). Ordinary citizen-users, who comprise the vast majority of #KOT, too often fail to get the traction that they hope for with their tweets, simply because they are unlikely to have a similar number of followers to the tens of thousands, sometimes millions, held by elite actors. Digital media therefore reproduce the political narrative of traditional media logics, but all the while giving users the illusion of having their voices heard and influencing the debate (Diamond 2012).

Finally, access to diverse and pluralistic opinions is also contingent on the user's decision to follow those with different political opinions to their own. Too often, an individual's decision to follow other users is dependent on mutual interests, socio-economic, political or religious commonalities, or for the purposes of professional networking. Moreover, Twitter algorithms are likely to use these preferences when determining which posts to display on a user's newsfeed and in suggesting new accounts to follow. As a result, the social media space is one that is fragmented and polarised. Instead of enhancing the quality of democratic politics, social media therefore can function as an 'echo chamber', leading to polarisation and separation rather than meaningful debate.

The Operation Usalama Watch case study clearly demonstrates these trends. It highlights homogenised, yet totally polarised, conversations, shaped by political, media and celebrity personalities. In this way, narratives on print media appear almost replicated online. These findings therefore raise important questions about the value and function of social media in the context of an increasingly restricted traditional media space.

Kenya's 'war on terror' and Operation Usalama Watch

Following the intervention of the Kenyan Defence Forces (KDF) in Somalia from 2011 to combat the threat posed by terrorist group Al Shabaab, a number of retaliatory guerrilla-style attacks have taken place throughout the country, particularly along the Kenya–Somalia border (for example, see Molony 2019). Al Shabaab has also demonstrated the intent and capacity to mount large-scale attacks in major cities, including in Mombasa and Nairobi. These events generated national and regional debates (as explored in the context of Mombasa in Diepeveen, this volume). These included the September 2013 attack on the upscale Westgate shopping mall in Nairobi, in which 67 people were killed, and the 2015 attack on Garissa University College, where gunmen brutally murdered at least 148 people, mostly students.

Operation Usalama Watch began in April 2014 following grenade and gun attacks in Mombasa and Nairobi the previous month that killed twelve and injured at least eight. In response, Kenya's then Interior Minister, the late Joseph Ole Lenku, announced that 6,000 police had been deployed to Nairobi's Eastleigh neighbourhood to arrest foreign nationals who were in the country unlawfully and anyone suspected of terrorist links. Eastleigh has long been regarded with considerable suspicion, with the external imagery of the neighbourhood as a place of danger, harbouring terrorists and terrorist sympathisers, funded by illicit financial flows, piracy and tax and duty evasion. Arrests and detentions have been common since the time of Moi, and Somalis have often been targets of extortion. As Carrier (2016: 221) writes in his ethnography of Eastleigh, 'the resonance of the nickname "Little Mogadishu" is strong here, reflecting the continued perception of the estate as a piece of the Somali Republic transported to Kenya as a result of civil war'. Shaped by migration dynamics, Eastleigh has become increasingly securitised alongside the Kenyan government's 'war on terror', which has frequently been employed as a rationale for government and security forces to act with relative impunity (Carrier 2016; Burbidge 2015; Lochery 2012). Operation Usalama Watch profiled Eastleigh's Somali and refugee population as terrorists, detaining thousands (as well as Ethiopians and South Sudanese) in Nairobi's Kasarani Stadium (Human Rights Watch 2014). A scathing report by the Independent Policing Oversight Authority (2014) found that the operation 'was not conducted in compliance with the law, respect for the Rule of Law, democracy, human rights and fundamental freedoms'.

Contesting narratives of Kenya's 'war on terror' in print media

To understand how Operation Usalama Watch was framed in print media, a quantitative and qualitative content analysis of the major Kenyan print newspapers, the *Daily Nation*, the *Standard* and the *Star* was undertaken from March 2014, just before the start of Operation Usalama Watch, to May 2014, after the majority of those detained were either released from custody or deported. Both news stories and op-ed pieces were studied in order to cover the wide range of commentary and reaction to the security forces' operation, as well as to identify the major positions taken in the coverage. Through this study, a number of important findings emerge, which will be briefly summarised before being explored in more detail. Firstly, there were two distinct narratives of Operation Usalama Watch, demonstrating the polarising nature of the operation. On the one side, some pieces strongly agreed with the government's 'war on terror' and the operation's objectives to flush out the threat posed by Somalis, framing them as dangerous terrorists who had accumulated wealth in suspect ways. On the other, a large part of the commentary condemned the unconstitutionality of the operation, the profiling of Somalis as terrorists, the conditions detainees were subjected to, and the failure of the operation to meet its stated objectives. Secondly, within these narratives, it was mostly the op-ed pieces that were critical of Operation Usalama Watch. News pieces, and to a large extent the in-house editorial leads, backed the government's approach. To some degree, this highlights the influence the government holds over the media. Finally, very few pieces gave a voice to those who had been affected by the abusive round-ups, with most articles citing comments made by either government and security force actors, prominent domestic and international civil society organisations, and even the international diplomatic community.

The polarisation in narratives around Operation Usalama Watch was marked on one side by pieces that saw Somalis as potential terrorists and felt a hard-hitting police response was justified. In this coverage, many voices within the Kenyan print media landscape drew links between Somalis and the Somali-based militant group Al Shabaab. In one particularly incendiary op-ed by Kwamchetsi Makokha, Somalis were framed as 'other' and were explicitly referred to as terrorists: 'it would appear that every little two-bit Somali has a big dream – to blow us up, knock down our buildings and slaughter our children' (Makokha 2014 (*Nation*)). The same piece explicitly referred to Somalis as 'relations of al Shabaab' (Makokha 2014 (*Nation*)), making reference to their 'Cushitic features' and 'billowing robes', as well as their amassed wealth, as reasons to hold them in deep suspicion. In what amounted to hate speech and incitement to violence, the op-ed ended with a call to arms: 'We are at war. Let's start shooting' (Makokha 2014 (*Nation*)).

While no other pieces in the sample used such egregious language, many referenced the preceding terrorist attacks in Likoni and Mombasa to justify the need for a strong police response. In doing so, they implicitly reinforced links between Somali refugees and Al Shabaab. In one op-ed for the *Star* newspaper, journalist Faith Muthoni wrote, 'Kenya has borne the brunt of being too good and too soft to foreigners' (Muthoni 2014, *Star*), while another news piece in the *Standard* quoted then Interior Minister Joe Ole Lenku stating, 'These terrorists had made Eastleigh their launching pad. We will not relent' (Lenku 2014). As a result, Makokha wrote, 'arresting 657 Somalis in Eastleigh, holding them in cages at Kasarani stadium, and taxing them for illegal presence in Kenya should teach terrorists a lesson' (Makokha 2014). These pieces made little distinction between Somalis and terrorists. Praising Operation Usalama Watch, the government was seen as 'finally winning the war against terror and crime' (Kuria 2014, *Standard*), when it had previously been too 'casual and lax' (Gaitho 2014 (*Nation*)).

However, there were as many journalists criticising Operation Usalama Watch, with no discernible difference between media houses. Not only did they call out against the poor conditions that detainees faced, but they opined that the operation was unconstitutional, careless and ultimately counter-productive. Opinion pieces made it clear to readers that men, women and children were held in custody for more than 24 hours, without 'access to food and water' (Obala & Kithi 2014 (*Standard*)) and 'in degrading conditions, showing little regard to basic human rights and fundamental liberties as enshrined in the Kenyan Constitution and international and regional human rights law' (Aling'o 2014 (*Standard*)).

Writing directly against their peers who drew strong links between Somalis and terrorists, this narrative criticised the unfair profiling that led to detention, which was described as being 'akin to saying that if someone speaks Somali, looks Somali and is dressed like a Somali then he is a terrorist, or at least a potential terrorist' (Kiai 2014 (*Nation*)). As Billow Kerrow wrote in the *Standard*, 'the [Somali] community has been stigmatised and portrayed as "terrorists" by the xenophobic narrative of the State, and other Kenyans psyched against them' (Kerrow 2014). Kerrow and some of his peers also noted that the operation 'was reminiscent of the kind of humiliation the Somali people have been undergoing since Independence under successive regimes in Kenya' (Guleid 2014 (*Standard*)), referring to historical injustices against Somalis such as the Shifta War (1963–1967) and Wagalla massacre (1984).

With the launch of Operation Usalama Watch coming shortly after the release of the Westgate report, which highlighted unprofessional, ineffective and corrupt policing, the role of the police was also questioned in many of the articles. For many, their rejection of Operation Usalama Watch centred on criticism of Kenya's ineffective and corrupt police force and the ideology underpinning Kenya's 'war on terror'. Also drawing on the many raids in Eastleigh over previous decades (see Lochery 2012), journalists stated that 'members of the Kenyan Somali community have always been a milking cow for police officers, immigration officers and any government agency that is required to enforce the law' (Kerrow 2014 (*Standard*)), and suggested that 'police action in Eastleigh [aimed] to disenfranchise the community economically by disabling its main business hub' (Kerrow 2014 (*Standard*)). Highlighting the evidence of unconstitutional detention and degrading conditions, journalists made clear that the only result of Operation Usalama Watch was 'the fattening of wallets of corrupt policemen who took advantage of the operation to arrest Kenyan citizens and demand bribes' (Waitherero 2014 (*Nation*)).

This criticism was also intimately linked to Kenya's 'war on terror'. Op-ed commentators made it clear that the security operation was harmful and ineffective: 'we are becoming victims of terrorism because of easily corruptible security forces [...] poor intelligence gathering and downright incompetence' (Warah 2014 (*Nation*)). Given this, the excessive force and unconstitutionality of Operation Usalama Watch would be 'inefficient, ineffective and unsustainable' (Waitherero 2014 (*Nation*)) and ultimately counter-productive. As Mohamed Wato writing in the *Nation* summarised: 'carrying out indiscriminate arrests or effecting disparate measures like profiling Somalis in general are short-term, half-hearted measures that are bound to become counter-productive in the long term' (Wato 2014). As such, Usalama Watch would end up as 'a smokescreen that would result in bitterness, isolation and alienation amongst Kenyans' (Aling'o 2014 (*Standard*)), with journalists also calling out the poor logic of the Interior Secretary's strategy which they saw as 'trying to solve a seemingly intractable problem by demonising people who are already victims of violence in their own countries' (Ngwiri 2014 (*Nation*)).

The role of elites in framing news coverage and shaping print media debate

Both interesting and important to note is that the vast majority of critical pieces were contained in the op-ed sections rather than news features. Generally, news pieces about the operation were much more moderate in their tone, with the government narrative clearly promoted in some. News features also quoted government sources extensively, including then Interior Secretary Joe Lenku and Inspector General of Police David Kimaiyo, as well as President Uhuru Kenyatta, Vice President William Ruto and many more MPs.

For example, in its news coverage of Operation Usalama Watch during its first week, the *Nation*, Kenya's most widely circulated newspaper, clearly toed the government line – not only in news features but also in editorial leads. As the operation began, a *Nation* editorial called on the public to unquestioningly support government security measures: 'It is the cardinal duty of the government to guarantee security for all. It follows, therefore, that all those who want to live in peace and safety must support any measures to eliminate terrorists' (*Nation* Editorial Team 2014). In the double page spreads that followed, the government narrative was promoted by either direct quotes by government and police officials or commentary seen to endorse the operation or to describe the gains made. In a feature entitled '500 more arrested as police carry out swoop in Eastleigh' on 6 April, journalists Aggrey Mutambo and Angira Zadock painted a picture of the Somalis picked up by police in Eastleigh as suspect and dangerous:

> The men, probably in their mid-20s, could speak neither English nor Kiswahili, and police had to use sign language. They had no identification documents and they too, were bundled into the lorry ... The building next door had six occupants – three women and three men. Four had genuine IDs and two had waiting cards. But just as police were about to leave the house, they noticed two others hiding under the mattress. They too boarded the lorry. (Mutamo & Zadock 2014 (*Nation*))

The news feature also cited a local truck driver, Ali Hussain, to highlight how the Somali community itself endorsed the crackdown: 'This operation will help make this place safer. The police should take away those who do not belong here and take them to the camps of their countries' (Mutamo & Zadock 2014 (*Nation*)). Even the photos reified the role of the police and made those Somalis arrested look suspicious. Given that journalists were prevented from entering Kasarani Stadium, there were no pictures of the conditions that detainees faced for days on end.

Another *Nation* headline read '"Bomb factory" found in police terror crackdown', with a report telling of the chemicals, equipment and manuals for making bombs, as well as rifles and ammunition, that had been seized. A featured quote from President Kenyatta stated: 'we are not fighting any religion or tribe, but fighting terrorists who are killing innocent Kenyans'. This news commentary mirrored the government's narrative, praising its approach and, in descriptions of Usalama Watch, it strongly associated Somalis with potential terrorists, and painted Eastleigh as a suspicious, dangerous and illicit place. The piece also used the international community's pledges to support the government's efforts to fight terrorism as an endorsement of the operation: 'Britain, US, Canada and Australia have pledged to support the government's efforts to fight terrorism' (*Nation* Team 2014). Despite scathing criticism of Operation Usalama Watch – including from Nation op-ed contributors literally adjacent to this coverage – the *Nation*'s lead editorials affirmed that the operation was important and ethically conducted, and had had public support: 'the feeling among the majority of Kenyans is that the campaign, should, in fact, be stepped up' (*Nation* Editorial Team 2014). This commentary arguably demonstrates the influence of the government in shaping the media debate.

Finally, few news pieces and op-eds actually gave a voice to those who had been directly impacted by the round-ups. Instead, most articles cited government and security actors – including publishing an op-ed from Joe Lenku himself – as well as prominent civil society organisations such as the Kenyan National Commission on Human Rights (KNCHR), Muslims for Human Rights (MUHURI) and Amnesty International. Only three pieces in the sample quoted from citizens who had been affected by the round-ups, and only one of these in depth. Ultimately this meant that the commentary around Usalama Watch was centred on the government's 'war on terror', rather than, for example, on questions of citizenship, identity, as well as the conditions faced by those who were detained and the racial profiling and extortion to which they may have been exposed.

Similar stories, similar voices: Twitter responds to Operation Usalama Watch

The response on Twitter to Operation Usalama Watch was analysed using the Mecodify platform,[1] which can be used to gauge the influence Twitter users had and to assess the content of their tweets. Given that responses to news events on Twitter typically occur rapidly before dropping off, only the period 6–11 April 2014 was studied, in order to just cover Operation Usalama Watch. Casting too wide a net produced more 'noise' as tweeters used 'Usalama Watch' to reference the government's wider campaign, particularly after Al Shabaab terrorist attacks in Mombasa and Pangani. Twitter hashtags were predominantly chosen to analyse the case study for a number of reasons. Hashtags have the ability to serve as communities, discourses and discursive formation; they are recognised as an individual event and an effective amplifier, and form and subtend particular publics (Rambukkana 2015: 2). As Bruns & Burgess (2015: 5) argue, 'to include a hashtag in one's tweet is a performative statement: it brings the hashtag into being at the very moment that it is first articulated, and – as the tweet is instantly disseminated to all the senders' followers – announces its existence'. Put differently, using a hashtag allows users to frame a debate, as well as to situate themselves and others in a particular digital modality, with the hashtag taking on a particular agency in its own right. The selected hashtags for analysing this case study were #Usalama, #UsalamaWatch and #Kasarani, and the text 'Kasarani'. These were chosen because they were among the most trending hashtags and widely used text during the conflict, and were not associated with a positive or negative value judgement. Focusing on the most prolific hashtags also highlighted the most prominent and influential online discourses in order to assess how Operation Usalama Watch was framed, and by whom.

Two notable findings emerged from quantitative and qualitative analysis of Twitter commentary during this period, which this chapter will analyse in greater depth. Firstly, the government, media houses/ journalists and celebrity bloggers were the most influential actors on Twitter by a considerable margin. Secondly, the same polarised narratives outlined in the op-ed pieces in the print media were replicated on Twitter. This shows that while Twitter may have opened access to new users, crucially, many of the same actors identified in print media were among the most active and influential. This included government voices, such as Joe Lenku (@joelenku), David Kimaiyo (@IGkimaiyo) and the official Ministry of the Interior (@InteriorKE). Echoing findings of the print media analysis, major media houses tweeted less prolifically and were altogether more reticent to come down on either side of the debate, focusing instead on the reporting of news, reaffirming earlier discussions of close connections between government and media. For instance, the *Daily Nation* on 6 April tweeted, 'Today's front page: Police hold hundreds in Kasarani Stadium'. Ultimately, despite opening up the space for an alternative and more inclusive debate, the same narratives were propagated on Twitter, and with the migration of influential actors online, it was typically these same actors that were prominent in shaping the debate.

Twitter influence was assessed by using three metrics: 1) the number of followers each user had; 2) the number of retweets they received; and 3) the number of 'mentions' received. Users with a high degree of influence would have their tweets disseminated more widely and were therefore more likely to shape the online debate. Firstly, analysis of the number of followers each actor had shows that those users with the most followers were overwhelmingly media outlets: eight of the top 10 Twitter accounts covering Operation Usalama Watch were either accounts of print or broadcast media, radio stations or journalists. The other two top 10 Twitter accounts were among the most famous Kenyan citizen activist bloggers, Robert Alai (@RobertAlai) and Thee Trend Setter (@xtiandela). Robert Alai is a Kenyan blogger and cyber-activist that has become one of the foremost bloggers in Kenyan social media space through a strategy that has involved a high volume of tweeting and covering events as they break. For example, during the Westgate terror attack, Alai provided coverage that directly contested some of the statements put out by the government, which brought with it both national and international exposure. Xtian Dela is a Kenyan YouTuber, blogger, social media personality and radio presenter, who won the Best Personal Blog in the African Bloggers Awards and the Most Influential Twitter Personality in the Kenyan Social Media Awards. He also gained international media coverage when he started a Twitter campaign in 2014 called #BringBackOurKDFSoldiers. While both are examples of how a digital community has leveraged Twitter to hold the government to account, such followings are reserved for a very narrow elite that should not be conflated with the everyday Twitter user as they are better seen as professional social media personalities.

The total number of retweets each user received was another measure of their influence on Twitter. The most popular tweets are not only displayed more prominently when searching for a specific hashtag, but through the process of retweeting the reach of the tweets also extends further. If User A retweets a tweet by User B, and User A is followed by User C, then User B's tweet is more likely to appear on User C's newsfeed upon logging on to Twitter. In an exponential fashion, the process of retweeting extends the sphere of influence of the original tweeter's message and in the process can also lead to the original user gathering more followers. Retweets also facilitate engagement as users are able to quote the tweet alongside their own commentary. In the case of Operation Usalama Watch, the data highlight that there is a considerable degree of concentration, with the top three users gaining more than five times as many retweets as the user with the fourth largest number of retweets. Critically this highlights the significant degree to which these tweets were able to penetrate the online space and ultimately influence Twitter users. Again, the trends here highlight that the aforementioned actors have the most influence, in some part facilitated by the number of followers they have. Robert Alai, Mohammed Ali and Al Jazeera Africa journalists Haru Mutasa (@harumutasa) and Shailja Patel (@shailjapatel) all feature. Notably, the number of times some government actors, including the Ministry of the Interior, and Inspector General of the Kenyan police David Kimaiyo, were retweeted is also high. Again, this indicator highlights that journalists, government officials and elite bloggers are engaged with the most and dominate Twitter.

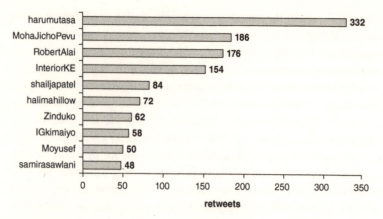

Figure 12.1 Top 10 tweeters by number of retweets

The majority of Twitter users get little to no traction on Twitter. As seen in Figure 12.2, the modal number of retweets is 0 for the vast majority of users. In this case, over 1,300 users failed to get a single retweet, while just over 300 got between one and two retweets. Therefore, the vast majority of Twitter users tweet into a void, and will be unlikely to be able to influence or change the agenda.

Government actors also featured prominently when gauging influence through the function of mentions – another measure of influence. Echoing findings from Diepeveen (this volume) in her study of Facebook

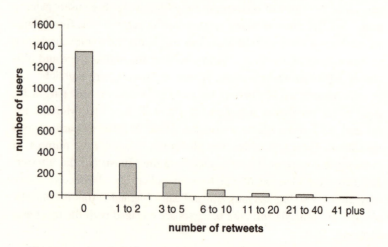

Figure 12.2 Number of retweets each user received

use in Mombasa, the debate was centred on politicians. Interior Minister Joe Lenku received considerably more mentions than other users, with the related tweets both containing affirmation and criticism of the crackdown he spearheaded. Similarly, Inspector General David Kimaiyo and the Ministry of the Interior were the second and third biggest recipients of mentions. While these mentions have the ability to facilitate communication between government and citizens, this episode highlights that communication predominantly remains one way.

Taken together, these measures demonstrate that media houses, journalists, celebrity bloggers and government actors hold considerably more influence than everyday citizen-users, indicating that the agenda setters offline are the same as those online, replicating existing hierarchies and discourses. The Operation Usalama Watch case study shows that the use of Twitter was less about creating a new community and connecting with like-minded individuals. Instead, users replicated existing patterns of communication and engagement, with agenda setting remaining driven by those with the most political, cultural and symbolic capital.

Turning to the content of the tweets that gained the most traction, similar narratives to those articulated in the print media op-ed pieces can be identified. Other than tweets from the aforementioned government actors, the most popular tweets were much more critical of the government's hard-line approach. Such critical tweets called on the government to be more transparent about the goings on at Kasarani Stadium. For instance, then Investigations Editor of KTN, Mohammed Ali, received 97 retweets from his tweet 'Dear @IGkimaiyo allow the

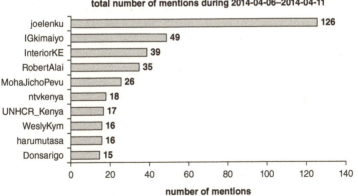

Figure 12.3 Top 10 tweeters by number of mentions

media to cover the other side of the story. We need to know what's going on at Kasarani'. Another journalist, Mohammed Yusuf (@Moyusef) shared one of the few pictures of Somalis detained in what appear to be cages within Kasarani, accompanied by the text 'For most Somalis in police stations & Kasarani it's hard to think about the future when the present is so harsh'. Gado, the satirical cartoonist who was working at the *Nation* at the time, had the second most retweeted tweet, with his own version of Martin Niemöller's poem, 'First they came ...', adapted for Operation Usalama Watch. The most retweeted tweets all came from journalists, somewhat unsurprising given the levels of influence they hold both on and offline. Just as importantly, the majority of the most popular tweets directly mentioned government actors such as David Kimaiyo and Joe Lenku, highlighting the extent to which one elite addressed another online, with ordinary citizens more passively retweeting. In this way, the content appeared almost indistinguishable from that published in traditional print media.

As well as being mentioned by others, the Kenyan government was also active on Twitter. Despite the barrage of social media criticism against Operation Usalama Watch, government actors reiterated the importance of the operation and affirmed their approach. For example, the Ministry of the Interior tweeted the words of Minister Joe Lenku many times during the episode. For example, '@joelenku: Eastleigh has operated as if it isn't part of Kenya and it is time Govt restores sanity #UsalamaWatch'; '@joelenku: We'll not allow sideshows to distract us from the main goal #UsalamaWatch'; '@joelenku: States of lawlessness has existed in Eastleigh for more than 20 years'; and '@joelenku: Kasarani isn't a concentration hall. It's a screening area. #UsalamaWatch'. However, these tweets were not as influential as those more critical of Operation Usalama Watch, despite the significant number of followers the Ministry of the Interior had. Many Twitter users also critically retweeted or replied to these tweets, highlighting that such platforms can allow citizens to directly challenge and criticise the government. Nevertheless, the actors they attempt to engage remain the same, and communication remains unidirectional.

Conclusion

The framing of Operation Usalama Watch on print media and Twitter highlights the complex print and social media nexus in Kenya.

The analysis demonstrates that there remains an elite on Twitter – mostly politicians and journalists – who retain the influence and economic and symbolic capital that they are afforded in traditional print media. As use of social media has proliferated, journalists and politicians have also seized digital channels and used them as a key method of communication with a growing number of citizens, but critically these channels are unidirectional. Mirroring Diepeveen's study of Facebook use in Mombasa (this volume), this chapter demonstrates that the online narratives of Operation Usalama Watch were not only markedly similar to those of the mainstream print media, but critically that the debate was centred around the same government actors that were directly cited in newspapers. Those social media personalities that have emulated these actors are best seen as professionals or celebrities, commanding respect or serving as key interlocutors who are to be followed, referenced or engaged in dialogue. Linked to this, there was a great degree of homogeneity in the content of news and opinion, both on and offline. In many cases, social media directly replicated and recirculated what was published on print media, demonstrating the influence of traditional media actors in setting and normalising the agenda. There was also a significant degree of polarisation, with the debate in this case revisiting familiar narratives condoning the government's 'war on terror' or condemning the persecution of the Somali community.

This study therefore invites us to consider the ways in which social media can reproduce traditional media logics – often heavily influenced by the government in many settings – rather than privileging alternative discourses. While some of the literature on social media, particularly its role during the Arab Spring, showed how social media could act as a platform for the creation of communities and the organisation of virtual and actual forms of protest, this case study highlights how the democratic potential of social media can be undermined by its replication of traditional hierarchies, as well as the polarisation that comes with its vast scale. As increasing numbers take to social media, they enter an echo chamber where elites gain prominence, and users centre around hashtags and ideas that conform to group norms and discourses. Given the evolving political economy of Kenya's media, and similar patterns within the region, this has important consequences for citizens' ability to access and participate in meaningful and varied debate, organise and mobilise, and ultimately advance democratic outcomes.

Note

1 Available at www.mecodem.
eu/mecodify/

References

Abdi Ismail, J. & Deane, J. (2008) 'The Kenyan 2007 elections and their aftermath: the role of media and communication'. Policy Briefing No.1, BBC World Service Trust, London.

Aday, S. & Livingston, S. (2008) 'Taking the state out of state–media relations theory: how transnational advocacy networks are rewriting (some of) the rules about what we think we know about news and politics'. *Media, War, and Conflict*, 1, 1: 99–107.

Alling'o, P. (2014) 'We need a new approach in terror investigation'. *Standard*, 11 May. www.standardmedia.co.ke/article/2000119707/we-need-a-new-approach-in-terror-investigation (accessed 10 March 2018).

Atieno-Odhiambo, E.S. (1987) 'Democracy and the ideology of order in Kenya'. In M.G. Schatzberg (ed.), *The Political Economy of Kenya*. New York: Praeger, pp. 177–201.

Bennett, W.L. & Segerberg, A. (2012) 'The logic of connective action'. *Information, Communication and Society* 15(7): 39–68.

Bourdieu, P. (2005) 'The political field, the social science field and the journalistic field'. In R. Benson and E. Neveu (eds.), *Bourdieu and the Journalistic Field*. Cambridge: Polity.

Bruns, A. & Burgess, J. (2015) 'Twitter hashtags from ad hoc to calculated publics'. In N. Rambukkana (ed.), *Hashtag Publics: the power and Politics of Discursive Networks*. New York: Peter Lang, pp.13–27.

Burbidge, D. (2015) 'The Kenyan state's fear of Somali identity'. Accord, 23 October. www.accord.org.za/conflict-trends/the-kenyan-states-fear-of-somali-identity/ (accessed 8 March 2018).

Carrier, N. (2016) *Little Mogadishu: Eastleigh, Nairobi's Global Somali Hub*. London: Hurst.

Chadwick, A. (2013) 'The hybrid media system: politics and power'. New York: Oxford University Press USA.

Cheeseman, N, Mwende, J & Ouma, S (2016) 'Peace? But at what cost? Media coverage of elections and conflict in Kenya'. Mecodem Working Paper. https://s3.amazonaws.com/academia.edu.documents/56414469/Peace_but_at_what_cost__Media_coverage_of_elections_and_conflict_in_Kenya.pdf?AWSAccessKeyId=AKIAIWOWYYGZ2Y53UL3A&Expires=1553787194&Signature=qAe%2F8nvhfVZUGDR7pP9%2FUl9QxWc%3D&response-content-disposition=inline%3B%20filename%3DPeace_but_at_what_cost_Media_coverage_of.pdf.

Diamond, L. & Plattner, M.F. (eds.) (2012) *Liberation Technology: Social Media and the Struggle for Democracy*. Baltimore: Johns Hopkins University Press.

Freedom House (2018) 'Freedom in the World Kenya profile'. https://freedomhouse.org/report/freedom-world/2018/kenya.

Gaitho, M. (2014) 'We have a war on our hands: it must be fought with everything we possess'. *Daily Nation*, 25 March. www.nation.co.ke/oped/opinion/We-have-a-war-on-our-hands/440808-2256208-cimuo2/index.html (accessed 10 March 2018).

Guleid, M. (2014) 'Ethnic profiling runs against basic human values'. *The Standard*, 13 April. www.standardmedia.co.ke/article/2000109268/ethnic-profiling-runs-against-basic-human-values (accessed 10 March 2014).

Gustafsson, J. (2016) 'Media and the 2013 Kenyan election: from hate speech to peace preaching'. *Conflict and Communication Online*, 15(1): 1–13.

Howard, P.N. & Parks, M.R. (2012) 'Social media and political change: capacity, constraint and consequence'. *Journal of Communication*, 62(2): 359–362.

Human Rights Watch (2014) 'End Abusive Round Ups'. www.hrw.org/news/2014/05/12/kenya-end-abusive-round-ups.

Independent Policing Oversight Authority (2014) 'Monitoring Report on Operation Sanitization Eastleigh publically known as Operation Usalama Watch'. www.regionalmms.org/images/sector/IPOA%20report%20on%20Usalama%20Watch%20operation%20in%20Eastleigh,%20Kenya.pdf (accessed 8 March 2018).

Keane, J. (2013) *Democracy and Media Decadence*. Cambridge: Cambridge University Press.

Kerrow, B. (2014) 'Is Operation Usalama Watch a Somali Gulag?' *The Standard*, 13 April. www.standardmedia.co.ke/article/2000109277/is-operation-usalama-watch-a-somali-gulag (accessed 10 March 2018).

Kiai, M. (2014) 'Mass arrests and assassinations will only make our borders more insecure'. *Daily Nation*, 13 April. www.nation.co.ke/oped/Opinion/Mass-arrests-and-assassinations/-/440808/2276020/-/10d7yg2/-/index.html (accessed 10 March 2018).

Klinger, U. & Svensson, J. (2015) 'The emergence of network media logic in political communication: a theoretical approach'. *New Media Society*, 17: 1241–57

Kuria, M. (2014) 'Radicalisation of terror is the petrol that keeps the fire burning'. *The Standard*, 13 April. www.standardmedia.co.ke/mobile/article/2000109296/radicalisation-of-terror-is-the-petrol-that-keeps-the-fire-burning (accessed 10 March 2018).

Lasarosa, D.L., Lewis, S.C. & Holton, A. (2012) 'Normalising Twitter: journalism pratice in an emerging communication space'. *Journalism Studies*, 13(1): 19–36.

Lenku, J.O. (2014) 'Our war against terrorism is unstoppable'. *The Standard*, 6 April. www.standardmedia.co.ke/article/2000108719/our-war-against-terrorism-is-unstoppable (accessed 10 March 2018).

Lochery (2012) 'Rendering difference visible: the Kenyan state and its Somali citizens'. *African Affairs*, 111(445): 615–639.

Makokha, K. (2014) 'Politically correct: turning screws on Somalis will force them to reveal attacks'. *Daily Nation*, 23 March. www.nation.co.ke/oped/opinion/Turning-screws-on-Somalis-will-force-them-reveal-attacks--/440808-2276024-ol9qrl/index.html (accessed 10 March 2018).

Mazzoleni, G. (2014) 'Mediatization and political populism'. In F. Esser & J. Strömbäck (eds.), *Mediatization of Politics: Understanding the Transformation of Western Democracies*. Basingstoke: Palgrave Macmillan: pp. 42–57.

Molony, T. (2019) 'Social media warfare and Kenya's conflict with Al Shabaab in Somalia: a right to know?' *African Affairs*, 118(471): 328–351.

Mutambo, A. & Zadock, A. (2014) '500 more arrested as police carry out swoop in Eastleigh'. *Daily Nation*, 6 April (accessed 10 March 2018).

Muthoni, F. (2014) 'Security swoops are perfectly legal'. *The Star*, 17 April. www.the-star.co.ke/news/2014/04/17/security-swoops-are-perfectly-legal_c924320 (accessed 10 March 2018).

Nation Editorial Team (2014) 'Terse Uhuru warning on security welcome'. *Daily Nation*, 5 April.

Nation Editorial Team (2014) 'Go for specific targets in anti-terrorism drive', *Daily Nation*, 8 April.

Nation Team (2014) 'Police hold hundreds in Kasarani stadium: "Bomb factory" found in police terror crackdown'. *Daily Nation*, 7 April.

Ngwiri, M. (2014) 'Minister's decree and shoot-to-kill order wrong solutions to insecurity'. *Daily Nation*, 29 March. www.nation.co.ke/oped/opinion/Minister-s-decree-and-shoot-to-kill-order-wrong/440808-2261250-3ws41jz/index.html (accessed 10 March 2018).

Obala, R. & Kithi, N. (2014) 'Police operation illegal, inhumane, claims civil society'. *The Standard*, 13 April. www.standardmedia.co.ke/mobile/article/2000109305/police-operation-illegal-inhumane-claims-civil-society (accessed 10 March 2018).

Ogola, G. (2011) 'The political economy of the media in Kenya: from Kenyatta's nation-building press to Kibaki's local-language FM radio'. *Africa Today*, 57(3): 77–95.

Ogola, G. (2017) 'How African governments use advertising as a weapon against media freedom'. The Conversation, 18 April. Available at: https://theconversation.com/how-african-governments-use-advertising-as-a-weapon-against-media-freedom-75702 (accessed 8 March 2018).

Ogola, G. (2018) 'How Kenyatta has gone about stifling the free press in Kenya'. The Conversation, 7 February. https://theconversation.com/how-kenyatta-has-gone-about-stifling-the-free-press-in-kenya-91335 (accessed 8 March 2018).

Pew Research Center (2018) 'Technology Use in Africa: Internet'. www.pewglobal.org/interactives/technology-use-in-africa-internet/ (accessed 11 February 2019).

Phillips, A. (2010) 'Old sources: new bottles'. In N. Fenton (ed.), *New Media, Old News*. London: Sage, pp. 87–102.

Rambukkana, N. (2015) 'Hashtags as technosocial events'. In N. Rambukkana (ed.), *Hashtag Publics: the Power and Politics of Discursive Networks*. New York: Peter Lang, pp. 1–13.

Singer, J.B. (2005) 'The political j-blogger: "normalizing" a new media form to fit old Norms and practices'. *Journalism*, 6(2): 173–198.

Somerville, K. (2011) 'Violence, hate speech and inflammatory broadcasting in Kenya: the problems of definition and identification'. *Ecquid Novi: African Journalism Studies*, 32(1): 82–101.

Stremlau, N. & Gagliardone, I. (2015) 'Media, conflict and political transitions in Africa'. In J. Zielonka (ed.), *Media and Politics in New Democracies: Europe in a Comparative Perspective*. Oxford: Oxford University Press, pp. 289–305.

Voltmer, K. & Sorensen, L. (2016) 'Mediatised transitions: democratisation in an age of media abundance'. Mecodem Working Paper. www.mecodem.eu/wp-content/uploads/2015/05/

Voltmer-Sorensen-2016_Mediatised-transitions.pdf.

Waitherero, B. (2014) 'Lack of moderate, circumspect leadership hampers the war against terrorism'. *Daily Nation*, 20 April. www.nation.co.ke/oped/blogs/dot9/waitherero/2274550-2286972-6bqoo3/index.html (accessed 10 March 2018).

Warah, R. (2014) 'Kenya sliding down a slippery path leading to lawlessness and anarchy'. *Daily Nation*, 7 April. www.nation.co.ke/oped/opinion/-slippery-path-to-lawlessness-and-anarchy--/440808-2275548-73dx85/index.html (accessed 10 March 2018).

Wato, M. (2014) 'Change of tack needed to crush terrorism'. *Daily Nation*, 3 April. www.nation.co.ke/oped/opinion/Change-of-tack-needed-to-crush-terrorism-/440808-2269364-w89gixz/index.html (accessed 10 March 2018).

Youmans, W.L. & York, J.C. (2012) 'Social Media and the activist toolkit: user agreements, corporate interests, and the information infrastructure of modern social movements'. *Journal of Communication*, 62(2): 315–329.

13 | FROM WHISPERS TO THE ASSEMBLAGE

Surveillance in post-independence East Africa

Denis Galava

Introduction

> Surveillance always carries with it some plausible justification
> that makes most of us content to comply [...] The advantages of
> surveillance for its subjects are real, palpable, and undeniable.
> (David Lyon 2001: 3)

Achille Mbembe's (2001: 109) anatomy of how post-colonial African
strongmen perform power through surveillance and violence recalls
an incident that happened in Busia, a town in western Kenya, in
1990, where policemen reportedly clobbered a man who they found
sitting when the national flag was being lowered. At a historical time
when all Kenyans were expected to show unquestionable loyalty to
the then President Moi, the mundane transgression of the unnamed
man who sat when one was expected to stand could be interpreted
as either lack of patriotism or attempted treason. The 'seriousness'
of such minor transgressions was usually seen in the violent response
of the police and its newsworthiness.[1] If the violent reaction by the
police was excessive, it was because of the prevailing logics of state
surveillance and domination – both processes critical in maintaining
the myth of post-colonial Kenya, and the whole of Africa, as anchored
on 'order', which was in turn both necessitated and then reinforced
by cultures of surveillance. Regimes of surveillance are characterised
by dual logics that render surveillance both necessary but potentially
dreadful, the latter often noticed only when there are individual or
systemic lapses. 'Surveillance systems are less and less obvious and
overt', writes David Lyon (2001: 2), 'but more and more systematic
and subtle. Thus, they tend to be visible only when by mistake or
misdemeanour we fall foul of them or when they fail publicly. They
are, in a sense, best seen in the breach'.

Like the unfortunate Busia man whose plight found its way, via a
newspaper report, to Mbembe's analysis of the state in Africa, many

other people have encountered the African state through violence. Such violence has sometimes been physical, but more often merely symbolic, through relentless documentation of otherwise private data in processes that engender anxiety and strife among the victims. Yet, the practices and processes of surveillance are not entirely unnecessary, as Lyon's observation that I adopt for my epigraph demonstrates. On the contrary, the post-9/11 era of global vulnerability to terrorism, the spread of the internet and the emergence of politically conscious virtual communities have created good reasons for state surveillance.

But lurking in the shadows of these morally justifiable reasons for surveillance are the traditional claws and fangs of state power, of domination, and of an insatiable desire to extract compliance from citizenry. This, then, is the burden of my chapter: to demonstrate that while the regional political economies of the state in East Africa have been unmistakably and forever transformed by the spectres of terrorism and disruptive powers of the internet, these are but new excuses that the same states currently deploy to carry on with their old habits of systemic surveillance with intent to dominate and control their citizens, sometimes violently so. My intervention will make three different but related contributions: firstly, it will speak to the troubled relationships between the states and their citizens in the region, which have led to the coups and attempted coups of the 1960s to 1980s, dictatorial regimes and political assassinations. Secondly, while scholarship exists on surveillance in other regions such as North America (Lyon 2014, 2001), South Africa (Breckenridge 2014) and even Rwanda (Purdekova 2015), no similar study exists for Kenya, Uganda, and Tanzania. Yet, in these countries, like the rest of the world, surveillance has become part of everyday life. The third contribution relates to the gap in current theories of both surveillance and of the state in East Africa, partly because of spatial–temporal distance of ideas associated with Lyon and Manuel Castells (2010), but also because of the paucity of research on surveillance from eastern African perspectives. Therefore, I shall treat these ideas as what may be theories, rather than actual theories, of surveillance in eastern Africa. I shall consider surveillance as 'a process in which special note is taken of certain human behaviours that go well beyond idle curiosity' (Lyon 2014, p. 13); as 'any collection and processing of personal data, whether identifiable or not, for the purposes of influencing or managing those whose data have been garnered' (Lyon 2001: 2). I argue that as the region has deepened democratic processes and institutions, so has it intensified its surveillance practices by developing an ambivalent outlook to technology of communication: using it when it suits the regimes, and constraining its usage by common citizens when such technology is perceived to pose a threat to state apparatuses.

(Dis)Continuities of surveillance in East Africa: an overview

Although the practices and processes of surveillance in East Africa date back to colonial times, socio-political and technological advances in the past thirty years have impacted extensively on the nature, forms and degrees of surveillance, as well as the individual and group responses to surveillance. Two notable developments with direct bearings on surveillance are worth highlighting; firstly, the shift towards political plurality through a multi-party order that began around the 1990s, which included the rise of a rights-based approach to discourses of development, the emergence of an audible and influential civil society sector, and a more competitive political climate in the three main East African countries that reconfigured how power is acquired and exercised. The second development relates to what I will call the 'digitalisation of populations' in the region at the beginning of the 21st century, when the mobile phone increasingly became the communication technology of choice, disrupting pre-existing social hierarchies. The work of Manuel Castells (2010) is especially useful in understanding how internet-based technologies can be deployed to imagine virtual communities that may be within definite geographical boundaries. These same communities nonetheless superimpose more amorphous boundaries in virtual spaces that defy the strictures of physical surveillance and control because, essentially, they operate at different levels of reality. For Castells (2010: xviii),

[t]he shift from traditional mass media to a system of horizontal communication networks organized around the Internet and wireless communication has introduced a multiplicity of communication patterns at the source of a fundamental cultural transformation, as virtuality becomes an essential dimension of our reality.

Although the accuracy of this observation is contentious in the African context where the 'digital divide' is rigged against many citizens, it remains a useful projection into the future of networked communities in Africa, given the growing numbers of East Africans with access to internet-enabled mobile telephony. In statistical terms, East Africans are increasingly embracing this technology. According to the Privacy International's Impact Report (2017), 41 million Ugandans, 33 million Kenyans, and 23 million Tanzanians had access to smartphones by the end of 2017. Some of them also used social network platforms such as WhatsApp, Facebook and Twitter to create smaller variants of what Castells (2010) had earlier called 'networked communities' in the region. These, as I shall argue below, have implications on the course and nature of surveillance and the reactions to it.

East Africa was a late starter in dealing with the threats and opportunities associated with these advances in technology. Commenting on the American situation, Campbell and Park (2008: 372) demonstrate how 'information and communication technologies of the 1980s and 1990s nourished a shift in social organisation characterised by decentralised, flexible, network nodes based on shared interests rather than shared geographic state', posing a real threat to officialdom's quest for forging a singular nation that coincides with the geographical state boundaries. Similarly, in East Africa, developments in digital communications also altered the terms of engagement between the states and their citizens, posing challenges to the surveillance machinery of the former, while opening up new expressive spaces for the latter. As Keith Breckenridge (2014) writes about the South African context, but which is equally applicable to East Africa, what had previously been a matter of the slow routine of documentary surveillance for the state, and a predicament of abstract helplessness for the people, suddenly changed to complex processes of biometric data farming for the state and real-time assertion of expressive freedoms for the citizens. How were the states to continue with their surveillance in the wake of the disruptions posed by internet innovations that could collapse geographical boundaries and remain invisible? How could non-elite people enjoy the conveniences of such technology while avoiding the risks associated with state surveillance? These were the key questions that emerged at the beginning of the 21st century, for the state and the citizens, respectively. The questions, and the conundrums that they hinted at, reflected a delicate situation of great uncertainty associated with internet-based technologies of communication and the shifting relationship between the states and their subjects in the region. The delicateness of these interactions is best captured by Lyon's analysis of the practical implications of state surveillance in North America, which also resonates with East Africa.

He argues, 'the coordination of social activities in time and space, the growing perception and production of risk, the role of privacy in generating as well as trying to contain surveillance societies are all practical issues' (2001: 5).

That is why, in this chapter, I examine the changing forms of surveillance in East Africa to argue that despite differences in the approaches that states currently adopt, the underlying logic has remained the same since the 1960s: to control public thought and secure political centres. The old ways of documentary domination have been rendered obsolete by technology and a greater awareness of privacy rights. Now, governments have devised ways to surreptitiously infiltrate social media spaces to monitor their subjects without invoking litigation, or have circumvented old legislation by enacting new regulatory frameworks, such as stringent licensing requirements and taxation of social media usage, in order to control information flows (Ugangu 2015). In 2018, the Tanzanian government enacted the Electronic and Postal Communications (Online Content) Regulations prescribing heavy fines for breaches, apparently to curb hate speech and 'abuse' of the cyberspace, but clearly meant to control the space (see Cross, this volume).[2] In Uganda, the Museveni government introduced similar measures, braving popular protest against the legislation.[3]

Clearly, these laws have subterranean political motives of control, even though they are packaged and justified in the rhetoric of the common good. Thus, they demonstrate the existing slippages between what David Barnard-Wills (2011: 548) calls 'appropriate surveillance' and 'inappropriate surveillance' – the former aimed at crime prevention, the latter at encroachment on personal spaces. Surveillance, as earlier scholarship (Lyon 2014) and these laws show, operates in a systemic manner, with a kind of central command that draws in information on an individual in different ways and from different sources. The systems of surveillance, 'afford control of people through the identification, tracking, monitoring or analysis of individuals, data, or systems' (Monahan 2010: 96). Because systems of surveillance rely on a blend of Althusserian ideological and repressive state apparatuses, they are all held together in organic coherence through 'connections between seemingly disparate and previously discrete surveillance technologies, sites, practices, and agents traditionally studied in isolation' (Barnard-Wills 2011: 549). This results in an assemblage[4] of surveillance tools and approaches that adhere to the political cultures of domination and resistance pitting the state against citizens. For instance, in Kenya, the work of Angelique Haugerud (1997), which I shall revisit later, demonstrates how a unique blend of traditional patriarchal structures of communal mobilisation on the one hand, and provincial administrative tools on the other, can facilitate structured state observance and the flow of information in an uncanny performance of what Hannah Arendt elsewhere called the marriage of bureaucracy and despotism (cited in Breckenridge 2014: 20). All these factors impact on the relationship between democracy and social media – in the broader sense that includes word of mouth – highlighting the need for studies on how these two influence state politics in East Africa.

I drew the data for this chapter through a desktop review of the current literature on global cases, firstly because it relates to historical occurrences, and, secondly, because I am concerned more with the logics of surveillance rather than its empirical recurrence. I also draw on critical works of fiction that, I propose, have extensively deployed semantic trickery such as irony and satire to poke regimes out of their delusions, while allowing ordinary people to take moral positions by association. Such qualitative discourse analysis and close textual reading is suitable for normative research that seeks to deepen an understanding of knowledge, social processes and social action.

In the rest of this chapter, I address the facets and trajectories of surveillance in East Africa, first by demarcating contextual issues of surveillance in the region, then attempting to theorise rumour and humour as critical products in regimes of surveillance. I show how the phenomenon of 'dramaturgy of power' (Outa 2001) manifests itself in the contests of engagements between the powerful and their subjects, and ultimately argue that although time and means change, the states' anxiety of surveillance over their subjects remain and become more sophisticated and vicious.

Two caveats are necessary. The first is that if, in all this, Kenya seems to be the main source of illustrative examples, it is because of its seeming prominence as the regional hub in technological and socio-political advancements. It is also the country in which existing theories of state practices have been most tested, first through its internal ethnicity-propelled politics (Atieno-Odhiambo 2002), and then as the worst hit by the recent spectre of global terrorism that necessitates state surveillance. The second is that since I locate this analysis in post-colonial East Africa, I appreciate the expansive breadth of social media as both a subject of study and as an analytical category. A book chapter of this kind is therefore limited and does not allow for effective engagement with the entire spectrum of social media, about which earlier studies exist (Ligaga 2012). Therefore, I specifically focus on digital technology that, in my view, has greater potential to mobilise communities across the geopolitical boundaries of East Africa, and therefore justify an East African perspective, as opposed to other forms of social media – such as rumour and gossip – that would be captive to intra-state particularities. However, where necessary, I draw on illustrations from social media to buttress my arguments.

Tracking surveillance in East Africa

Post-independence East Africa was characterised by divergences across nations, mainly because of the different ideological positions taken by independence leaders Julius Nyerere of Tanzania, Milton Obote of Uganda and Jomo Kenyatta of Kenya. These positions were reflected in different policy guidelines that were inward-looking rather than regional; Nyerere's Tanzania embraced *Ujamaa*, a people-centred form of socialism, while Kenyatta's Kenya adopted and hyped the Sessional Paper No. 10 of 1965, a market-driven economic compass that put Kenya on the path to the currently derided neo-liberal capitalism. In Uganda, Milton Obote summed up his ideas in the Common Man's Charter, a somewhat vague prescription of a social-liberalist economic philosophy. Apart from the clearly nationalistic aura in all these, there was the subsequent if inevitable emergence of the heads of state as cult figures around whom ideas of development, patriotism and so on revolved. Well-meaning as they were, these leaders, and especially Obote, remained vulnerable to the menace of violent military coups that were common in Africa – a reality that pushed them towards paranoia. Thus, the desire to inaugurate economic development was punctuated by institutionalised suspicion, even within the top political circles (Odinga 1967; Mboya 1986).

Subsequently, state surveillance was entrenched; the state infiltrated public lives of common people to enforce compliance under the rubric of 'ideology of order' (Atieno-Odhiambo 1987), to which I shall return later in this chapter. In early post-independence East Africa, surveillance was more physical and manual; snoops were implanted in various places to pick out rumours and gossip about the state. Any divergent views on the surveillance operations could either only be expressed in whispers (Ogola 2005), hence the prefix to my chapter title, or silenced within. This was the reality in greater eastern Africa, where citizens responded by perpetuating a culture of conspiracy theories (Sunstein 2014) that cast the state as a dreadful yet unavoidable monster.

During the 1970s and 1980s, however, there were growing voices that called for the expansion of democratic spaces through the legalisation of multi-partyism. But such voices were severely punished, and states intensified their surveillance strategies, incarcerating many individuals on spurious charges of dissidence. In Kenya, Uganda, Ethiopia and Somalia, the regimes were particularly intolerant and dramatically used detention without trial, forced disappearances and even assassinations as political weapons to impose silence and fear among individuals with politically divergent views. In Kenya, the implications of terror as a weapon included innovative use of subversive strategies, such as the culture of whispers mentioned above, and conspiracy theories manifested through subversive rumours, gossip and laughter, to create sites of freedom within terror-filled regimes.

Presidents Jomo Kenyatta and Daniel arap Moi relied on surveillance both to govern and to intimidate and neuter real and imagined political adversaries. Sometimes, as Joyce Nyairo (2013) observes in her study of the cultural histories of Kenya's first 50 years of independence, surveillance during the peak of the Moi regime would often focus on the petty and the banal, not because they portended any danger to the political status quo, but because they allowed Moi to instil fear in prominent politicians and civil servants by illustrating that he knew them and their supposed schemes in detail. Because many legitimate avenues for information had been closed by the regime of surveillance, for those who sought alternative sources of information to the propaganda that was circulating via mainstream media, rumours, gossip and conspiracy theories became the default references. Hence, for Moi, even rumours and gossip – which were the most dominant and influential forms of social media at that time – were to be controlled through surveillance and 'policing loose talk' (Nyairo 2013: 119), and offenders would often be punished through detention without trial for middle-level actors and the so-called 'dissidents and subversive elements', dismissals for 'disgraced' civil servants and politicians and, in some extreme cases, assassinations similar to those of Robert Ouko and Bishop Alexander Muge.

All these were forms of moral armament similar to the more recent Rwanda scenario. Andrea Purdekova (2015) demonstrates how Paul Kagame's post-conflict Rwanda used civic education and other state-led neo-traditional methods such as camps and retreats to indoctrinate the populace to mould the desired Rwandese citizen and, in the process, entrench the political status quo. Using idioms associated with 'the politics of depoliticisation' (Purdekova 2015: 13), and 'politography of unity' (2015: 10), the Rwandese state perfects and deploys surveillance for political uses. All these strategies in the larger East Africa resulted in political cultures of sycophancy, or the 'dramaturgy of power' (Outa 2001), which we theorise in the next section.

Rumour, humour and the dramaturgy of power and politics

The public response to systemic surveillance, and how brutally 'suspicious' actors were treated, led to both strategic acquiescence to the will of the government and creative criticism. Playwrights, musicians and other creative artists deployed what Odera Outa, while writing about Ngugi wa Thiong'o's protest drama, calls 'the dramaturgy of power and politics' (2001: 345). Upon critiquing Ngugi's plays that were set in post-colonial Kenya, Outa concludes that they survived censorship because they were structured and woven around ambiguous strategies of expression that enabled them to discursively communicate otherwise politically unacceptable content. Such strategies, which were also used to beat surveillance in other forms, included 'telling the truth laughingly' (Ruganda 1992), a way of speaking truth to power without provoking its ire. This enabled Francis Imbuga, for instance, to critique the state in his widely staged play *Betrayal in the City* (1976), without suffering the same plight Ngugi wa Thiong'o did for *I Will Marry When I Want* (co-authored with Ngugi wa Mirii). Its performance at the Kamirithu Theatre was stopped by government, the theatre was destroyed, and the playwright was hounded into exile. By 'telling the truth laughingly', Imbuga's *Betrayal in the City* seeped through the censor's mesh, unlike Ngugi and Ngugi's *I Will Marry When I Want*, which seemed to mount a frontal attack on the neo-colonialism of Daniel arap Moi.

Musical artists similarly used versions of semantic trickery to add a satirical edge to their works while still preserving themselves, because semantic distanceation creates spaces for ambiguities. For instance, Daniel Misiani used allegory and zoological metaphors – 'the cat that ended up eating the homestead chicken' – to lament political assassination in Kenya (Ogude 2007). Using techniques such as irony and satire, these artists conscientiously responded to, and commented on, socio-political issues in Kenya while beating the censorship trap.

With time, multi-partyism was reintroduced in Kenya (1991), Tanzania (1992) and Uganda (2005). This created new political economies that allowed citizens to officially hold different opinions from those of the ruling party, which created a deeper sense of uncertainty for the regimes and rendered their need for surveillance more urgent. While the region was grappling with the challenges of multi-partyism, the recently liberated airwaves democratised the kind of information and propaganda that the people could consume. With more FM stations and rediscovered freedoms, the conflicts that had been simmering at the subterranean levels were brought to the surface through call-in sessions for the many community radios that were now operational (Odhiambo 2007). The new cultures of self-expression through the radio stations threatened national unity because previously buried subjects were excavated and debated publicly, leading to government efforts to moderate such commentaries to avoid ethnic and other sectarian incitements in the region.

Hiding behind the walls of anonymity afforded by social media platforms, users of internet-based smartphones across East Africa opened debates on politically taboo subjects such as land problems, regional marginalisation, and government atrocities such as massacres and assassinations. These debates were not so much valuable for their factual content, but because they affirmed the existence of alternative sites for national discourse and reified them above the official ones. They created what Ogola (2015: 74) calls a 'heteroglossic discursive space' in which multivocal narratives compete with and outstrip the official narratives. They also invited stronger surveillance as a response. The proliferation of these micro-narratives was because of the multivocality that was enabled by the digital disruption of the states' regimes of surveillance. As Ogude (2007) and Musila (2015) demonstrate, surveillance engendered silences that could only be broken through strategic use of multi-layered language codes such as allegory, and of emergent technologies and cultures of social media such as Twitter and hashtag mobilisation.

At the same time, the global 'war on terror' has altered the rationales and methods of surveillance. Thus, the war on terror is an amorphous means that allows governments to persecute some individuals on the pretext that they are terrorists. Subsequently, states have intensified surveillance in cyberspaces, where apparently hate informs terrorism, and the coordination of terror attacks occurs. That is why, as I suggested earlier, the legislation which has been enlisted in the war on terror is itself dependent on surveillance. East African governments have taken turns to institute regulatory measures to control the number of actors and extent of their involvement in digital spaces. In Kenya, such initiatives include the Kenya Information and Communications (Amendment) Act (2013) and the Kenya Security Laws (2014) (see Ugangu 2015: 6), and the establishment of the Communications Authority of Kenya and the Media Council of Kenya for state and self-regulation of media conduct in Kenya. Other East African countries have replicated similar measures, for example, the Uganda Communications Commission, and some statutory controls, including the Electronic and Postal Communications Regulations (2018) in Tanzania. Thus, as the region has become more digitalised and democratic, the governments have implemented mechanisms of policing the dynamics enabled by the advances in communication technology.

Surveillance: the East African experiences

At the heart of all efforts at surveillance is the performance of and resistance to power, either through creation of an omnipresent state, or through bureaucratic domination by documentation, which is made possible by the state's accumulation of inventorised information about the individual or group of individuals. This has been the modus operandi of states from time immemorial, as summarised by Michel Foucault, who argues that 'there is no power relation without the correlative constitution of a field of knowledge, nor any knowledge that does not presuppose and constitute at the same time, power relations' (1977: 27). Although Foucault makes this observation in a different spatial–temporal context, it is relevant to East Africa where surveillance is driven by the state in a bid to legitimise and secure its power over the citizens.

Knowledge of the subject to be controlled is thus critical, as seen in the forms that the government addresses its subjects, such as the case of the *baraza*[5] phenomenon in Kenya. As Haugerud (1997) argues, state control of public discourse also involves controlling who speaks in *barazas*, and thus what is spoken. Essentially, these hierarchies of speakers in *barazas* and the clear demarcation of the speakable and taboo subjects are all part of strengthening what Atieno-Odhiambo calls the 'ideology of order' (1987: 191). This is reinforced by calculated comparisons between Kenya's relative tranquillity and the chaos in other parts of Africa including Somalia, Sudan, Liberia, Ethiopia, and the Democratic Republic of Congo, all of which are deployed to work as 'weapons of fear' with the aim of ensuring that the citizenry 'obey the government' (Haugerud 1997: 76).

But this approach cannot possibly work when the technology of communication creates virtual spaces that transcend physical boundaries and make policing difficult. Elsewhere, but on a related plane, Campbell and Park argue that 'information and communication technologies of the 1980s and 1990s nourished a shift in social organisation characterised by decentralised, flexible, network nodes based on shared interests rather than shared geographic state' (2008: 372). These possibilities to mobilise beyond the gaze of the state threaten the latter's preoccupation with control, and weaken the chances of officialdom succeeding in its desire to 'know' each of its subjects as a *sine qua non* for the ultimate domination of individual freedoms and national psyche. By imagining virtual communities and going beyond the state's surveillance machinery, the subjects subsequently conquer the fear that was engendered by the state's control over their imaginative and expressive possibilities.

Ironically, the internet-driven dispersal of power from traditional centres is because of the limits of Foucault's regime of power; deviation from the norm currently, unlike in Foucauldian times, only leads to sanctions when there is a breach. Significantly, therefore, the governments no longer have monopoly over knowledge on their subjects and what they are up to; even commoners now also have knowledge about each other and about the government, which ultimately makes it harder for the government to achieve its desire to dominate the common people while relying on traditional means of information access and surveillance.

The amorphousness of power flows currently speaks to the idea of the rhizome, an analytical metaphor that was popularised by Gilles Deleuze and Felix Guattari (1987). This botanical metaphor is a 'form of plant-life which spreads, such as mushrooms or crabgrass, without a central root, spot or origination or logical pattern; the rhizome itself assumes very diverse forms, from ramified surface extension in all directions to concretion into bulbs and tubers' (Deleuze & Guattari 1987: 29). In the current context of multiple spaces of power and its effects, I find the rhizome to be a useful metaphor in understanding the dynamics of surveillance because the gaze that informs it has 'neither beginning, nor end, but always a middle (milieu) from which it grows and spills' (Deleuze & Guattari 1987: 23). The outcomes of such surveillance, similarly, have no discernible shape. Therefore, the metaphor of the rhizome, in its disavowal of linearity of power flows, reflects the complexities facing surveillance, and refracts the uncanny resemblance between surveillance networks and those of rumour and gossip which, interestingly, thrive in situations where the regimes engage in surveillance. In East Africa, thus, it is difficult to study the nature and trajectories of surveillance without paying regard to rumour and gossip as discourses that generally necessitate simultaneous state surveillance in contestation with people's deflection of the same.

The relatively recent departure from the widely embraced panoptic model of studying surveillance – thus assumptions that surveillance only occurs from singular centres being debunked by later observations of multiple centres and directions of surveillance – may be understood in this context. Indeed, if the previous understandings of the dynamics of surveillance in East Africa (and the rest of the world) derived from a blend of influences ranging from African patrimonial logics (Haugerud 1997), Christian ethos of omnipresent father figures (Mudimbe 1994), and even technocratic imaginations of the Orwellian type, the idea that there can be a single omnivoyant state symbolised in the father figures of East Africa's presidents has been undone by technologies of communication that are used to both mock the central powers of the patriarch, priest or president, and disperse their powers in multiple directions (Mbembe 2001). If a panopticon – as envisaged by Foucault (1979) – is characterised by 'clarity, docility, and utility' (François Debrix 1999: 269), then post-colonial East Africa is anything but the model panoptic society because the political economies of the respective countries are fuzzy, their peoples almost always subversive, and societies are generally more preoccupied with human dignity – and not necessarily utility – in much of what they do.

Yet, despite the changing political economies of the region, advances in communication technology, and more politically conscious populations, governments of East Africa continue to initiate and impose surveillance measures, targeting the virtual spaces in which a lot of (un)wanted and (un)necessary information circulates. As I indicated earlier in this chapter, Barnard-Wills' categorisation of surveillance applies; where 'good' surveillance has been done to weed out terrorist elements within the region and to stop other forms of crime, for instance, and 'bad' surveillance has been conducted for reasons of moral policing in Kenya and Tanzania especially, and in Uganda to a lesser degree. And then, there are slippages in between, which are used by the regimes to settle political scores in the name of upholding a given country's morality or culture. The three major East African countries – Kenya, Uganda and Tanzania – thus continue to assert control over virtual space to silence or otherwise frustrate the so-called 'dissident voices'. In Kenya, some legal instruments have been adopted to control the flow of information within digital circuits: the Computer Misuse and Cybercrimes Bill (2017) targets internet users with fines and prison sentences for circulating 'fake news' on blogs and other social networks, and those who engage in cyber-bullying. Those found guilty of publishing false information are punishable by a two-year jail term, or a fine of up to 5 million Kenyan shillings ($50,000 USD). This may arguably be a good thing because it is meant to protect the reputations of public figures that can become damaged under uncertain circumstances. However, it leaves gaps in implementation because, often, truth has many perspectives and falls prey to the dynamics of power. Therefore, the net effect of such legislation is to engender self-censorship and discourage the kind of investigative journalism which often unearths deeply concealed truths. The Bill enables the police to violate citizens' private lives because, although generally the police require a court order before accessing individuals' records, security services may still access the same information if they deem an investigation too urgent to await a court order.

The Computer Misuse and Cybercrimes Bill (2017) allows police to build digital dossiers on cyberspace users, meaning it is impossible for any individual to proclaim absolute privacy at any one time. The greatest challenge regarding this law is that given how it is tailored, it is virtually impossible not to breach sections of it. For instance, all computer users are required to report cybercrimes to the National Computer and Cybercrimes Coordination Committee. Yet, reflecting a typical assemblage model of surveillance, the Computer Misuse and Cybercrimes Bill (2017) works in sync with the National Intelligence Service (NIS) Act (2012), which allows the government to investigate, interfere with and monitor a person's communications if the person is suspected to have committed an offence, even though the service is required to obtain a warrant before doing this. But the breadth of the provisions – investigate, interfere with and monitor – simply means that individual rights are more likely than not to be violated because, once the security agents show any interest in a person, intrusion in their cyberspace lives become legal.

Other legal instruments of surveillance include the Prevention of Terrorism Act (2012) which allows state agencies to limit freedoms and monitor people's communication, and the Security Laws (Amendment) Act (2014), which augments the Prevention of Terrorism Act. Clearly, surveillance driven by genuine concerns about enhancing national security gives security agents more authority to infiltrate people's private lives without guaranteeing the integrity of the information gathered.

As I indicated earlier in this chapter, a similar scenario is occurring in Uganda, where President Museveni's regime has drafted several legislative tools to enhance surveillance. For Museveni, however, the approach has also entailed making the internet more expensive, thus limiting the number of users. From July 2018, the Government of Uganda started taxing social media usage at a daily rate of 200 Ugandan shillings ($0.05 USD) for active mobile phone users of services including WhatsApp, Viber, Twitter and Skype. The move came after President Museveni wrote a letter to the Ugandan Treasury complaining that idle talk was costing the country too much. He asked the Treasury to institute the tax as a way of avoiding frivolity on the net. This was a long-winded way of silencing many Ugandans.

Other regulatory instruments in Uganda include the Regulation of Interception of Communications Act (RICA) (2010), which authorises intelligence officials to intercept specific communications subject to a court warrant; the Anti-Terrorism Act (2002) which gives the state permission to conduct surveillance without seeking judicial oversight; and the Computer Misuse Act (2011) which forbids access to various computer systems that are deemed to be dangerous. All these legal tools have been extensively deployed in limiting the freedoms of Ugandans. For instance, in April 2011, the Ugandan Communication Commission reportedly instructed ISPs (internet service providers) to block access to social networking sites Facebook and Twitter for 24 hours at the request of security agencies concerned over 'Walk to Work' demonstrations linked to opposition leader Kizza Besigye. In May 2013 the government set up a Social Media Monitoring Center to weed out those 'wanting to damage the government's reputation' (New Vision 2013). For the same reasons, the Ugandan government blocked access to Facebook, Twitter and WhatsApp during the 2016

General Election and, in March 2017, it tried to force Facebook to reveal the identity of government critic Tom Voltaire Okwalinga by suing the company in an Irish Court. These examples demonstrate both how legislation can be abused to serve frivolous anxieties of those in power, and the capacity for an uncensored social media to mobilise solidarities across class and political interests and, ironically, occasion the need for surveillance. Generally, in East Africa, legislation on surveillance is enacted to address short-term definite challenges and to pre-empt the long-term fears of the powerful.

In Tanzania as well, the government has sought to enforce its surveillance agenda through legislation. For instance, using the Electronic and Postal Communications (Online Content) Regulations (2018), President John Magufuli's government outlines a series of prohibited content, including 'content that causes annoyance [...] or leads to public disorder' – vague wording that is subject to abuse by aggrieved government agencies, especially in situations where unseen factors determine perception of the supposed offender. Bloggers are required to pay a total of $930 USD a year before working in Tanzania; they also require a licence from the Tanzanian Communication Regulatory Authority, renewable every three years, and a Tax Clearance Certificate. Critically, the same law requires bloggers to reveal the ownership of their blogging outlets, and the citizenship of those working at the blog. For those who break these laws, the punishment upon conviction is imprisonment of at least one year, or a fine of at least 5 million Tanzanian shillings ($2,200 USD), or both.

Conclusion

This chapter has engaged with surveillance in East Africa from a historical perspective. It has demonstrated that the practice has a clear pattern within which both states and subjects have innovated; the former working to enhance the efficiency of surveillance, while the latter creatively adapts to the circumstances. In all, effects of surveillance have been seen in four different but related manifestations of state power. The first is the savage brutalisation of common people who are adjudged to have disrespected the state, such as the beating up of citizens who appear to ignore important state functions such as the lowering and raising of the national flag. The anecdote of the man in Busia who was assaulted by police for such trivial reasons shows that surveillance enables the state to announce itself in all corners of the republic by inflicting physical pain on some of its subjects, in order to send a message about the need for compliance to the rest, much in the way Foucault (1977) argued. Secondly, the spread of internet-based technologies of communication has forced states to tighten legislative responses that are purportedly engineered with good intentions, but which serve the old preoccupations of state domination of its citizens. Thirdly, these legislations have engendered a climate of fear that necessitates self- and systemic censorship. At the core of all these initiatives is the old political logic of self-preservation for the political class – silencing critical voices to control public thought and secure the political centre.

Lastly, the ubiquitous spread of internet-based communication technologies and their corresponding cultures have bequeathed the ordinary person with more knowledge about politics and political leaders. The fact that we are now living in the middle of a digital revolution has collapsed social boundaries that were previously considered safe, created opportunities for issue-based mass mobilisation that was impossible just a few years ago, and rendered obsolete traditional, panoptic approaches to surveillance. As the people become more conscious of their political rights and freedoms, they demand more of their governments, critique them more, and render the whole business of governance harder.

As I have shown, governments in East Africa have responded to this informal dispersal of power by restricting human freedoms, informally punishing the masses by charging them exorbitantly for using internet-based social media platforms, enacting legislation that limits the extent of individual expression in digital spaces, and punishing convicted offenders with stiff penalties. At the same time, the governments have adopted the more effective assemblages model of surveillance; putting real and imaginary observatories everywhere to ensure that the subjects are aware of the omnipresent state, and behave compliantly or be punished.

Notes

1 'Police Beat Up Man over Flag'. *The Standard* 23547, 8 February 1990, 1–2 (Mbembe 2001: 136).

2 See *The Citizen* reporter (n.d.), 'What new regulations mean to social media users'. *The Citizen*, www.thecitizen.co.tz/news/1840340-4375404-3861hz/index.html.

3 See Patience Akumu, 'Uganda introduces social media tax despite criticism'. www.aljazeera.com/news/2018/06/uganda-introduces-social-media-tax-criticism-180630180322121.html.

4 Paul Patton (1994: 158) defines an 'assemblage' as a 'multiplicity of heterogeneous objects, whose unity

comes solely from the fact that these items function together, that they work together as a functional entity'.

5 The precise meaning of this word is difficult to pin down, but its etymology is reportedly traceable to Persia. In the context of Kenyan politics of state–subject engagement, Haugerud writes that 'the term connotes contrasting social contexts of hierarchy and relative equality: a sultan holding a public audience, a colonial administrator addressing the public, the master of a house receiving his male friends, or a council of elders meeting to adjudicate a local dispute' (Haugerud 1997: 61).

References

Atieno-Odhiambo, Elisha Stephen (2002) 'Hegemonic enterprises and instrumentalities of survival: ethnicity and democracy in Kenya'. *African Studies*, 61(2): 223–249.

Atieno-Odhiambo, Elisha Stephen (1987) 'Democracy and the ideology of order in Kenya'. In Michael Schatzberg (ed.), *The Political Economy of Kenya*. New York: Praeger.

Barnard-Wills, David (2011) 'UK News Media Discourses of Surveillance'. *The Sociological Quarterly*, 52(4): 548–567.

Breckenridge, Keith (2014) *Biometric State: the Global Politics of Identification in South Africa, 1850 to the Present*. Cambridge: Cambridge University Press.

Castells, Manuel (2010) *The Rise of the Network Society*. Sussex: Wiley-Blackwell, England.

Campbell, Scott W. & Yon Jin Park (2008) 'Social implications of mobile telephony: the rise of personal communication society'. *Sociology Compass* 2(2): 371–387.

The *Citizen* reporter (n.d.) 'What new regulations mean to social media users'. *The Citizen*, www.thecitizen.co.tz/news/1840340-4375404-3861hz/index.html (accessed 2 April 2019).

Debrix, François (1999) 'Space quest: surveillance, governance, and the panoptic eye of the United Nations'. *Alternatives: Global, Local, Political*, 24(3): 269–294.

Deleuze, Gilles & Guattari, Felix (1987) *A Thousand Plateaus: Capitalism and Schizophrenia* (Transl. Brian Massumi). London/Minneapolis: University of Minnesota.

Foucault, Michel (1977) *Discipline and Punish: the Birth of the Prison*. New York: Vintage.

Haugerud, Angelique (1997) *The Culture of Politics in Modern Kenya*. Cambridge: Cambridge University Press.

Imbuga, Francis (1976) *Betrayal in the City*. Nairobi: East African Educational Publishers.

Ligaga, Dina (2012) '"Virtual Expressions": alternative online spaces and the staging of Kenyan popular culture'. *Research in African Literatures*, 43(4): 1–16.

Lyon, David (2001) *Surveillance Society: Monitoring Everyday Life*. Buckingham: Open University Press.

Lyon, David (2007) *Surveillance Studies: an Overview*. Cambridge, England: Polity.

Lyon, David (2014) 'Surveillance, Snowden, and big data: capacities, consequences, critique'. *Big Data & Society*, 2014: 1–13.

Mbembe, Achille (2001) *On the Postcolony*. Berkeley: University of California Press.

Mboya, Tom (1986) *Freedom and After*. Nairobi: EAEP.

Monahan, Torin (2010) *Surveillance in the Time of Insecurity*. New Brunswick, NJ: Rutgers University Press.

Mudimbe, Valentin (1994) *The Idea of Africa*. Bloomington & Indianapolis: Indiana University Press.

Musila, Grace (2015) *A Death Retold in Truth and Rumour: Kenya, Britain and the Julie Ward Murder*. Rochester: James Currey.

New Vision (2013) 'Gov't plans to monitor social media'. 31 May. www.newvision.co.ug/new_vision/news/1321505/gov-plans-monitor-social-media (accessed 2 April 2019).

Ngugi wa Thiong'o & Ngugi wa Mirii (1977) *I Will Marry When I Want*. Nairobi: EAEP.

Nyairo, Joyce. 2013. *Kenya@50: Trends, Identities and the Politics of Belonging*. Nairobi: Contact Zones & JKF.

Odhiambo, Christopher Joseph (2007) 'Reading FM radio stations in Kenya: opening a Pandora's Box'. In Kimani Njogu and G. Olouch-Olunya (eds.), *Cultural Production and Social Change in Kenya*, previewed in *Art Culture and Society*, (1) 2007:151–161.

Odinga, Oginga (1967) *Not Yet Uhuru*. Nairobi: EAEP.

Ogola, George (2005) 'Popular culture and politics: *whispers* and the "dramaturgy of power" in Kenya'. *Social Identities*, 11(2): 147–160, DOI: 10.1080/13504630500161581.

Ogola, George (2015) 'Social media as a heteroglossic discursive space and Kenya's emergent alternative/citizen experiment'. *African Journalism Studies*, 36(4): 66–81. DOI: 10.1080/23743670.2015.1119490.

Ogude, James (2007) '"The cat ended up eating the homestead chicken": murder, memory and fabulization in D.O. Misiani's Dissident Music'. In James Ogude and Joyce Nyairo (eds.), *Urban Legends, Colonial Myths: Popular Culture and Literature in East Africa*. Trenton, NJ.: Africa World Press, pp. 173–202.

Outa, Odera. 2001. 'The dramaturgy of power and politics in post-colonial Kenya: a comparative rereading of "forms", in texts by Ngugi wa Thiong'o and Francis Imbuga'. *Nordic Journal of African Studies*, 10(3): 344–365.

Patton, Paul (1994) 'Metamorpho-Logic: bodies and powers in a thousand plateaus'. *Journal of the British Society for Phenomenology*, 25(2): 157–169.

Privacy International (2017) 'Track, Capture, Kill: Inside Communications Surveillance and Counterterrorism in Kenya'. https://privacyinternational.org/sites/default/files/track_capture_final.pdf (accessed 2 April 2019).

Purdekova, Andrea (2015) *Making Ubumwe: Power, State and Camps in Rwanda's Unity Building Project*. Oxford: Berghahn Books.

Ruganda, John (1992) *Telling the Truth Laughingly*. Nairobi: East African Educational Publishers.

Sunstein, Cass (2014) *Conspiracy Theories and Other Dangerous Ideas*. New York: Simon and Schuster.

Ugangu, Wilson (2015) 'Political influence and shifts in Kenya's Media Policy'. In Rose Lukalo Owino, *Exploring Kenya's Media Policy 1963–2013*. Nairobi: Media Policy Research Centre, pp. 3–20.

Research trajectories in African digital spheres

Bruce Mutsvairo and Kate Wright

The future of social media research in Africa

The rapid spread of social media in Africa has been remarkable, along with the emergence of other applications that enable new forms of social interaction, exchange, dialogue and online collaboration across borders (Mutsvairo & Sirks 2015). Yet social media is not inherently progressive, nor can it 'do' anything to Africa, without Africans first adopting it, and using it in particular ways. The question for researchers must therefore be: what different kinds of social media practice are in operation, rather than what 'impact' social media is having on Africa.

Although social media scholarship has been expanding in much of the West for some time, research into African social media has only started gaining ground in the last five years or so. Researchers in this area build upon the cross-disciplinary approach emerging from existing studies, which span anthropology (de Bruijn 2016), journalism and media studies (Wright 2018; Mutsvairo 2018; Bosch & Mutsvairo 2017), political communication (Mutsvairo & Karam 2018; Mpofu 2013) and business studies (Oji et. al. 2017).

Scholars examining social media practice in Africa also benefit from the growing acceptance of social media as a source of scientific data (boyd & Ellison 2008; Sloan et al. 2013; Vishwanath 2015). Indeed, the proliferation of endlessly flowing, easily and quickly available digital data can seem like a veritable gold mine for academics, eager to use social media as a research tool, or to focus on online platforms as new objects of study in their own right. So, studies such the 'Social Media and Security in Africa' project, which culminated in the publication of this important volume, have started to gain academic traction.

Yet we must be careful not to engage in a kind of scholarly 'Scramble for Africa': research ethics remain vitally important, and difficult. Few sub-Saharan countries have data protection laws, and even outside Africa, ethical issues continue to dominate debates on digital research.

As boyd and Crawford (2012: 672) have argued, 'it is problematic for researchers to justify their actions as ethical simply because the data are accessible'. The key problem underlying their statement is whether social media should be conceptualised as a public or private space.

This is not easy to establish in Africa, where some people are registered as social media users, even though they do not know about it, and where others do not have the ability to fully participate in discussions taking place on these platforms. It remains extremely difficult to trace who people registered on social media actually are, which both facilitates identity fraud and helps to protect those living in authoritarian states, who fear reprisals. Should social media be treated as 'public' or 'private' communication in such circumstances? Can data obtained from such sources be regarded as valid and trustworthy?

Moreover, how can we ensure that all individuals who feature in an online data set fully consent to participating in a research project? Even when researchers inform participants about their research by posting a letter on an online platform, that simply is not enough by Eurocentric standards because it does not allow the respondents to actively approve their involvement in the project. In fact, for the most part, many participants take part in large-scale online research without even knowing about it, let alone consenting to it. This challenge is easily tied to problems of digital illiteracy, where people posting in social media groups, such as WhatsApp, may be unaware that everyone else in the group can see what they post.

Additional questions can be raised about the representativeness of data that emerges from social media networks. For example, language barriers can often impede participation in online discussions, especially on platforms that are dominated by European languages. Social or religious norms could also prohibit participants from fully and openly sharing their opinions. Thus researchers working in African digital environments need to continue to think about how offline norms and social practices shape who is able to engage in social media discussions, and the conditions of that engagement, so that the validity of their findings is not called into question.

Several other factors will be central in determining the future role of social media in Afrocentric settings. For example, questions can be raised about the universality of research methods. Should Eurocentric forms of research – such as empirically driven examinations – be the only acceptable kinds of study? This is important because, for many African scholars or those studying Africa, Europe and America are generally viewed as the source of theory, while Africa can only provide case studies for testing Western theory (Comaroff & Comaroff 2012).

So far, research in social media settings has been favourable to Eurocentric approaches, which for some is perfectly fine – and, in a way, understandable given the colonial influence on Africa's recent history. However, if research, as Chakrabarty (2000: 12) argues, cannot 'transcend places of [its] origin', is it not therefore important to rethink the epistemological consequences of conducting social media research deprived of context-specific methodological and theoretical frameworks? When, for example, will researchers in African settings move beyond case study research to attempt to theorise digital research using concepts developed through Afrocentric accounts and lenses?

We can also ask: how representative and relevant is social media research, if access to digital platforms is not open to all, or even the majority, of Africans? Empirical accounts have persuasively demonstrated that the exponential growth in the use of ICTs (information and communication technologies) replicates the existing inequalities associated with accessing and using the telecommunications infrastructures, the internet and other digital technologies (Ragnedda & Muschert 2013). Therefore, digital inequalities cannot be reduced to a simple matter of access to the internet (Mutsvairo & Ragnedda 2017).

Researchers can do little to improve Africans' patchy access to digital media, as this is caused by the combination of several structural factors, including widening differences in income, infrastructure and literacy. What they can do, however, is to continue exposing, through their research, growing inequalities in African societies in the hope that affordable access to social networks and the internet will one day diminish the 'digital divide'. It is from that perspective that editors of this volume deserve nothing but praise in producing such an important book, which clearly contributes to on-going conversations about growing social media research in African digital communities.

Equally important for many researchers is how African governments will react to global data concerns in the wake of the Cambridge Analytica scandal (Tarran 2018; Kang & Frenkel 2018), which saw personal data belonging to over 80 million users being used in an attempt to influence voter opinion. Seeking to safeguard laws determining the collection, storage, use and protection of all data connected to the identification of its citizens, the European Union launched its General Data Protection Regulation in May 2018. This raises questions about how African countries will now seek to protect their own citizens. Will they implement similar measures to those introduced in Europe? New regulations or legal frameworks could also affect the way online research is conducted in Africa, forcing some, like Makulilo (2016), to update their works should African countries choose to amend their digital laws.

Some issues also have the potential to upset the accomplishments being made in cross-disciplinary research across Africa. For example, it remains a challenge to locate diverse research emerging from non-Anglophone parts of the continent. This is worrying, especially when we consider that many Africans are not conversant in English. How are their stories being told? Who is telling their stories? What translation techniques are being used? If these studies are not available in English, does that make research in these equally significant parts of Africa less important or influential? What can be done to improve access to research coming out of these regions of the continent? Even in the Anglophone world, research in a few countries such as South Africa tend to dominate publications. Greater attention to more neglected regions and languages would be a welcome addition to further develop our understanding of the effects of social media across the continent.

The importance of this book

When reading this book, three achievements immediately spring to mind. The first, and most obvious, involves the incredible variety and empirical richness of this volume. This richness pertains not only to the range of countries included, many of which are rarely studied in relation to social media practice, but also in terms of the very varied case studies which scholars have chosen to interrogate. These include analysis of the approaches to social media taken by rappers, police-men and students, as well as new insights into the practices of more frequently studied actors, such as politicians and voters.

Secondly, the scholars in this volume have made a decisive break away from old, techno-determinist arguments which portray social media as inevitably 'doing something' to Africans (Mare 2014). Instead, this research builds on the work of previous studies (Bunce, Franks & Paterson 2016; Gallagher 2015; Mutsvairo 2016a) by focusing on African actors' lived experience of different forms of social media, and the varied uses to which they put it. In order to interrogate this, researchers bring together many different academic traditions, blending research in human rights with studies of governance, international development and the digital humanities. This innovative interdisciplinarity enables researchers to illuminate the recursive relationships of social media to mainstream media, and other forms of political communication.

But at the same time, the chapter authors revisit many of the structural issues raised by previous researchers: paying careful attention to the relevance of patchy material infrastructure, unequal socio-economic positioning, political and military instability, and the existence, in some sub-Saharan countries, of harsh media laws and other restrictions on freedom of expression (Wasserman 2011). In so doing, this book moves the study of social media into new territory theoretically: making a decisive break from old notions of the 'digital divide', which relied on the notion of media access. Instead, they explore the conditions shaping participation in social media, including who is most able to frame and circulate national and issue-based narratives, which involve important legitimacy claims.

Thus, the third contribution of this book is the way in which it develops our understandings of how and why different kinds of social media practices arise from interactions between the agency of various actors and socio-economic structures. These more nuanced theoretical approaches are used to explore the preconditions of effective digital activism, as well as other forms of democratic participation, without presuming that the spread of the internet, mobile phones or other kinds of ICT will trigger a widespread 'African Spring' (Mutsvairo 2016a). Indeed, this book challenges the oft-held assumption that mass participation in social media is likely to have progressive effects. Instead, authors show that the dominance of political, economic and military elites can be reinforced just as effectively in populations where there is widespread participation in social media, like Kenya, as in contexts where only a very small proportion of the population are able to participate, such as Burundi.

Such conclusions may be seen to have emerged from a long-standing body of research about the strategic uses of social media by African elites to gain political and economic advantages (Gallagher 2015), including using Twitter and Facebook to stir up ethnic and other forms of hatred (Mäkinen & Kuira 2008). However, we are now able to make much more detailed links between the conditions shaping social media participation, and the means through which elites 'capture' mainstream media discourse (Schiffrin 2017).

In so doing, this book enables us to develop more nuanced theoretical approaches to analysing the relationships between social media and the nation state. One can make useful links here with previous research carried out in relation to the so-called 'Arab Spring', as well as previous studies about African countries, which examined how social media is used to both challenge, and entrench, the power of authoritarian states (for example Gagliardone & Pohjonen 2016; Mare 2016). Yet this earlier research still tended to revolve around binary tensions. That is to say, it tended to portray social media as having affordances which enable pro-democratic activists to collectively resist overweening forms of state power, while also facilitating greater state surveillance and repression of activists.

What this book does is to break down that over-generalised binary paradigm by analysing social media practices in relation to many different kinds of states, including nascent and post-conflict states. Even when these scholars do discuss the legal and regulatory regimes of authoritarian states, they tend to avoid conceptualising 'the state' as a homogenous, unified and stable whole. Instead, they often take a more diffuse and dynamic approach: examining how different state and non-state actors interact (and often conflict) with one another through intersecting forms of media in order to challenge, legitimise and/or reproduce particular visions of statehood, and forms of state power.

By exploring the often-pivotal roles played by diasporic groups, these authors then break down a further binary division, between that which is 'African', and that which is 'not African'. Thus their work speaks to the broader literature about social media, mobility and diasporic identities, as well as research into intersectional identities, understandings of belonging, and socio-political responsibilities to others. These include issues of race, gender, generation and sexuality, which have been tackled before (Currier & Moreau 2016; Mhiripiri & Moyo 2016). But what is new about this book is that it portrays social media as simultaneously a site of discursive contestation between actors with different legitimacy claims and strategic objectives, and also as a deliberative space, wherein new forms of intersectional identity, consensus and community can be built.

However, what is perhaps the most intriguing theoretical contribution of this book is the way in which so many scholars have begun to address the significance of visual images within social media texts. This is a refreshing change, as work on social media practices in Africa tends to be overly focused on the dissemination of written texts, engaging far less with social media as a multimodal phenomenon, involving the interplay of many different kinds of written, oral and visual text, as well as other kinds of interactive participation (such as likes and shares). These scholars have even begun to engage with broader arguments about remediation (Chouliaraki 2015), by attending to the ways in which mediated images are repeatedly reframed as they pass through successive social media accounts.

To bring the analysis of visual images and film into the study of social media is not only to engage with contemporary arguments about the ways in which visual images are used to privilege certain narratives, make legitimacy claims and manage doubt within social media (Chouliaraki 2015). It is also to re-engage with old arguments about the kinds of 'gaze' used to view 'Africa', which stem from colonial times (Spurr 1993). Thus we can see how this edited collection has the potential to enrich both African Studies and Media Studies.

Yet to say so is to openly address the critical elephant in the room, for, with the exception of some notable scholars, there remains a slight air of scepticism about researching media amongst Africanist scholars. There seems to be a lingering suspicion that studying tweets, Facebook likes and YouTube video-streams might be somehow less serious, less intellectually challenging and worthwhile than researching more traditional topics like conflict, economics and governance. But as the chapters in this book show, it is virtually impossible, these days, to discuss any of those time-honoured topics in depth, without dealing with the veritable saturation of such activities in intersecting forms of mainstream and social media discourse.

Moreover, scholars specialising in research about sub-Saharan countries may play a vital role in helping to 'de-Westernise' academic research about social media – so much of which has focused on Europe and North America. It is important to explore distinctive, African forms of media practice, but we need to be careful to avoid exceptionalism: that is, treating sub-Saharan Africa – and the study of it – in isolation from the rest of the world (Mabweazara 2015; Willems & Mano 2016). Instead, the next step is to spell out how such interdisciplinary research 'talks back' to the existing body of scholarship: reshaping our understandings of social media more broadly in order to develop 'a shared intellectual core' of academic thought (Waisbord 2015, cited and discussed by Mabweazara 2015: 5).

References

Bosch, T. & Mutsvairo, B. (2017) 'Pictures, protests and politics: mapping Twitter images during South Africa's Fees Must Fall campaign'. *Ecquid Novi: African Journalism Studies*, 38(2): 71–89.

boyd, d. & Crawford, K. (2012) 'Critical questions for big data'. *Information, Communication & Society*, 15(5): 662–679,

boyd, d.m. & Ellison, N.B. (2008) 'Social network sites: definition, history, and scholarship'. *Journal of Computer-Mediated Communication*, 13(1): 210–230.

Bunce, M., Franks, S. & Paterson, C. (eds.) (2016) *Africa's Media Image in the 21st Century: from the 'Heart of Darkness' to 'Africa Rising'*. London: Routledge.

Chakrabarty, D. (2000) *Provincializing Europe: Postcolonial Thought and Historical Difference*. Princeton: Princeton University Press.

Chouliaraki, L. (2015) 'Digital witnessing in conflict zones: the politics of remediation'. *Information, Communication and Society*, 18(11): 1362–1377.

Comaroff, J. & Comaroff, J. (2012) *Theory from the South: or, how EuroAmerica is Evolving toward Africa*. Boulder: Paradigm Publishers.

Currier, A. & Mureau, J. (2016) 'Digital strategies and LGBTI organising'. In B. Mutsvairo (ed.) *Digital Activism in the Social Media Era: Critical Reflections on Emerging Trends in sub-Saharan Africa*. London: Palgrave Macmillan.

de Bruijn, M.E. (2016) 'Citizen journalism at crossroads: mediated political agency and duress in Central Africa'. In B. Mutsvairo (ed.), *Participatory Politics and Citizen Journalism in a Networked Africa: a Connected Continent*. Houndmills: Palgrave Macmillan, pp. 90–104.

Gagliardone, I. & Pohjonen, M. (2016) 'Engaging in polarised society: social media and political discourse in Ethiopia'. In B. Mutsvairo (ed.), *Digital Activism in the Social Media Era: Critical Reflections on Emerging Trends in sub-Saharan Africa*. London: Palgrave Macmillan.

Gallagher, J. (ed.) (2015) *Images of Africa: Creation, Negotiation and Subversion*. Oxford: Oxford University Press.

Kang, C. & Frenkel, S. (2018) 'Facebook Says Cambridge Analytica harvested data of up to 87 million users'. *The New York Times*, 4 April. www.nytimes.com/2018/04/04/technology/mark-zuckerberg-testify-congress.html (accessed 30 January 2019).

Mabweazara, H. (2015) 'Mainstreaming African digital cultures, practices and emerging forms of citizen engagement'. *African Journalism Studies*, 36(4): 1–11.

Mäkinen, M. & Kuira, M.W. (2008) 'Social media and post-election crisis in Kenya'. *The International Journal of Press/Politics*, 13(3): 328–335.

Makulilo, A. (ed.) (2016) *African Data Privacy Laws*. Berlin: Springer.

Mare, A. (2014) 'Social media: the new protest drums in Africa'. In B. Pătruţ & M. Pătruţ (eds.), *Social Media in Politics: Public Administration and Information Technology*, vol. 13. New York: Springer, Cham.

Mare, A. (2016) 'Baba Jukwa and the digital repertoires of connective action in a "competitive authoritarian regime": the case of Zimbabwe'. In B. Mutsvairo (ed.), *Digital Activism in the Social Media Era: Critical Reflections on Emerging Trends in sub-Saharan Africa*. London: Palgrave Macmillan.

Mhiripiri, N.A. & Moyo, S.B. (2016) 'A resilient unwanted civil society: the gays and lesbians of Zimbabwe use of Facebook as alternative public sphere in a dominant homophobic society'. In B. Mutsvairo (ed.), *Digital Activism in the Social Media Era: Critical Reflections on Emerging Trends in sub-Saharan Africa*. London: Palgrave Macmillan.

Mpofu, S. (2013) 'Social media and the politics of ethnicity in Zimbabwe'. *Ecquid Novi: African Journalism Studies*, 34(1): 115–122.

Mutsvairo, B. (2016) 'Dovetailing desires for democracy with new ICTS' potentiality as platform for activism'. In B. Mutsvairo (ed.), *Digital Activism in the Social Media Era: Critical Reflections on Emerging Trends in sub-Saharan Africa*. London: Palgrave Macmillan.

Mutsvairo, B. (ed.) (2018) *Palgrave Handbook of Media and Communication Research in Africa*. London: Palgrave Macmillan.

Mutsvairo, B. & Karam, B. (eds.) (2018) *Perspectives on Political Communication in Africa*. London: Palgrave Macmillan.

Mutsvairo, B. & Ragnedda, M. (2017) 'Emerging political narratives on Malawian digital spaces'. *Communicatio: South African Journal for Communication Theory and Research*, 43(2): 147–167.

Mutsvairo, B. & Sirks, L. (2015) 'Examining the contribution of social media in advancing political participation in Zimbabwe'. *Journal of African Media Studies*, 7(3): 329–344.

Oji, O. et al. (2017) 'Social media adoption challenges of small businesses: the case of restaurants in the Cape Metropole, South Africa'. *African Journal of Hospitality, Tourism and Leisure*, 6(4): 1–12.

Ragnedda, M. & Muschert, G.W. (2013) *The Digital Divide: the Internet and Social Inequality in International Perspective*. London: Routledge.

Schiffrin, A. (ed.) (2017) *In the Service of Power: Media Capture and the Threat to Democracy*. New York: Center for International Media Assistance.

Sloan, L. et al. (2013) 'The tweeters: deriving sociologically relevant demographics from Twitter'. *Sociological Research Online*, 18(3): 7.

Spurr, D. (1993) *Rhetoric of Empire: Colonial Discourse in Journalism, Travel Writing and Imperial Administration*. North Carolina: Duke University Press.

Tarran, B. (2018) 'What can we learn from the Facebook–Cambridge Analytica scandal?' *Journal of the Royal Statistical Society*, 15(3): 4–5.

Vishwanath, A. (2015) 'Habitual Facebook use and its impact on getting deceived on social media'. *Journal of Computer Mediated Communication*, 20(1): 83–98.

Waisbord, Silvio (2015) 'My vision for the *Journal of Communication*'. *Journal of Communication*, 65: 585–588.

Wasserman, H. (2011) 'Mobile phones, popular media, and everyday African democracy: transmissions and transgressions'. *Popular Communication*, 9(2): 146–158.

Willems, W. & Mano, W. (2016) 'Decolonizing and provincializing audience and internet studies: contextual approaches from African vantage points'. In W. Willems & W. Mano (eds.), *Everyday Media Culture in Africa: Audiences and Users*. London: Routledge.

Wright, K. (2018) *Who's reporting Africa now? Non-Governmental Organizations, Journalists and Multimedia*. London, New York: Peter Lang.

INDEX

Note: Page numbers in italic indicate figures or tables; page numbers followed by *n* indicate an endnote with relevant number.

ZED

Zed is a platform for marginalised voices across the globe.

It is the world's largest publishing collective and a world leading example of alternative, non-hierarchical business practice.

It has no CEO, no MD and no bosses and is owned and managed by its workers who are all on equal pay.

It makes its content available in as many languages as possible.

It publishes content critical of oppressive power structures and regimes.

It publishes content that changes its readers' thinking.

It publishes content that other publishers won't and that the establishment finds threatening.

It has been subject to repeated acts of censorship by states and corporations.

It fights all forms of censorship.

It is financially and ideologically independent of any party, corporation, state or individual.

Its books are shared all over the world.

www.zedbooks.net
@ZedBooks